To
BILL MOXLEY
CHRISTMAS 1982

FRED SHORSHER

SLIM
THE STANDARDBEARER

Rommel as Military Commander
Montgomery as Military Commander
Churchill as War Lord
Freedom's Battle: The War on Land, 1939–45 (Ed.)
Man of Armour
A Study of Lieut-General Vyvyan Pope

The Chief of the Imperial General Staff addresses the Generals
of the Indian Army, Delhi, 1949.

SLIM

THE STANDARDBEARER

★★★★★

A Biography of
Field-Marshal The Viscount Slim
KG, GCB, GCMG, GCVO, GBE, DSO, MC

by
RONALD LEWIN

'Will you tell me, Master Shallow, how to choose a man? Care I for the limb, the thews, the stature, bulk, and big assemblance of a man? Give me the spirit, Master Shallow.'

Sir John Falstaff

LEO COOPER

LONDON

First Published in Great Britain 1976 by
LEO COOPER LTD
196 Shaftesbury Avenue, London WC2H 8JL

Reprinted 1977
Reprinted 1978

Copyright © 1976 Ronald Lewin
ISBN 0 85052 218 8

Set in Monotype Fournier by
Western Printing Services Ltd, Bristol
Reproduced and printed by photolithography and bound in
Great Britain at The Pitman Press, Bath

To
Bill's Son
John

CONTENTS

MAPS

ILLUSTRATIONS

All the photographs are reproduced by kind permission of the family of the late Viscount Slim, except nos 14–18 and 20–21, which are reproduced by kind permission of the Imperial War Museum and nos 25 and 27 by kind permission of Mr Robin Adshead.

AUTHOR'S NOTE

To Aileen, Viscountess Slim, and her son and daughter, Lieutenant-Colonel the Viscount Slim and the Hon. Mrs Nigel Frazer, my debt is beyond words.

My text reveals the value of Slim's personal papers, which his family so willingly placed at my disposal. To the late Philip Pratt, and to Miss Margaret Pratt, I am indebted for access to a life-long correspondence illuminating areas of Slim's career for which little or no other material is available.

Admiral of the Fleet the Earl Mountbatten of Burma assisted and advised me with unfailing generosity. Brigadier Michael Roberts brought to his reading of my drafts the eagle eye and deep knowledge which he applied to the original text of *Defeat into Victory* and throughout his service as an Official Historian of the war against Japan. To Lieutenant-General Sir Ian Jacob and Brigadier the Lord Ballantrae I am also grateful for devoting much time to the scrutiny of what I have written.

Many others made this book possible by the information, advice and encouragement which they provided in consultation, correspondence, or by commenting on passages in my text about which they had special knowledge. In particular, I must record my gratitude to Major-General W. V. Abraham, Robin Adshead, Field-Marshal Sir Claude Auchinleck, the late Air Marshal Sir John Baldwin, Lieut-Colonel A. J. Barker, Lieut-General Sir Edric Bastyan, Brigadier R. G. S. Bidwell, Major-General R. L. Bond, Lord Boyd-Carpenter, Doreen Lady Brabourne, Lord Brabourne, Antony Brett-James, Nigel Bruce, Brigadier Michael Calvert, Alan Campbell-Johnson, Lord Carrington, Sir Paul Chambers, General Sir Philip Christison Bt, Dr John Clayton, Brigadier H. V. L. Collingridge, Major-General D. T. Cowan, Lieut-General Sir Richard Craddock, the late Major-General H. L. Davies, Dr Norman Dixon, Major-General Sir Charles Dunphie, Colonel Peter Dunphie, Major-General Nigel Duncan, Major-General G. M. Dyer, Professor Joel Egerer, Marshal of the RAF the Lord Elworthy, Lieut-Colonel R. A. R. Fanshawe, Lord Franks, General Sir Richard Gale, Lieut-Colonel H. R. K. Gibbs, Sir Martin Gilliat, the late Christopher Gimson,

xiii

Lieut-General Eric Goddard, Major Michael Hankinson, Field-Marshal Lord Harding, General Sir Charles Harington, Major-General W. F. Hasted, the Viscount Head, Philip Howe, Miss Judy Hutchinson, Lieut-General Sir Thomas Hutton, Arthur Johnson, Lieut-General Sir Brian Kimmins, Major-General A. W. Lee, Lieut-General Sir Oliver Leese Bt, Dr Hugh L'Etang, Major George Llewellyn, General Sir Rob Lockhart, The Rev Dr Donald MacDonald, Philip Mason, Major-General Sir John Marriott, Sir Roy Matthews, Sir Robert Mackworth-Young, the late General Sir Frank Messervy, Lieut-Colonel Michael Mitchell, Lieut-Colonel Brian Montgomery, General Sir Cameron Nicholson, Nigel Nicolson, Lieut-General Sir Denis O'Connor, General Sir Richard O'Connor, Lieut-General Sir William Oliver, Frank Owen, Mrs Anson Paul, Sir Harald Peake, Bill Richardson, General Sir Ouvry Roberts, Douglas Robertson, Major-General J. A. R. Robertson, Admiral the Hon Sir Guy Russell, Lord Savile, Lieut-General Sir Reginald Savory, the late General Sir Geoffry Scoones, Major-General Sir Reginald Scoones, the late Major-General Bruce Scott, Lord Shinwell, General Sir Frank Simpson, Marshal of the RAF Sir John Slessor, Colonel Sir Henry Abel Smith, Brigadier Sir John Smyth, the late General Sir James Steele, Brigadier John Stephenson, Alex St Pierre, Brigadier John Swinton, Major-General G. W. Symes, Field-Marshal Sir Gerald Templer, C. H. W. Troughton, Colonel Tyrwhitt-Drake, Lieut-General W. G. H. Vickers, the late Air Vice-Marshal S. F. Vincent, General Sir Walter Walker, Major-General F. J. Walsh, Major Weber-Brown, Major-General Douglas Wimberley, Group Captain F. W. Winterbotham and the Rt Rev. Robin Woods (Bishop of Worcester).

I am grateful to the Leverhulme Trust for the award of a Research Fellowship which facilitated my visits to Australia and India.

I owe particular thanks to the Governor-General, His Excellency Sir John Kerr, for his kindness in enabling me during my Australian visit to familiarize myself with Government House, Canberra, and Admiralty House, Sydney. To say that Sir Robert Menzies gave up for me the last afternoon o a Melbourne Test Match is to indicate the measure of his concern. Sir Murray and Lady Tyrrell opened a mine of information and many doors. Others who in Canberra, Sydney, Melbourne, Adelaide and England gave me helpful advice about Slim's Governor-Generalship, as well as their ready hospitality, include:

The Rt Rev. Gordon Arthur, Sim Bennet, Lieut-General Sir Frank Berryman, John Breadmore, Sir Allen Brown, His Excellency Sir John Bunting, Lord Casey, Lieut-Colonel Ralph Connor, Sir Robert Crichton-Brown, Professor L. F. Crisp, His Excellency Sir Roden Cutler, Lieut-General Sir Thomas Daly, Sir Alexander Downer, Sir William Dunk, Geoffrey Fairbairn, Mrs Betty Foott, Professor Sir Keith Hancock, Mrs Kay Hargrave, the Rev. Hector Harrison, Lieut-General the Hon. Sir Edmund

Herring, Alec Hill, John Howse, the Hon. Davis Hughes, A. G. W. Keys, Sir Daryl Lindsay, Major-General Sir Denzil Macarthur-Onslow, Ion Macarthur-Onslow, Sir William Morrow, Keith Oliphant, Dr Robert O'Neill, Professor Murray Pheils, John Pringle, Lieut-Colonel Tim Rodriguez, the late Lieut-General Sir Sydney Rowell, Deric Thompson, Dr Cyril Tonkin, Professor L. C. F. Turner and Major-General the Hon. Sir Victor Windeyer.

The High Commissioner for India in London, His Excellency B. K. Nehru, and his Military Advisers at India House, assisted me greatly over my visit to their country, particularly in obtaining permission for me to enter the restricted areas of Assam and enabling me to enjoy the notable hospitality and efficient facilities of the Indian Army. The Defence Adviser to the British High Commissioner in Delhi, Major-General T. S. Richardson, was an unfailing support. In Delhi I also benefited from discussions with General G. G. Bewoor, Lieut-General S. G. Gupta, Major-General S. K. Korla, Major-General D. K. Palit, Lieut-General N. C. Rawlley, and Lieut-General S. K. Sinha; Dr K. N. Pandey, Director of the Historical Section of the Ministry of Defence, kindly placed his files at my disposal. In Calcutta the Commander-in-Chief, Eastern Army, Lieut-General J. F. R. Jacob, showed me great kindness at Fort William and in smoothing my path; Major-General Asoke Banerjee, General J. N. Chaudhuri and General I. S. Gill also contributed insights and information. At Dimapur, Kohima and Imphal my investigations owed everything to the kindness of Major-General G. S. Rawat (GOC 8th Mountain Division). At Kohima Macdonald da Silva's intimate knowledge of the topography, and his recollections of the battle itself, were inestimable aids.

To my wife I can only express my inexpressible thanks in words used by Bill Slim when he dedicated *Defeat into Victory* to Aileen: she 'followed the drum'.

RONALD LEWIN

CHAPTER ONE

THE LAUNCHING PAD

History is lived forwards but it is written in retrospect. We know the end before we consider the beginning and we can never wholly recapture what it was to know the beginning only.

C. V. Wedgwood, *William the Silent*

THERE EXISTS a short section of film on which one may observe the Commander of the 14th Army arriving in a light plane at a muddy airstrip somewhere in Burma. As he emerges, his trousers droop and flap. With a supreme lack of self-consciousness he makes all safe. Then he steps down and strides towards the reception committee, smiling, unruffled, in complete control. No other Army Commander in the Second World War could have managed this trivial incident with such instinctive ease or so effortlessly retained his full military dignity. But in those few seconds one detects in quintessence the qualities which caused a future Field-Marshal to be known simply as Uncle Bill throughout a great army. Its love, respect, and something close to dedication, were earned by an instinctive honesty of mind and deed, a natural authority, a mastery over circumstance. Few have surpassed William Joseph Slim in that gift which Liddell Hart attributed to Marlborough—'the power of commanding affection while communicating energy'. His military distinction was founded on his humanity.

This was his true *métier*, yet in his early childhood neither he nor his parents could have thought it possible. The reasons were social and economic. In the 1890s the son of a man modestly engaged in the whole-sale hardware trade had no prospect of becoming an officer, and to 'go for a soldier' by enlisting in the ranks was inconceivable. Late in life

Slim recalled that 'Even when, one day, a school friend's elder brother, who had run away and enlisted in the Life Guards, re-appeared swaggering down the road in tight overalls and white serge pea-jacket, spurs jangling, riding whip under arm, pill-box hat over one ear, I felt no urge to emulate him.'

It was at 72 Belmont Road, Bishopston—then a village on the outskirts of Bristol—that Slim was born on 6 August, 1891; and it was to the Lord Mayor of Bristol that he would write in 1960 for permission to adopt the title of Viscount Slim of Yarralumla in the Capital Territory of Australia and of Bishopston in the City and County of Bristol. He was a younger son; Charles was the first-born of John Slim and his wife Charlotte, the daughter of Charles Tucker of Burnham, Somerset. Here, and from 1897 at 12 Maurice Road, Slim's childhood slipped by in what the Victorians understood as a respectable way of life, which left clear impressions on his mind of W. G. Grace at the wicket, or his father reading from the newspapers about the Sudan campaign of 1896 and a man called Kitchener—whose name cropped up so often that Bill became confused, for up to now it had stood for the old-fashioned black-leaded cooking range.

His father made a habit of reading to the two boys—Dickens, Thackeray, Scott and much poetry—during the gas-lit evenings. Those were the days of copious publications in weekly or fortnightly parts, and there was one to which John Slim subscribed, a thin, pale green journal called *British Battles by Land and Sea*, which his son marked as the beginning of his interest in soldiering.

> Almost every battle, from Saxons and Normans lambasting one another with great axes at Hastings to Wolseley-helmeted British soldiers firing steady volleys into charging Fuzzy-Wuzzies in the Sudan, was there. I pored over these pictures and through them I first began to daydream of myself as a soldier. In my childishly romantic visions I saw myself plunging forward in the most desperate assaults, while somewhere in the background bands played, men cheered and colours waved. Strangely enough, among all these exciting pictures it was one of a sailor which most riveted my attention. In it a cabin-boy, Cloudesley Shovell, was swimming from one three-decker to another bearing a vital message. Above him the great broadsides roared and crashed; the sea all around, covered in wreckage, was beaten to a foam by round-shot and musket-ball.*

---

* Towards the end of his life Slim was working on a further autobiographical

What particularly impressed Slim, who cannot have been more than five or six at the time, was Cloudesley Shovell's subsequent distinction as Admiral and Knight of the Bath. Forty-seven years later he himself became a Knight of the same order. As he stood with his three Corps Commanders waiting to be dubbed by the Viceroy of India on the Imphal plain, where his 14th Army had just shattered a Japanese invasion, the cabin-boy's picture suddenly flashed into his mind. Honours were even.

The South African War converted romance into reality—though nobody from Slim's world 'went out'. There was glamour, of course, in the cigarette cards of generals, the battalions marching through Bristol, the relief of Mafeking. But Slim was an inconvenient name at a time when one always referred to 'the slim Boers'—clever, crafty, treacherous. This coincidence was manna to Bill's school-fellows, who naturally derided him for being a Boer. 'The gibe outraged my pride, my patriotism, my whole being. I remember battering away ineffectually at a bigger boy and blubbering hard, not because he was giving me a hiding, as most of them did, but from sheer frustrated rage and indignation.'* It was a cross he had to carry for a long time. In 1945, when Alanbrooke as CIGS was recommending him to the Prime Minister for the post of Commander-in-Chief, Allied Land Forces, South East Asia, in what was still expected to be a long war against Japan, something stirred in the memory of the old campaigner who had fought beside Alanbrooke's brother at Spion Kop and ridden with him into relieved Ladysmith. 'I cannot think', grunted Churchill, 'that a man with a name like Slim can be any good.'

At the turn of the century even a respectable life could be precarious for a man in a small way of business. John Slim was an admirable father, but better, perhaps, at reading *David Copperfield* aloud than at mastering accounts. By 1903 his affairs were in disorder, and the family moved to Birmingham, that traditional home of the self-employed worker, or dealer, in metal goods. There was great competition, but there was also opportunity. At 144 Poplar Avenue the Slims made a fresh start,† and a place for Bill was found in St Philip's, Edgbaston,

---

memoir, from which these words are taken. Subsequent quotations will be indicated as *Memoir*.
* *Memoir*.
† John Slim set up as a hardware merchant and factor, in the firm of Sellers and Slim, Dean Street, Birmingham.

a Catholic grammar school run by the Fathers of Birmingham Oratory. Those who only knew Slim in his maturity are sometimes shocked, sometimes incredulous, but always taken aback when they discover that he had a Catholic upbringing. This is not surprising, since by his thirties he had ceased either to profess or to practise a faith which had never penetrated his core. When he married a Presbyterian in 1926 no religious difficulties arose, and his children were not brought up to be Romans. His chaplains in Burma knew, indeed, that here was a man who insisted on their putting spiritual ministry before the provision of mere physical comforts, but the insistence was impartial. Slim required soldiers who believed in more than material things; he was not concerned about their creeds. Nor, for that matter, did he make Montgomery's mistake of suggesting that he and God were a Private Company. His attitude was that of the Colonel of the 75th Foot at the siege of Delhi during the Indian Mutiny, who, before the assault, allowed a Catholic priest, Father Bertrand, to give his blessing to all denominations. 'We may differ some of us in matters of religion, but the blessing of an old man and a clergyman can do nothing but good.'

The deepest truths about a man's inner life are often reflected in his preoccupations when death approaches. During his last few years Slim was troubled in mind, so evidently distressed that some of those most intimately concerned for his well-being felt that he was in need of spiritual advice and guidance. It emerged that he was pricked by a sense of guilt—guilt that he had broken a youthful promise to his mother never to abandon the Catholic faith. The point was not that he was aching, with the emptiness of an apostate, for what he had rejected; the point was the pledge to his mother. And here is the clue. Charlotte Slim was a totally and fervently committed Catholic, a passionate devotee. She had a strong personality—complementing, it is clear, the gentle failure she had married. Her son retained a dutiful regard for her and cared for her comfort to the end of her long life, as a proper filial activity, not because in any of the well-known ways she dominated him. Thus it was the natural and inevitable step for Bill Slim to receive a Catholic education and he accepted it as natural and normal. But manhood made him ask questions which the dogmas of his early indoctrination were unable to sustain. Gently, but irrevocably, he lapsed.

When he was at Quetta in 1927 his first child, John, was born. The Chaplain of the 2nd Battalion the Cameronians, Donald MacDonald, received an unexpected visit, which led to a lifelong friendship and a profound mutual understanding. Dr MacDonald recalled:

He came to the point at once. Would I christen the child? I reminded him of the law of his Church concerning Baptism, but he surprised me by saying that for some time, and recently more intensely, he had become dissatisfied with many RC tenets. At the time this appeared to me to be more of an intellectual aversion than a spiritual reformation. In further talk I gathered that it was not 'the faith once delivered to the saints' that gave him disquiet but rather the claims, demands, and obligatory dogmas which the Church had clustered round the central core. A man could not see the wood for the trees. His mental process was of the type that liked the direct approach. Like Shaw and his Basic English, Bill had a leaning towards basic Christianity. The Ten Commandments which all Churches term the Moral Law were to him the basis of human progress and stability, whether revealed in the Old Testament or not. To his soldier's mind a 'Command' had tremendous appeal. It was the same with the Lord's Prayer—no dreamy, woolly, out-of-this-world stuff but a direct cry for help to meet the basic needs. Many years later, when he was GOC 14th Army and I was the Senior Staff Chaplain at 11th Army Group, I frequently flew into his Tac HQ, and on one occasion, when our mutual friend Punch Cowan was battling for Meiktila with his 17 Div., Bill and I were sitting outside his caravan at Kalewa and he turned to me, saying, 'Now, Donald, get your chaps to pray *flat out* for this victory.' That phrase 'flat out' has lived in my memory—so different from Rubric language! Yet it was his idea of what a real prayer should be. He would have been at home with the Cromwellian Ironsides, for he was the kind that 'took the Kingdom by storm'.*

There is nothing in Slim's career, nothing in his private world as disclosed by his family and intimate friends, nothing in writing and nothing in deed which makes it necessary to qualify Dr MacDonald's assessment. He was *anima naturaliter Christiana*, a man to whom belief came instinctively; but it was a belief uncomplicated by dogma. One calls it, according to one's judgement, unsophisticated or unspoiled.

St Philip's, however, was not taken by storm. During his time there Slim gave no evidence to the staff or to his contemporaries that his quality was exceptional. Looking back, the student of his career can find it significant that the one subject in which he excelled was English, and that the one corporate activity in which he shone was the Debating Society, for throughout his life a second theme runs in counterpoint with his public preoccupations—the private world of words and

* Letter to the author.

writing. But there was nothing remarkable about a schoolboy who could produce good English essays and make a forceful speech. From one small episode, however, much may already be learned about his character.

For some peccadillo the Headmaster forbade him, as a punishment, to attend the school play and speechday in Birmingham's Botanical Gardens. Slim's sense of justice was outraged. He felt that the Headmaster ought to have no control over his actions after school hours, and he therefore presented himself at the Gardens. Here he was observed by the Second Master, a sterling man called Leighton, who pointed out that the Head had forbidden him to come. 'Well, sir, I don't feel he should dictate to me out of school hours.' 'All right,' said Leighton, 'you've made your protest. Now clear out before he sees you.' The relevant points are, first, that Slim accepted the logic and departed without argument, and, secondly, that though he was soon to leave the school he and Leighton exchanged Christmas cards every year until the latter's death in the 1950s. He was never so fettered by authority that his natural independence was inhibited. On the other hand he never allowed his independence to become outrageous. Life must be conducted within a ring-fence defined by duty and discipline. These were deep-seated convictions, which never weakened under stress and never permitted compromise.

The chief bequest of St Philip's, however, was an enduring friendship. A boy called Philip Pratt at first disapproved of the newcomer's *savoir faire* and self-sufficiency; in later years he remembered how he hurled 'opprobrious names'. Yet he was drawn to Slim by the fact that he never replied in kind, but used to walk away with a private, amused smile that made Pratt himself feel small. Then they came to terms and found that they shared similar tastes. ('It is amusing that our youthful ambitions were: his to command a body of mercenaries like Brazenhead of Milan, and mine to be a trooper in the Hussars of Conflans like Brigadier Gerard.'*) They meshed in a close companionship, which continued until Slim's death even though the pattern of their lives was utterly dissimilar. During the First World War Pratt was prevented from taking part, until, towards the end, he contrived to fulfil his boyhood ambition by riding as a trooper in the Hussars. Because he wore spectacles, he had been compelled to work in the explosives industry until the reverses of 1918 caused the standards for enlistment to be

* Philip Pratt, letter to author, 20 August, 1975.

lowered, and he passed out as a fully fledged cavalryman – in Armistice week. Between the wars he was a faithful member of the Warwickshire Yeomanry and in 1939, though he was considered a little long in the tooth, he contrived once again to join the colours, as a Sergeant, when the Yeomanry was sent out to Palestine. In civil life he pursued a quiet industrial career in Birmingham. But from August, 1914, when their paths parted as Slim entered the army, they maintained an unbroken flow of correspondence and would meet when it was possible. Slim was a man of many friendships. His spontaneous and outgoing nature drew others to him and held them by the affection and admiration he aroused. But only Pratt and he had their youth in common.

Indeed, their association had been signed and sealed. They decided that money might be made in buying stamps and selling them at a profit—Pratt to purchase and Slim to sell. On the twelfth day of October in the year Nineteen Hundred and Seven, therefore, a Deed of Partnership was executed. Drawn up in Slim's bold copper plate, it began, 'We, the undersigned, do hereby agree to enter into partnership for the sale of postage, official and fiscal stamps, until such time as is mutually agreed upon to disolve [sic] the afore said partnership.' Stringent conditions were laid down, though their rigour was perhaps qualified by the final clause. 'Any of the above rules may be suspended, struck out, or added to, when agreed upon by both partners.' Above the signature of Philip Claude Pratt appears the impressive William Joseph Slim, A. A. (Oxon).* The whole deed was wrapped in a sheet of paper which had been used by Pratt for elementary shorthand notes at the Midland Institute, and suitably adorned with two red waxen seals.

To Birmingham had come the volumes of *British Battles*. Slim was now studying them in a more practical way, working out from diagrams how the battles had actually been fought. Could he become an officer? The move had brought no greater prosperity, and Sandhurst was beyond imagination. His hero, Hector Macdonald, 'Fighting Mac', had risen from the ranks to become a General, but Slim realized that this was exceptional. He retained his dreams but behaved realistically, and in September, 1908, transferred to King Edward's School, where the educational standard was excellent and where he could qualify as a teacher. Once again English was his best subject, the rest being un-

---

* In those days, to pass the Oxford Senior Local Examination at school avoided the need to take a matriculation examination before entering a University, and earned the title 'Associate in Arts (Oxon)'.

distinguished. However, it was at King Edward's that he stepped out as a soldier, for he joined the Officer Training Corps and was promoted Lance-Corporal.

> Soon I had no option. I was sixteen when my father's business, in spite of his energy and courage, proved increasingly unsuccessful. He had then, late in life, to find other employment—no easy task. Our whole standard of living was drastically reduced. My brother was still a Medical Student at the University, and this at a time when all education beyond the elementary school had to be paid for. Obviously I must, and quickly, relieve my parents of some at least of the expense of supporting me, and of my education. The only job I could get immediately was in elementary school teaching, and so, without much thought and with no knowledge at all of teaching, I became a pupil-teacher at seventeen shillings and sixpence a week.*

Slim spent some two years, first as a pupil-teacher and then as an uncertificated elementary teacher, working in the poorest category of school in Birmingham. Though the city had been a pioneer in overcoming Victorian squalor by civic administration, the slums were still a noisome presence and Slim's pupils were their product. Most were unwashed—a shared tap at an alley's end did not make for cleanliness— some were lousy and he discovered that it was unwise to lean over them too closely 'for fear of enterprising fleas seeking fresh pastures'. Their clothes were threadbare and in summer many lacked boots.

Experience of such poverty has turned some men, in their rage, to seek a political solution. But Slim was not, and would never become, a political animal. He reacted differently. Instead of protesting at the human condition he got to know the human beings. He discovered, for example, that his fellow teachers, in spite of their lowly status, were men and women of vocation for whom he learned to feel respect and affection. As for his pupils:

> These boys were rough and tough; they knew more of the crude facts of life, of sex, disease, drunkenness and petty crime than I did. They daily suffered hardships and deprivations I had never felt. Their enemies to be feared, evaded and out-witted were, generally speaking, rent collectors, school attendance officers, the police, and sometimes even a heavy-handed, not-too-sober parent. Yet these boys, all in all,

---

* *Memoir.*

were cheerful, manly fellows, enduring stoically, taking punishment without whimpering. They had an immensely attractive *gamin* humour and a quick-wittedness that was more than a match for me. Loyal to their own standards and their comrades, generous in thought and action to those they accepted, and, when under difficulties, good sons, especially to their mothers.*

It was said of Slim, when he became Chief of the Imperial General Staff and titular head of the Army, that he had the inestimable merit of never having forgotten 'the smell of a soldier's feet'. That ingrained understanding of the ordinary Other Rank, his psychology, his hopes and fears, which was worth more than divisions when he came to fight the Japanese, had roots stretching far back to a crude classroom in a Birmingham slum, where victory consisted in ending the day without disorder.

Unless one had a sense of vocation, however, the elementary teacher's existence was hardly tolerable. 'So', Slim would put it in his self-mocking way, 'I broke loose and entered industry.' In other words, after searching for a job for some time he was taken on as a junior clerk by Stewarts and Lloyds, the metal tube makers. He had moved from one part of a Dickens novel to another, from the dreadful environment of the novelist's working-class scenarios to one of his City counting-houses, for, like a Dickensian clerk, Slim's bulk now perched on an old high stool in front of an old high desk. James Alford, who perched beside him, particularly remembered that he was always referring to 'this little red book of his dealing with military exercises and tactics'. 'Jim,' he used to say, 'if I were doing this I certainly wouldn't do it this way.'

For the dream was only dormant. It was, at least, a para-military exercise to cycle out at the week-ends on camping expeditions with two friends from Stewarts and Lloyds—one of whom, Mackenzie, had worked as a ranch-hand in the States—and to execute *Operation Sinking Can*. They took the name from their habit of practising shooting at empty tins floating downstream past their second-hand army bell tent; shooting, incidentally, with a formidable armoury which included a ·22 rifle, an automatic pistol and a ·45 Colt revolver, all well supplied with ammunition. But the idea of a military career still nagged. His father wisely pointed out the difficulties, which Slim knew only too

---

* *Memoir.*

well, but added that in his view Germany and England were on a collision course. When the crash came in a few years time there would inevitably be a demand for officers. To get some sort of military qualification without interrupting the business routine might prove a good investment.

Slim now moved fast. His brother Charles was still reading medicine at Birmingham University, where there was, of course, an OTC. Slim was not an undergraduate, but what was a minor technicality? By diplomacy and determination he was enrolled in the Corps in 1912, attending enthusiastically all evening parades and all the week-end and annual camps. His favourite reading now was *Field Service and Musketry Regulations*, and rifle exercises were practised in the solitude of his bedroom. He was like one of the dedicated in Kitchener's Army, a few years ahead of his time. Once again he became a Lance-Corporal (though legend has it that he was temporarily reduced to the ranks because he fell out to get a drink during a route march). He also obtained his Certificate 'A'—through one of those short cuts well known to the army. All had gone well except his drilling, which had ended with the rear rank where the front rank should have been. The regular officer who was examining considered him compassionately. 'Well, that's not too good, is it? But you've got a decent word of command. Tell you what I'll do. March a platoon to the other end of the square, then give them an order from here. If they can hear it—I'll pass you!'

Slim was a ruminant. Life seems to glide past some people without leaving an impression; others absorb and digest. Slim was a pondering man, chewing the cud of experience, and it is striking to observe how often during his time of high command he would draw on what he had deduced from episodes, often apparently trivial, which had occurred many years ago, He was always a pupil-teacher in the classroom of the world. So when he was pushed off his high desk in the office of Stewarts and Lloyds and sent round the various departments, he was bored by accounting and invoicing but found his weeks in the metal works of absorbing interest. There was perhaps no more hard-bitten a character than the Black Country iron worker of 1913, but Slim perceived that he was simply a grown-up version of the boys he had tried to teach. He might gamble, drink and fight, but he was a four-square human being under whose bravado lay the permanent dread of unemployment, accident or sickness, against which he could make small provision. Accepted by this tough society as an equal rather than an interloper, Slim learned much about men—and about skill. He particularly admired

Billy the Bulger, 'a grizzled man of over fifty who, in a disreputable morning coat without collar or tie, but sporting a bowler hat—the badges of superior status—stood beside the press where boiler tubes had the bulge put in one end'. Here he remained by the hour in the raging heat (refreshed occasionally by a jug of beer). Poised, with finger upraised, he would wait patiently for the moment to signal for the tube to crash into the press at precisely the correct temperature.

In one of his pauses I asked Billy how he judged the exact moment of impact. 'By the colour', he answered, but what that colour was he would not say; a man had to hold on to the secrets of his job. Years later, I watched his task being done scientifically by a man seated at what looked like the console of an organ, pressing buttons, throwing switches, peering through a spectroscope. Very impressive, much quicker, and much cleaner; but I wondered if the quota of split tubes was much less than old Billy the Bulger's.*

Here was a useful insight for a man who, in Burma, would have to instil into his forgotten Army the principle of 'do it yourself'.

But he was less satisfied with his employers. He had been promised that he would be sent abroad, probably to South Africa, but nothing stirred. Then he met a young man who had recently been taken on by the Asiatic Petroleum Company, a subsidiary of Shell, and gathered that others were being recruited to go East. His friend was a university graduate who had entered Shell through introductions to the right people. Undeterred, Slim found out from him the name of one of the top executives (which he then characteristically checked for himself in the Company's Annual Report), and took a day excursion to London. Outside the Company's head office in the Strand he carefully dusted his shoes, then ran the gauntlet of the commissionaire and reached the outer room of the executive's sanctum. Without an appointment he carried the position by storm, first overcoming the secretarial outpost and then obtaining an interview. Several other people were next asked to look at him. The result was that he left St Helen's Court, Bishopsgate, in a dazed condition but with instructions to report for a period of probation on 1 September, 1914. He had landed just the job he wanted, but he never returned to St Helen's Court. When he was Governor-General of Australia, however, he had to open a vast new Shell refinery

---

* *Memoir.*

and amused himself and his audience by telling the story. Shell, he added, seemed to have done pretty well without him.

In July he took a fortnight's holiday. Over and over again, in the letters, diaries and autobiographies of his generation, the same fact—incredible as it now seems—is repeated, that war came to them out of a clear sky. Certainly Slim had no inkling of what was imminent. In a few years, perhaps: and it was with this middle-distance contingency in mind that he decided the best way for Lance-Corporal Slim to spend his vacation would be to examine the German Army. He had little money, he had never been abroad before, he did not speak German; but 'Time spent in reconnaissance is seldom wasted', so he went to Metz. Everything he saw, the drill, the bearing and turnout of the troops, the faultless elegance of the officers impressed him with a sense of effortless efficiency. And he lost his first encounter with the German Army, for when he foolishly entered a barracks by an unguarded gate, and started to prowl around, an enormous bellowing NCO ejected him as though he had committed sacrilege.

Still, he handsomely won the next round in his amateur game of Intelligence. It was his daily custom to watch the changing of the guard outside the *Kommandantur*. The normal dress was blue tunics, white trousers and *pickelhaube*, but there came a day when the old guard in its colourful uniform was relieved by a new guard in field grey, equipped with knapsacks and helmet-covers. Since he was unable to read the local newspapers Slim knew nothing about the current international situation except that some time ago an Austrian Archduke had been murdered, but instinct told him that field grey meant trouble. This was confirmed when he got back to his cheap little hotel and ran into another Englishman, a seedy-looking individual who explained that he was a jockey, that he had been riding in Germany, that war between Austria and Serbia must start in a matter of hours and involve Germany too, and that they must get away immediately. Throughout the day the streets were filled with troops, transport and cavalry, all moving westwards and all in field grey. Next morning Slim was *en route* for home.

He paused in Birmingham only to pick up his uniform, and then joined his OTC in camp on Salisbury Plain, just beating the outbreak of war. His emotions were typical of his innocent generation—would it all be over before he got into the fighting? The unit was quickly ordered back to Birmingham and the cadets were told not to enlist, but to await orders. Slim used to describe with relish his first independent command,* which came his way when they arrived home at Snow Hill station. He was left with all the ammunition and two men, and instructed to get it safely to the Drill Hall. With the high authority of a Lance-Corporal's stripe he extracted from the Station Master not only a hand trolley, but also three porters to drag it, and with bayonets fixed they escorted the Great Western Railway through the heart of Birmingham. After a short wait he learned, on 22 August, that he had been gazetted a Second Lieutenant in the Royal Warwickshire Regiment. Four days later a Lieutenant in a regular battalion of the Warwicks, one Bernard Montgomery, went into his first attack in Flanders.

It was good for morale during the Second World War to spread the word that 'Uncle Bill' had risen from the ranks to the military heights, but this was not the case. Hector Macdonald had done so. 'Wully' Robertson had ascended from being a trooper in the 16th Lancers to the rank of Field-Marshal and the office of CIGS. One of Slim's own contemporaries, Sir Archibald Nye (also of the Royal Warwicks) became a VCIGS after serving in the ranks during 1914/15. But Slim was no different from the multitude of other young men who provided the officers for Kitchener's Army after peacetime service as cadets in their Officer Training Units at school or university. That he had slipped into his OTC sideways was merely to his credit. Anyway, he was launched—and Cloudesley Shovell would have approved.

---

* Notably in October, 1947, in his speech on receiving the freedom of the City of Birmingham.

CHAPTER TWO

THE RIVER OF DEATH

They then addressed themselves to the water; and entering,
Christian began to sink, and crying out to his good friend
Hopeful, he said, I sink in deep waters; the billows go over my
head, all his waves go over me, Selah.
Then said the other, Be of good cheer my brother, I feel the
bottom, and it is good.

John Bunyan, *The Pilgrim's Progress*

FOR MOST of the young subalterns who were Slim's contemporaries at the beginning of the Great War the pilgrimage, as Bunyan described it on his title page, 'from this world to that which is to come' was short and ugly. Few survived the River of Death; the waves and the billows went over them. But Slim was lucky. Though he was twice wounded—once almost fatally—he recovered, without being maimed or seriously weakened. But he was even more fortunate in that chance took him to Gallipoli and Mesopotamia and not to the Western Front. He saw hard fighting and harsh conditions, but he was spared the interminable erosion of Flanders—that reiterated slaughter at Ypres, the Somme and Passchendaele which, in its course, could destroy several times over the complete muster of an infantry battalion. The effect of their experience as young officers in this theatre was marked in a number of the senior British commanders during the Second World War. Slim came through unscathed in spirit. Like Hopeful, he was able to keep in touch with the bottom, to retain a cheerful sanity in the midst of the River of Death. A naturally robust temperament might have preserved his equanimity even in the wilderness of the Salient, or at Mametz Wood, or during the March Retreat; as it happened, he was certainly subjected to strains but was never mentally overstrained. It might be said that by 1918 he had learned a great deal about war without knowing too much. Still, while Christian was 'troubled with apparitions of hobgoblins and evil spirits', it was Hopeful who got them over the River. Slim never lost buoyancy, and this would be of profound importance in Burma when he carried a whole army on his back.

In appearance the 23-year-old Second Lieutenant who reported to the 9th Battalion of the Royal Warwickshire Regiment at Tidworth, on Salisbury Plain, was a prototype of the stalwart figure beneath his bush hat which so many photographs of the Burma campaign were to present as a personification of the will for victory. He already had the bearing and presence that pick a man out in a crowd—the upright, self-confident stance, the steady, candid eyes. And the chin had already begun to jut, the strong, pugnacious chin which would later remind one of T. E. Lawrence's insight about Allenby, that a battleship does not require the razor-edge bow of a destroyer because the power-drive of its engines is so much greater. Unfortunately that September afternoon the Assistant Adjutant in the orderly room was blind to these features of the subaltern who had spent the whole of his time in the train checking and re-checking his unfamiliar new uniform. 'You', he observed coldly, 'are improperly dressed.' And, after a suitable pause, 'Your whistle cord is on the wrong shoulder.'* *Malbroucke s'en va t'en guerre!*

One day he stood on a bunker on Tidworth Golf Course and surveyed his platoon. It was his introduction to his first command—60 of them. All the old romantic day-dreams instantaneously dissolved. Only he, his sergeant and his lance-corporal were in uniform; the rest wore a crumpled and dusty miscellany of clothes above which could be observed a mixture of caps, panamas, bowlers and straw boaters. This was Kitchener's First Army, the First Hundred Thousand, 'K1' as they proudly put on their Battalion Orders. But the spirit of Slim's raggle-taggle platoon was the spirit of its army, unquenchable, in spite of shortage of weapons, clothing and every other warlike store. It was a spirit summed up in the reply of one of his men to his platoon commander's tactful suggestion that, patriotism apart, he was rather old for an infantryman. 'What! Me! Too old! Father's here!' And though they

---

* He had much to learn. In his subaltern's pride he gave a lackadaisical response to a sergeant's smart salute, unaware that his Colonel was watching. The CO reprimanded him, stuck his cane in the ground, and ordered Slim to stand correctly and salute it properly for half an hour.

had no rifles, they had reminders about what lay ahead. On 6 December Slim wrote to Pratt: 'We have some wounded Germans here; they looked pretty horrible when they arrived but are much fatter and cleaner now. We have also some British prisoners from the Front undergoing imprisonment for self-mutilation. One poor devil is doing two years for sleeping on guard—he's in hospital with enteric.'

Most of Slim's men came from the Black Country, miners and workers in iron and steel, the hard cases he had learned to understand in the days when he met Billy the Bulger. That proved a useful apprenticeship, for it was the miners who first put him to the test. They mutinied. Slim was informed that they had barricaded themselves in their barrack room and refused to go on duty. When he arrived he found that their complaint was that they had been defrauded of their pay. Slim realized that they were simply miners on strike, making the only protest to which they were accustomed; their obligations as soldiers had been overlooked. The sergeant-major and sergeant having failed to make them see reason, Slim persuaded them that he—and he alone—should be allowed into their fortress. 'My miners meant business. I sat rather nervously on a bed, surrounded by a ring of angry faces.'

As he talked to them, gently but firmly, he gradually extracted that the reason for 'witholding their labour' was that the family allotments they had made had been based on their miner's pay. A private's was even less than a miner's, and as a result they found that after all deductions the amount of cash they actually handled on pay day was derisory. The bosses must be cheating, so they had downed tools. Slim won them over, squatting in the stuffy barrack, with a promise that each man's account should be scrupulously examined by himself, the company pay clerk, and the man concerned. The strike ended. There had been no malpractices. The soldiers were satisfied; the matter was kept from the Colonel's ears. It was a small and early lesson in man-management, but as usual Slim thought much about its implications. He became convinced that in his training an officer should be taught what causes mutinies, how to avoid them, and, if they occur, how to deal with them. Many an officer faced with the outbreaks of 1919 would have been grateful for such instruction. (However, when Slim was teaching at the Staff College in the thirties, and proposed an exercise in mutinies, it was rejected on the grounds that it was in rather bad taste even to contemplate the possibility.)

Esprit de corps came easily, for all were Midlanders, and their motto was ' 'E ain't polite enough to come from the South; 'e ain't honest enough to come from the North; 'e must 'ave come from Bermigum!' Efficiency improved, as proper scales of equipment arrived, and, more importantly, as 'our training, based at first on the tactics of the South African War, the fire fight, building up to the assault by short rushes under cover of rifle fire, soon gave place to the methods being so inexorably imposed at The Front, the digging of defensive systems, the routine of trench warfare and staged mass attacks with the maximum artillery support.' But the omens began to change. First, inoculation against enteric, 'done with a syringe like a football pump in one colossal dose'; Slim noted a small signaller crashing to the floor in a dead faint as soon as he felt the prick, and the next time he remembered the event was in battle, as he watched the man out in the open, under heavy fire, calmly mending a telephone cable. Then bales of drill uniform arrived, and boxes of sun helmets. It must be Gallipoli. 'At last the evening came when, after dark, we fell in on the parade ground; the Colonel said the Lord's Prayer as the battalion stood silent in the gloom, and very quietly we moved off to the little country station from which we were to entrain for Avonmouth.

'It is a most serious military offence to strike a superior officer; it is an even more serious one to strike a subordinate. I have committed both, the first once only, the second twice—if I count what happened now.'* Unfortunately for military history the two other improprieties are unrecorded.† But what happened now was that as he walked along the platform to see that his platoon was entraining properly Slim heard the voice of a tall and drunken Irish private proclaiming that he was 'off to Gally-poly in the morning'—somewhat irrelevantly, since he was refusing to get into his compartment. When Slim remonstrated he was violently attacked by flailing fists, and had to fight back until support came up and the Irishman was hurled aboard, to start his journey to Armageddon flat on the floor beneath a dozen army boots.

The embarkation of the Royal Warwicks was the by-product of a new mood in Whitehall and Westminster. The disappointing failure of the Navy to break through the Dardanelles had been followed by the miracle of the landings on the Gallipoli peninsula, but when footholds

---

* *Memoir.*
† When he was Governor-General of Australia Slim told Sir William Morrow that he had once knocked down a Colonel when he was a Brigadier in Eritrea. If so, this could only have been at Gallabat. (see p. 65).

secured at the Anzac and Helles beachheads in April led only to stalemate and slaughter there was a deep sense of disillusion. Churchill paid
the price. 'How art thou fallen from heaven, O Lucifer, son of the
morning!' But in May the pendulum swung back, 'For a period,
enthusiasm for the Gallipoli operations reached unparalleled heights in
London.'* Encouraged by Kitchener, the Cabinet on 9 June authorized
a reinforcement for Sir Ian Hamilton of three New Army divisions,
10 (Irish), 11 (Northern), and 13 (Western), as well as extra naval units.
A month later two further divisions, 53 and 54, were ordered out. Thus
Slim, whose battalion was in 39 Brigade of 13 Division, was riding in
on the second great wave of the Gallipoli campaign. A breathless post-
card to Pratt from Malta on 2 July was pardonably dramatic. 'Dear
Phil, Put in here for water. Leave for unknown destination (supposed
to be the Isle of Blank) in twenty minutes or so. Uneventful voyage so
far. This is beginning to look a little more like business.' It was; on 13
July the Warwicks relieved the Worcesters in their trenches on Cape
Helles.

Of the Helles bridgehead, at the top of the peninsula, it has been
observed that it 'looked like a midden and smelt like an opened cemetery',
and that it was 'a prison, which became a tomb'. Here on the low ground
beneath the critical but unconquered height of Achi Baba the Expeditionary Force was trapped. Between the beginning of June and
13 July, the day Slim arrived, an advance of only 500 yards had been
achieved at a cost to the Allies of over 17,000 casualties and 40,000 to
the Turks. No wonder that the infantry, as one signals corporal noted,
were beginning to look 'like old, tottering men, bowed stooping, and
most of their faces were colourless, except that they were grey or dirty.
Now and then we heard some odd remark, but there was very little
talking and less laughter. There was so little to laugh about, now . . .'†

In this graveyard 9 Battalion endured for 15 days . . . 'for a short
spell of duty at Helles while waiting for the 10th and 11th Divisions to
arrive', as the *Official History* puts it in a dismissive manner about
which Slim, the author of *Unofficial History*, would have had something
mordant to say. There were strict orders that this New Army Division
should only be used defensively, since Hamilton wanted all his fresh
reinforcements for the big assault he was planning for August. Never-

---

* Robert Rhodes James, *Gallipoli*, p. 216.
† Ibid.

theless the daily attrition of bombardment, trench raids and minor local attacks took its toll.

On the extreme left of the British line, we and the enemy had been so near together that in places we held one part, he another, of the same trench, with a block between us, over which we lobbed our improvised jam-tin—literally jam-tin—bombs and got in return his more sophisticated German cricket-ball and stick grenades. Indeed we did not exaggerate too wildly when we sometimes wryly said we shared the parapet with the Turk and took turns with him at the loopholes.*

Over everything there glittered the metallic green of the obscene and bloated blow-flies; over everything spread the inescapable odour of decay. So close were the Warwicks to the Turks that it was impossible to bury the hundreds of bodies lying between them—bodies which, as on the Western Front, were often embedded in the very walls of their trenches.

During a short period out of the line—not that anyone was ever truly out of line at Helles—an episode occurred which could be discounted as part of the mythology that envelops a famous soldier were it not authenticated by Slim himself. He described it to Philip Pratt. His platoon was at rest on the sun-drenched beach and he had secured for it the one patch of shade, formed by a large rock which stood detached from the main cliff. 'Instead of relaxing, he stood out in the sun watching the spasmodic shelling of the beaches by a far-off, invisible Turkish gun. He watched the shells exploding at intervals and saw how each was nearer than the last. Noticing the even timing as well as the even spacing, Slim fell to calculating times and distances. He came to the startling conclusion that the fourth shell from then would fall in the very shadow of the rock under which his men were lying.'† To move a platoon of battle-weary men from shade to Mediterranean sun for no ostensible reason demands conviction and courage. Slim got them away, listened to their protests, watched a platoon of another regiment move into their place, and shortly afterwards saw a shell burst in the midst of the new arrivals.

When they pulled out after this 'short spell of duty' the Warwicks had lost in killed and wounded four officers and 510 other ranks. Colonel Palmer, who had sent them off from Tidworth with the Lord's

---

* *Memoir.*
† Philip Pratt, 'Care for His Men', *British Army Annual No. 2*, 1955.

Prayer, had died from a sniper's bullet through the head. The survivors were riddled with dysentery. In this state they were dumped on the island of Lemnos to recover themselves for the Big Push, and in a centipede-ridden vineyard they counted their blessings. These, apart from life itself, were few. Sickness was increasing, and rations of half molten bully beef, hard-tack biscuit and over-chlorinated water gave no encouragement to queasy stomachs. Slim was ordered to go to the HQ of the Lines of Communications to get authority to draw extras, particularly tinned milk, and money for local purchase of eggs, fruit, goats and chickens. Above all he was instructed, against the direst penalties, to lay hands on the battalion's mail, which was thought to have been lurking in the L-of-C HQ for weeks.

The next few hours had a radical and lasting effect on the future commander. He saw in an extreme form what happens when the principle is forgotten which Montgomery, in his own *Memoirs*, records as a main lesson he learned in 1914–18—that 'the staff must be the servant of the troops'. The reasons were manifold. Hamilton consistently disregarded his administrative officers. Kitchener insisted on retaining distant Alexandria as the expedition's base, so that the Lemnos L-of-C had all the responsibilities of a base but only the power and capacity of a forwarding unit. The good officers, who achieved miracles in equipping, maintaining, watering and feeding a large army, were over-worked and overwrought; the bad officers, who were not in short supply, cultivated an attitude of superiority towards the front line troops which was inexcusable, and their headquarter ship became a byword. 'Certainly', wrote the war correspondent Henry Nevinson, 'to anyone coming fresh from the dug-outs, dust-storms, monotonous rations and perpetual risks of the Peninsula, the *Aragon* was like an Enchanted Isle.'

He might have been describing Slim, whose first problem was how to reach this paradise. None of the many craft in the harbour were interested in him. He finally hitched a lift from a naval Captain in his spotless pinnace, only to be stopped by a sergeant as he climbed on board the *Aragon*. He was told, apologetically, that he could go no further. A notice on the rail stated: 'No visiting officers or other ranks will be permitted to board unless they are on duty and wearing correct uniform with jackets and badges of rank.' Slim was in his cleanest shirt and shorts. A compromise was achieved. The sergeant lent him his own jacket, and wearing this Slim stepped on to the deck in acceptable order.

It was lunchtime. Nobody offered him lunch, or even a drink. Everybody passed him on to the next man. He watched the white-jacketed stewards serving the Overlords in their deck chairs and struck out for himself, waylaying one for sandwiches and another for a gin and lime with *ice*. Thus fortified, he continued his quest.

> I got the impression that visitors from the fighting troops, especially those who interfered with the pleasant tenor of staff life by asking for things, were not really welcome. I also felt increasingly that the staff was not itself very efficient: at least they did not seem to know how to help me, even if they were willing, nor to what departments I should go for my requirements or where in the maze of this great ship they were located.*

At last he discovered a Major who obviously would have preferred to be in action on the Peninsula, and who offered to act as guide. He got his cash; then the battalion's mail, from under a vast pile of undelivered bags; then the authority to draw extra rations. Finally his friend solved the problem of a return voyage by getting him on to a water barge heading for shore. As he looked back, and saw the clusters of red-tabbed staff officers taking their drinks in the evening breeze, he thought maliciously of the story then current in the trenches of Helles. *Aragon* was said to be so deeply aground on gin bottles that she would never sail again.

But August was now approaching, and the time for Ian Hamilton's great new plan to unfold—a plan so shrouded in secrecy that for long it was withheld even from the staff at GHQ. In essence it was simple: a powerful reinforcement of the troops in the Anzac bridgehead to enable them to break our successfully, accompanied by an entirely new landing, a little further north at Suvla Bay.

Slim's part in the operation was brief, if intense, and it is therefore unnecessary to review the many causes for the failure of this ambitious but promising concept—the deadening lethargy of General Stopford, the lack of push at the right time on both fronts, the disastrous assaults which were ordered at the wrong time, the absence of a co-ordinating control. For Slim the point of interest was that 13 Division (with which he sailed from England), a brigade of the 10th, and 29 Indian Brigade were allocated to General Birdwood as reinforcement for the Australians and New Zealanders he commanded within the Anzac beachhead. The Warwicks, therefore, were among the 20,000 men who, by a remarkable

---

* *Memoir.*

achievement, were ferried over the sea on three successive nights, landed at Anzac, and concealed successfully in caves and trenches without being observed by the enemy.

The object of the attack from Anzac was to capture and secure the Sari Bair ridge, that massive central spine dominating the battle-area of the Peninsula with its high-points of Koja Chemen Tepe, Hill Q and Chunuk Bair. By seizing this crest-line Hamilton could deny the Turks observation of his own ground, and also obtain a commanding view of the straits themselves and the enemy-held territory between Sari Bair and the Dardanelles. Here lay the key to the whole campaign. A Right Assaulting Column was to make for Chunuk Bair, and a Left Assaulting Column for the other two summits—a double commitment which, in view of the distance and cruel ground, and the enfeebled condition of the infantry, was excessive. And so it proved when, during the last hours of 6 August, the battle began. At dawn next morning the New Zealanders, with elements of 1/5th and 2/10th Gurkhas, were within 1,000 yards of Chunuk Bair; a company of 1/6th Gurkhas was a similar distance from Hill Q, but little progress had been made towards Koja Chemen Tepe. And all forward movement had now been halted either by the exhaustion of the troops, lack of information, or the inertia of local commanders.

Attention is now focused on Hill Q. As the fighting was renewed throughout the 7th and 8th, in desperate self-sacrificial attempts to make up for time that had been irrecoverably lost and to overcome constantly increasing opposition, it was towards this feature that Slim found himself drawn. The Warwicks were part of the Left Assaulting Column, and very soon Slim had to act as Company Commander because all his superiors had been shot. (When the operation was concluded, every officer of 9th Royal Warwicks had been killed or wounded, and only 175 men answered the roll-call after the battle.) During the night of the 7th/8th he had pressed forward and upwards to a position close to that group of Gurkhas who, under their brilliant commander, Major Allanson, had almost reached the summit of Hill Q in the first night attack. (Allanson was wounded and recommended for the VC, but received the DSO.) The Major, having been ordered to attack again at dawn on the 8th, went in with his small force alone, since he had been unable to contact the two regiments with whom he was supposed to assault. By the mountain-craft of the Gurkhas he manoeuvred his men to within 300 yards of the summit before being pinned down.

As he trudged up towards the heights Slim had passed through the area of the ANZAC brigade commanded by John Monash, whose biography by A. J. Smithers recaptures this chance of war.

> For a moment of time, in a myrtle-covered ravine without a name, the paths of two great soldiers crossed, one who was in a few years to become Australia's first general of international reputation, the other who, a generation later, would prove himself to be the greatest fighting commander the army had known since Wellington. At the head of the company of the Royal Warwicks on its way to join Allanson on Hill Q walked its commander, a Territorial soldier holding a temporary commission, William Joseph Slim.

But now Allanson was under the lip of the summit.

> This magnificent advance, executed with great skill and enterprise and at relatively minor cost, had been seen by Slim, whose company of Warwicks were occupying a cramped and dangerous position on Allanson's left. Slim had some Gurkhas with him, and led them across with him to a line of men lying in a row in cover; there he found Allanson, with whom he shared a 'dirty envelope of raisins', and discussed the situation, agreeing to act together as far as possible as a single unit.*

This was one of the turning-points in Slim's life. It has often been noted that when he transferred to the Indian Army he joined the Gurkhas because of the admiration he formed for them at Gallipoli, but it has not been sufficiently stressed that his first introduction to them was to the very battalion, the 1/6th, which he subsequently joined; that he and they came together at the extreme spearpoint of the British thrust from Anzac; and that what he witnessed was one of the most gallant actions on a Peninsula where absolute bravery became a commonplace. Not only that, but by putting himself under Allanson's command at that moment of danger he became a sort of acting member of the Gurkha Brigade whose motto is 'It is better to die than be a coward'.

At 6.30 next morning Allanson reported: 'All the troops concerned had an extremely bad night last night, and only just clung on.' By that

---

* Robert Rhodes James, *op. cit.* p. 284. Allanson's group contained survivors from all three Gurkha battalions, 1/6th, 1/5th and 2/10th.

time, however, Slim was *en route* for the beaches, wounded, and Allanson had seen the Dardanelles—he and his handful of men being the only Allied soldiers to do so from the inland heights.

The night had indeed been bad—constant shelling, no replenishment of water, food or ammunition, near misses from the guns of the Navy, a searchlight playing over the hill-side to prevent the Turks from making a surprise attack. An attempt on their right, by the New Zealanders and four British battalions, to gain Chunuk Bair had failed; the British got lost, and the New Zealanders were stopped in their tracks. At 5.15 am a vicious naval bombardment, which was intended to herald an attack all along the line, came to its end, but the only troops available to follow it up were Allanson, his Gurkhas, and the elements of the Warwicks and South Lancashires who had joined him—making three companies in all. They went straight for the top 'and then', Allanson wrote, 'for about ten minutes we fought hand to hand, we bit and fisted, and used rifles and pistols as clubs; blood was flying about like spray from a hair-wash bottle'. The summit was conquered. They had their historic view. Then, unsupported, they were at last called back.

But Slim never reached the crest. He was directing his company, now reduced to fifty men, up the steep and scrub-covered slope.

At that moment someone hit me hard between the shoulders with a huge, flat shovel. . . . The blow pitched me heavily on my face, but after a dazed moment I managed to sit up. I felt no pain and was surprised to see blood spurting from the point of my left shoulder and already spreading in a dark, damp patch over my jacket. . . . I sat there wonderingly for a second and then Gregson, one of my two surviving officers, was kneeling beside me. The firing was heavier now, clapping just over our heads, and as Gregson leant towards me to speak, he suddenly slumped forward across my feet.*

Slim had enough strength to put his only remaining subaltern in command, and then his batman shuffled him down the hill to an Aid Post, where the doctor, after examining him, cried out, 'By God, you're shot through the ticker!' However, he bandaged Slim up with the yards of muslin wrapping from his topee, and his batman, having made him comfortable, gave him a rifle butt salute, then trudged back up the hill to his death . . . a small untidy man, Greenway, an ex-footman

* *Memoir.*

and an epileptic whose fits his mates helped to conceal, fondly believing
that his officer knew nothing about them. Shortly afterwards Slim was
on the Anzac beach, unconscious, tossing in a barge which responded
rhythmically to the incoming waves.

This eternally repeated *lift* . . . *pause* . . . *bump* was the first thing I
became aware of, and mistily I half-wondered about it—but I was not
very interested. I was conscious that I existed, but how or where I did
not bother; I lay in a vague contentment, almost without thought and
quite without feeling or emotion. *Lift* . . *pause* . . . *bump, lift* . . . *pause*
. . . *bump*. I was not asleep but I might be dreaming.

Then one wave, larger than the rest, broke the rhythm, lifted the
barge higher and dumped it on the sand with a shuddering jar. Automatically I tensed my muscles against the shock and pushed my head
back on the rough canvas of the stretcher. At once, a stab of pain
thrust through my chest, so severe and sudden that I cried out—at
least I would have cried out, but hardly any sound beyond a strange,
stifled gurgling came from my throat. There was blood in my mouth;
I fought for breath as if I were drowning.*

'Poor bastard,' said a half-naked Australian, whose right leg was held
together by two splints made of the helves of entrenching tools. 'Poor
bastard. Feelin' crook?'

There followed a terrible passage through the darkness, as the barge
was towed from ship to ship in search of one that was not already full of
wounded. At last they reached a craft which, though crowded to the
gangways, accepted them. Slim was now very ill. After they sailed he
was mainly unconscious; the foetid air in the confined deck-space,
packed with broken bodies, oppressed him; a time came when he knew
he was dying. As he gasped for air a little steward noticed him, got
help, and moved him out into the dark, cool night. Then the steward
talked him back into life. It was wrong to wish to die; it was wrong to
let oneself die. He had wanted to die once and he knew. He was still
talking when Slim fell asleep.†

Next day they reached Lemnos harbour and were transferred to the
Aquitania, one of the transports which had brought out the New Army

* *Memoir.*
† Years later, in India, he re-enacted this moving episode. A fellow-officer wanted
to commit suicide. Slim prevented him by talking to him all through the critical
night. When he was asked how he managed to hold his attention he said, 'I
discovered he was interested in butterflies.'

Divisions and was being used as a temporary hospital ship. Slim was taken to a comfortable ward, where at last he found himself between white sheets—after one hitch: when they lifted him the stretcher came too, since the canvas was gummed to his bloody back and shoulders. But though the voyage home seemed to go smoothly (because he was under sedation) he was disturbed, when the *Aquitania* docked at Southampton, to discover that an orderly had pinned on him a label shouting 'DANGEROUS. Not to be moved by train'. So it was in a jolting ambulance, semi-conscious, that he was conveyed to the Royal Victoria Hospital, Netley, where the first thing of which he was aware was a rhinoceros—only a trophy on a wall, but to him a monstrous part of that nightmare which had started, so long ago, high on the scrub-strewn slopes of unconquered Sari Bair.

At Netley Slim was nearly made a cripple for life. The process began with a formal examination by an RAMC Colonel, surrounded by the usual cohort of juniors. After sinister mutterings and consultation of X-ray photographs he pronounced: 'The left lung is completely collapsed, with lesions. The heart is displaced into the resulting cavity some three inches. It is evident, from the track of the bullet and from the area of local paralysis and insensitivity, that the bracheal plexus has suffered injury. The scapula is fractured and the head of the humerus shattered.* He then looked at Slim with what the patient felt to be a wintry gleam of approbation, and addressed his flock. 'This, gentlemen', he said with satisfaction, 'this is *really good clinical material!*'

The Colonel's conclusion was that the shoulder joint and upper arm of this excellent material should be wired together. The joint would be immovable but—with luck—the hand might be raised to the mouth. As to the lung, its future seemed dubious. 'You've finished', he said cheerfully, 'with soldiering for good.' All was dust and ashes. 'I have known since what it is to lose battles,' Slim wrote in his old age, 'but I have never suffered so morale-shattering a defeat as that.'

Yet the battle was not lost. There was a Blücher at his Waterloo. When the ward was quiet a young Territorial doctor who had been caring for Slim slipped furtively through the door. 'It's against all military discipline and what not, but I'm a doctor not a soldier. *Don't have that operation!* Refuse to have it; you can, you know. Don't have it!' He explained that if Slim refused the operation he couldn't be worse

---

* For all this Slim ultimately received a disability grant of £125.

off, whereas there was a good chance that new methods would make the shoulder function again, if only partially. He knew a place in London—massage, latest electrical treatment and so on. Strengthened by this reinforcement, Slim counter-attacked the authorities, avoided the operation—and remained a soldier.

His improvement is charted in letters to Philip Pratt. On 26 August he wrote: 'I suppose you heard I got pipped. It was a bit of a knockout—thro' the lung, smashed the left shoulder to blazes and bust the top of my arm. I couldn't breathe for a few days. . . . On the *Aquitania* I met Fr Sebastian who gave me the Last Sacraments . . . yours slightly damaged, Will. PS. I haven't told my Mother my wound is serious.' By 6 September he is reporting: 'There seems little doubt I shall get back at least part of the use of the arm. They give me a terrific doings every morning—so far they have succeeded in getting my wrist to work as well as the hand and incidentally they have given me hell.' On the 26th his letter begins, 'I believe I leave here some time this week', and he describes how, in his typical way, he had got back on to the *Aquitania* to seek out the doctor who had looked after him. 'He was surprised and told me he thought when he had me that I had splinters of bone in my big arteries and should die of haemorrage (that's spelt wrong but you know what I mean.)' Then he added 'I was boarded day before yesterday and declared permanently disabled but fit for active service in three months.' As he reasonably commented, it was the verdict of a fat-headed old Colonel; but it was a verdict.

CHAPTER THREE

EAST OF SUEZ

URING THE next two years the course of Slim's life turned
decisively in a new direction. By chance, rather than by calculation, he was drawn first to Mesopotamia and then to India. While
it is true that in 1914 he had inserted himself into the Asiatic Petroleum
Company, this was only for the sake of getting abroad and earning
more money; the East, as such, had never particularly tempted him.
Though he had indeed been impressed by the Gurkhas at Gallipoli,
there was nothing inevitable about his ultimate arrival in the Indian
Army, from which so much was to flow. Still, 'things and actions are
what they are,' as Bishop Butler observed in the eighteenth century,
'and the consequences of them will be what they will be.'

The immediate question, however, was whether Slim would ever
again be able to return to active service. By the end of October he was
in London convalescing, taking treatment, and writing to Pratt, 'I'm
getting disgustingly fat and flabby. The sooner I'm given a job of work
the better for me, if it's not too strenuous. Can't say I'm bursting to
return to Gallipoli or Serbia.' His real destination, however, was
Dorset, for during the winter he was posted to the 12th (Holding)
Battalion of the Royal Warwicks at Bovington. 'I am most annoyed
with the WO,' he wrote to Pratt on 2 February, 1916. 'They have
transferred me to this Battalion, strafe 'em, without consulting me in the
least. I don't want to join this blank regiment. The old 9th was good
enough for me (see daily papers). The prospect of stopping here for
the duration of the War fills me with gloom.'

The company in a wartime holding battalion was inevitably mixed,
and not always to Slim's taste. 'There are many capts and senior lieuts

who have never, and will never, go out and get killed. They don't want to!' But enforced leisure now allowed him to start developing that practice of writing about his experiences which he would pursue, at times from economic necessity but always with satisfaction, for the rest of his life. His style was still callow, his spelling unreliable, his thoughts conventional. He was not yet ready for the market. But an assiduous and self-critical habit of composition evolved, over the years, the techniques which made *Defeat into Victory* not only the most modest, but also the best written, of all books published by those who held a senior command in the Second World War.

Pratt played a large part in this process. As young men in Birmingham they had shared their thoughts about everything, from literature to comparative theology. Now they began a routine of sending each other their manuscripts and exchanging detailed criticism. Indeed, one observes in a letter from Bovington an important embryo. Slim to Pratt, 2 February, 1916: 'I am enclosing MS of latest effort. I have polished it up a bit since you last read it but don't think I have improved it at all. Let me have your opinion, or if you think it good enough get it typed and send me the bill. Do you think it might get accepted anywhere "at our usual rates"?' Here was the germ of a useful arrangement in later years, when Slim was in India and writing marketable material, whereby Pratt in England acted as his honorary 'agent', placing articles and stories and guarding Slim's interests. Pratt himself had high ambitions, for in March Slim was writing to him about what he called his 'gypsy senario' [*sic*], of which he sagely remarked that its lack of humour was a weakness, 'as for a long film people hardly want all love and scrapping'. He added that he wasn't actually up-to-date in film techniques. In 1916! At Bovington!

Among the miscellany of officers in 12 Royal Warwicks there was fortunately one with whom he became friendly and who was to act as an important catalyst in his career. This was Lieut R. E. Barnwell, who had already served in France. He and Slim would go riding together, and one day he mentioned how he had heard in the trenches that the War Office was offering Regular Commissions to temporary officers; his own application, he explained, seemed to be going smoothly. Slim took fire at the idea, but worried about his lack of private means. However, in 1973 Colonel Barnwell recalled, in a BBC Television programme about Slim, that he later reported: 'I find there's a thing called the West India Regiment where the chaps go when they're broke. And so I'm going to apply to them.' As he did; his War Office

Record of Service shows him as commissioned in the Regiment on 1 June, 1916. But it was not in the Caribbean that his destiny lay.

Nor on the Western Front. When Slim died *The Times* declared in its obituary notice that after being wounded at Gallipoli 'he reappeared in the firing line, this time in France'. The implications flatter his gallantry, but the facts are different. He was, of course, in no condition to endure the trenches of the Western Front in the spring of 1916. His own account characteristically sets the matter in perspective. Slim to Pratt, 3 April, 1916: 'Dear Phil, I leave for France in three hours. Sounds awfully dramatic but it only amounts to this—I'm conducting a draft of 38 men to Étaples or somewhere. Not a very exciting job but a rather aggravating one as half the men aren't a bit keen on going and two at least I'm sure are going to try to cut in London when it's a bit difficult to shepherd them. . . . They are a pretty tough lot when the drink is in 'em, too, bless 'em.' His *Record of Service* shows that he went to France, as a draft-conducting officer, but under the heading 'Battle, siege, action' there appears, uncompromisingly, 'NONE'.

Later in the year, nevertheless, he found himself in charge of another draft; but this time it was to Mesopotamia, and to reinforce his beloved old battalion, the 9th Royal Warwicks. Officially (as it later emerged), he was still unfit for active employment, but his *Record of Service*, which deals only with facts and not with nuances, firmly shows him as posted to the 9th in Iraq, with the rank of Temporary Captain, as from 2 September, 1916. When he was brought back to England from Gallipoli Slim had feared that the shattered 9th would never be reconstituted, but, on the contrary, the battalion was withdrawn to Lemnos, reinforced, and returned to Cape Helles to cover the final evacuation from the Peninsula. Then it exchanged the Dardanelles for the Tigris, and moved with 13 Division to Mesopotamia.

In *Unofficial History* Slim gave an engaging account of this new turn in his fortunes which, in the event, would commit him to East of Suez for the major part of his military life. Conscription was authorized in March, 1916. At Bovington it was decided to segregate the conscript intake into a separate company which would become a draft for the battalion in Mesopotamia; Slim, as senior subaltern, applied for and obtained command of this draft. But in view of the official excitement after he was wounded a second time it is clear that someone, somewhere, was persuaded to turn a blind eye; he seems, in fact, to have escaped back to active service while still being technically unfit. However that may be, he had a lively voyage out, including the Mediterranean evening when a submarine first tried to torpedo and then shelled his transport, while 200 Welsh Territorials fell in on deck and sang 'Nearer, My God, to Thee'. They reached the 9th to find them resting outside Kut el Amara, whose humiliating surrender by Townshend (after the Turks had rejected a bribe of £2,000,000) left a stain that must now be effaced. 'Resting in Mesopotamia', Slim wrote, 'meant that, instead of sitting in trenches dug in the desert, one sat in tents in the same desert. It was just as hot, just as uncomfortable, just as depressing, and more monotonous. But it was something to be back with the battalion again and to find myself commanding my old company.'

Once more, as at Gallipoli, he found himself about to ride on the back of a breaking wave—but this time it was irresistible. 'The elderly relics of the Indian army were at last passed over by the elevation of a junior major-general in Mesopotamia.'* Stanley Maude, who had done well in France and at Helles, and on the Tigris had commanded 13 Division (to which Slim's battalion of the Warwicks belonged), took over the whole Expeditionary Force on 28 August by the direct intervention of the CIGS, 'Wully' Robertson. His effect on the campaign may be compared with that of Montgomery when, in another August, he transformed the Eighth Army almost overnight. Spirits rose. Administration improved. The wounded had a chance of surviving. An expectation of victory replaced an assumption of defeat.

But, like Montgomery, Maude refused to be rushed. Before he began his advance up the Tigris he had much to correct that was wrong—and a Government to placate which was anxious to contract rather than to expand its Mesopotamian commitment. Instead of being hurled straight into action, as had happened at Helles, Slim therefore had a more tranquil period of initiation before, on 10 December, Maude concentrated his divisions for the attack. Continuous action followed throughout the next two months, until Kut was finally entered on 24 February. The Warwicks were frequently engaged, but never with more distinction than on the morning of 25 January. In one of the innumerable attacks in the Hai Salient south of Kut, 39 Brigade was performing the usual Mesopotamian operation of advancing over open ground without adequate artillery support against strongly held enemy trenches. By mid-morning the two forward battalions, the Worcesters and North Staffs, began to falter and fall back, and the Warwicks were ordered to

---

* C. R. M. F. Cruttwell, *A History of the Great War*, p. 606 (Oxford University Press, 1934).

restore the situation. They pressed through their retiring friends and captured the objective; both the Colonel and the Adjutant were awarded VCs, the Colonel's, tragically, being posthumous.

With the fall of Kut the Turks moved precipitately northwards, harried and hampered by British river-craft on the Tigris, until, early on the morning of 11 March, an officer of the Buffs hoisted the Union Jack above the citadel of Baghdad, thus marking the thirtieth seizure in history of this Caliphs' capital with minarets in the skies and feet in the mud. Slim and his men were among the first troops to reach the city.* It was the freedom to manoeuvre, the skirmish, the independent action to outwit the enemy which gave him the most satisfaction, not the Somme-like assault by lines of plodding infantry which was too often the feature of this campaign. His pleasure in the more cavalier style of war comes through vividly in 'Tigris Bank', the article in *Unofficial History* in which he describes a little operation with the first mixed force he ever commanded—two companies of infantry, a section of machine-guns and two 18-pounders. But he kept silent about another occasion when, with his own company, he neatly outflanked a line of Turkish trenches and earned the Military Cross.

On 28 March Slim had a premonition of death. It was a feeling he had never previously experienced on the battlefield. He cannot have had anything more than a vague recollection of that moment after his first wound when he *knew* he was dying, but on the evening of the 28th he identified precisely the significance of what he was feeling. At 1.30 next morning his brigade would begin to take up positions for a battle known to the *Official History* as 'the affair of Duqma', but to Slim as 'the Marl Plain'. He sensed that the plan was wrong, and that he would pay for it. Looking back, with all the experience of a second World War, he could see what was wrong.

In the drive north from Baghdad the British had run up against a Turkish position protecting the track beside the Tigris which was the main axis of the Turkish retreat. From the river-bank, entrenchments formed a sickle-shaped curve running due north to a point behind which lay some broken buildings, the Ruins, which nevertheless gave the

---

* 'We did come in for a triumphal march of sorts, too—we had to search a part of Baghdad and I came thro' with two Coys. The Jews all turned out and clapped and cheered so much that I nearly spoilt the whole show when my fierce steed went mad. Fat Jewesses leered at us from balconies, while father spread his palms and said, "You are very velgome." He then opened shop and robbed us.' Letter to Pratt, 22 May, 1917.

enemy good observations. Apart from marsh-land down by the river, the ground in front of these defences consisted of a huge, bare and flat expanse of hard-baked, off-white clay, the Marl Plain, an emotive name which, in view of what was about to happen, calls up images of the scene in the first book of *Paradise Lost* when Satan, to summon his legions, took

> '... uneasy steps
> Over the burning marl ...'

The plan of the divisional commander, General Cayley, was to tackle the Tigris end of the defences with two brigades while 39 Brigade, after getting onto a start line during the night, made a direct assault from the east on the trenches below the Ruins. (Slim's mature view was that this was unsophisticated; the correct plan would have been to feint down by the river and turn the whole line of trenches by outflanking it in the north.)

Thus it was that in the half-light before dawn on the 29th the three battalions of 39 Brigade formed up, the men six paces apart, in long drab lines which stretched away into the murk. Slim studied his watch, signalled to his company, and trudged forward. He and his soldiers, he recalled in his *Memoir*, were apathetic. They were not alone. In his semi-autobiographical novel about the campaign, *These Men Thy Friends*, Edward Thompson summarized the mood of the army at exactly this point, the end of March.

> There had been a splendour in the name and thought of Baghdad; we had been walking in the glow of mighty memories and deeds, and a kingdom had fallen, even in the universal clang of the world war, re-soundingly. But now we were fighting for nameless stretches of sand and pebbles, for the foul middens which marked where pretty villages had once existed, for dry ditches that watered no fields. Over useless dust men had to walk on, and on, and on, from one indistinguishable line of earth-scar to the next, while they were torn to pieces or shot down.

So the Warwicks marched steadily onwards over the marl, amid spasmodic shelling, until the morning heat threw up a mirage which prevented them from seeing the enemy's earth-scars below the Ruins. A halt was called. Even the comatose flies failed to keep men awake. For three torpid hours they lay in the merciless sun until, some time in the afternoon, the order to advance was given. Now they were closing on the Turkish line, and the machine-guns were working. One of Slim's four officers died as he spoke to him. The battalion was racing with bayonets at the charge, while shrapnel poured down to deny the last stretch before the trenches. Through a gap in the dust-clouds Slim saw for the only time in his life not just the flash of enemy guns, but the guns themselves. Then something hurtled out of the sky and thudded into the ground at his feet. He realized it was the case of a shrapnel shell, and next that in its passage it had scooped out of his right forearm a large chunk of sleeve and flesh. Nevertheless, he kept pace with the charge, and in the captured position was bandaged by a Turkish medical orderly. The battalion had lost over a third of its officers and men.

Things had changed since the early days, when the handling of the wounded in Mesopotamia indelibly stained the record of the British (and Indian) Army. Competent treatment at a Dressing Station, a trip in a spidery Ford ambulance, a river steamer past Baghdad and Kut, and cool drinks in the comfortable hospital at Amara—all this was to the good. More sinister was the amount of attention that far too many doctors seemed to be paying to Slim. His wound was genuine, but hardly critical. Eventually the truth emerged: there was a file of signals from London protesting that he had no right to be on active service at all, still less to be wounded. No record existed that a Board had passed him as fit. Had Slim placed too much trust in the verdict of that 'fat-headed old Colonel'? In any event, he was returned to bed, re-examined, and told that one lung was in poor condition while there was only restricted movement in his left arm, shoulder and hand. Yet he had just marched beyond Baghdad, fighting for most of the way.

The explanation was simple. So far-reaching had been the repercussions of the medical scandal in Mesopotamia that no doctor was now prepared to risk a repetition, however minor. 'With my bundle of incriminating papers round my neck like the Ancient Mariner's albatross, nobody wanted me; no one would have me in his hospital.' As a result he was rushed down to Basra, far ahead of serious cases, and placed immediately on a hospital ship bound for Bombay. Here tensions seemed less, for the Medical Officer to whom he reported allowed him, instead of living in hospital, to be entertained as a guest by the welcoming, if aged, members of the Byculla Club, whose uniform for dinner each night was an impeccable white dinner jacket, silk cummerbund, black evening trousers and patent leather shoes. After a period of remedial treatment he was removed from these luxuries and sent up to the Hills to convalesce. He asked for Mussoorie, having heard of its delights and its ladies. Nobody below the rank of Lieutenant-Colonel, he was told. How dull, he thought, for the ladies, and opted for Simla. He never regretted Mussoorie.

In fact the doctors had good grounds for suspicion. On 18 June Slim wrote to Pratt from The Crags, Simla:

> I'm about as fit as I shall ever be. The lung is as you were. I no longer spit blood and chunks of lung—the sands of Mesopot I suppose made that start on the way to Baghdad. The arm has healed at last, there's only a scar left now. It was rather beastly at one time at Amara and Basra—very septic all down my arm. But that's all over—of course I didn't tell Mother so there's no cause to tell her at all.

The Himalayas were healers; by the autumn he had been placed on light duty, and temporarily attached to the General Staff. At this stage it is clear from his letter that he assumed he would be returned in due course to Mesopotamia, or even to England.

In November, 1917, however, he was formally appointed a GSO III at Army Headquarters, India, as a temporary Captain, becoming a temporary Major and GSO II in November, 1918. Superficially it was a period of profound boredom, which lasted until early 1920. As he wrote to his friend, now 69073 Trooper P. C. Pratt, in June, 1918: 'I'm still stuck up here getting fedder and fedder up daily. It's an appallingly dull existence—I'm reduced to reading Shaw to keep awake.' But this investment in the experience of staff disciplines would pay good dividends in the future. Moreover, his Annual Reports were consistently good. Energy, initiative, resourcefulness, common sense, tact, ability to keep his head in emergencies—these are the qualities his superiors noted and approved. His report in 1919 ended, however, 'before being trained for further staff work, at which he should eventually do well, he requires a thorough grounding in regimental work.'

At home, now, in India, Slim had already obtained a transfer from the West India Regiment to the Indian Army list, which made it possible for him to join an Indian regiment. But the transfer had not been achieved without an acrimonious exchange of signals between Delhi and London. On 8 January, 1919, a telegram passed from the office of the Viceroy to that of the Secretary of State for India 'in London, recommending Slim's application. 'This officer has an excellent war record and exceptional qualifications. He has done consistently good work in his present appointment and we consider him suitable in every respect for Indian Army.' London replied that while all such applications were being refused, Slim's case was recognized as a special one, but he ought to transfer with the rank of Lieutenant and not Captain, as was proposed. 'As reward for good service, Chief strongly recommends that he be transferred in rank of Captain,' replied Delhi. On 26 February the Secretary of State for India morosely capitulated. 'In consideration of Commander-in-Chief's strong recommendation I reluctantly agree to the acceptance of Slim. As I have been rigidly rejecting all similar applications since Armistice unless acceptances had been actually issued Slim's acceptance will cause embarrassment here. . . .'

Abandoning London to its fate, Delhi went ahead and gazetted Slim as a Captain in the Indian Army from 31 May, 1919—thus putting his mind at rest, for a week earlier he had told Pratt that 'I'm still talking about joining the Indian Army, but I've had a difference with Montagu*—the stinker—so I don't know what the end will be.' With this hurdle cleared, he was eager to get away from desk-work, even though it would mean losing Staff pay and dropping a rank. All went well, and on 27 March, 1920, he was posted as a Captain to 1/6th Gurkha Rifles. The idea half-formed during the death grapple on Sari Bair had become a reality.

Slim's Annual Report for 1919 carries a final scribbled endorsement by the responsible Brigadier—'Yes, a good spell of regimental work will do him more good than anything.' This was a right judgement. In war he had given all the necessary proofs—to others and to himself— proofs of courage, enterprise, determination. There was nothing wrong with him as a fighting animal. But he had won a secret and greater victory. Without ever losing heart he had risen from deeps of frustration and despair. Between the moment at Netley when the RAMC Colonel had told him he was finished with the army and the day when he joined the Gurkhas he had steadfastly refused to admit defeat. His moral strength, in fact, had matured as much as his military skills. He knew what he could do. There would always be a streak of the self-deprecatory, of something modest and humble in his character,† but as

---

* Edwin Montagu was Secretary of State and responsible for the passing, in December, 1919, of the Government of India Act, generally known as the Montagu-Chelmsford reforms. Harold Nicolson described him as possessing 'simple tastes like bird-watching and oppressed nationalities'.

† After his obituary appeared in *The Times* someone wrote in to recall how Slim had once remarked, 'I was lucky after the war was over—they gave me a job at the War Office.' He meant that he became CIGS. His career produced many such

a soldier he had acquired the inner confidence of the true professional. Nothing could be better, in 1920, than to try this out in the test-bed of regimental duty.

1/6th Gurkha Rifles provided precisely the right kind of challenge. Their long tradition of service under the Crown stretched back to the days when their parent, the Cuttack Legion, fought in the Burma War of 1824. In November, 1919, the regiment had returned to its home station at Abbottabad, on the North-West Frontier, after an odyssey which had taken it via Gallipoli through Mesopotamia and deep into northern Persia. Already three officers and 200 men had been detached as reinforcements for Waziristan, where operations still continued in spite of the formal conclusion of the Third Afghan War in September, 1919. Here was a regiment with a fighting past, an active present and a future which promised service in the field rather than loitering in a cantonment. The officers would be good, for Gurkha standards were high and self-perpetuating, in that the battalion would normally choose its own new members. As to the men, Slim spoke for himself when, now a Field-Marshal, he contributed a preface to the Battalion's history.

> I spent many of the happiest, and from a military point of view the most valuable, years of my life in the Regiment. The Almighty created in the Gurkha an ideal infantryman, indeed an ideal Rifleman, brave, tough, patient, adaptable, skilled in field-craft, intensely proud of his military record and unswervingly loyal. Add to this his honesty in word and deed, his parade perfection, and his unquenchable cheerfulness, then service with Gurkhas is for any soldier an immense satisfaction. The Gurkha expects from his officers a standard as high as his own.

Such, then, was the challenge awaiting Captain W. J. Slim, MC, late West India Regiment, when he presented himself at the Adjutant's office in Abbottabad.

---

throwaway lines, but it is a sign of his total integrity that nobody ever felt they were spoken to create an effect.

CHAPTER FOUR

'AYO GURKHALI'*

IN *Bugles and a Tiger*, the first volume of his autobiography, John Masters described his early years as a subaltern in the 4th Gurkhas and his prejudiced impressions of the other regiments in the mid-thirties. 'The 1st Gurkhas were earnest,' he said, 'the 2nd idle, the 3rd illiterate, the 5th narrow-minded, the 6th down-trodden, the 7th unshaven, the 8th exhibitionist, the 9th Brahminical (they enlisted high-class† Gurkhas), and the 10th alcoholic.' An attractive list, owing as much, perhaps, to the author's gift for writing fiction as it does to the partiality of a member of the 4th Prince of Wales's Own! Certainly down-trodden would have been the last adjective to pin on to the 1/6th during the period from 1920 to 1925, Slim's initial years of service—years when this remarkable battalion contained officers who would subsequently supply the Army with two Major-Generals and one Field-Marshal.

At first his reception was cool. The battalion was a family, accustomed to select for itself the additions to its circle. Slim had not been applied for, he had been posted—a subtle but critical distinction. More immediately relevant was the current excess of officers within the Gurkha Brigade, as wartime expansion was followed by peacetime cuts. But he was disarming. Those qualities which later made him, for Vinegar Joe Stilwell, the only Limey whose command was acceptable overcame without difficulty the resistance of a Gurkha mess. Moreover, the war-hardened battalion assessed military capacity with the eyes of connoisseurs, and Slim was so obviously a man with whom to march to the

---

* The Gurkha battle-cry—'The Gurkhas are here!'
† Masters presumably meant 'high-caste'.

sound of the guns that the Gurkhas and his brother-officers alike soon gave him their respect and accepted his authority.

This was fortunate, for the 1/6th was soon mobilizing and off, once again, to the front. Slim had only a few months for assimilating the station which was now his home, Abbottabad, with its simple bungalows scattered among the trees; the mess, with its formally panelled dining-room and the glittering silver; its leather-armchaired anteroom; its snarling shooting trophies; the open sea of the parade-ground; the Gurkhas' lines. 'The marches of Empire as represented by Abbottabad are very uninteresting', he wrote to Pratt in June; but this was only the anti-climax of having to work in a hot office, when, as he said in the same letter, 'all the talk of War that was going on round here has fizzled out.' He was doubly wrong; he was finding his men from Nepal intensely interesting, while in October 1/6th Gurkhas moved to Thal to join a field force of brigade strength for operations against the Tochi Wazirs south of Thal. For a short while Slim's company was given the task of supporting the Kurram Militia in its task of bringing troublesome villagers to heel. This offered the considerable freedom of action that suited Slim, and also gave him a glimpse of the route to the Peiwar Kotal which Lord Roberts had used to gain surprise in his brilliant advance to Kabul during the Second Afghan War.

Meanwhile plans were being made for the destruction of the fortified Wazir village of Panch Pir, some 12 miles to the south of Thal. 1/6th Gurkhas had to piquet the final section of the route for the village destruction party, a battalion of the Frontier Force, whose task was to pass through and beyond the village to cover the Sappers while they blew up the big fortified tower which is a feature of every frontier village. In *Unofficial History* Slim sketches with quick vivid strokes the whole course of this hectic little affray. His description of the tower-blowing is particularly telling.

> A few shots came our way, and everybody got under cover, the colonel and I sitting with our backs against a big rock, while he cursed the delay.
>
> 'They'll be on top of us properly if we hang about now,' he complained. A bullet smacked into the rock and went shrilly ricochetting off into the blue. 'And to think', he groaned, 'I've only six months to go for pension!'
>
> We sat mournfully contemplating the distant tower. It stood straight and defiant, dominating the drab landscape, one side in full sunlight, the other in dark shadow. Suddenly a puff of white smoke

shot out from its base, the great square tower rose bodily, and for a
second hovered in the air. Then it sank gently back again and, as a dull
boom came to us, dissolved completely. A swelling bronze beehive of
smoke and dust bellied up, looking as solid as the tower it had replaced.

'As many pounds of gun-cotton as the diameter of the tower in feet
plus five,' murmured the colonel. Then we really got busy.

When retirement began they were chased by the wasps disturbed from
the nest. Angry Wazirs harried them all the way back. They marched
32 miles in 24 hours, over rough country and many river-crossings, to
arrive so exhausted that one officer from the rearguard could only gasp
'This running about . . . this running about!' A game of toys and
puppets, it may be thought, by comparison with the 'real' war of
Passchendaele, but then one suddenly comes across a reference to the
Wazirs in one of Slim's letters. 'They scuppered the escort to the
Surveying Party that is drawing maps of the delightful district last week.
Only one wounded man got away—the bodies of the rest were recovered that night, having been subjected to what we call "the usual
Eastern indignities".' The perspective alters; castration by a woman of
the Wazirs is as 'real' as castration by a shell on the Somme. To get all
the wounded away was a point of honour on the Frontier, even if to
recover a single man meant mounting a full scale counter-attack by the
rear guard.

The following March Slim became Adjutant of the 1/6th, remaining
so until November, 1924. It was a measure of his acceptance by his
battalion and, in particular, by his commanding officer. In addition to
the heavy routine responsibility of an Adjutant—training, discipline,
administration—there were special problems recalled by Lieut-Colonel
H. R. K. Gibbs, who was then Quartermaster.

> It was in that time that Slim showed not only his professional ability
> but also his strong character and leadership. Many senior officers began
> to rejoin the battalion after long spells of staff and extra-regimental
> service; officiating commanding officers were continually changing.
> All this gave rise to a certain amount of resentment by those officers
> who, though junior, had commanded companies, knew the men, and
> in many respects were much more up-to-date than their seniors. They
> expressed their opinions forcibly. Slim promptly stopped all this talk
> and told us all to cut out the bellyaching and get on with our jobs.
> Everyone respected him and he remained as popular as ever.

A man's nickname is often a guide to what others think of him. Throughout his Gurkha service Slim was universally known as 'Slimbo'.*

The two men from 1/6th Gurkhas who ultimately became Major-Generals were each at the head of one of the two divisions constituting the Burma Corps when Slim arrived, in March 1942, to take command during the long retreat. 'Punch' Cowan had the 17th Indian Division and Bruce Scott the 1st Burma Division, an unexpected bonus. As Slim pointed out in *Defeat into Victory*, 'We had served and lived together for twenty-odd years; we—and our wives —were the closest friends; our children had been brought up together in the happiest of regiments . . . I have never heard of any other occasion on which the corps commander and both his divisional commanders came not only from the same regiments but from the same battalion.' Scott had a special reason for remembering the Adjutant, since he came to the battalion from the Tochi Scouts and was put in Slim's hands to learn the intricacies of Gurkha regiments. What particularly impressed him was the capability which struck Colonel Gibbs—of maintaining strict discipline while spreading content, 'commanding affection while communicating energy'. He noted, too, Slim's perfectionism. 'Under his eye the guard mounting and bugles very quickly became as good as they had ever been; he spoke the language well, knew the men intimately and they in turn had a respect and an affection for him.'

If he was a disciplinarian without being a martinet, he also retained his privacy without becoming anti-social. His wounds did not prevent him from being a warrior, but tennis, polo, hunting were out of his orbit—not that a horse was much more to him than a mode of conveyance. (There are frequent accounts in his letters to Pratt of his 'fiery steed' taking charge of him, though one of his reports says of him that 'he rides well—for an infantry officer!') Still, he would climb up into the snows of Chitral to shoot an ibex, or take an afternoon off for duck or snipe, and no guest night in the mess was complete without his performance as Number One in the gun team of either Pip or Squeak, the two mountain 7-pounders on which an unorthodox drill would be performed after dinner. He was a hearty participant in High Cockalorum. From this time onwards, whenever one comes across a contemporary comment on Slim it is always about a man with a future, yet nobody ever complained about his present company. He was intimately

---

* This friendly diminutive was a frequent practice at this time. One Gurkha battalion contained a Baldo, a Busso, a Robo and a Gasso.

one of the family—but then he would walk away to his quarters and become a private person, reading and thinking not as an intellectual, not as an aesthete, but with a massive common sense and a mind that sought answers to unconventional questions.

He must have had an aura, something distinctive and noticeable which set him apart. During his first year as Adjutant Birdwood spotted him as outstanding. At the end of 1923 he countersigned Slim's Annual Report (in his capacity of General Officer Commanding-in-Chief Northern Command, India) agreeing to his recommendation for the Staff College and adding, 'A first class officer. Best of his rank in the Battalion.' Now Birdwood, who had mastered the mercurial Australians and New Zealanders at Gallipoli, had learned to judge an officer in a hard school. Yet the impression was strong, for in 1930 Birdwood, now a Field-Marshal and Commander-in-Chief, India, wrote a special letter to Slim to congratulate him on his brevet-Majority and to say that 'I have always remembered how much struck I was with your good work when I first inspected you when commanding the detachment of your regiment at Abbottabad.'

At the end of 1922 the battalion moved for two years to Malakand, a post built to command the route through the Malakand Pass to Chitral—that region about which, in 1898, Winston Churchill published his first book, *The Story of the Malakand Field Force*. Slim was content. He told Pratt on 29 November:

> Malakand isn't a bad spot. It's easily the pick of the frontier stations. Awfully windy and getting very cold now. But what with stone houses to live in with electric light installed, it's almost too good to be true. I always wanted as a small boy to live in a fort and here I am. It's just like a toy fort—with a round tower on top and a big flag flying over all—and I'm certainly living right inside.

But would there be any action?

> The staff evidently think so as they did a big Staff ride up the Pass. Rather amusing, big cars dashing about, excited generals and all complete. About half of 'em are now in hospital—one lot capsized their car into a nullah full of water, two got out of their cars and tried to climb the hills and almost died of exhaustion, while more than one got such a sore backside from riding that they are in bed still.

As it happened, the remote and reasonably tranquil Malakand was an ideal setting in which to prepare for the next step—the Staff College at

Quetta. Bruce Scott, who shared the same quarters with Slim, found this a time when close proximity cemented their friendship but a time, also, when Bill was close to his books. Fortunately the battalion now had a brilliant teacher for a commander, Lieut-Colonel G. M. Glynton, a meticulous little man whom Slim rated as the best peacetime trainer he ever met. Like a good Colonel, he believed that the more Gurkha officers there were at the Staff College, the better for the Gurkhas. But he was sometimes over-meticulous. Colonel Gibbs watched Slim curb his zealous commander.

> He made a bad start by quoting his previous regiment to us as superior in all respects. It came to a head over a trivial matter. We were told that the men did not know how to pitch tents in the correct way. If there was one thing we could do it was just that! The battalion had marched from the end of Mesopotamia to the shores of the Caspian Sea, 589 miles between 18 September and 28 November, 1918, and during the hot weather of 1919 marched most of the way back—as far as Kut. On return to India the battalion was for the most of the next two years under canvas. The men were so used to pitching tents that they could have done it with their eyes shut! I was told by Slim to pitch two tents, one according to the sketch made by the CO and one in the normal (correct) way. When the demonstration was over Slim and I went into the CO's office. Slim then said that much as we admired the Nth Gurkha Rifles we did not consider ourselves in need of instruction from that unit and that, in any case, we were the 6th and not the Nth Gurkha Rifles. For a moment it seemed that the storm would burst and that we were for the high jump. However, after a brief silence the CO suddenly said, 'Right, I understand, so that now is settled, thank you.'

Gibbs and Slim were side by side in more than one sortie. In 1924, for example, they found themselves on leave together in London, and with a couple of friends paid a visit to *The Desert Song* at Drury Lane. In this production a live camel was led on to the stage. From their experience of transport camels in India they knew the way to make a camel fold up and lie down—an appropriate tug on the nose rope, and an appropriate vocal encouragement. It seemed to them reasonable to invade the stage and demonstrate this technique to the audience. An experienced Theatre Management remained master of the field.*

---

* By chance, Colonel Gibbs was also a Birmingham man and had even been, for a time, a boy at St Philip's Grammar School. During this leave he observed

The long leave Slim took in 1924 gave him his first sight of England since 1916, and its consequences transformed the rest of his life. All is implicit in the dedication at the front of *Defeat into Victory*.

To
AILEEN
a soldier's wife who followed the drum
and
from mud-walled hut or Government House
made a home

While Slim was relaxing in London Aileen, the daughter of the Rev. John Anderson Robertson, minister of the Church of Scotland at Corstorphine, Edinburgh, was having no less delightful a time in the north. This presented her with a dilemma. A wealthy aunt, whose husband had died during the Great War, in which she had also lost two of her sons, felt life to be void, and wished to fill it by visiting her remaining son in Kashmir. But she disliked the idea of travelling alone and asked Aileen to join her. Edinburgh life was good; why waste time with a widow? The Minister, however, summoned his daughter to his study and sternly informed her that she was being selfish. 'Moreover,' he sensibly added, 'I myself shall never be able to afford to send you round the world.' Aileen capitulated. When she and her aunt reached Dover, on the first stage of their journey, they were shown on board the Channel steamer with a certain attention, and Aileen casually noticed a man observing them from the deck. After they joined their boat for India she discovered that he was sitting at their dinner table.

This was the beginning of an operation in which Slim applied the classic rules of war—surprise, concentration of force, economy of effort, maintenance of the objective. At first his generalship failed. A quick arrangement with the purser to put him on the right table led to his sitting next to the aunt for the whole of the voyage. But that proved to be a little local difficulty which did not prevent him, by the time they reached India, from achieving an understanding. He already sought an engagement, but Aileen required more time. Time! What general has enough? But Slim was undefeated. When they landed at Bombay he

---

Slim transferring his mother and two ageing aunts from Birmingham to a house he had acquired for them in Bournemouth—a move, he said, worse than shifting an Army Corps. But, camels apart, Slim spent most of his time in England studying for the Staff College.

remained there for four days, seeing Aileen constantly—and over-staying his leave. A few weeks after he got back to Abbottabad he approached Bruce Scott, who was temporarily in command of the 1/6th, and requested a further ten days' leave to enable him to visit Kashmir, where, he said, he was 'on to a good thing'. Scott, guessing what was in the wind, risked the reprimand which inevitably followed when his Colonel returned, and Slim proceeded to Kashmir, where he obtained a houseboat and moored it near the one on which Aileen and her aunt were staying. This settled the matter. Privately, they became engaged.

Slim then wisely arranged for Aileen to visit Abbottabad so that she could get the feel of the regimental family and decide for herself whether she would be at home in this very specialized existence, so different from the douce delights of Edinburgh. This caused no problem for one who was so happily to follow the sound of the drum. But there still remained Corstorphine. It was no easy matter, across half the world, to explain that a penniless Captain in the Indian Army, of Catholic origins and no apparent prospects, was a suitable husband for the daughter of a Presbyterian minister in Scotland. They therefore made no public announcement until all doubts had been allayed. (Even to Pratt, for example, Slim made no mention of Aileen until he could speak openly.) The striking photograph of the Adjutant of the 1/6th Gurkhas (Plate No. 8) no doubt assisted their cause. It has been reproduced in other books, and rightly so; but their readers did not know that it was really taken as a propaganda exercise, to impress the parents in Corstorphine with the manly bearing of their future son-in-law.

Slim was now moving into his maturity. The first half was ending of a natural span whose full course would carry him to pinnacles of power and distinction. But there is a sense in which, during the famous second half of his life, his apparent imperturbability concealed too much from the world. Excelling in crises—like Marlborough, 'most master of him-self amid the din of battle'—he calmed and elevated by the example of his insouciance. The records and recollections of the Burma campaign are studded with accounts of his magisterial poise in the midst of chaos. Nor is this mere legend or hagiography; it is authenticated truth. But there was another truth, realized by few of those who watched and admired. It was only at a great price that he purchased his freedom. Behind the façade lived another man, deeply sensitive, deeply un-certain, deeply self-critical—a man of quick conscience and all that the

Quakers mean by concern. In a crisis, therefore, his cool response was
not phlegmatic or nerveless; it was the result of a superb self-control.
If such a character is not to disintegrate under prolonged stress, there
must be at least one person in the world with whom he is absolutely
safe, from whom nothing is concealed, by whom all is understood.
From beginning to end, from mud-walled hut to Government House,
Slim found this person in Aileen. He was a man of size—great in his
nature and great in his achievement; she enlarged him.

But in 1924 and 1925 neither leave nor love diverted him from the
goal of Quetta. His nomination went forward with a flattering cluster
of recommendations. Colonel Glynton assiduously set, marked and
discussed his practice papers. All this effort, all the lonely reading in his
quarters at Malakand were rewarded when he learned at the end of May,
1925, that he had passed the Staff College entrance examination at the
head of the list. Very prudently he had organized an intelligence
system, and a friend in the bowels of Army Headquarters wrote: 'First
of all let me congratulate you again most heartily on passing into
Quetta top. You got 6,225 marks which would *easily* have got you
into Camberley had you competed for the latter instead of Quetta. You
need have no doubt about the results as the War Office cypher cable
came straight to the G1 who works in the same room as I do ... you've
got the result "from the horse's mouth" so to speak and can now throw
a quiet blind in perfect confidence!'

His studies at Quetta began in February, 1926. One of the most
endearing things about Slim, so much the paragon of military virtue,
is the knowledge that among all his Annual Confidential Reports
between the end of the First and the beginning of the Second World
War there is only one which contains a sharply critical comment—
that for his first Staff College year. 'Is much above the average,' it
stated. '*Could do very well, if he worked—which he has not.* Might be
brilliant. Has ideas and originality. Does not play games, but is
sufficiently active.' The notion of Slim not working is so strange that
an unusual explanation must be sought—and found, perhaps, in the
marriage of Captain W. J. Slim and Miss A. Robertson at St Andrew's
Church, Bombay, on New Year's Day, 1926*. So far he had always
been—the cliché is inevitable—a man's man. He had not avoided

---

* This Church of Scotland ceremony was followed later by a marriage in the
Catholic Church at Quetta, but (as indicated in Chapter One), this was little
more than a formality.

society, but a talk in the mess or at the bar had always been preferable
to dances or dinner-parties. Now the world was new; with a partner
beside him, he entered the social merry-go-round with relish. But after
four months he was summoned and told, 'Your honeymoon has lasted
long enough.'

Was there another reason? On the same course was an Ulsterman,
Captain James Steele, who like Slim had been commissioned in 1914—
in The Royal Irish Rifles—and, like Slim, had survived the European
War to serve on the North-West Frontier.* He, too, was recently
married, and Slims and Steeles formed a friendship. But the Ulsterman
would often watch from his bungalow this Gurkha fellow-student
striding masterfully down the road to the Staff College, and say to
himself, 'There goes a loner.' It was noticed, too, that at the beginning
of lectures Slim would quietly pull out a novel. Was he, for once, too
high in the clouds? Over-confident? Or was there a more subtle cause?
The officers on a Staff College course are a hand-picked selection of
potential high-fliers—the Army's future. Since his quiet beginnings in
Birmingham Slim had never competed in a group of such quality. Was
diffidence concealed by the defence mechanism of an affected superiority? Certainly he was already marked as *primus inter pares*. Michael
Roberts, who later commanded with distinction a brigade in Burma and
subsequently became a joint author of the *Official History of the War
against Japan*, first met Slim at Quetta in 1926. A friend ran into him
on the steps of the Gurkha mess and said, 'Come inside. I want you to
meet a man who's going to be a Commander-in-Chief.'

The swift and successful conversion of 14th Army from the jungle-
bound force that fought at Imphal to the fast-moving armoured,
mechanized and air-supported divisions which swept across the
Irrawaddy and down to Rangoon had many of the qualities preached
by the British pioneers of mobile warfare in the twenties and thirties.
It is not irrelevant, therefore, that in 1926 perhaps the greatest of those
pioneers was in his last year as an instructor at Quetta and that Slim
took to him and became his friend. This was the future Major-General
Sir Percy Hobart; the significant point is that these Quetta years were
the period in which Hobart first thought out, and developed in his
teaching, the theories about mobile war which he subsequently applied
so effectively in practice. There could be no better summary of the

---

* The late General Sir James Steele, GCB, KBE, DSO, MC, next served beside
Slim in 1948 when he was Adjutant-General and Slim was CIGS.

principles which Slim adopted at Meiktila and thereafter than some lines Hobart wrote in 1926 in a paper on the 'Light Division of the Future':

> Pace is Protection, Rapidity means Surprise. . . . Increased mobility and range entail great calls not only on endurance . . . but on intelligence and initiative in all ranks. . . . A new sort of discipline is required. The 'You're not paid to think' variety is obsolete.

Nobody who knew the dynamic and merciless Hobart can imagine him wasting his time over a Staff College student of lazy habits—and, of course, Slim's truancy was not long-lasting even if it was ever more than superficial. 'Punch' Cowan followed him as a student in 1927. For his special subject Slim had chosen the history of British India, and Cowan, no shining master of the text-books, borrowed his fellow-Gurkha's file for illumination. He was astonished by what he saw. Everything relevant was there, beautifully and lucidly organized, implying an amount of work and a grasp of the subject which Cowan had never anticipated.

Slim did things his own way, accepting neither the easy answer nor the received idea. Ten years later, when he was an instructor at the Staff College at Camberley, a fellow-instructor* noted that 'he gave the impression that before he spoke about something he had already given a great deal of thought to the subject—there was little spontaneity in his views about things and what emerged was the result of careful and mature thinking.' When he got into his stride at Quetta, therefore, the integrity and independence of his judgement had its effect—laced, as it often was, by a humour so dry that the less sensitive palates found its tang too sharp. All this was reflected in the triumphant conclusion of the course, for he passed out top with an 'A' grading, the distinctive mark given to 'officers of exceptional merit and outstanding ability'.

'He is an original quick thinker,' reported the Commandant of the Staff College, 'with very decided views and personality. He is critical, has apparently read widely and can take a broad view on any subject. He is a good speaker with considerable powers of command and not afraid of expressing his own views. *He is not always tactful, but an interesting man to have dealings with.*'

---

* The late Lieutenant-General Sir Archibald Nye, VCIGS.

$$\bigstar\bigstar\bigstar\bigstar\bigstar$$

CHAPTER FIVE
MR ANTHONY MILLS

I want to know a butcher paints,
A baker rhymes for his pursuit,
Candlestick-maker much acquaints
His soul with song, or, haply mute,
Blows out his brains upon the flute.

Robert Browning

RILLIANT SUCCESS at Quetta was inevitably followed by service on the Staff. Between 1928 and the outbreak of the Second World War Slim spent the greater proportion of his time in this region where, as Montgomery once put it, 'the pen is mightier than the sword'. Four years at Army HQ, India; two as Instructor at the Staff College, Camberley; a year at the Imperial Defence College and some time as student and then as Commandant at the Senior Officers' School, Belgaum—these duties were only briefly interspersed with a return to 1/6th Gurkhas as a company commander and a year in command of the 2/7th.

But all the time Slim's pen was active in a way very different from what Montgomery had in mind. From the mid-twenties onwards he was writing and getting into print a stream of short stories and occasional articles. The prime motive was cash. Even his Lieut-Colonelcy was delayed until 1938—a reflection not on his ability but on the sluggish rate of promotion in his profession. With no capital, two young children* to raise and educate, a wife who believed in high standards for her household, and the constant movement from one post to another Slim was always short at the bank. Indeed—perhaps because of the

---

* John was born in 1927, Una in 1930.

circumstances of his youth, perhaps because of the insight into poverty which he gained as a teacher—anxiety about money was a recurrent motif throughout his life. The concern of a young subaltern about his bank balance in 1915 was echoed by the CIGS and the Constable of Windsor Castle. One reason, undoubtedly, was an inability to set the same high valuation on himself as others did. Genuine humility combined with some inner uncertainty to prevent him from seeing that he would never want for appropriate employment. The truly humble man is so rare a specimen that when one appears he lacks credibility; Slim was just such a person—not humble before God in the religious sense, but simply a human being devoid of vanity, self-complacency, *folie de grandeur.* He was certainly not short of ambition or worldly wisdom, but neither tarnished his integrity nor made him pitch his hopes too high. The man who passed top into Quetta wrote to Pratt that he had been expecting just to scrape by.

Since every guinea counted, Slim turned pleasure to profit. He was a natural writer—more specifically, he was a natural teller of tales. He had an eye for incident and character, an instinctive sense of attack enabled him to get a story going, an excellent command of English kept him on the move without faltering, and he learned how to shape, how to cut, how to pattern. So it was that every year during the thirties his stories appeared with impressive regularity in a variety of journals, particularly the *Daily Mail* and its sisters, the *Evening News* and the *Daily Sketch.* Another frequent patron was *The Illustrated Weekly of India. Blackwood's* and *Chambers'* were homes for his articles, a number of which were to reappear in *Unofficial History.* For this considerable output (and much was written, of course, that never reached the public) he required the cover of a pen-name. By reversing Slim a new author was created—Anthony Mills.*

The profit was not large; at rates rising to 15 guineas per story, and 30 per article, even with a suitable adjustment to the pound, this does not imply riches. Slim was no Somerset Maugham. In terms of a Major's pay, however, the extra income was worth the midnight oil. Many years later, Slim had the tentative idea of assembling his stories for publication as a book, and the opening paragraphs of the introduction he drafted ruefully reflect this aspect of his literary life.

---

* Slim's stimulus was Cecil Hunt, literary editor of the *Daily Mail* and *Evening News*, who developed a great interest in him and warmly encouraged his writing.

Some time ago, my bank received a letter from the Superintendent of Taxes, who kept, I hoped, a more or less benevolent eye on my Income Tax affairs. The letter read something like this:

'Looking through the Field-Marshal's file recently, I came across an item in the magazine *Men Only*, which stated that he was one of the most highly paid short story writers in the country, but that he wrote always under a top-secret *nom-de-plume*. I have not been able to trace, in the Field-Marshal's tax returns submitted by you, any record of earnings from this source. I shall be grateful if you will comment.'

By then Slim had not written a short story for a quarter of a century, he had never been highly paid and Mr Mills was defunct. But in the thirties everything was amateurishly professional. Anthony Mills's address was that of Philip Pratt, who acted as Slim's honorary agent, placing his stories, collecting his fees (Slim had a special 'literary account' in a bank in Bournemouth, where his mother lived), criticizing and even rewriting the texts. This was no sinecure. Slim to Pratt, 18 October, 1932, about a new story: 'I've sent it first to *Britannia and Eve*, who will no doubt return it in due course to you. Will you then be kind enough to circulate it as follows: *Women's Journal, Good Housekeeping, Pearson's Magazine, Windsor, Cassell's, London, Cornhill, Cover Magazine, 20 Story Magazine?* After that anywhere you like.' In 1933 there was even the question of French translation rights. Slim's North-West Frontier material acquired an extra flavour in the pages of *L'Illustrée*. ' "*Sahib*", *protesta le Patan, homme de haute stature à la barbe hirsute, s'exprimant en un Pouchtou guttural. . . .*'

The stories were more a matter of craft than of art—neatly tailor-made to meet the requirements of a Fleet Street which, with newsprint cheap and before television had started to compete for advertising, could still afford large daily editions whose short story was a staple item. Within its brevity must be comprised a definite beginning, middle and end, a single, attention-holding situation, no wasted words, sentimentality, perhaps, but no vulgarity; and the mix must be such that the morning or evening commuter could understand and be stimulated without having to pause. Slim read the blueprint perfectly, and his finished models matched the market's need. Like Kipling, he realized that the commonplaces of life in India could become mystery and magic in London. Once he had acquired the knack, he was always able to draw a theme from the routine of soldiering on the North-West Frontier, and though he wrote hard for at least a decade, in the middle of an active professional and family life, he was never stale or mechan-

ical: his subject was always close to his heart. Close indeed, for apart
from Pratt and Aileen, very few shared the knowledge of his secret life.
(In all their journeyings, from the Frontier to Camberley and back,
Slim insisted on Aileen posting his stories and articles—'to bring me
luck'.) At most, his contemporaries suspected him of going in for what
they suspiciously termed 'journalism'.

From the point of view of literature this was all, of course, very small
beer. From the point of view of a commander who one day would have
to achieve a *rapport* with hundreds of thousands of men there was much
to be said for learning how to grip the attention of the readers of a
popular daily newspaper. In any case, Slim was enjoying himself.
Pleasure in their partnership glows in his letters to Pratt—and gratitude:

> As a literary agent you indubitably delivered the goods. Your
> share in disposing of this brainchild of mine was so much more than
> acting as a post office that I insist on your sharing a portion at least of
> the spoils. I enclose a cheque for three guineas with which I suggest
> you take the most attractive young woman you know out for the even-
> ing or failing that buy yourself a cigarette holder or some small thing
> that will remind you of how you have helped the deserving and strug-
> gling author. But I prefer the first use of it. Above all don't use this
> three quid to pay debts or insurance.*

The ability to express his thoughts clearly and cogently—which later
would make his speeches and broadcasts so effective—was not the least
of the attributes which struck his contemporaries. It is true that the days
were past when the Commanding Officer of the Bengal Sappers and
Miners could enter on the Annual Report of one of his subalterns, as an
adverse comment: 'This officer reads poetry.'† Still, a man who could
think on his feet and compose a lucid paper tended to stand out in the
ruck, particularly when his communications were backed by a forceful
and uncompromising intelligence. Slim's qualities in the field were now
well established; his years at Army Headquarters as a staff officer, from
February, 1929, to December, 1933, confirmed in the minds of his
superiors the important fact that he was as capable at a desk as in a
trench. Lieut-General Wigram, the Chief of the General Staff, Indian
Army, rounded off Slim's Annual Report for 1932 with prophetic
words: 'By reason of his special qualities I would like to bring his name

---

* From a letter of 14 June, 1933.
† As happened to Hobart, in his pre-1914 youth.

to the notice of those under whom he will serve in the future as one who, in the interests of the Service, is worthy of special attention.' Indeed, every senior officer who commented on his work during this period used superlatives.

A biography is an account of a man's growing up; it is during these early thirties that one can observe Slim advancing from adolescence to maturity in an area of the commander's art which is of pre-eminent importance. His popular reputation is that of a *battle* commander, a front-line general. But though this is right—though his own preference was always for the sharp end and his battle skills were exemplary— victory in Burma owed as much to administration and organization as it did to the men at the front. The famous definition by Socrates, which Wavell used to such good effect in *Generals and Generalship*, was rarely more relevant.

> The general must know how to get his men their rations and every other kind of stores needed for war. He must have imagination to originate plans, practical sense and energy to carry them through. He must be observant, untiring, shrewd; kindly and cruel; simple and crafty; a watchman and a robber; lavish and miserly; generous and stingy; rash and conservative. . . . He should also, as a matter of course, know his tactics. . . .

What struck Wavell was that Socrates placed administration, 'the real crux of generalship', first; for, as he remarked, 'there are ten military students who can tell you how Blenheim was won for one who has any knowledge at all of the administrative preparations that made the march to Blenheim possible'. For Blenheim substitute Meiktila and the same applies to Slim. It is in this sense that the thorough grounding in staff work he received at Delhi and Simla paid dividends later. He knew the administrative necessities and he knew how to pick the men for the job; they, in their turn, found they were dealing with a general who spoke their language and understood their problems. Few good fighting commanders evoke the same praise from their quartermasters and engineers as they do from the front line. Hasted and Snelling, Slim's chief sapper and 'Q' officers, were among his most ardent admirers.

It is not to be supposed, however, that Slim won golden opinions simply by avoiding censure and behaving conventionally. As a GSO2 in the Operations Directorate he shared an office with 'Phil' Vickers*

---

* Lieut-General W. G. H. Vickers, CB, OBE.

(who in 1942 became Quartermaster-General in India) and Rob Lockhart.* Vickers and Lockhart were responsible respectively for 'Q' and 'I'. Vickers naturally had a continuing concern for supply on the North-West Frontier, and as Slim was responsible for Operations they used to discuss possible means of freeing a force from the need to move along valley bottoms, tied to its supply train, so that it could be as unhampered as tribesmen in its use of the higher ground. Out of their talks came the concept of air supply, and that had consequences in both the short and the long term. It was Slim who first took action, reaching for the telephone to speak to an RAF staff officer and tell him that the Army was proposing to develop air supply. Had he any views? Could the RAF co-operate? The results were disastrous. This revolutionary proposition was immediately reported to the RAF Commander-in-Chief, who roused the Army Commander from his quarters to voice his instant protests. The latter not unreasonably denied all knowledge of any such project and then, with some asperity, sought the culprit. Slim, the obvious suspect, was summoned and roasted.

But in the long term this initiative was fruitful. 'Victory has many parents, but defeat is an orphan.' Certainly the victorious use of air supply in the Burma campaign has been attributed to a variety of begetters, though by then the idea was hardly new. Tactical and even strategic air supply had been undertaken by 1918. 'But I think one can claim', General Vickers affirms, 'that so far as India was concerned the original idea started with Bill Slim in our little second-grade Operations Office at Army HQ in Simla about 1931–1932.'† For it was Vickers who then went on, as Deputy Director of Staff Duties, to arrange at Kohat the first experiments with 'free drops' of containers without para-chutes—a complete failure—and then, as Director of Supplies and Transport, to encourage a more scientific approach to the problems of packaging and providing inexpensive non-silk parachutes. At the same time 'theoretical exercises were carried out on landing grounds or on dropping areas'. All this predated the Burma campaigns. It was not with a virgin mind, therefore, that Slim faced the problem of air supply when he himself became an Army Commander.

Apart from the works of Mr Anthony Mills, Slim was now engaged on another literary task. As he wrote to Pratt in May, 1930, 'In addition to my other duties I have become a full-fledged editor—not a very

---

* General Sir Rob Lockhart, KCB, CIE, MC.
† Letter to author, 23 April, 1974.

highly paid one, but still enough screw to make it worth while. I've taken over the editorship of the *United Service Institution Journal.* We publish quarterly and it's rather fun. But, my God, the tosh people send in for publication. . . . What about an article on "War Poetry"?' When Pratt produced this Slim replied, 'I get such maunds and maunds of dry technical tripe that any reasonably readable article of your type is sure of a good reading. If you know any other struggling authors, put them on to it too.' But it was the editor who was struggling. He had committed himself to a forlorn hope in trying to invigorate the *Journal,* and was glad to shed the responsibility when he departed from GHQ.

New vistas now opened. It was customary to include among the instructors at the Staff College at Camberley one specially selected officer from the Indian Army, who could represent the interests of Delhi and amplify the Westerly-orientated teaching out of his particular experience of warfare further east. The Indian incumbent from 1931 to 1934 was Jackie Smyth,* who was consulted about a suitable successor by the Commandant, John Dill. As it happened, Smyth put forward the names of two men who, ten years later, would win in combination the battle of Imphal—Scoones who commanded 4 Corps and Slim who commanded the 14th Army. Dill had not heard of Slim. Smyth said 'You will,' and held forth about his qualifications. By chance, Slim had already been noted in India as a promising candidate for the post, and thus slid easily into a new phase of his career.

The Camberley attachment (for the three years 1934–36), meant a drop of £400 a year from his Indian pay, and other expenses were inevitably involved. Slim never hesitated, and indeed he would have been imprudent to miss one of the turning-points in his life. The Staff College is a caravanserai of military quality, a meeting-place where gifted instructors and students pause for a while in their professional journeys and learn, perhaps, as much by their association as they do in formal lessons. Here a man's character and capacity are mercilessly assessed—but he who survives the assay has a brighter future. Slim survived, and his Camberley years, followed by his time at the Imperial Defence College, meant that though he was often concerned about his age and his prospects, in fact he was already a marked man. Moreover, though the mid-thirties was hardly a period when the Home Army was at its most flourishing, Slim had lived long enough on and thought enough about the North-West Frontier; his mental health required that

---

* Brigadier the Rt Hon Sir John Smyth, Bt, VC, PC, MC.

he should be exposed to new problems, new techniques, new men. Camberley refreshed and replenished him.

Smyth handed over his accommodation, and at No. 6 Bungalow in the College quarters Bill and Aileen started their first home in England. But there was another useful item handed over to the incoming tenant. In 1962, when Field-Marshal Slim was dining at a guest night of the Farriers' Company,* whose Master was his host, Brigadier Sir John Smyth, Slim made public in his speech the fact that in 1934 Smyth had passed on to him all his notes for lectures, and that he had survived his first year as an instructor by relying on them. Since after-dinner speeches should be taken with a pinch of salt, and since Slim was incapable of existing for long on second-hand opinions, perhaps a more exact record may be found in the memory of Marshal of the RAF Sir John Slessor, whose period as Air Force member of the Directing Staff at Camberley just overlapped with Slim's. He remembered that Slim had put his own very individual gloss on the original text.

Certainly it was his personal style that commended him to the students. By the 'eleven o'clock rule' it became the custom for teachers and taught to drift into the anteroom about 11 pm for a final drink and a free-for-all discussion, in which students were at liberty to criticize as they wished anything to do with the course. Major-General A. W. Lee used to attend these debates as an instructor. 'It gave us a chance to see ourselves as others saw us,' he recalled, 'and to learn much more about the students when they let their hair down. The senior division instructor whom the great majority of students seemed to regard as outstanding was Bill, not only because of his breadth of vision and incisiveness, but also because he seems to have got on so well with them all. This did not apply to all the DS by any manner of means.'†

He was infectious—and how could he not be when, as Nigel Duncan‡ saw him, he 'commanded instant respect; he was broad and burly, standing four square to all the winds that blew, full of common sense and with a delightful friendly manner'? Duncan came as a student in 1935 from 1 Army Tank Brigade where that great pioneer of armour, Hobart, was driving at top speed and against time to demonstrate to a

---

* Slim himself was then a Freeman of the City of London and Master of the Clothworkers' Company.
† Among Slim's pupils was the late Duke of Gloucester. During one exercise, after the students had stormed a hill the Duke sat down on the objective and said, 'You know, I'm not built for this sort of thing.'
‡ Major-General Nigel Duncan, CB, CBE, DSO.

reluctant military Establishment the practical possibilities of mobile warfare. Inspired by Hobart's zeal, Duncan tended to find Slim's doctrines a shade out-moded—Slim who, ironically, was Hobart's pupil and friend.

Bill's *pièce de résistance* was the Frontier warfare scheme which took place in the Welsh hills behind Harlech. We did a considerable amount of preparatory work on this and studied the art of picketing the heights, forming camp and so on, and one's conversation became inter-larded with 'sangars' and Pathans and the like. The effort expended on one of the Frontier punitive expeditions to burn a few villages was prodigious, and it became too much for me and a fellow Tank Corps officer. We stood up and announced that we thought the whole affair was a load of rubbish; results could be just as well achieved by using tanks up the valleys. They would escort a few infantry forward and would themselves be protected by aircraft while long range guns and howitzers would provide additional cover and also complete the des-truction of the villages in very quick time. The result exceeded our wildest expectations. Bill rose in his wrath, proved it couldn't work, and damned us into heaps as spoilsports who sought to take away the chance of training the Indian soldier and depriving him of the fun of fighting the Pathan. When we interrupted to say that we disapproved of amateur approaches to war we got a rise again. Of course, it all passed off, but it made me feel that he was a proper old died-in-the-wool Indian Frontier soldier despite his common sense.*

A few years later, with enthusiasm modified by experience, Duncan would no doubt have asked himself what was the likelihood, in 1936, of Britain being able to assemble a force of howitzers, long-range guns, tanks and aircraft to punish Pathans and Wazirs. Still, his conclusions were different:

He was a chap that we all looked up to immensely because he was the only one who had had actual experience of war†—even though the enemy were only tribesmen. He was apparently very skilful at the game—there were other Indian Army Officers there who spoke of him on the Frontier with bated breath. Slightly confused by the apparently archaic approach which he seemed to advocate, contradicted by the

---

* Letter to author, 27 October, 1973.
† War, that is, on the Frontier. The Directing Staff at Camberley in the thirties had all been to the wars in one theatre or another.

evidence of our companions who had seen him in operation on the
Frontier, we went our ways after the two years with a feeling that out
of all our DS Bill was one of the two or three with whom we should
like to go to war.

Another student at the time, a Gunner who later served with distinction in armour, Charles Dunphie,* made a similar judgement. 'We had
a most able and later highly distinguished batch of instructors and we
were all of the opinion that Slim was one of the best. . . . I don't think I
have learned more from anybody.' It is not surprising, therefore, that
at the end of 1934 the Commandant, Major-General Armitage, reported
that 'I look on him as one of the best instructors I have had at the Staff
College', and that in 1936, at the end of his tour of duty, no less a person
than Lord Gort, now the Commandant, declared him to be 'obviously
a commander. I consider him to be well above the average of his rank.
In my opinion his promotion to Colonel should be accelerated as much
as possible.'

The natural next step for an officer of exceptional qualities was a
course at the Imperial Defence College. Here, mixing with his equivalents from the other two services, and a few picked men from Whitehall,
he should find the opportunity to lift his mind from the infinitesimal
details of Staff College studies to the broad horizons of high strategy.
Theoretically, at least, he should have the chance to 'think big'. Slim
had been marked down in India several times as a suitable candidate for
the IDC; it was therefore an obvious progression for him to move on
from Camberley to London, as a member of the course for 1937.†

During that year he was surrounded by men who were shortly to
make or enhance their reputations. After 1939 the Commandant, Air
Marshal Sir Arthur Longmore, would control the Middle East air force
in the hard early days, and one of his directing staff, Air Commodore
Portal, would outstrip him to become a great Chief of Staff, while a
fellow-student of Slim's, Keith Park, played a main part with his 11
Group of Fighter Command in winning the Battle of Britain. From the
Navy came Captain Warburton-Lee, soon to earn a posthumous VC
at Narvik, and Captain the Hon. G. H. E. Russell, whose *Duke of York*

---

* Major-General Sir Charles Dunphie, CB, CBE, DSO.
† The move was not obvious to Slim. Brigadier Roberts met him by chance just
after he had heard of his nomination to the IDC and found him worried because
he had been away from regimental duty for too long. In fact Slim begged to be
allowed a year with his regiment before going to the IDC.

brought doom to the *Scharnhorst* and who, as Admiral Sir Guy Russell, would himself become Commandant of the IDC in 1956. One of the Army students, Alan Cunningham, would make a name against the Italians in East Africa only to fail against Rommel, and another, Rowell, later became Chief of the Australian General Staff. There was only one New Zealander, Colonel Puttick; but he, after leading his compatriots in Greece and Crete, became Chief of the New Zealand General Staff.

Yet these were uneasy months for Slim. Sir Guy Russell acquired a special ability to assess him in the context of the IDC, for besides being a fellow-student and ultimately Commandant, he came back in 1946 as Chief Naval Instructor when Slim re-started the College. Looking back, he felt that the man who had made so distinctive an impression at Camberley was not in any particular way outstanding in 1937. This is a surprising judgement, made by one who was Slim's admiring friend, but several reasons support it. To begin with, he was absent for a period because of a lowering operation on the gall-bladder.* The second reason was the IDC itself. No student of the British Army in the latter thirties, and particularly of its upper echelons, is unaware that this was a phase when strategical thinking was at its nadir. There was no common doctrine understood and shared by the armed services and the government. By air and sea and land the heads and staffs of the different forces followed different paths—if a path could indeed be discerned. All these uncertainties about Britain's role in the event of war—uncertainties displayed in her military posture both before and after 3 September, 1939—were inevitably reflected at the IDC. The theatre where Grand Strategy should hold the stage was short of a cast. What was offered to the students tended to be tepid, conventional, archaic. Slim was not a man to dwell contentedly in a world of received ideas, and after the lively intercourse of the Staff College he now lacked a stimulus.

But the malaise bit deeper. That concern about his professional future which had been evident for some years in his confidential letters to Pratt became intense in 1937, and for good reason, since it seemed at the time that his whole career was in the balance. H. L. Davies (known throughout his service as Taffy) who would become Slim's Chief of Staff during the retreat from Burma in 1942, was in Whitehall during this year as a GSO2 at the War Office. He saw a good deal of Slim, and noted how he seemed to be hard pressed financially and pessimistic about promotion. It must be remembered that one of the curious facts

---

* The stone removed was enormous and required a jamjar for preservation.

about the Regular Army at this period is the way many of its officers discounted the possibility of war. Ignorance, optimism, belief that Hitler would behave rationally, excessive confidence in the French— the causes are manifold. The point in Slim's case is that in 1937 he was weighing his promotional chances in terms of a normal peacetime advancement, and here his age had become a disadvantage. There was no lack of pressure in his support. Gort had recommended him for a Colonelcy, and in India a number of powerful papers had been put forward supporting his preferment—even as a special case. His depression was nevertheless well justified; he knew that his shining record might not overcome the forces of tradition—he knew his Indian Army—and it did indeed happen that, at the Promotions Board which at last brought him, in 1938, a substantive Lieut-Colonelcy and a battalion command, the majority was in favour of passing him by (on grounds of age) until the late General Coleridge swung the Board in his favour. Had he been overlooked the result would have been agony for Slim and an incalculable loss for his country. He himself, torn between love of his profession and love of his family, might well have resigned his commission and sought a more rewarding career. If he had done so he would, of course, have returned to the colours in 1939, but who can tell what effect a break in service might have had on his military destiny?

In the event all went smoothly, and almost as if the sequence had been pre-ordained. He returned to India early in 1938 to take the course at the Senior Officers' School at Belgaum, then obtained command of the 2/7th Gurkhas, only to return as Commandant to Belgaum in April, 1939 (which gave him the local rank of Brigadier) and to remain at the SOS until the outbreak of war.

Mr Anthony Mills was still active. Shortly after arriving at Belgaum, on 20 April, 1938, he wrote to Pratt thanking him for the news that *Blackwood's* had taken his article 'Elizabeth succeeded Henry' (reprinted in *Unofficial History*), and reporting on his recent efforts to write short stories. He added: 'I don't feel much like work but it's very good for me to argue about where a platoon should be put after messing about for so long with Grand Fleets and groups of armies.' He didn't reveal, however, that he had made such an impression as a student that the Directing Staff began to consult him as a reliable adviser—a form of flattery whose subtle distinction only those who have attended such places of instruction can fully appreciate.

The 2/7th Gurkha Rifles were at Shillong in Assam. Slim arrived in July and was not joined by Aileen until the end of the year. He was lonely and not entirely happy, partly because 2/7th was not 1/6th, partly because he had to pull the battalion together, and partly because he had to act as Garrison Commander of Shillong, which involved responsibility for one other battalion and sundry extras, and also for providing assistance over such local problems as the native bazaar, whose staple industries were brothels and illicit stills. 'I'm a cross between the chairman of a Parish Council and a brigadier,' he wrote to Pratt. He would have preferred, of course, to have been commanding his old battalion, but there was no vacancy. As it was. . . .

> I know no one here—not a single officer of my new battalion even and so I'm rather on my own. There are a lot of unpleasant jobs to be done as my two predecessors were all for a quiet life and peace in their time. Today for instance I had to tell two worthy Gurkha havildar majors (i.e. sergeant-majors) that they could not become officers because they were over 40 years old. Unfortunately before I arrived they had been told they would be promoted—it's forbidden by regulation to promote after 40 and of course they ought to have been told. Now, poor devils, they think it's entirely due to the arrival of a shit of a new Colonel. They would willingly kill me and I don't altogether blame them—but people who put off unpleasant duties so that their successors will have the unpleasantness and the blame want a particularly warm corner of the next world.*

His spirits were not improved by the Munich crisis. 'I'll never forgive Hitler for it,' he wrote to Pratt in December. 'I was on my way for a most marvellous month or so in Java at King George's expense to do a spot of liaison at the Dutch manoeuvres there, when Hitler stopped it all and I had to hand back fifteen hundred rupees entertainment allowance and scuttle back to my battalion, curse it.' Still, Aileen had now arrived, and if their new home together was not a Government House it was more than mud walls, for they had a pleasant thatched cottage with all modernities, from which base she supervised the hundreds of Gurkha babies produced by the battalion (900 strong), while Slim, as he put it, made an unpleasantness of himself to their fathers.

John Slim once remarked to the author that 'You must make it clear that we were a very *Indian* family.' To the post-1947 and perhaps post-1939 generations it is almost impossible to identify the full flavour of that phrase. The Slims, parents and children, experienced that total

---

* Letter to Pratt, 2 August, 1938.

immersion in Indian life which had been a commonplace for the best representatives of Britain in India since the mid-nineteenth century. In its first and highest form, this produced in the ruler a self-dedicated commitment to the well-being of the ruled. Plato declared that 'all who are in any place of command, in so far as they are indeed rulers, neither consider nor enjoin their own interest but that of their subjects on behalf of whom they exercise their craft.' It was in this spirit that Philip Mason, in his masterly study of the Indian Civil Service, *The Men Who Ruled India*, christened its members 'The Guardians'. For a sound, hard-working Army family like the Slims there would have been something exalted and idealistic, perhaps something high-falutin' in such concepts. Nevertheless, in their domestic way of life and in Slim's professional attitudes they approached them by instinctive and natural processes. There was no sense of *apartheid* in a good Gurkha regiment—that is to say, in a Gurkha regiment; nor, for that matter, was there anything paternalistic. Wife, children, husband—all were part of a larger family, a close-knit society whose fibres ran from cantonment and parade ground into the distant valleys of Nepal; for all of them India, in a sense that has now disappeared, was home. It would be Slim's great strength, when he came to lead a largely Asian army out of defeat into victory, that because he and his family had inherited the outlook of The Guardians, however unconsciously, there could never be a moment when he might look on Sikh or Pathan, Dogra or Jat, Garhwali or Gurkha as a thing apart. They were his and he was theirs.

★★★★★

CHAPTER SIX

WAR ON A SHOESTRING

SLIM WAS Hitler's beneficiary. By 1939 he had acquired all the main qualifications available to a middle-grade officer in peacetime; old for his rank, he might nevertheless have been carried by his record and reputation a rung or two further up the promotion ladder, but the highest places were inaccessible. A war was needed to open a new career for his talents. He was neither a man of blood nor a man of iron. Since he was a realist, however, he would have pointed out that the war happened in any case and that he simply did his duty. But the logic is inexorable. No war, no Field-Marshal.

Certainly Hitler's first gift to Slim was an infantry brigade. Immediately hostilities were declared, he hastened to Army Headquarters, determined to find himself an active command at the outset, and not get left on the shelf. On 23 September, in consequence, he was posted as the commander of 10 Indian Brigade at Jhansi, consisting of one Baluchi, one Garhwali and one Punjabi infantry battalion. Trained for the Frontier, these troops had now to be prepared for operations in the Western Desert of North Africa, as units made mobile by motor transport which they had not received and which they were unable to drive or maintain. Slim rose to the challenge. Taffy Davies, now commanding the Garhwalis, found him 'a memorable Brigade commander. Slim had completely overcome his pessimism regarding the future of his career. He was now sure of himself.' Improvisation reigned. Four officers from the Brigade were made into a special unit for training in mechanization—including Davies and Captain Brian Montgomery of the Baluchis (a younger brother of Major-General Bernard Montgomery, then commanding 3 Division in France). For practice, Slim selected some of the horse transport and said, 'These are vehicles'— with which road movement, dispersion, breakdown drills and so on

63

were realistically rehearsed. Montgomery was impressed by the spirit in which the troops accepted this make-believe; they treated the horse transport as actual motor vehicles *because the Brigadier had said that was what they were.* Apart from three old 3-ton lorries, no proper trucks arrived until March, 1940. In the meantime Slim got the District Commissioner to produce driving instructors from the local garages and civilian volunteers, and designed long and realistic tactical exercises to test and train his officers. Davies noted that 'by his personality, the confidence he inspired, and his friendly manner, he very soon welded the brigade into a happy and enthusiastic team'.

It was not the Führer, however, but the Duce who brought the Jhansi Brigade to battle. By the autumn of 1940 the situation of Mussolini's East African empire was brilliant but hopeless. The troops and aircraft assembled in Ethiopia had an immense numerical superiority over those Wavell could bring to bear; three British battalions, and the other sundries with which General Platt* was manoeuvring on the Sudanese frontier, were hardly a counter-weight. Yet Wavell was about to initiate a campaign whose result was a classic example of quality's power over quantity, and when, on 2 August, 5 Indian Division (containing Slim's brigade) was diverted from Iraq to Port Sudan, it was destined to strike the opening blow.

By 24 October, when Eden, the Secretary of State for War, had a meeting in Khartoum to discuss prospects with Wavell and General Smuts, the stage was already set. Pressure would be exercised on the Italians from within and from outside Ethiopia; a British mission was already in touch with the native Patriots, while Haile Selassie awaited in Khartoum the signal for his return. General Platt's first intention, therefore, was to recover the little frontier post of Gallabat (one of the few specks of Sudanese territory abandoned to the Italians), and thereafter to foster an internal revolt while pressing, further north, on the boundaries of Eritrea. Slim's task was to recapture Gallabat. There was a secrecy worthy of D Day, 1944; when they met, Slim even refrained from mentioning the operation to Eden until the latter, as he departed, said: 'Thanks for your hospitality and showing me round, and the best of luck on Wednesday!'

In retrospect this minor conflict caused Slim almost as much heartsearching as some of the great controversies in Burma. It was the first action on any scale in which he was the senior commander, and in his

---

* Major-General William Platt, CB, DSO, Commander-in-Chief in the Sudan.

view it was a failure. That was arguable, but what haunted him was the feeling that with more self-confidence, with the moral courage he later made habitual, he might have turned failure into triumph. 'When two courses of action were open to me I had not chosen, as a good commander should, the bolder. I had taken counsel of my fears.'

Slim had to start on the wrong foot. Platt held back one brigade of his division down at Port Sudan and to make up a divisional strength on the frontier from the rest—9 and 10 Brigades—he gave Major-General Heath, the divisional commander, the three British battalions which had previously been showing the flag in the Sudan. Heath, following standard practice, replaced an Indian with a British battalion in 9 and 10 Brigades, completing his divisional order of battle with a third brigade composed of the spare British and two displaced Indian units.* Slim thus lost his Punjabis, whom he had trained and trusted, for a battalion of the Essex Regiment. He protested vigorously against this disruption of his well-knit team, but he was over-ruled. He felt anxious and angry. Not surprisingly, because his directive was of the type so much easier to issue than to implement; while he was to attack, at the same time his over-riding duty was to prevent any Italian advance via Gallabat into the Sudan.

Nevertheless, by 6 November his plan and preparations were complete. Gallabat itself consisted of a mud and stone fort surrounded by strong perimeter defences, and standing above a deep rift, in fact a dry stream bed, which formed the frontier between the Sudan and Ethiopia. Beyond this *Khor* stood the larger and more powerfully protected post of Metemma. The two areas had been organized for mutual protection, and while the Italian and African troops available were about equal in number to Slim's, they had the immense advantage of barbed wire, thorn *zaribas*, field-works and solid buildings. Their air superiority was overwhelming and they had substantial reserves close at hand. For his part Slim had better artillery and the six light and six cruiser tanks of 6 Royal Tank Regiment. Deployment of the guns and route-reconnaissance for the armour had been carried out undetected.

The obvious answers to the technical problem presented by the Gallabat-Metemma complex were surprise and shock. Slim achieved both. At dawn six ancient Wellesley bombers—all he had on call—

---

* Peacetime fears that Indian formations required British stiffening were proved in war to be as groundless as the theory that Indians could not be trusted with artillery, could not operate armour, and could not function effectively in the air.

accurately plastered Gallabat, his field regiment put down concentrations and the tanks rolled from their hiding-places. The Garhwalis went through the wire and over the walls, and Gallabat fell without much resistance. Slim moved up to the fort to set in motion the second phase of his plan—the capture of Metemma—but now ill luck compounded with the inexcusable to produce anticlimax. In spite of route-reconnaissance, nine of the twelve tanks were immobilized with tracks damaged by mines and boulders invisible in the long grass. To conceal their reconnaissance, the Tank Corps men had substituted tropical helmets for their black berets; on going into action they naturally wore berets, and some, mistaken by the Indians for Italians, had been fired on and even killed, including their sergeant-major. The nine Gladiator fighters, Slim's frail air cover, were not supposed to operate except in their greatest strength—never in ones or twos; inexplicably, orders were ignored and they were eliminated piecemeal by an Italian air force superior in numbers and performance.

The sky was thus free for the Capronis. By mischance, a heavy raid on Gallabat secured a direct hit on the lorry carrying the only tank spares, which effectively destroyed Slim's hope of keeping up the momentum of his attack on Metemma by directing his repaired tanks on probably demoralized Italians. Nor was it the Italians whose morale cracked. After the bombing, the Essex battalion broke and cascaded to the rear, Slim himself having to take part in checking the fugitives— and this was the battalion he had meant to send in against Metemma.

Next morning, after a night's brooding, Slim could no longer avoid a decision. Further bombing of Gallabat made it clear that to remain in possession meant clutching on to a death-trap. To advance on Metemma was out of the question. But 1,000 yards to the east the ridge of Jebel Mariam Waha ran from north to south, completely commanding from the rear the Italian defences. Following the principle which he and Wavell used so coolly to apply, he laid his own troubles on one side and put himself in the enemy's place: what was worrying *him?* He couldn't know about the turn-tail Essex, or that the armour which had surprised Gallabat was completely unavailable for Metemma. There had been significant desertions, and indications of flight. Suppose Slim moved his Baluchis by night on to Mariam Waha. Might another shock, this time from the rear, finally unnerve the garrison and make them run for Gondar and safety?

His brigade major, his gunner (the brilliant Welchman), and the colonel of the Garhwalis were adamant in opposition. Suppose the garrison stuck? Suppose the rumoured reinforcement arrived? Two native battalions and some Italian troops were reported to be coming up from Gondar. The Baluchis would then be perched unsupported on a bare and waterless hill, more exposed than Gallabat to the bombers, incapable of assaulting Metemma without tanks. 'These three men were each of them braver than I was,' Slim modestly reflected. 'Would they hesitate if the risk were a reasonable one?' Webb clinched the opposition case by reminding Slim of his standing commitment—to protect the Sudan from an Italian advance. If his new plan failed his brigade would fall into useless fragments. He withdrew after nightfall, to positions commanding Gallabat from which his artillery by day and patrols by night could prevent the Italians from re-occupying the ruins of the fort.

The episode was certainly mortifying; the casualties were 42 killed and 125 wounded, and the best that the Official Historians could subsequently say in mitigation of the reverse was that the Ethiopian Patriots were encouraged to know that 'the Italians had been attacked by forces armed with modern weapons'. Slim's sense of failure was increased when, a few days later, it became clear from intercepted signals and the stories of many deserters that there had been panic in Metemma; the garrison had been ready to retreat before another attack.

Soon afterwards, however, the point of emphasis shifted north to Kassala, the Eritrean border, and pursuit of a defeated enemy. On 22 January Slim and his men took their revenge by cutting the escape route of the Italian 41 Colonial Brigade and capturing its Commandant with his staff and 800 troops. But was Slim's self-flagellation over Gallabat justified? His basic plan was sound. The inadequate reconnaissance of the going for his armour was scarcely his fault, nor was the destruction of the Gladiators or the collapse of the Essex battalion—a unit softened by internal duties in the Sudan which later developed into a praiseworthy combination. It can be argued, in view of his lack of air cover, that he crammed too much too soon into Gallabat, and as for his main concern, it is a nice question whether his staff was right and he was wrong about Jebel Mariam Waha. Still, there was an immeasurable gain. Whenever in the future Slim was tempted to take counsel of his fears he remembered Gallabat.

One anticlimax was now followed by another. During the advance into Eritrea his brigade, fully committed in action, was suddenly ordered to disengage and move 60 miles at right angles to the axis of advance, to cut off an Italian force retreating on his flank. 'Move with all speed. Repeat all speed.' Slim disentangled his battalions, pushed his

Sudanese armoured car company ahead to intercept and harass the enemy, and followed himself, escorted by only one truck, to reconnoitre the new area of battle. As they raced over open country he half dozed, exhausted by lack of sleep and lulled by the heat. Suddenly the instrument panel in front of him disintegrated. He stood on the brake and yelled 'Get out', to find that Welchman beside him was already hit in the arm and the driver of the escort truck was slumped over his wheel. Slim himself waited for a second, remembering instinctively that he must switch off the engine, and as he did so the two Italian CR42 fighters made another run. He jumped for safety, but his boot caught between the side of the truck and the spare wheel bolted to it. He had just flung himself desperately to the ground when the world all round him erupted in shattering noise, and a huge kick from behind propelled him, face downwards, into the sand. 'I lay still in what seemed a sudden and extraordinary silence. I felt no pain but I was certain I had been shot to pieces, that my back was broken, my legs paralysed, my vital organs destroyed. I would never move again. Strangely enough I was no longer frightened. "What a pity!", I thought, gently sorry for my wife, my children and myself. "What a pity!" And I lay quite still.'*

In fact he had been hit in the bottom and was able to move, with pain, sufficiently well to be able to take stock. Of the men in the two trucks eight had been wounded, three seriously. The escort vehicle was a write-off. They piled on to Slim's truck and retraced their tracks until they met the advancing brigade. Seeing his condition, Webb, the brigade major, administered some doped whisky, and he survived the ambulance journey back to the railhead at Gedaref in the Sudan. Here an Indian surgeon operated on him immediately, for the wound was complex. The belts of the CR42 machine-guns were loaded in a series of three with first an armour-piercing, then an incendiary, then an explosive bullet. Slim had the benefit of all three. The first had tunnelled through his posterior, fortunately missing all bones. The second had also burrowed into the flesh, but the third, passing straight through, had exploded on the ground and peppered him with slivers of metal. He was kept under chloroform for a considerable time, spending it in repeating *verbatim* the orders he had given for the interception of the Italian column. Welchman, who was in the bed beside him, swore that he issued them much more effectively when he was unconscious.

He was next transferred uncomfortably by train and Nile steamer to Gordon College at Khartoum, now converted into a hospital. Here was

---
* *Memoir.*

civilization and a ward cared for by nurses, two of whom, by the elaborate manipulation of hand mirrors, enabled him to inspect the damage. 'Doesn't it look beautiful?' said a sister, professionally concentrating on the surgeon's achievement. 'No,' said Slim, 'it looks to me like a cross between a night watchman's fire bucket and my aunt's string bag!' A few days later he received a consolatory present from his brigade. A procession escorting a loaded stretcher halted outside the ward, and a note for Slim was produced. It stated that here with the compliments of his brigade was the commander of the Italian column he had set out to intercept. The figure on the stretcher was lying *face downwards*—a colonel, ignominiously wounded like Slim, but by a British anti-tank rifle. 'And thus', the fool in *Twelfth Night* observed, 'the whirligig of time brings in his revenges.' But so does bureaucracy. To anticipate the official telegram he sent a private cable to Aileen: 'Wounded. Nothing to worry about but shall not sit down comfortably for some weeks.' A month later he found that his message had not been delivered, so he hobbled angrily from department to department in the Khartoum Telegraph Office until, at last, he came across a senior censor. After much research the reason was produced. Under a particular subsection of the Censorship Instructions, the official said triumphantly, 'No private cable will be passed for transmission unless its meaning is clear.'

Slim was now a brigadier without a brigade. The doctors refused to let him return to the field, and he was despatched to Cairo *en route* for India. In Cairo Wavell, who had with him the CIGS, Sir John Dill, heard of Slim's presence and summoned him. One of the few recorded instances of Wavell's breaking into hearty laughter occurred when Slim described to his two superiors the nature of his disability. But soon it was sick leave and Simla, snow-sprinkled and sparkling under cloudless blue skies. He had not seen John and Una for two years,* but snowballing is a great mixer. The champagne air, the children and Aileen's cherishing soon restored him to fitness. But, for what?

His luck was on the turn. Rob Lockhart, his old friend and roommate at Simla ten years before, was now Director of Staff Duties at GHQ, where, in his view, there were inadequate arrangements for forward planning. To Slim's fury, because he wanted another active command, Lockhart drew him into the GHQ staff (where he had a desk at which he could *stand*), and here Slim applied himself to a study of the

---

* The children had been at school in England. They came out to India in a 1940 convoy.

Iraq situation. His task was to prepare plans to meet a German success in the Caucasus—that long nightmare of the British in the Middle East— or to deal with the possible defection of the Iraqis to the Axis. These precautions were wise, for on 31 March, 1941, the Regent of Iraq, hearing of a plot against him, escaped from Baghdad to Basra, leaving the field clear for the pro-German Rashid Ali and 'the Golden Square', his military adherents. Lieut-General Quinan was appointed to command the expeditionary force which must assemble in Iraq to meet this threat, and Slim flew off to Basra with him as his Chief of Staff. They had been preceded by advance elements of 10 Indian Division, under Major-General W. A. K. Fraser, which had disembarked on 18 April. But shortly afterwards Fraser fell ill, and a replacement was urgently needed. Who better than Slim? On 15 May he was appointed to command the Division, with the temporary rank of Major-General.

As it happened, the crucial action had already been fought. Towards the end of April superior forces of Iraqi troops assembled on the high ground overlooking Habbaniyah, the British air base and flying school on the Euphrates some 50 miles west of Baghdad. The thousands of non-combatants, the obsolete or instructional aircraft, the exposed position of the garrison offered little hope of an effective defence. However, some 300 infantry were flown in, eighteen Wellington bombers were moved to Iraq from Egypt, and Colonel Ouvry Roberts, G1 of 10 Indian Division, who had flown up from Basra to assess the situation, decided to remain and assume command of the land elements. (Roberts, who by good fortune had been a pupil of Slim's at the Staff College, would become his right-hand man until the following spring, and later continue under him in 14th Army the distinguished career which took General Sir Ouvry Roberts, GCB, KBE, DSO to the post of Quartermaster-General.) The Wellingtons, the pugnacity of the Flying School pilots, and Roberts's aggressive leadership so unnerved the Iraqis that by 6 May they were in full retreat. Thereafter the British situation steadily improved, while the threat of German intervention waned; at the end of the month, as the reinforcing Habforce column from Palestine reached the outskirts of Baghdad, Rashid Ali and the Golden Square fled over the frontier of Persia and armistice terms were agreed.

Slim reached Baghdad early in June, a quarter of a century after he had first entered the city as a victor. But this time his troops had contributed little, splashing slowly northwards through the inundations on the route from Basra. A detachment had flown up to Mosul, where the Germans had tentatively used the airfield. It was time to make the division feel it was an entity and to start imposing his ideas. He talked to them. In a hangar at Habbaniyah all the available officers of 21 Brigade were gathered to listen to him—among them John Masters, then adjutant of his 4th Gurkha battalion. All the regulars in Slim's audience had listened to many such lectures in their time, and often taken away the impression that their general was 'a pompous old blatherskite'.

The quiet that fell in the hangar when Bill Slim entered was not, therefore, entirely of awed expectation. It was, in part, a judicial hush. We waited.

Slim was squarely built, with a heavy, slightly undershot jaw and short greying hair. He began to speak, slowly and judiciously, with no affectation. He told us first that we had done a good job in the Iraqi campaign. What he wanted to do was to prepare us, practically and above all mentally, for the heavier fighting that we must soon meet.

By now he had our whole attention . . . he began to speak about the nature of modern war, of what it was really like when you engaged an enemy as determined, as numerous, and perhaps better armed than yourselves. . . .

'We make the best plans we can, gentlemen, and train our wills to hold steadfastly to them in the face of adversity, and yet to be flexible to change them when events show them to be unsound, or to take advantage of an opportunity that unfolds during the battle itself. . . . But in the end every important battle develops to a point where there is no real control by senior commanders. Each soldier feels himself to be alone . . . the dominant feeling of the battlefield is loneliness, gentlemen. . . .'

I went back to camp in a thoughtful mood. Slim's sort of a battle wouldn't be much of a lark, after all.*

It was by a curious coincidence that a few days later the division was on the move towards a battle in which Slim, having made his plan, would have to show steadfastness in sticking to it. But now the enemy were the Vichy French. To prevent the Germans picking up the Middle East countries by what Churchill called 'petty air forces, tourists and local revolts', a reluctant Wavell was impelled by London to invade Syria, where hatred of the Free French had driven their countrymen to reject all Allied overtures and start opening the door to Hitler. The

---

* John Masters, *The Road Past Mandalay*, p. 44.

main thrust, powered by 7 Australian Division, came northwards from Palestine. A subsidiary move against Palmyra was made from Iraq by Habforce and the Arab Legion. Finally Slim, in mid-June, was ordered by Quinan to concentrate 10 Indian Division at Haditha, 150 miles to the west of Baghdad, with the ultimate object of advancing into Syria as far as Aleppo. To protect his columns against the known strength of the French airforce he had one 'squadron' of fighters—four Gladiators and four Hurricanes. It was appropriate to the character of this shoe-string war—his transport was also inadequate—that the codename for the operation was DEFICIENT.

One of Slim's favourite sayings was a description of Mesopotamia which he had heard a disillusioned soldier utter during the Great War: 'Miles and miles of sweet Fanny Adams, with a river runnin' through it!' He was reminded of its accuracy as with great exertions he got 21 Indian Brigade up to Haditha and then forward another 100 miles to Abu Kemal, a fortlet just inside the Syrian frontier (a brigade only, because nothing larger could be maintained). For transport it had been necessary to strip virtually every formation in Iraq Command. Even then vehicles were lost or delayed, partly because French superiority in the air imposed movement by night, and partly because the desert tracks were a convenient hunting ground for Fawzi Qawukji, a Syrian Arab who had learned his trade as a guerrilla in Palestine. Shortage of rifles left many of Slim's drivers unarmed; knowledge of this encouraged the Arabs to ambush, murder and loot. And then there was the perennial bane of long-distance travel—until the jerrican brought salvation—the paper-thin four-gallon petrol tin whose leakages, in North Africa and the Middle East, wasted millions of pounds and imperilled many an operation. Fortunately Slim had extracted from the Lines of Communications Area Lieut-Colonel Alf Snelling to handle his administrative problems—as, in posts of increasing responsibility, he continued to do throughout the war. Slim said of Snelling that 'his great faculty was conjuring—producing rabbits out of hats, making bricks without straw'. Ouvry Roberts who, as Slim's chief Staff Officer, worked closely with Snelling, felt that nevertheless his great merit was that he never promised Slim what he was unable to perform. By using every possible British vehicle, civilian trucks from Baghdad, native boats on the Euphrates and even the ubiquitous donkey an essential minimum was humped forward to enable Slim to tackle his main task, the capture of Deir-ez-Zor.

The importance of this capital of Eastern Syria was its position.

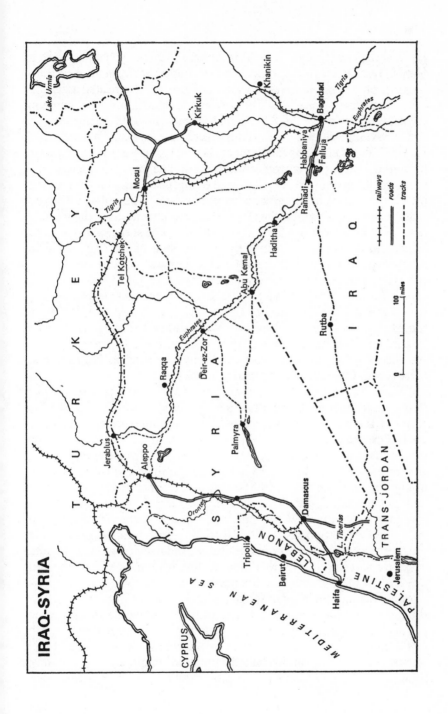

IRAQ-SYRIA

Here, at the only bridge over the Euphrates in all the 500 miles between Habbaniyah and Turkey, desert routes converged from all directions. Its garrison was not large—informers and prisoners indicated a strength of an augmented battalion. To its west and south, however, covering the routes to Palmyra and Abu Kemal, there were good defensive posts, concreted and well dug-in. And the French bombers and fighters, which harassed Slim's columns throughout their advance from Haditha, could be counted on for a vigorous contribution. The problem, therefore, as so often in desert warfare, lay in the approach march. A slogging-match in front of fixed defences would be fatal. The bulk of his force must inevitably move by the direct river-bank route over the 84 miles between Abu Kemal and Deir-ez-Zor. How could surprise be achieved? Slim decided to send the main body of 21 Brigade under Brigadier Weld by the river route, and at the same time despatch a motorized column (of 13th Lancers in ancient armoured cars, a troop of field guns and 4/13th Frontier Force Rifles) to make a wide 100-mile sweep, cutting round and behind Deir-ez-Zor by the south and west and halting on the Aleppo road north of the town. Weld should then be poised for the assault, and as soon as the motorized column made its presence felt in the enemy's rear, and distracted the Vichyites facing 21 Brigade, both forces would launch a simultaneous attack.

'We make the best plans we can, gentlemen'; this was the best plan in the circumstances. On the evening of 1 July, however, after the first phase of the manoeuvre had started, Slim was unexpectedly informed by Roberts that Brigadier Weld had called in the outflanking column to join him by the Euphrates; there would be no surprise at dawn in the enemy's rear. After driving 30 miles through the night over the rough going Slim reached Weld, to find that in the darkness dust storms and bad ground had defeated the drivers. Too many engines groaning in low gear had consumed too much petrol, and there was no hope of reaching the Aleppo road. Weld had therefore recalled his column, given it what little petrol could be spared, and decided to make another effort the same night, but this time sending his outflankers to the west rather than further round to the north of Deir-ez-Zor.

Slim was in a quandary. Weld's scheme was not good enough, for the much stronger western defences of the town would deny the surprise which might be achieved by an attack on the unprotected north. Yet if he waited to collect enough petrol from his distant rear and then pursue his original plan, his halted formations might be caught in daylight by the French bombers—as they would put it, *en rase campagne*, in the open desert. According to Weld, the four Gladiators had already been shot down and two of the four Hurricanes were missing. Slim felt naked. Nevertheless, he trusted Snelling's mastery over the impossible, and signalled back to him that he must collect fuel immediately from every available source and rush it forward in all available transport— by not later than 1800 hours on the evening of the 2nd. Snelling had the nose of a gun-dog and the drive of a bulldozer. By 1900 hours 5,000 gallons had arrived in 'signal trucks, engineer, baggage and ammunition lorries', an issue had been made and the mobile column was ready to move. On an optimistic calculation it could reach the Aleppo road, as originally planned, but there would only be 10 miles per vehicle in hand. Slim quite consciously remembered Gallabat. This time he responded to the feeling in his bones rather than the arithmetic in his head.

'In the end every important battle develops to a point where there is no real control by senior commanders. Each soldier feels himself to be alone.' Slim endured agonies of self-reproach before a message came through—not at dawn, but at ten o'clock—that the column was in the right place. The double attack he had planned succeeded painlessly.* The Euphrates bridge was captured intact, the Vichy Chief of Police became an Instant Gaullist, and Slim enjoyed the *déjeuner* which had been prepared for the late Governor of Deir-ez-Zor. The whole affair, in fact, was a minor episode which rightly receives no more than a half-page in the *Official History*.

Yet the side-show had its comic turns. In 1950 Desmond Young, who was on Slim's staff at the time of Deir-ez-Zor, sent his former commander a personal copy of his book on Rommel.

Under an appropriate inscription the author wrote the words '*à bruler*'. The origin of this enigmatic phrase may be found in Slim's own account in *Unofficial History* of how, when they took over the office of the Governor of Deir-ez-Zor, the key of the safe in his study was missing—a temporary disappointment, for gelignite soon solved the problem. The safe was easily blown, but the hopes of Slim and his intelligence staff, that they might lay their hands on instructive papers,

---

* But not necessarily so. During the attack Slim was at the HQ of 2/10th Gurkhas, whose history, *Bugle and Kukri*, records that 'half a dozen aircraft appeared, but unfortunately they were French and proceeded to bomb Battalion Headquarters and a nearby Field Ambulance. . . . During this incident General Slim had a narrow escape from one of the sticks of bombs.

were foiled. Inside the safe lay a file containing a collection of porno-graphic photographs, marked '*à bruler*', and a set of black silk ladies' underwear.

But there was a more serious dimension. From the point of view of Slim's development as a commander Deir-ez-Zor was of immeasurable importance. His character will be misunderstood unless it is seen as a composition in which self-assurance balances in counterpoint with self-doubt. After Gallabat two things were necessary before he could pro-ceed, as he did with such apparent ease, to larger responsibilities. The first was technical. He had to re-affirm for himself that he possessed the professional skill to evolve the right battle-plan. But he was so persistent an interrogator of his own conscience that a second require-ment was the greater. Having evolved the right plan, he must prove to himself that he could stick to it because it *was* right. He needed another test of his own moral strength; and this time he must not be seen, by his own standards, to fail. Some commanders have had to face such a private inquisition after major and critical battles. It was Slim's good fortune that he was able to stiffen his self-confidence in the course of a side-show.

A fortnight later all French resistance ended. The Germans had never, in fact, been a serious threat in Syria. But in Persia, where a substantial Fifth Column had long existed, matters were different. Railways and government services were being infiltrated, a nuisance which became a menace after 22 June and the German invasion of Russia. Trans-Persian rail and road routes were suddenly a prime means of keeping Russia in the fight, and as suddenly it was necessary to demand the expulsion of the Germans. A joint Anglo-Russian note to this effect was rejected on 17 August. Guns took over from dip-lomacy, and from north, south and west the new Allies moved in to obtain a firm grip on the vital communications. The inevitable followed when on 28 August the Shah abdicated in favour of his more co-operative son, and on 17 September British and Russian troops occupied Teheran.

It was not so much a war as an Arabian Night's Entertainment. Slim first heard of it when he was urgently summoned back to see Quinan while his plane was taking him to a conference at Jerusalem. He pon-dered, recalling that when Quinan himself was recently returning from the Holy City he had demanded of a young officer why the aircraft was littered with amorphous packages. 'Instruments for a jazz band, Sir. General Slim sent me to buy them in Jerusalem.' Unpopular—as was the time when Snelling sniffed out beer in Haifa and they brought it from 600 miles away in the French lorries they had captured at Deir-ez-Zor, but made the mistake on the return journey of forcing Quinan's car off the road. What could his Army Commander want now? It was a relief to discover that he was to take charge of a brigade group from his own division, and 2 Indian and 9 British Armoured Brigades, and penetrate Persia from the west. It was even more relaxing to discover that his force was to assemble on the frontier at Khanaquin, about which he could only recall four lines from the First World War:

> The Khaimaquam of Khanaquin
> Is versed in every kind of sin,
> For all the grosser forms of lust
> He makes a gorgeous bundobust.

At dawn on 25 August Slim crossed his fifth frontier in twelve months. There was virtually no action, which was just as well, since he was faced by a full Corps of the Persian army, with modern weapons, while his own two armoured brigades possessed, between them, one regiment of light tanks. Another Operation DEFICIENT. The only point of difficulty came when the divisional column was winding up the Pai Tak Pass, which climbs some 3,000 feet towards Kermanshah and is the chief defensive position in all the 400 miles to Teheran. John Masters moved in the vanguard with the 4th Gurkhas. There was much gunfire; the shells, as Masters put it, burst 'with tremendous authority'. The vanguard began to feel that some difficult work lay ahead.

> A khaki saloon appeared, coming down to us from the direction of the pass. The leading riflemen dropped and prepared to open fire. But the car was obviously unarmed and flying a red divisional flag from the radiator cap. It stopped beside us and General Slim got out. 'How the hell did he get past us?' I muttered. Willy hurried forward. 'Morning, Willy,' the general said. 'There's nothing until you get round the fourth hairpin. They've got an anti-tank gun there.' There was a large hole through the back of the car body.

Slim's own phrase for the Persian occupation was *opéra bouffe*. That he enjoyed all its scenes with immense zest and a keen eye will be plain to readers of the last two chapters of *Unofficial History*. His senses were always alert, and he had the great gift, for a soldier as for a writer, of a retentive visual memory. Ouvry Roberts drove beside him for many hundreds of miles between western Syria and northern Persia, and he was constantly struck by the number of times that Slim would say to him, at the end of a journey, 'Did you notice that. . .?' He himself was noticing now; noticing the serio-comic Persians, caught between the British presence and their fear of both Russians and Germans, the exquisite arts of Isfahan, the superb mountain scenery, the Kurds, who recalled the Pathans. Roberts and Slim performed a comic turn themselves when they were sent ahead in secret to contact the British legation in Teheran, which involved dressing up in locally purchased civilian clothes and the ubiquitous cloth cap. So successfully did they disguise the truth that every Persian military post along the road turned out the guard and presented arms!

The Russians were a source of much joy and some discomfort. This was a honeymoon season with a partner who was nevertheless, as the Americans would say, 'out for grabs'. Slim therefore took a certain Machiavellian pleasure in thwarting their inevitable attempts to gain an advantage, whether territorial or psychological. But the bitterness and suspicion of later days were not yet evident; in the main, it was the amiability and consideration of his allies that impressed him. His opposite number, General Novikov, 'the rugged old soldier, lean, weather-beaten, with humorous glinting eyes under shaggy brows, a chest of medals, and a great flow of hearty talk', became a boon companion. There was a joint party for the troops inside the Russian zone, and the mandatory banquet for officers at which Slim, to Roberts's admiration, drank toast for toast without flagging (until he retired to bed)—a true victory, for he was always abstemious about liquor. Nor did he smoke; Roberts, who was addicted to cigars, would never have dreamed of lighting one in Slim's office.

But the Russians were soon to provide a very different preoccupation. 10 Indian Division was pulled back from Persia for a more appropriately combatant role in Iraq. The danger of a German penetration through Caucasia looked larger or smaller according to the effect of the weather or temporary Russian successes, but it was always there, and Slim's troops spent many weeks practising for the counter-attack, preparing strong-points, studying the ground. By the spring of 1942 he was proud of his division—and himself. He had forged a weapon. And then, early in March, he was summoned, in his headquarters at Habbaniyah, to speak to Quinan on the telephone. Within three days, he was informed, he must be in India.

CHAPTER SEVEN

THE SLOUGH OF DESPOND

> WORLDLY WISEMAN: I see the dirt of the Slough of Des-
> pond is upon thee: but that slough is the beginning of the
> sorrows that do attend those that go on in that way: hear me, I
> am older than thou; thou art like to meet with, in the way
> which thou goest, wearisomeness, painfulness, hunger, perils,
> nakedness, sword, lions, dragons, darkness, and, in a word,
> death, and what not?
>
> John Bunyan, *The Pilgrim's Progress*

IT WAS Help who extricated Bunyan's struggling pilgrim from the
Slough, and Help who explained to him, when they reached safe
ground, that the filth and mire were a kind of precipitate from previous sin. To get through to the future a man must march through the
consequences of the past. Nothing could be a more precise symbol for
those who led the British out of Burma in the great retreat of 1942.
They were expiating the errors of their predecessors, and they emerged
from the slough mainly because they helped themselves. Moreover,
their emergence was only the beginning of sorrows.

Once the Japanese decided to move aggressively into Burma no
commander, living or dead, could have sustained by his genius the
indefensible British position. It was a house of cards, erected on the
quicksands of false hopes. Wrong decisions in the twenties about the
defence of Singapore bred an assumption that this vital base was
impregnable; therefore Burma was safe; therefore nothing need be done
to protect it—except to toss responsibility for its care backwards and
forwards between India and the Far East Command. There were no
reliable land routes over the mountainous Indian frontier. The few
civil airfields were not strategically sited. Army HQ at Rangoon was an
administrative, not an operational organization. Fighting stores, trained

troops, intelligence, communications were all deficient. And the legacy of Imperial rule was a native population which, apart from the hill tribes, was largely apathetic. When the foundation of Singapore unexpectedly subsided the frail and rickety structure of Burma needed no more than a confident push to hurl it to the ground.

In such earthquake situations it is often the British way to censure men who, through no fault of their own, have found themselves faced with the responsibility of shoring up a tumbling ruin and have done their honest but hopeless best. This role of sin-eater now fell to Lieut-General Hutton, Wavell's able CGS in India, whom the Commander-in-Chief sent to Rangoon on 27 December, 1941, to take charge of the Burma Army. With its widely dispersed and semi-amateur Burma Division, and the newly arrived, under-trained, ill-equipped 17 Indian Division* he loyally sought to implement his directive to win time by refusing to give up space, i.e., by holding Rangoon and keeping the Japanese as far to the east as possible—a directive based on a misjudgement by Wavell of the enemy's military capability (as he himself would later freely admit). With the Sittang bridge blown, the Japanese at the gates of Rangoon and the Allied air force dying in the skies, Alexander took up command in Burma on 5 March, 1942. Adhering to Wavell's instructions, and ignoring the informed advice of Hutton and his staff, the new general nearly precipitated disaster by refusing to abandon Rangoon. He was quick to accept the inevitable, however; yet when, on the 6th, he ordered a withdrawal it was only by a miracle that he and the substantial force in the city were not captured as they sought to escape. In this lamentable sequence of events there was one positive act, often overlooked, which was to have profound consequences during the coming months. Hutton and his staff had wisely and properly arranged for vast quantities of supplies to be removed from Rangoon and stock-piled further inland—resources which proved to be the iron rations of the retreat.†

---

* The remarkable performance of 17 Division in the 1942 Burma campaign could hardly have been predicted from its condition in December, 1941. See Appendix Two in *The War against Japan*, Vol. 11, for a hair-raising account of the Division's weaknesses in equipment, personnel and readiness for jungle warfare. Wavell's curious optimism at this time was partly due to an assumption that the Indian troops in Burma were of the same quality and efficiency as 4 and 5 Indian Divisions which had served him so superbly in the Middle East.

† One essential war-store disappeared in the process—the stocks of maps. As the retreat proceeded, this deficiency severely hampered Slim and his subordinates. Colonel Brian Montgomery recalled that 'Before we reached the Kabaw

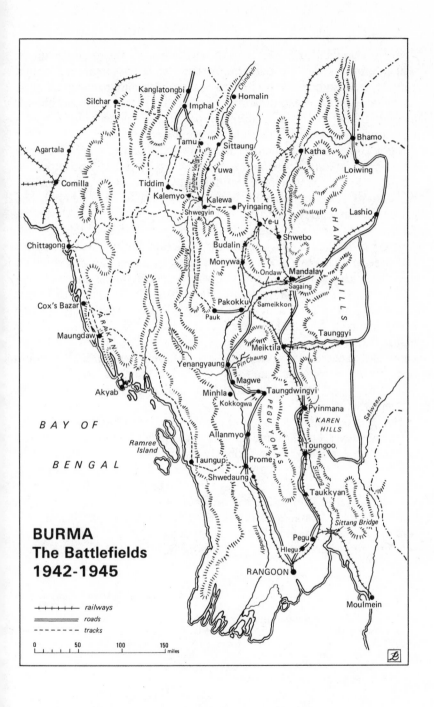

Silchar
Kanglatongbi
Imphal
Homalin
Chindwin
Agartala
Tamu
Sittaung
Katha
Bhamo
Yuwa
Loiwing
Comilla
Tiddim
Kalemyo
Kalewa
Pyingaing
Ye-u
Lashio
Shwegyin
Kabaw Valley
Irrawaddy
S H A N
Chittagong
Budalin
Shwebo
Monywa
H I L L S
Ondaw
Mandalay
Cox's Bazar
Pakokku
Sameikkon
Sagaing
Pauk
Maungdaw
Taunggyi
A R A K A N
Meiktila
Yenangyaung
Pin Chaung
Akyab
Magwe
Minhla
Taungdwingyi
Kokkogwa
Pyinmana
KAREN
HILLS
BAY OF
Allanmyo
P E G U   Y O M A S
Salween
Ramree
Island
Toungoo
BENGAL
Taungup
Prome
Shwedaung
Sittang
Taukkyan

BURMA
The Battlefields
1942-1945

Sittang Bridge
Pegu
Hlegu
RANGOON

Moulmein

++++++ railways
====== roads
------ tracks

0   50   100   150
miles

Such, sketched in broad strokes, is the back-drop to the stage on which Slim was about to perform. As so often in his career, chance and coincidence played their part in his casting. Alexander realized that he must have a Corps Commander to fight the battle while he himself handled the many administrative and political problems of his complex war-zone. Prompted by his staff, he asked London for Slim, whom he did not know. As it happened, his need for a Commander had already been appreciated in Whitehall. Alanbrooke, only recently promoted to CIGS, was examining a list of candidates. On the list was Slim's name, and the VCIGS was General Nye who, it will be remembered, had formed at Camberley a high opinion of Slim's qualities. Like Alexander, Alanbrooke knew not Slim; but Nye persuaded his Chief, and the future Field-Marshal was moved into position for the next act in the Burmese drama. On 13 March he reported to Alexander at Prome on the Irrawaddy, commander-elect of what was now called 1 Burma Corps or Burcorps.* Set out in this orderly fashion the sequence of events seems to have a certain inevitability, but in truth there was nothing predetermined. Suppose Alexander or Alanbrooke had rejected this Major-General, personally unknown to them, whose experience of high command in action had so far been at a relatively low level. Slim would certainly have made a name elsewhere, but there is no doubt that Burma in 1942 offered the challenge which perfectly matched his particular qualities.

Before Alexander left England for Burma Mountbatten advised him to ensure that Churchill understood what he could and could not do; he must state that he would probably be unable to save Burma, but he would seek to save the army, and then he *must* be brought home. 'If they regard this as a defeat for which you are responsible, it will damage you irretrievably.' But Slim was unable to make such conditions, nor, indeed, would it have been in his character to do so. As Quinan told him when he protested about leaving his division in Iraq, 'A good soldier goes where he's sent and does what he's told.' He settled into

---

valley all I had was an out-of-date road map *devoid of all contours*. Taffy Davies wanted that anyway!'

* He had first arrived in Burma a few days earlier and met Alexander, who disclosed nothing about his future. Slim feared that he might be made Alexander's Chief of Staff, which he knew was not his *métier*. He went back to India still in the dark about his prospects, but in Calcutta was summoned by Wavell and ordered to return immediately in command of the Corps about to be formed from 17 Division and the Burma Division.

his headquarters in the Law Courts at Prome and assessed his new command.

This was not the first, nor was it to be the last, time that I had taken over a situation that was not going too well. I knew the feeling of unease that comes first at such times, a sinking of the heart as the gloomy facts crowd in; then the glow of exhilaration as the brain grapples with problem after problem; lastly the tingling of the nerves and the lightening of the spirit, as the urge to get out and tackle the job takes hold. Experience had taught me, however, that before rushing into action, it is advisable to get quite clearly fixed in mind what the object of it all is.*

During the later stages of the retreat its object—that is to say, an object clearly defined by the highest authorities—became intermittently obscure, but at the time of Slim's arrival Alexander was in no doubt about his orders. On his way to Burma he met Wavell at Calcutta airport, on 3 March, and as they talked he received a brief which the *Official History* convincingly paraphrases:

The retention of Rangoon is a matter of vital importance to our position in the Far East and every effort must be made to hold it. If, however, that is not possible, the British force must not be allowed to be cut off and destroyed, but must be withdrawn from the Rangoon area for the defence of upper Burma. This must be held as long as possible in order to safeguard the oilfields at Yenangyaung, keep contact with the Chinese and protect the construction of the road from Assam to Burma.

When Slim reached Prome Rangoon had already gone, though 'the British force' had fortunately not been cut off. For the rest, the directive laid down sufficiently clear objectives for the immediate future—as clear, perhaps as was possible. The Chinese and oil, these were the two great preoccupations—for though destruction of the refineries and other installations at Rangoon had been a considerable loss, the experts calculated that the oil-fields up-country could supply the fuel for Alexander's army and his allies over at least two years. Yenangyaung was therefore a treasure-house.

To count one's blessings is usually a good beginning, and Slim

---

* *Defeat into Victory*, p. 27.

discovered several. He had a principle, to which he adhered right up to his period as CIGS, of not bringing with him to a new appointment his own group of preferred staff officers. 'I don't', he would say (thinking of Montgomery and others) 'travel with a circus.' In practice this proved unnecessary since he would either fall among old and trusted friends or, with his immense gift for inducing affection and loyalty, soon weld his new staff into an efficient and happy team. At Prome he was in luck. Taffy Davies of the Garhwalis, whom he had last seen in his Jhansi Brigade in 1940, and who had been acting as BGS to Hutton at Rangoon, now became the BGS of Burcorps.

The danger of using military terminology is that the word is assumed to represent a standard thing. A Corps implies a normally staffed and equipped HQ. But throughout the story of the retreat it must be remembered that Slim's headquarters were deficient in almost every item of equipment that makes effective service possible—virtually no wireless sets or even signallers, little transport, less office stores. Davies, according to Slim, 'got—and kept—that scratch headquarters working. From nothing and almost with nothing, he formed, organized, and fused it with his own spirit.' And then, by another coincidence, there was Brian Montgomery, 'who never seemed to need sleep', and who doubled the parts of several junior staff officers until, after the retreat had reached the Yenangyaung oilfields, he was reinforced by a G3 from 1/8th Gurkhas in the shape of the future General Sir Walter Walker. Slim also recognized with delight a Brigadier in 17 Division, the trusted Welchman, whom he had last seen in the next bed at Khartoum; he was immediately switched to Slim's headquarters and put in charge of the Corps artillery—such as it was. Above all, of course, good fortune supplied Slim with two divisional commanders whose high qualities he knew from the intimacy of service in the same battalion—Bruce Scott of the Burma Division, and 'Punch' Cowan who was to have the experience, almost certainly unique, of leading 17 Indian Division for the rest of the war, until, in 1945, they returned to Rangoon.

The danger of military terminology is once again illustrated by the use of 'Division' to describe the two main formations in Slim's command. Before the invasion the Burma Division had never functioned as a whole; after the invasion those of its units which were Burmese became progressively unreliable as distance and defeat drew them further from their homes. 17 Indian, which on its arrival was under-equipped and largely untrained, was reduced by the Sittang bridge disaster to a force of some 4,000 exhausted men. Reinforcement,* a minimal re-equipment, and Cowan's dynamic leadership kept it battle-worthy, but neither division had the power for major operations. Only 7 Armoured Brigade,† with its two regiments of light tanks and its experience of war against Rommel, supplied Slim with a core of battle-hardened troops; yet the tanks had only a limited value, because their guns fired solid shot without the alternative of high-explosive shell and their narrow tracks were inefficient in paddy fields. By the end of March all Allied aircraft had been destroyed or driven out of Burma.‡ The only direction in which Slim could look for help, outside his own command, was China. (To whose forces the same terminological point applies. A Chinese 'Army' or 'division' was always far weaker in numbers and equipment than its British name implies.)

After Pearl Harbor Wavell had been reluctant to accept in full Chiang Kai-shek's offer of Chinese divisions for Burma, on the grounds that such troops would require supplies and maintenance beyond the facilities of Burma Army. These regimented locusts could indeed look after themselves, but their methods of 'living on the country' were un-welcome. Nevertheless, the umbrage of the Generalissimo had not prevented the movement of his V and VI Armies in the general direction of the Sittang valley, with Toungoo prescribed by Chiang as the most southerly objective. This enabled Alexander to pull out Burma Division from the Sittang and transfer it westwards, beyond the range of the Pegu Yomas which divide the Irrawaddy from the Sittang valley. Here, in the latter part of March, the Division re-assembled to the north of Prome, and with 17 Division operating to the south of the town Slim could at least begin to feel that his command was coming together under his thumb, and that an intelligible defensive pattern was emerging in which Burcorps would hold the Irrawaddy, and the Chinese the Sittang, along the general line Prome—the Yomas—Toungoo. So long as these points could be held, the Japanese would be baulked. But

---

* After the Sittang its 46 Brigade was broken up and replaced by a spare brigade 63.

† 7 Armoured Brigade arrived from the Middle East just before Rangoon fell. In spite of its habituation to the African Desert, this veteran formation adapted itself with remarkable efficiency to the conditions of Burma.

‡ The main destruction was on the ground, at Magwe, owing to bad dispersal on the airfield. 'I so well remember Slim's dismay and Taffy Davies's rage, when the news reached us at Prome that our air-cover had vanished overnight. We sensed it had gone for good, and so it had.' Colonel Montgomery to author, 28 Novem-ber, 1975.

nothing remained stable for long in Burma, and this was a scheme containing too many incalculables—the performance of the Chinese, in particular, and the intentions of the Japanese 15th Army, whose 55 Division was thrusting up the road to Mandalay while 33 Division made for the Yenangyaung oilfields via Prome.

To discern the broad scope of those intentions was not difficult; to obtain detailed information about the enemy's dispositions was less easy, for Slim was practically blind—no air reconnaissance, no well-established intelligence network, a lukewarm native population infiltrated by active dissidents. In the whole of Slim's Burcorps there was only one officer linguistically competent in Japanese. At Prome, therefore, he encouraged and expanded the improvised *Yoma Intelligence Service* which Cowan had initiated by recruiting British civilians, traders, forestry men etc., with first-hand knowledge of the country and its people. It was one of these, Philip Howe, a *teakwallah* in the great firm of Steel Bros, but transformed overnight into an Intelligence major, who actually housed Slim and his staff in his own senior assistant's house and 'dined in' the new Corps Commander on the night of his arrival. Howe went all through the retreat and out into India with 17 Division. His first official meeting with Slim, however, was less friendly.

The day after Slim's arrival Howe learned that a local police official, a Eurasian, was to be given a post of authority in the new Intelligence Service. As he believed, from recent experience, that the man was wholly unsuitable for the job, and as he himself had until the previous day been an independent and self-reliant civilian, he dared to speak his mind to Slim. Slim had obviously received different advice from those he believed to be qualified, and he was brusque with this intrusive *teakwallah*. Yet many exhausting weeks later, and many miles further up the Irrawaddy, he suddenly volunteered to Howe that among the many things he had discovered since his arrival was the fact that Howe had been right. Howe never forgot the spontaneous gesture.

One discovery came all too soon—the unreliability of the Chinese. The Prome–Toungoo line was vital, for in the west it provided forward protection to the oilfields at Yenangyaung, on which the Burma Army now relied for its fuel, while Toungoo itself was a buttress of Central Burma. There were the air-fields—invaluable to the advancing Japanese. More importantly, Toungoo commanded the bridge over the Sittang which gave direct access to the route running north to Lashio and the Burma Road to China. Thus the fall of Toungoo would mean the cutting of their communications for the Chinese forces in Burma;

it would also allow the Japanese 33 Division to join the 55th in a converging attack on Mandalay. Yet so it went; the Chinese 200 Division was first cut off in Toungoo and then forced to retreat, with the loss of 3,000 casualties and most of its guns and equipment.* An incompetent higher command, internal jealousies and primitive methods of waging war were not compensated for by the stubborn bravery of the individual soldier, and the Chinese front swiftly disintegrated. (To look ahead, by 29 April the Japanese were in Lashio, by 4 May in Bhamo, and by 8 May in Myitkyina.) The whole eastern face of Burma was soon to be slashed open, and Slim was right in judging that the loss of Toungoo was a major diaster, second only to the loss of the Sittang bridge which had brought down Rangoon.

It was the pressure on Toungoo that precipitated Slim's first operation in the Burma Campaign. In the latter half of March his prime concern was to concentrate effectively his newly formed Corps in the area round Prome. With 17 Division as a shield to the south, he was allowing the tired Burma Division to reassemble and reorganize. Suddenly, on the 28th, he received a signal from Alexander (then with Chiang Kai-shek at Chungking) instructing him to take the weight off the Chinese at Toungoo by attacking on his own front. To maintain solidarity with Chiang such sops were unavoidable, though it is difficult to see how the investment of Toungoo could have been substantially affected by operations at Prome. If he had been commanding a properly organized Corps Slim might well have been able to improve the situation on his own front as well as marginally assisting the Chinese. As it was, however, he could do neither. Burma Division was not yet ready, so the best he could do was to order Cowan to thrust southwards with 17 Division and tanks from the armoured brigade. In a bloody scramble at Shwedaung the force was cut off by the usual Japanese tactics of infiltrating and encircling; after extricating itself, it had lost 10 tanks and 350 casualties—with no compensating profit. For Slim the mathematics were inescapable. Next time there would be less armour available, and next time less still. It was a one-way process. When his Corps left the Chindwin for the last terrible tramp into Imphal each of his divisions had been reduced to the equivalent of a weak brigade.

Prome was now in danger. Slim therefore moved his Corps HQ

---

* This was not the fault of 200 Division, which was of unusually high quality. Another Chinese division sent to its relief disobeyed orders. Such non-happenings were characteristic of Chiang Kai-shek's armies.

some 35 miles up river to Allanmyo, and it was here that he was visited
on 1 April by Wavell and Alexander, to be told that he must expedite
back-loading of the supply dumps in Prome and withdraw his troops
further north. This, in effect, was a recognition that the time had come
for a final stand to save the oilfields. It was a serious moment—with
one light note, recorded by Philip Howe:

> I kept out of the way and sat quietly reading a book on a swing seat
> in a corner of the garden. My peace was rudely shattered by three army
> captains bursting into the garden and demanding beer. 'We know it's
> here and we intend to get it,' they said. 'Where is it hidden?'
> 'There's beer here,' I said. 'And it's quite easy to obtain. All you
> have to do is to go upstairs where you'll find Generals Wavell, Slim
> and Alexander in conference on the verandah. I'm sure they'll be only
> too happy to give you a bottle of beer each.'
> They crept out on tiptoe.

The seriousness of the situation was underlined within a few hours, for
during the night of the 1st Cowan's division was driven out of Prome.
As it fell back to the north, moreover, there were fears that the outflanking Japanese might cut the division off from the rest of Burcorps.
Fortunately this threat was imaginary, but after a hard night's fighting
and a dispiriting defeat 17 Division had to endure the miseries of retirement through heat and dust, without water, and under constant attack
from the air.* By 3 April, however, they had linked up with the Burma
Division, and Slim's Corps was re-united.

But this concentration was only temporary and Slim was now under
great strain. The atmosphere at Allanmyo, Howe noted, was one of
crisis; during the Prome battle neither Slim nor Davies slept all night.†
Their burden was not lessened by Alexander's decision to withdraw
still closer to Yenangyaung, since the new line to be held by Burcorps
was, in truth, over-extended—though for good reasons. The Burma
Division was now split, one of its brigades being detached as a flank
guard to the west bank of the Irrawaddy at Minhla. From here on an
eastward arc of some 40 miles the front ran through waterless, roadless,
sparsely clad hill country to Taungdwingyi, whence a railway creeps

---

* 'April in Burma is one of the hottest months of the year, and the division was
now entering the most arid region of the country.' *The War against Japan*,
Vo . 11, p. 160.
† General Davies confirmed this to the author.

down into the Sittang valley. Like Slim, Alexander was fully aware that such a frontage was hardly defensible by so small and so weak a formation as Burcorps; nevertheless, their obligation to the Chinese still existed, and he instructed Slim to hold Taungdwingyi firmly, as a junction point with the two Chinese Armies, V and VI, who, in theory at least, were to prolong the allied line across the Sittang and over the Karen Hills. Slim therefore moved 17 Division into the general area of Taungdwingyi.

He did so reluctantly. His long, thinly protected front invited the very tactics of infiltration in which the Japanese excelled. Moreover, his pugnacious spirit still cherished the hope of somehow concentrating his force and recovering the initiative by aggressive action. A careful reader will note how often in the pages of *Defeat into Victory* which describe this phase of the retreat he introduces the words 'attack' and 'counter-attack'. Merely to contemplate such action, even if its effect could be little more than deterrent, was a remarkable feat of resilience. Considering the physical and mental strain on Slim's men, they were certainly marching and fighting with a laudable stoicism. For the British troops there was no mail from home to bring comfort, and home itself was a prospect increasingly remote. The Indians were steeled by their strong loyalties, to the regiment and to the Raj, but the imperial aura of the British must sometimes have seemed frail. Yet all but the weak endured, harassed by thirst, harassed from the air, harassed most of all, perhaps, by the unknown. The men of Burcorps were indeed a gallant and long-suffering company. But nobody, least of all Slim, could consider them a well-tuned military instrument, or apt—except in desperation—for a large-scale assault.

There were, moreover, many practical impediments to thwart Slim's generalship. The effort to control his widespread troops with a handful of wireless sets, whose batteries were re-charged by a bicycle-driven machine, was itself a nightmare, particularly since the Japanese threat had driven from their posts almost all the civil service and the staffs of public utilities. The telephone network had collapsed. Even an improvised system of messengers and liaison officers was put at risk by murderous gangs who used the current chaos to exploit Burma's oldest profession, dacoity. These also thrived parasitically on the drifting swarms of refugees, whose tragic presence affected both operations and morale as they blocked the roads with their non-stop embodiment of misery and despair. The most elementary necessities now conditioned planning, for in the Dry Belt of Burma the water-courses, at the end of the pre-monsoon period, were exhausted. When putting his troops in new positions, therefore, Slim was sometimes forced to take as his first criterion the accessibility of the nearest water-point. The truth was that he was fighting in the circumstances of a nineteenth-century colonial war.

Yet Slim never lost heart. All eye-witness accounts of the retreat single out for emphasis the unbroken calm and good humour which he consistently displayed. He was drawing on deep wells of fortitude. As a conscious act he used every possible opportunity to make direct and personal contact with his soldiers, talking cheerfully to them, letting them learn from him, carrying in his hands the gifts of faith and self-confidence. Perhaps his true achievement during the retreat was to prevent military disaster by winning a moral victory. He did well in manoeuvring his divisions, but he did better in making them the partners of his spirit.

Like any good commander, in fact, Slim hid his inner disquiet behind a mask of assurance—and this could sometimes be counter-productive, as happened one day at Taungdwingyi, where he had set up his head-quarters in the hope that he could make effective arrangements with the Chinese. As 17 Division sought to turn the town into a stronghold there were regular air attacks, for by now Japanese planes ranged freely, pattern-bombing in comfortable unimpeded groups, and one by one the population-centres burned—Mandalay, Meiktila, Thazi, Pyinmana, Maymyo, Lashio. A raid came in on Taungdwingyi just as Slim, his staff and two divisional commanders were finishing breakfast before starting a Corps conference.

> I remember shouting in Hindustani, 'There's plenty of time. Don't hurry!' a remark that almost qualified for the Famous Last Words series. At that instant we heard the unmistakable scream of bombs actually falling. With one accord two or three generals and half a dozen other senior officers, abandoning dignity, plunged for the nearest trench. Scott, being no mean athlete, arrived first and landed with shattering impact on a couple of Indian sweepers already crouching out of sight. I followed, cup of tea and all; the rest piled in on top, and the whole salvo of bombs went off in one devastating bang. Poor Scott, crushed under our combined weight, feeling warm liquid dripping over him, was convinced that I had been blown into the trench and was now bleeding to death all over him.*

---

* *Defeat into Victory*, p. 53.

To place the headquarters of a Corps on the extreme left of its front is hardly orthodox. Slim set up his command post at Taungdwingyi because on the 6th, under pressure from Alexander, Chiang Kai-shek agreed to send one of his divisions there from V Army, as a reserve for the over-extended Burcorps, and Slim sensibly wished to make personal contact with his allies. The hope was vain, for with typical deviousness Chiang cancelled his order, and all efforts to make a Chinese soldier materialize faded. 'It was rather like enticing a shy sparrow to perch on your windowsill.'* One small 'guerrilla battalion' did appear—and disappear. Cowan and 17 Division were thus left in the air at Taungdwingyi.

It was during these abortive arrangements with the Chinese that Slim first met what he called 'the most colourful character in South East Asia', General Joseph Stilwell. Recently appointed Chief of Staff to Chiang Kai-shek, as well as being Commanding General of the US Army Forces in the China-Burma-India theatre, Stilwell was nevertheless no plenipotentiary, for Chiang had carefully refrained from giving him the all-important *Kwang-Fang*, or seal of office as Commander-in-Chief.† Chinese generals were therefore always at liberty to ignore his instructions and delay matters by referring back to Chungking.

Stilwell's extensive pre-war service in China had opened his eyes to the Byzantine character of his new allies. He well understood that for one of Chiang's generals his division was a kind of personal fief, not to be lightly dissipated in engagements with the enemy. He knew, for he had noted it before 1939, that to a senior Chinese officer rarities like war stores—artillery, say, or tanks—represented both a treasure and a private insurance-policy which it was better not to exploit immediately but to preserve against a rainier day. Harsh on the surface (but with a tender core), anglophobe, suspicious and necessarily ruthless, Stilwell was an uncomfortable partner. Yet from the beginning Slim seems to have sensed his qualities and shrewdly gauged his difficulties; until the very end, when in late 1944 Chiang finally disembarrassed himself of 'Vinegar Joe', this awkwardly matched pair achieved an effective symbiosis. Neither during the war nor afterwards was Slim prepared to join in the fashionable denigration of Stilwell. This acidulous American,

---

* *Defeat into Victory*, p. 52.
† Stilwell was not empowered with the vermilion seal of command until December, 1943, when he wrote to his wife, 'Put down 18 December, 1943, as the day when, for the first time in history, a foreigner was given command of Chinese troops, with full control over all officers and no strings attached.'

dressed like a shabby duck-hunter, with the haircut of Uriah Heep and
one skin too few, never caused his colleague to lose his temper or stand
on hurt dignity. For Slim Stilwell was unique, the one man who could
impel the Chinese to battle, and he unswervingly respected both the
character and the military capacity which made possible so unlikely an
event. Yet even Stilwell was unable to plant a Chinese division in
Taungdwingyi.

The inevitable soon followed. On 10 April the Japanese began to
probe and thrust along the whole front, working their way up the east
bank of the Irrawaddy and, on the left flank of Burcorps, engaging 48
Brigade at Kokkogwa in what Slim considered to be 'one of the most
bitterly fought actions of the campaign'. The problem of checking
infiltration through a wide front was complicated; to the weary men of
Burcorps any group of Burmese with a bullock cart could be, and
sometimes was, a party of Japanese with a concealed machine-gun. And
so, by the 14th, after confused and vicious fighting, the Burma Division
had fallen back to the line of the Yin Chaung. The significance of this
channel, which wriggles westwards through the hills from the Taungdwingyi–Kokkogwa region to the Irrawaddy, is that if it had to be
abandoned the next watering-point* would be another 40 miles away,
on the Pin Chaung to the *north* of Yenangyaung. The enemy was on
the threshold of the oilfields.

Preliminary arrangements for their denial to the Japanese had been
put in hand as early as January by the local technicians. They were
strengthened in mid-May by the arrival of W. L. Forster, a civil
engineer who was an expert in the highly skilled craft of putting oil-
fields out of action and had already applied his knowledge in the Middle
East, in the Caucasus (after the German invasion of Russia) and in
wrecking installations at Rangoon. Under Forster the preparatory
stages were efficiently completed, and it was at some point during the
evening of 14 April that Slim, seeing the situation was irrecoverable,
gave instructions for the final demolitions to commence.

The immediate responsibility for this grave decision was borne by
Slim alone. He was aware that he was executing the broad policy of
Alexander and the Government in London who, apart from the struggle
in Burma, were determined to deny to the Japanese facilities valuable
for the general conduct of the war. This point became absolutely clear

---

* The Yin Chaung itself was running dry, and its sandy bottom, though an im-
pediment to tracks or wheels, was no barrier to Japanese feet.

some twenty years later, in 1963, when Slim's testimony was sought during an appeal to the House of Lords in which the Burmah Oil Company was seeking compensation for the destruction of its equipment. The important fact which emerged was that the installations at Yenangyaung were demolished not primarily through 'battle damage' but by a conscious act on Slim's part in implementation of the overall policy of his Government. This was a difficult and distracting issue for a commander in the middle of a desperate battle. Thanks to the skill of the experts and the timing of Slim's orders all went well—to the chagrin of the Japanese who, it was noticed, had been meticulous in keeping their bombers away from the key installations.

By the 16th the Burma Division, exhausted and somewhat disorganized, was slowly withdrawing northwards under pressure to the outskirts of Yenangyaung, where the flames and smoke from millions of gallons of burning oil provided an apocalyptic backcloth. To Slim and his staff, who had moved Corps headquarters to the far or northern side of the Pin Chaung, these towering columns of crude black cloud must have symbolized the dead end of one road and the beginning of another. But whither? This was no time for speculation. Late on the night of the 16th, just as the transport of Burma Division had crossed the Pin Chaung, moving ahead of the main body, a Japanese road-block was inserted ahead of it on the north side of the Chaung, while another appeared on the south, at Twingon. The bulk of the Division was therefore effectively cut off in the burning stinking shambles of Yenangyaung.

Next day there reported to Slim a man who was to provide him with a yardstick of how good a Chinese commander might be. This was Lieut-General Sun Li Jen, whose excellent 38 Division, in spite of shuffling by Chiang Kai-shek, had been diverted by Alexander and Stilwell to the support of Burcorps. Sun, a product of the Virginian Military Academy, is reckoned in retrospect to have been pre-eminent among the Chinese leaders, honest, calm, pugnacious. Slim immediately arranged for his troops to join in a counter-attack next morning, and even, with a shrewd stroke of diplomacy, put the available British artillery and armour under his command. Not only to have armour, but to have *foreign* armour under one's *command* meant an immeasurable accession of 'face' for General Sun, and when the attack went in early on the 18th Slim, observing of course from the front line, assessed the Chinese performance professionally and found it good. Yet not good enough. Neither this attack from the outside nor the Burma Division around Yenangyaung, fighting to by-pass the road-block between themselves and the Chaung crossing, succeeded in breaking the Japanese stranglehold. The temperature was 114 degrees. The air was foul with the fumes of burning oil. There was no water.

A loss of one half of Burcorps now seemed imminent. Slim arranged for a renewal of the attack next day, and then, at 4.30 in the afternoon, spoke by radio to Bruce Scott in his defensive perimeter beside the ruins of Yenangyaung. Scott's men were exhausted by marching, fighting and thirst. The torrid, poisonous air and the blazing sun were taking their toll. He therefore asked for Slim's permission to destroy his guns and transport and attempt a breakout during the night. To condemn others to the probability of imprisonment or death is pain enough for a sensitive man; so to condemn an old friend when you yourself are under extreme pressure is indefinably harder. This was now Slim's private purgatory. Scott, his wife and his children were bound to the Slim family by years of shared living. It was Scott who had risked trouble for himself in allowing Slim that extra leave in Kashmir which had enabled him to win Aileen's hand. Now the commander of 1 Burma Division must be told to hold fast, endure the night, and co-operate next morning in the attack by British and Chinese which should release him. His soldiers were now little more than paper tigers.

Nevertheless, the orders were given—and accepted without argument. Brian Montgomery, who was watching and listening to Slim, noted how gently and courteously he talked to Scott, never relaxing the iron grip of authority but never domineering or dictating.* This was the occasion about which Slim wrote in *Defeat into Victory* some oft-quoted and self-revealing words:

> I stepped out of the van feeling about as depressed as a man could. There, standing in a little half-circle waiting for me, were a couple of my own staff, an officer or two from the Tank Brigade, Sun, and the Chinese liaison officers. They stood there silent and looked at me. All commanders know that look. They see it in the eyes of their staff and their men when things are really bad, when even the most confident staff officer and the toughest soldier want holding up, and they turn

---

* 'Throughout the Retreat,' Montgomery observed, 'when speaking on the wireless Slim always began "This is Bill speaking". Later on, in 14th Army, he changed to "Uncle Bill". To me, at any rate, "Bill speaking" at a time of crisis was psychologically superb, for it breathed *friendship*, not necessarily avuncular!' Was it more valuable than the loss of security?

where they *should* turn for support—to their commander. And sometimes he does not know what to say. He feels very much alone.

'Well, gentlemen,' I said, putting on what I hoped was a confident, cheerful expression, 'it might be worse!'

One of the group, in a sepulchral voice, replied with a single word: 'How?'

I could cheerfully have murdered him, but instead I had to keep my temper.

'Oh,' I said, grinning, 'it might be raining.' Two hours later, it was —hard.*

During this episode Walter Walker, who had just joined Slim's staff, was preparing some orders for distribution. After Slim emerged from talking to Scott he noticed, in spite of his preoccupation, that Walker had omitted the Chief Medical Officer from the distribution list. He immediately read the young man a sharp lecture about the need for precision of detail in staff-work at such times, and the vital importance of keeping medical officers in the picture during a battle. Walker never forgot the lesson, and at the Staff College at Quetta would later quote it as an example of how things should and should not be done by junior staff officers in times of crisis.†

Next morning the troops to the north and the rest of Burma Division south of the Chaung attacked at 7 am, but the Chinese, who were due to begin at 12.30, hesitated and were only prodded by Slim himself into action at 3 pm. By this time Scott could do no more. His transport and guns stuck in the sand and had to be abandoned. He managed to withdraw his wounded on tanks and pulled out the rest of his division on foot across the Chaung to safety.‡ Four 25-pounders, four 3·7 howitzers, Bofors and mortars represented a loss out of all proportion to their numbers. Moreover, though the Chinese, once they started, fought with exemplary ardour and penetrated some way into Yenangyaung itself, Slim could not afford a house-to-house battle. His whole force therefore fell back to the north of the Pin Chaung.

---

* p. 68–9.
† After the Retreat a team of 'Burma Retreat' officers was sent to join the Directing Staff at Quetta. One exercise was devoted to staff duties in the jungle. It began with a playlet performed by the Directing Staff into which this incident was written.
‡ The badly wounded had to be left behind in their ambulances. An officer who volunteered to return by dark and investigate found that every man had had his throat cut or had died by the bayonet.

If the loss of the oil-fields was the end of one road, for what was it the beginning? It is clear that both Slim and Alexander, looking back after the war, felt that they were hampered in making their short-term tactical judgements during the retreat because of a lack of guidance from above about the central purpose of their operations. At the outset of his narrative in *Defeat into Victory* Slim wrote: 'All would be conditioned by the overriding object of the campaign. What that was we did not know. Indeed, it was never, until the last stages, clear, and I think we suffered increasingly in all our actions for this.' In 1955 he sent the draft of this chapter to Alexander, who replied on 15 April:

> You say we had no national Directive—and you are right. I was sent out to try to save Rangoon. When it was lost, I never received any further directive—in fact I had no wireless capable of even communicating with India! We hoped that the Chinese would be able to do more than they did—and perhaps we should have known how logistically weak they were, and what a rotten system of command they had from Chiang Kai-shek downwards. It soon became pretty clear to me that eventually it would probably mean falling back on India, but I also knew that if the Chinese thought we were planning that they would, I think, have disintegrated sooner than they did or Chiang K.S. would have withdrawn them.

Since the Burma Army was not starved of instructions—for in spite of his reference to inadequate communications Alexander received definite orders from Wavell at various stages of the retreat—how is this profound feeling on the part of its two senior commanders to be accounted for? It was obviously genuine and long-lasting—and each nursed it independently. The answer seems to be not that they lacked directives, but that those they received were too complex, too unrealistic and too self-contradictory to provide them with the single, simple and attainable objective which every battle-commander hopes to be given by his overlords. In the phase following the loss of the oil-fields such was certainly the case.

On 18 April Alexander did receive a directive from Wavell—by letter. He was told:

(1) To maintain close touch with the Chinese and support them with part of Burcorps.
(2) To cover the Kalewa–Tamu route from the Chindwin to India.
(3) To keep 'a force in being'.

(4) To retain as many 'cards of re-entry' as possible to facilitate future offensive operations into Burma.
(5) Contact with the Chinese was the paramount consideration. They must be given no grounds for accusing the British of running away into India.

Alexander had already made logistic preparations to carry out what he knew was Wavell's policy and, on the assumption that Burcorps might fail to hold Mandalay and the Irrawaddy crossings, had decided that 7 Armoured Brigade and one brigade from 17 Division would fall back with V Chinese Army via Lashio into China while the rest of 17 Division moved northwards from Mandalay through Shwebo, covering the line of the projected new Ledo road down the Hukawng valley. To the Burma Division he allotted the task of holding the approaches to India from Kalewa.

In loyally implementing Wavell's policy Alexander was thus committed to splitting up Slim's withering force and dissipating it across north Burma. It must be doubted whether he believed in his plan. Certainly the notion of sending what amounted to a token force back to China appealed neither to him, nor to Slim, nor, it seems, to the military authorities in London. General Davies, Slim's Chief Staff Officer, who was himself appalled at the idea, wrote to the author on 1 September, 1974:

> I can assure you that Slim never had any intention of sending part of his Corps into China. He told me this himself, but he did not say how he would avoid doing it if he was finally ordered to do so. I think he appreciated that Alexander felt the same way as he did and would not insist on this action if the horrible decision to take it was made by Wavell.

As for London, the Director of Military Operations at the War Office, Major-General Kennedy, noted in March that, when Wavell first proposed a withdrawal towards China, 'if this had been accepted, our troops would have been almost entirely cut off from supplies, and could have had nothing more than a guerrilla value. We felt that Alexander should make for Assam.'*

In fact the time soon came when Alexander had to forget Wavell's instructions and write his own directive. The situation was changing daily. First, at a conference on the 19th, he and Stilwell agreed with a

---

* Major-General Sir John Kennedy, *The Business of War*, p. 210.

proposal from Slim that the Japanese advance up the Irrawaddy had exposed their enemy's right flank to a counter-attack. Stilwell promised to send the Chinese 200 and part of the 22 Division across to Slim, which, with 38 Division already supporting him, would give Burcorps a substantial lever against the Japanese flank. These plans were only beginning to mature, however, when they suddenly disintegrated and the last opportunity for a significant counter-move against the Japanese in Burma vanished.

The reason was the rapid development of that Japanese thrust through the eastern wing of the theatre, already mentioned, which threatened to drive their spearheads northwards, via the Shan States, towards Lashio and the China road. This meant doom for the Chinese formations in Burma. With an unannounced roar of engines 200 Division disappeared from Slim's side, and almost instantly V and VI Armies became a fugitive force withdrawing at speed and in some disorder towards the frontiers of China.

On 21 April, therefore, Alexander met Chiang Kai-shek's chief liaison officer, General Lin Wei, and concerted with him a reliable plan based on the assumption that evacuation of Burma was now inevitable. No British troops would make for China, and Slim's task with Burcorps would be to cover the Kalewa route to India—except 7 Armoured Brigade, which was to help those Chinese falling back west of the Irrawaddy via Shwebo. On the 25th, at a further meeting with Slim and Stilwell, Alexander ordered a general retirement of all his troops south of the Irrawaddy by the great bridge at Mandalay.*

One senses that at this moment Alexander and Slim felt a sensation of relief, dark though the future seemed.† Like Gort in 1940, when he finally abandoned the plan imposed on him from above for counter-attacking the German flank in France and decided to make for Dunkirk, they were now acting as they could see that the realities of the situation demanded. Alexander had no intention of allowing Burcorps to be cut

---

* Montgomery wrote to the author on 28 November, 1975: 'I so well remember that conference on 25 April, for Slim clearly dominated the scene, and made certain once and for all that no British or Indian troops would retreat into China. Alexander gave me, at any rate, the impression of being rattled. I think he needed Slim to help him compete with Stilwell.'
† For Slim the knowledge that none of his units was to withdraw to China was immensely heartening. He feared for the effect on their morale. Moreover news of famine in Yunnan suggested that the Chinese would have little with which to feed their own troops and none for the foreigner. And how could the British be evacuated? An airlift seemed difficult if not improbable.

off south of the Irrawaddy as, in the opening stages, 17 Division had been severed by the blowing of the Sittang Bridge. He had discarded Wavell's complicated instructions of the 18th. On the 28th, with the Japanese nearing Lashio, he gave Slim clear and specific orders for the final withdrawal to India. After immense efforts the last man and tank of Burcorps had crossed the famous Ava bridge near Mandalay by the evening of 30 April, and at one minute to midnight two of its massive spans were demolished—'a sad sight', Slim wrote, 'and a signal that we had lost Burma'. His next task was to shift his Corps westwards towards Monywa and the crossings of the Chindwin.

Now that India and safety were the only remaining objectives, Slim noticed that the psychological effect was curiously varied. The men-at-arms actually improved in morale and fighting power, while the lines-of-communication troops disintegrated.

> In its withdrawal the corps was from now on preceded by an undisciplined mob of fugitives intent only on escape. No longer organized units, without any supply arrangements, having deserted their officers, they banded together in gangs, looting, robbing, and not infrequently murdering the unfortune villagers on their route. They were almost entirely Indians and very few belonged to combatant units of the Army.*

In the main this was true, though it would be sanctimonious to pretend that there were not well-authenticated cases of British officers and men losing their nerve.† But the important point was that Slim—and his subordinates—had enabled the *fighting* troops to retain their morale. For the rest, the contemptible and sometimes criminal incidents were characteristic of all evacuations; it is those furthest from the front line who are the first to be demoralized. At Singapore as at Dunkirk, on Crete as when Rommel advanced on Cairo, the pattern was the same. For Slim the unfortunate consequence, which he was powerless to control, was that these undisciplined rioters were among the earliest to reach India. Their bearing and behaviour, as will be seen, left on those who received them an indelibly false impression of Burcorps' true stamina and achievement.

The mental and physical resilience of the Corps and its commander

---

* *Defeat into Victory*, p. 86.
† Not many. General Cowan's comment on this passage was: 'There were cases, I regret, when a few British and Indian troops panicked and were a dishonour to their rank and arm of service. But I never heard of a British officer doing so—anyhow on my front.' (Private communication.)

were in fact about to be exposed to a supreme test, for what had
momentarily appeared to be an orderly situation suddenly exploded in
violence and confusion. For over a week what should have been a
relatively smooth phase of the withdrawal now had to be conducted by
a series of hasty orders, breathless improvisations, and desperate
skirmishes. The reason was the unexpected loss of Monywa, which
immediately endangered the retreat. Slim was at his new headquarters
at Budalin, just north of Monywa, venting his frustration on a staff
officer from Army HQ.

> My litany was still in full swing when looking up I saw standing in
> the gloom two or three white-faced officers whom I did not know.
> 'And what do you want?' I asked, still in a bad temper.
> One of them stepped forward.
> 'The Japs have taken Monywa', he said, 'and if you listen you will
> hear them mortaring!'
> A deathly pause fell on the gathering.*

In his book on *Slim as Military Commander* Lieut-General Sir
Geoffrey Evans says of this moment:

> When the serious news was conveyed to him about 8.30 pm, those
> who were present affirm that he appeared quite unshaken. Having
> studied the map and quickly assessed the implications of the Japanese
> threat, within a quarter of an hour he issued orders to restore the situ-
> ation. His personality, combined with his calm confidence, had an
> electrifying effect on all; action was swift and orderly, and the panic
> which might well have set in was averted. In 24 hours he had reformed
> his front.

The cause of the crisis was immediately evident. Down river, at
Pakokku, there began a track which, running west and then north up
the Myittha valley, ended at Kalemyo, a few miles from Kalewa. From
Kalewa on the Chindwin, via Kalemyo, the Kabaw valley and the
mountain barrier, ran the only reasonable route whereby the bulk of
Burcorps could hope to reach India. Thus, if the enemy could infiltrate
up the Myittha valley he might cut off the Corps from safety. A report
that a Japanese force was moving up the west bank of the Chindwin to
do precisely this led Slim on the 28th (with Alexander's approval) to
order 2 Burma Brigade to withdraw up the valley and thus block a

---

* *Defeat into Victory*, p. 93.

potential threat to his main line of retreat. As the rest of the exhausted Burma Division was still short of Monywa, its approaches were now uncovered, and the town was wide open to an attack from the south by forces moving up the Chindwin. Slim discounted this possibility, but the enemy advanced with great energy, pushing up the river in boats and ignoring the temptation of the Myittha valley. At dawn on 1 May, therefore, a Japanese battalion took possession of Monywa.

Slim's headquarters were in a Buddhist monastery some miles north of the town. That night he spent a few uneasy hours on the hard wooden bed of the abbot, listening to the machine-guns and mortars, and wondering whether he was about to be separated from his Corps— whether, indeed, Bruce Scott and the men of Burma Division might not be badly mauled if not over-run.

By the rapid re-grouping of his diminishing force Slim very nearly recovered Monywa. Its final abandonment, however, was of less significance than the Japanese failure either to exploit the Myittha valley in an outflanking move which might have had fatal consequences, or to get into the rear of Burcorps on the eastern side of the Chindwin and cut the route for the next stage of its withdrawal. This ran north from Monywa to Ye-u. From here a track led westward to Shwegyin on the Chindwin, up which it would be necessary to use steamers for the few miles to Kalewa. Thereafter it was a matter of marching through the fearsome Kabaw valley into India. Had the Japanese been able to cut the route at any point between Monywa and Shwegyin the retreat would have been in jeopardy. As it was, by 3 May Slim had re-assembled his whole Corps at Ye-u, including 7 Armoured Brigade, since on 1 May Alexander, at his last meeting with Stilwell, had freed Slim of any further commitment to supporting the Chinese. The out-standing question, therefore, was whether Burcorps could reach Shwegyin overland before the Japanese reached it by water.

By 9 May Burma Division, which now consisted chiefly of British elements, had passed right through and was *en route* for India, while 17 Division and the armour brought up the rear. The heat was intense. The track was rough and sandy, crossing many water-courses which sometimes, though the season was late, were still awash. At one point a series of primitive bamboo bridges had to be negotiated. 'Anyone seeing this track for the first time', Alexander wrote in his *Despatch*, 'would find it difficult to imagine how a fully mechanized force could possibly move over it.' Yet somehow, in a few days, not only was the army kept supplied by vehicles moving on a one-way and even a two-way system, but 2,300 casualties as well as thousands of helpless refugees were helped onward. No soldier starved, and there was no shortage of petrol. With full wireless communications and a generous allocation of Military Police for traffic control, (there were never enough MPs in Burcorps), the task would have been formidable enough, but Slim and his tiny staff overcame the immense administrative problems without either. As the refugees and the soldiers were now more closely intermingled, smallpox and cholera became an even greater menace, while thirst was a constant agony.

In the event the Japanese were almost but not quite outstripped. By the evening of the 9th all troops except a brigade of 17 Division, the divisional HQ and 7th Hussars had been transferred up the Chindwin and on to the western bank at Kalewa. Once again, however, a plain statement summarizes an operation of great complexity. At Shwegyin the track ran down into a flat area some 1,000 yards broad, surrounded on three sides by a sheer 200-feet escarpment. On the fourth side was one frail improvised pier, from which everything had to be loaded on to steamers for the six-mile trip upstream to Kalewa. There were no cranes, so that all guns and vehicles had to be manoeuvred by hand on to decks never designed for the purpose. The 'Basin', as it was called, was not improved by hundreds of abandoned civilian cars. Slim called Shwegyin a bottleneck and a deathtrap. It might indeed have become one when Japanese bombing caused the native crews of the steamers to desert or refuse to return from Kalewa; only the determination of the Irrawaddy Flotilla's peacetime officers kept a service going.

A trap seemed even more likely at dawn on the 10th. Slim had just arrived by launch from Kalewa, and was walking off the pier, when tracer bullets began to stream over his head, and down to the south a whole orchestra of weapons opened up. A thin perimeter guard had been positioned to protect the rim of the escarpment, and a boom established two miles downstream. As at Monywa, the enemy had seized the initiative, for hundreds of Japanese, having landed several miles south of the boom,* had infiltrated inland along the banks to spring their surprise above the crowded Basin.

---

* This boom, by-passed by the Japanese, was built by the small detachment of Royal Marines (about 100 at the outset and a handful at the end) who from Prome to Shwegyin valiantly guarded the western flank of Burcorps on the Irrawaddy and the Chindwin. They were masters of improvisation.

Cowan counter-attacked as vigorously as possible, but his situation deteriorated as the Japanese were steadily reinforced. Until he fought his way into the Basin (his ADC wounded at his side), Slim stayed by the jetties, encouraging by his presence and striving to make order out of disorder. The 25-pounders of 7 Armoured Brigade were kept in action at the water's edge until the last minute before they were manoeuvred on board. So the struggle swirled until the evening, when the crews of the river flotilla refused to return to Shwegyin and the Japanese hold was obviously firm. The remaining guns therefore fired off as much ammunition as possible, while the mass of tanks and trucks was destroyed. The Basin screamed with the sound of hundreds of engines set to race at full speed after oil and water had been drained away, while flames belched where petrol tanks had been pierced and then thoughtlessly ignited. When no further delay could be risked Cowan led the column of those still at Shwegyin by a jungle track to Kalewa. This night march was a grim rehearsal for what lay ahead. The track, often no more than eighteen inches wide, made precipitous ascents and descents so that it was often necessary to use both hands and feet. Stoppages were frequent, and at times an advance of 100 yards took 20 minutes. The difficulty of maintaining discipline was not lessened by hundreds of feckless refugees.

From the chaos at Shwegyin Burcorps managed to rescue 30 jeeps and 50 trucks, mainly four-wheel-drive. (28 guns of various types also reached India.) For the majority, therefore, the final stage of their 1,000-mile adventure had still to be covered on foot. The main body trudged 90 miles up the Kabaw valley to Tamu, at its head, while the more fortunate 48 Brigade was conveyed further up river to Sittaung. Here the steamers were destroyed, but the march to Tamu, though a third as long, was often as arduous. It was the Kabaw valley, however, which was the real adversary; the source of a particularly virulent type of malaria, it was always avoided during the rainy season in peacetime, and rarely visited even in the safer cold months. The monsoon rains began to fall heavily about 12 May, as the column moved off, and within a week the downpour had become torrential. Out came the mosquito, to find a defenceless prey in troops who had never been trained in anti-malarial precautions. By the time Imphal was reached 17 Division had hundreds of men going sick each day with malaria and dysentery. Sanitation was impossible; the smell of death and excrement was everywhere. Corpses were even seen hanging from trees, a signal that some unfortunate had preferred suicide to suffering. Men marched barefoot

and clothed in rags. It was a symbol of the strain which he was enduring on behalf of all his command that when Slim followed the
fashion, and tried to grow a beard, the bristles emerged a pure white.

'Everyone realized,' General Davies wrote after the war, 'from the
humblest private soldier, that within the first few days of the initial
heavy main downpour the road to Assam, the lifeline of the Army,
would disintegrate into an impassable morass. There was a dreadful
tension in the air. Would the weather hold?' One development was
particularly demoralizing—cerebral malaria. A man would shiver one
evening and die next morning. Courage, endurance, self-control,
personal pride—all seemed powerless before this vicious scourge. Yet
still the march continued, to the iron bridge above a mountain torrent
which marks the boundary between Burma and India. And now it was
a matter of following a bridle path winding in 12 miles to the 7,000-foot
Shenam Pass, from which a sort of road covered the last 80 miles to
Imphal. The monsoon was already in full spate. Ambulances stuck.
Wrecked lorries lay like miniature toys in the valley bottoms. With
six jeeps 12 officers, running a non-stop service for 48 hours, ferried
800 incapable sick and wounded to the head of the Pass. Then,
suddenly, it was over, and the column wound down into the Imphal
plain.

Burcorps had not been overwhelmed in the Slough of Despond. The
cost had indeed been high: from 'wearisomeness, painfulness, hunger,
perils, nakedness, sword, lions, dragons, darkness, and, in a word,
death and what not' the casualties in killed, wounded and missing
were some 13,000, and many had still to experience the residual effects
of exhaustion and disease. All the same, as Slim stood by the roadside
to watch the last of his gaunt and ragged rearguard march in he felt
a proper pride. 'They might look like scarecrows, but they looked like
soldiers too.' Unfortunately, many of those responsible for receiving
the survivors of the retreat at Imphal behaved as though a contemptuous superiority was the right reaction. There are few bitter pages in
Defeat into Victory, but none more acrid than those in which Slim
describes the maltreatment of his men.

For the lack of preparedness in the reception arrangements there is
some excuse. There was a shortage of supplies of food, clothing,
medical equipment and comforts which had to be brought from a great
distance over the inadequate and overloaded Assam line of communication. For the lack of consideration shown to men who had endured a
retreat of 1,000 miles in burning heat, often short of water and food,

and pressed by a relentless and superior enemy there can be no excuse. They had fought back with courage and had come out in tatters with their discipline unimpaired and their personal arms intact. From Major-General Savory and his 23 Division, which had been hurried forward to hold the entrances to Imphal Plain to enable Burcorps to reassemble and reorganize in case the Japanese decided to follow up, they received the respect that was their due. But the staff and administrative services in Imphal seem to have been unable to distinguish between the rabble of refugees and the demoralized Line of Communication troops, who had been the first to reach Imphal, from the men of Burma Army who had endured and come out with their spirit unbroken.* A will can often find a way, but at Imphal the will to improvise, to organize, to energize, to *understand* was too often missing. When Slim arrived ahead of his troops he was greeted by Lieut-General Noel Irwin, whose 4 Corps HQ had been given the overall responsibility for the area. Irwin spoke harshly and critically. Slim said, 'I never thought an officer whose command I was about to join could be so rude to me.' Irwin replied, 'I can't be rude. I'm senior.'

This retort came from a man whose considerable intellectual gifts were marred by a dictatorial and egocentric temperament. Irwin had a way of treating subordinates like indentured coolies deserving neither trust nor consideration. One facet of this self-regarding mind was an inability to decentralize; since none could be trusted but himself, he must see to everything. But insensitivity and inflexibility were also dominant traits in this complex character. Put simply, therefore, Irwin was unsuited for the control of a situation in which the need was for imagination and sympathy, constructive improvisation, humanity. His presence and his attitude undoubtedly affected others at Imphal, for it was only too easy, in ignorance of the facts, to assume that what had recently happened in Burma was a repetition of what had happened in Singapore—a disgrace, as it then seemed, without alleviation—and to look down on the survivors.

When Burcorps first arrived, the offhand behaviour of its hosts was expressed in many ways. Slim remembered years later, when he was writing *Defeat into Victory* in Australia, that 'Taffy Davies, indefatigable in labouring to ease the suffering of our troops, wryly said,

---

* It should be noted that if conditions at Imphal were harsh for the troops who emerged from Burma in formed bodies and under their officers, for the civilian refugees, whether British or native, the state of affairs was even worse.

"The slogan in India seems to be, Isn't that Burma Army annihilated yet?" ' Philip Howe provides a chilling example. When General Cowan went ahead into Imphal to check the accommodation for 17 Indian Division Howe accompanied him. They were met by a smart Military Police corporal from 4 Corps, who said he had been sent to meet them and that he would conduct them to their camping site.

> All of us were absolutely horrified when we saw it. It was the bare side of the lower slopes of a mountain. There was not a tree to be seen. It had started to rain heavily again, and the water was rushing round our feet. . . . 'Punch' Cowan did not hesitate for a second. He told the corporal in no uncertain terms that his troops could not live in such a place and they must be put under cover, especially as many of them were sick and desperately needed medical attention. The corporal protested that this would be disobeying orders. So General Cowan snapped back that he was going to put his men under cover, orders or no orders.

The upshot was that use was made of uninhabited buildings in Imphal. All the same, 'there was a great row because of the General's refusal to let his troops camp at Kanglatongbi. The Commander of 4 Corps took him to task for disobeying orders, but General Cowan was fully supported by General Slim.'

The history of Burcorps may be said to have ended on 20 May, when Slim handed over his responsibilities to Irwin. The relics of the Burma Division were scattered—the natives, Karens, Kachins, Chins, being returned to their villages while the British and Indian elements filtered back to India to form the basis of a new 39 Indian Division. Cowan's 17 Division survived under its commander until the end of the war. But Slim, though he had said farewell, did not forget. He made his way down to Ranchi, in Bihar, and spent much of his free time there in visiting the hospitals of Eastern India where the sick of his old Corps were lying in what was often squalor and misery. The hospital provision, he wrote, was 'inadequate in amount, in accommodation, staff, equipment, and in the barest amenities'. Nor was the disease a respecter of rank: Davies was down,* and Montgomery. Slim himself, though

---

* Davies's health was permanently impaired. When he was taken back to India he was removed from the train unconscious, suffering from malaria, amoebic dysentery, jungle sores and anaemia.

drawn and thin, had not been undermined, either physically or mentally.

Indeed, the vigour of his mental resilience is demonstrated by the way he spent the rest of his time at Ranchi. He asked himself humbly, searchingly and comprehensively what had gone wrong. This was not a matter of looking for excuses or scapegoats. He had always been self-aware, introspective, his own confessor. It is typical, therefore, that, after reviewing all the relevant factors, he concluded, 'The most distressing aspect of the whole disastrous campaign had been the contrast between my generalship and the enemy's. . . . For myself, I had little to be proud of; I could not rate my generalship high.' His emotion at the time—or those emotions remembered in tranquillity as he composed *Defeat into Victory*—understandably account for Slim's sweeping self-condemnation. A cooler and more distant judgement, however, suggests that he was looking at himself in a distorting mirror.

Any attempt to reach the truth should properly begin by noting Slim's assets, of which the first—though this is often forgotten—was the Chinese. Unpredictable, ill-equipped, and often ill-led, they nevertheless attracted during the campaign about three-quarters of the Japanese strength in Burma. When the two original divisions of the Japanese 15th Army, 33 and 55, were reinforced by 18 and 56, all but 33 were mainly employed against the Chinese, yet even one more division on the front of Burcorps would have been overwhelming. A second asset was Alexander. It is sometimes argued that he was out of touch with the front line, and certainly when Burcorps reached Imphal men complained that they had never seen him. (Major-General Savory, incidentally, *did* see him, at the end of the retreat, riding into Imphal in his jeep—with an old Indian refugee sitting at his side!) These reactions are unjust. Alexander came up to the front regularly, as Slim recalled with vivid instances. But far more important was the fact that, having judged that Slim could handle the battle, Alexander left it to him without interfering and concentrated, instead, on the proper functions of a theatre commander. By doing so he freed Slim from all concern or responsibility for vexing negotiations and cor-respondence with London, Wavell and Chiang Kai-shek. Slim under-stood; perhaps he understood also that while the voice he heard was Alexander's the words occasionally came from somewhere else.

Within the region of the battle itself Slim had one human and one material advantage. The presence at the most senior level of men whose capacities he knew and trusted—Cowan, Scott, Davies, Welchman—

was sheer luck but also sheer gain. In a campaign where communications were normally bad and sometimes non-existent it was an inestimable benefit to have a command shared by officers who could read one another's minds instinctively. And as to communications, the material asset of 7 Armoured Brigade was invaluable, for over and over again the wireless sets in the tanks supplied the only network over which signal traffic could flow. Moreover, the desert-hardened veterans of the Brigade were the workhorses of the retreat, vanguards, rearguards, escorts, universal providers of firepower and reassurance. Beyond this, however, there was little either human or material that Slim could count on the credit side, except a hard core of officers and men in his two inexperienced divisions who refused to lose heart and managed to fight stoutly, if not always expertly.

The errors for which Slim reproached himself were mainly those of omission, and he was haunted, in particular, by the feeling that he had failed in aggression. 'I should have subordinated all else to the vital need to strike at them and thus to disrupt their plans, but I ought, in spite of everything and at all risks, to have collected the whole strength of my corps before I attempted any counter-offensive. Thus I might have risked disaster, but I was more likely to have achieved success.' This is very doubtful. It is significant that the next sentence of this passage in *Defeat into Victory* is almost word for word the same as that with which he concluded his account of Gallabat in *Unofficial History*: 'When two courses of action were open to me I had not chosen, as a good commander should, the bolder.' But boldness is not the only criterion for a general. Rational judgement as to the capability of his troops is at least as important. Setting aside, therefore, the inescapable fact that for reasons beyond his control Slim was never able to 'collect the whole strength' of Burcorps, it must surely be doubted whether his divisions were actually capable of mounting the kind of offensive he had in mind. Wretched communications, road-bound troops, no air cover, little artillery, a strong sense of the enemy's superiority—these were not the factors making for a successful co-ordinated corps attack in jungle conditions. Slim's motives were impeccable, but he was crying for the moon.

The central difficulty for Alexander and Slim was that ignorance, optimism and political necessity prevented both London and Delhi from supplying them with a single, definite objective. The existence of the Chinese and of the Sino-American relationship now seems an immense but unavoidable irrelevance, which continually blurred the obvious truth that once Rangoon had fallen the best course for the British was to evacuate Burma as tidily and quickly as possible.* By the time Mandalay was reached the Japanese had hammered that truth home. The real test of Slim's generalship, therefore, is the extent to which, in spite of divergent policies, he maintained the cohesion of his retreating Corps so that, when evacuation was finally accepted as inevitable, he still had a force to evacuate—a force, moreover, with sufficient spirit and stamina to endure the final terrible phase. In reproaching himself he modestly forgot this achievement—and forgot that it was *his* achievement.

Thinking of another famous retreat, that from Moscow, one recalls how Bernadotte remarked of Napoleon that God punished him because he relied exclusively on his intelligence. Slim certainly used his wits, but he never forgot that he was a human being. Thus his handling of Burcorps was a triumphant example of Napoleon's own principle, that in war the pre-eminent factor is the moral. He enabled his men to hope when hope seemed absurd, and their will to live sustained a will to fight. If his tactics were sometimes inadequate and his ambitions too large, this was a triviality by comparison with his leadership. And during these months he had learned a fundamental truth on which his future victories would be based. Man for man, he realized, the British and Indian troops were the equal of the Japanese. With the right training and sufficient material strength, they would return in triumph. He never lost faith in his soldiers and sepoys. Until the great days of 14th Army he did not become universally known as Uncle Bill, but it was during the retreat of 1942 that he unquestionably earned this affectionate accolade.

---

* A hindsight view. At this stage of the war, before Chiang Kai-shek's unreliability had become demonstrable, there were strong and tempting reasons, both military and political, for seeking to shore up the alliance and maintain contact with his armies. But the reasons were delusive.

CHAPTER EIGHT

THE HILL DIFFICULTY

'The engagement was not a defeat. We simply failed to take the position.'
The Times, February, 1881, on the battle of Laing's Nek

'We got run out of Burma and it is humiliating as hell. I think we ought to find out what caused it, go back and retake it.'
General Stilwell

URING THE twelve months after their retreat from Burma the British in India seemed, in Gandhi's phrase, to be 'on the toboggan'. Their glissade was accelerated by many forces—civil disorder, military weakness, material deficiencies, waning morale and vagaries in the higher direction of the war due to the divergent interests of the United Kingdom, the United States and their Chinese ally. Yet this was a superficial impression, for there were many countervailing factors. When Mountbatten took over South East Asia Command in November, 1943, the situation, though disturbing, was infinitely more promising than it had earlier threatened to be. Stout hearts, wise counsels and sustained energy off-set many of the consequences of error and debility. It was a period of growth as well as of decline. Among those who arrested the slide down the slope Slim was unquestionably outstanding.

But though he emerged from this phase of defeat into a sequence of classic victories he was the first to acknowledge, as he generously admitted in his book, that without the backing of an efficient administrative base the battle commander is impotent. This truism is peculiarly relevant to the Indo-Burmese theatre of war, with its vast distances, its hostile climate, its forbidding terrain. Slim was not alone in rejecting the idea of succumbing, and his final triumphs owed much to the far-sighted administrative plans which the Indian authorities set in motion during 1942—plans whose purpose is reflected in an instruction issued by Wavell, the Commander-in-Chief, on 16 April— at least a month before Slim's Burcorps finally debouched on the Imphal Plain. 'I want the Joint Planning Staff to begin as soon as possible consideration of an offensive to reoccupy Burma.'

It was in this spirit that 'during the spring of 1942, India Command began to consider the layout of the country *as a base for the larger forces which would eventually be required for the recapture of Burma, Malaya and the Netherland East Indies.'* Administrative planning for a total of 28 divisions, started in June, was amplified at the end of the year to cover 34 divisions and 100 RAF or USAAF squadrons. Immense efforts were devoted to improving the communications by road and rail to and within Assam and Arakan. A vast programme of airfield construction, ultimately involving a million labourers, was driven forward. Not all these enterprises succeeded immediately—it would require American technicians, for example, to extend the output of the railways—but the truth remains valid that while Slim, in 1942/43, was preoccupied with his own concerns, the face of India was being transformed by preparations on whose product he would ultimately depend. First Wavell and later Auchinleck, as Commander-in-Chief, were the responsible authorities. However much others, sometimes with justice, may have lampooned for lethargy their headquarters at Delhi, Slim never swerved in his gratitude for their constructive energy.

His private concerns were copious enough. By June he was established at Barrackpore, just outside Calcutta, as commander of 15 Corps, which with 4 Corps in Assam provided the main bulk of Eastern Army. With two divisions, 14 and 26 (neither of them battle-tested or jungle-trained), Slim was now responsible for internal security in the states of Bengal, Bihar and Orissa—some 185,000 square miles—and for defending the southern sector of the Indo-Burmese frontier and the Bengal coast. But British commanders were accustomed in those days to large responsibilities and small resources; Wavell had been more seriously stretched both in the Middle East and in his ABDA Command. Slim characteristically drew consolation from his Corps sign. Three Vs stood for Victory.

---

* *The War against Japan*, Vol. II, Appendix 24, 'Administrative Problems in India Command, 1942–1943'.

When he arrived, he was tired, thin, and had been ill, but there was ever a light in his eye and his humour—a gruff, no bloody nonsense sort of humour that was particularly his own—had certainly not left him.

The fact that we became a happy and efficient Corps HQ stemmed from the humanity of Slim himself. He was ready to speak personally to every man in the Corps from Divisional Commander to junior clerk or soldier. When speaking in English, Gurkhali, Urdu or Pushtu it was always as one man to another—never the great commander to his troops.*

The fact that he would sometimes chat happily in Gurkhali when he should have been using, say, Urdu enhanced rather than impaired his popularity.

As Slim slowly recovered his own strength and started to revitalize his Corps, two of the three dangers by which he was threatened diminished in scale. A landward attack by the Japanese on southern India was seen to be improbable until well after the monsoon period had ended. The reduction of the second threat was less immediately perceptible. Though the April sortie of the Japanese Navy against Ceylon and shipping in the Bay of Bengal had been repelled by Admiral Somerville—with considerable losses—the sea still lay open to the enemy, and Churchill sent urgent distress signals to Roosevelt. 'Even today the full gravity of the events of April, 1942, seems to have come home to us far less vividly than similar events in the Atlantic.'† In June Slim was unaware that the subsequent withdrawal of Japanese naval forces to the east would be permanent; still less could he instantly appreciate that the American victory at Midway, between 4 and 6 June, had destroyed all possibility of successful Japanese naval aggression by eliminating the Imperial Navy's carrier force. Thus, though it is now known that the Japanese never contemplated a seaborne invasion of India, on the inadequate evidence available to him in the summer of 1942 Slim was compelled to think and act as if one were imminent.

Defeat into Victory contains an inimitable account of how he and his staff scraped together a makeshift flotilla of light craft to guard the Sunderbans, that 200-mile delta through which Ganges and Brahmaputra filter into the sea, and along whose devious waterways an

---

* Note by Major-General O'Carroll-Scott, Slim's Brigadier General Staff in 15 Corps, quoted in Geoffrey Evans, *Slim*, p. 87.
† Stephen Roskill, *The War at Sea*, Vol. II, p. 32.

amphibious enemy might penetrate towards Calcutta and the communications with Assam. His craft were unsuitable. 'Most were old,
worn out and generally ill-found. It often seemed a toss-up which
would happen first—their cardboard-thick boilers blow up or rock
loose on their seatings and go through the fragile sides of the ships.'
The crews were mainly civilian volunteers, stiffened by Army gunners
and signallers and led by an ex-commando, Lieut-Colonel Feather-
stonhaugh, 'who had sailed before the mast, got a coastal mate's
certificate, and had his wings as an airman'. It is indicative of Slim's
intense sympathy for his men that his recollections are studded, to a
degree far greater than in the memoirs of his fellow commanders, with
such precise and vivid details about individuals. He thought in terms
of people, not of cyphers or units. A soldier was never a statistic. So
now he recalled the young officer who signalled: *Large Japanese
submarine reported off mouth of Meghna River. Am proceeding to sea to
engage.* 'His heaviest armament was a two-pounder, his speed, with the
safety valve screwed down, eight knots, and his rickety river steamer
was never meant to venture to sea, least of all in the monsoon. The
submarine would do eighteen knots on the surface and have a four-
inch gun. But he went to look for it!'

This second front, to which so much ingenuity and enthusiasm
were devoted, never in fact sustained an assault from the sea; it was the
third area of danger which exploded. Civil disobedience on a grand
scale, aroused by Gandhi's slogan 'Quit India', became the declared
policy of the Congress Party after its rejection, in April, of the Cripps
Mission, whose proposals for a post-war constitution and wartime
admission of Congress to the central government were unacceptable
to Hindus—largely because the package offered allowed for Moslem
secession. Propaganda for a fight to the finish against the British was
vigorously circulated during the summer, and on 1 August the All-
India Congress Committee in Bombay sanctioned 'The starting of a
mass struggle on non-violent lines on the widest possible scale.' That
night the police, after secret preparations, arrested Gandhi and all the
chief Congress leaders, the Mahatma being interned in a palace of the
Aga Khan. By mid-August the 'non-violent' explosion had occurred.

Calcutta was soon brought under control, but the city was virtually
isolated as planned insurrections cut the broad-gauge railways to
Delhi and Bombay, and the vital metre-gauge system to the north-
east on which the communications of 4 Corps depended. 'Large gangs',
Slim recalled, 'numbering often several hundreds, armed with primitive

but effective weapons and some fire-arms, assaulted railway stations all over the country. Signalling instruments were destroyed, station buildings burned and looted, lines torn up over a considerable distance, and European passengers dragged from trains to be hacked to pieces.' 15 Corps, in Bengal and Orissa, was at the heart of the storm. Eastern Army removed Bihar from Slim's responsibility, but with two key areas to pacify, with arson, murder and sabotage to contain, his resources were desperately strained. He was simply short of men. First reinforcement camps, then convalescent depots, then even venereal wards were emptied. Throughout India no less than 57 battalions were deployed in counter-insurgency, until, after six turbulent weeks, an uneasy peace was restored.

At the time Slim and other authorities suspected that Congress was acting in collusion with the Japanese. This was not so, though the disruption of the military communication network fitted such a scenario. But equally important, from the British point of view, was the delay imposed on preparations for the offensive which was always in the front of Wavell's mind.

> The training of certain field army formations and of reinforcements was retarded by some six to eight weeks; owing to the damage to the railways, Eastern Army's movement programme was delayed for at least three weeks; because of shortage of materials and labour difficulties, airfield construction in Assam and eastern India was held up for four to six weeks and there was a general loss of production in all factories turning out arms, clothing and equipment.*

For Slim this interruption of training was peculiarly frustrating. Like Stilwell he had been humiliated by the retreat from Burma. In searching self-examination he had drawn on his unique experience 'to find out what caused it'. He thought he now knew many of the answers, and had already begun to apply them for the instruction of his Corps.

The process which, from the nadir of 1942, raised in some eighteen months a confident and competent army, capable of defeating the Japanese on their own terms, may be said to have started in Delhi shortly after the evacuation of Burma, when Wavell summoned a conference of commanders and senior staff officers to review the lessons of the campaign. From these discussions and subsequent initiatives

---

* *The War against Japan*, Vol. II, p. 247.

many developments flowed—the reduction in mechanization of divisions to make them more jungle-worthy; the birth of Wingate's Long Range Penetration group; improved (though still inadequate) arrangements for training; the embryo of an airborne force. Slim's contribution, within the limits of his own command, was creative, but more important was the fact that in analysing the reasons for his defeat he formulated the principles on which he was to achieve victory. 'I do not think I changed them in any essential', he wrote, 'throughout the rest of the war.'

Slim did not invent the phrase 'The jungle is neutral', but he would have been happy to have done so, for his first and basic principle affirmed that 'the individual soldier must learn, by living, moving and exercising in it, that the jungle is neither impenetrable nor unfriendly'. It was not the private province of the Japanese. From that premiss his other doctrines logically followed: that the defence of long continuous lines should be avoided; that *frontal attacks should rarely*, and attacks on a *narrow front never*, be undertaken; that outflanking hooks should be normal; that the presence of enemy troops in one's rear should imply that the Japanese, and not one's own position, had been surrounded. There are no non-combatants in jungle warfare. Tanks can be used in almost any country except swamp. Patrolling is the master key to jungle fighting. Such were the texts of the sermons which Slim now continually preached—and he began applying the doctrine of mobility by transforming his own chairborne Corps HQ into one that could 'without repacking, be loaded at once on to either trucks, boats, aeroplanes or even mule transport'.

But the headquarters was now controlling an entirely different body of men. In July Noel Irwin had handed over 4 Corps in Assam to Geoffry Scoones, who would continue to command it until the end of the great battles of 1944. Irwin himself was promoted to Eastern Army, and at the end of August his HQ was installed at Barrackpore while Slim moved to Ranchi in Bihar. Here he had to sew together a new 15 Corps, whose only major formation was 70 British Division (seasoned in the Western Desert).

> I found also in Ranchi many of the Indian units that had been in the 1st Burma Division of the Retreat now formed into the 39th Indian Division. Not long afterwards however this division was taken from 15 Corps to become a training division. We had too a Special Training Brigade used to test new organizations and tactics suggested by the experiences of 1942. It had a battalion of Indian infantry mounted on

ponies, and another in jeeps, in the attempt to solve the problem of jungle mobility. . . . 50 Tank Brigade, equipped with Valentines, was the Corps armoured formation, and I liked the look of it very much. With these four formations, and an increasingly alive Corps Head-quarters, we began serious training.*

It was not many months, however, before the rhythm of training was interrupted by the discord of war. After a summer of stagnation during the monsoon Wavell, on 17 September, ordered Eastern Army to advance into Arakan with 14 Division, as a diversion from the main effort, which was to consist of a seaborne assault by two brigades on the island of Akyab. Akyab, lying off the southern tip of the Arakan peninsula, could provide a valuable base for future operations against Rangoon. This abortive project was born in frustration and culminated in chaos. Yet it proved to be another turning-point in Slim's career. During this first battle of Arakan his nerve and judgement were tested in the context of yet another retreat, and neither failed.

Second-best solutions are rarely satisfactory. The Arakan operation was no more than the minimal residue of a grand design sketched by Churchill in June, when the Midway victory encouraged him to inform Wavell that the small-scale sorties envisaged for the next winter cam-paign in Burma were 'very nice and useful nibbling', but that what he wanted was Rangoon, Moulmein and Bangkok. As an overture he proposed an advance in Arakan, followed by an amphibious landing further east by 'forty or fifty thousand troops'. Under the code-word ANAKIM Wavell set planning in motion. As the summer passed, how-ever, the contours of ANAKIM were eroded. Riots in August, the ravages of malaria, the crises in North Africa and Russia, the consequences of a heavy monsoon and the critical shortage of air power all combined to cancel any diversionary operations on 4 Corps front in the north, and, more seriously, to nullify the project of amphibious assault. By the end of October Wavell was left with ANAKIM's remnants—a divisional thrust down the Arakan peninsula, from whose tip at Foul Point his troops, it was hoped, might descend on Akyab in the few small craft now available.

While Slim was still at Barrackpore, and responsible for the southern flank, he had examined the situation in Arakan with Major-General Lloyd of 14 Division, the local commander, and decided that the weak

---

* *Defeat into Victory*, p. 141-2.

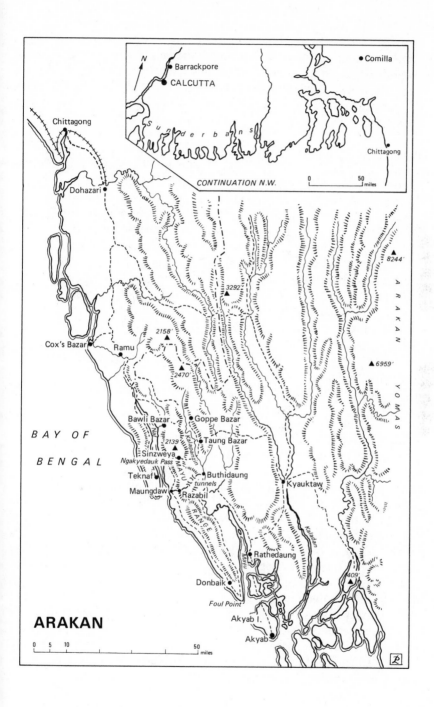

N

Barrackpore

CALCUTTA

• Comilla

Chittagong

S u n d e r b a n s

Chittagong

0   50
└─────────┘ miles

Dohazari

▲ 8244'

3292'

2158'

Cox's Bazar

Ramu

2470'

▲ 6959'

A
R
A
K
A
N

Y
O
M
A
S

BAY OF

Bawli Bazar   • Goppe Bazar

BENGAL

2139'   • Taung Bazar

Sinzweya
Ngakyedauk Pass

Teknaf   • Buthidaung
                tunnels
Maungdaw   Razabil

• Kyauktaw

Kaladan

• Rathedaung

Donbaik

409'

Foul Point

ARAKAN

Akyab I.

Akyab

0   5   10   50
└─┴───┴──────────────────┘ miles

Japanese holding force of four battalions would give Lloyd an initial
superiority in attack—allowing for the mud, the knife-edge ridges and
the treacherous tidal streams of the Mayu Peninsula. But the principles
of jungle warfare which he had distilled from his experience in Burma
made him reject the idea of a methodical march-to-the-front advance.
He therefore advocated a combination of frontal pressure with a series
of short amphibious hooks (using his home-made fleet), and a wide
outflanking move into the enemy's rear by Wingate's Long Range
Penetration brigade which, encouraged by Wavell, was now in being.
It was a day-dream. Wingate was switched by Wavell to the northern
theatre. Eastern Army dismissed the practicability of using the Sunderbans flotilla for coastal landings. Slim was transferred to Ranchi, and
Irwin in Barrackpore took control of the Arakan offensive.

This was ill-fated from the start. An operation never intended to
achieve dramatic results and unlikely to engage large Japanese forces
was launched as if the march on Burma had begun. Slim deplored the
unwise publicity. 'It is better to let a victory, if it comes, speak for
itself; it has a voice that drowns all other sounds.' In fact the promises
of victory were, as Gandhi said of the Cripps Mission's proposals, 'A
post-dated cheque on an overdrawn account,' for the tactics employed
in the battle were a barren, exhausted stock. 'From Ranchi', Slim wrote,
'we watched with growing anxiety the progress of the Arakan offensive,
now no longer our responsibility.'

By the beginning of 1943 Lloyd's division had almost attained its
objective, after leaning all the way down the peninsula on an enemy
inferior in numbers who fought a series of discreet delaying actions.
But on 10 January he was halted in his tracks, almost in sight of his
goal, for carrier patrols had probed to Foul Point. On the east side of
the Mayu Range, which bisects the peninsula, he was stuck outside
Rathedaung; on the west or seaward flank he was prevented from
advancing along the coastal strip by the inland defences at Donbaik.
Donbaik now became the Hill Difficulty of the Eastern Army; that
Hill where one of Bunyan's pilgrims 'took directly up the way to
Destruction, which led him into a wide field, full of dark mountains,
where he stumbled and fell, and rose no more'. So now, as frontal
attacks were launched across the open flats and up the foothills by
first one battalion and then, at Irwin's insistence, by two, against a
position held by a single company, many an Inniskilling or Punjabi
stumbled and died in the machine-gun fire from cunningly constructed
Japanese bunkers. These camouflaged strong-points, containing up to

two dozen men, sprung a tactical surprise to which the counter was not immediately evident. Their effect in January, 1943, was devastating.*

The relationship between Slim and Irwin is enigmatic. After the Field-Marshal's death Aileen received from his former commander a letter of deep and moving sincerity. But the old tension between them, generated by Irwin's callous reception of Burcorps at the end of the Retreat, was steadily heightened during the Arakan campaign. Slim found the almost contemptuous way he was personally treated to be unpalatable; more importantly, his professionalism was offended by Irwin's clumsy conduct of the battle. At Ranchi Slim had a complete, well-trained Corps headquarters available for immediate use— practised, indeed, in emergency moves. Yet as Irwin desperately pumped more and more units into Arakan, reinforcing failure until at last Lloyd, with one divisional headquarters, was handling no less than nine brigades, the Eastern Army's commander omitted to take the militarily obvious step of inserting a Corps HQ both to mediate between himself and the force in the field, and to lift from Lloyd's shoulders what had become an intolerable responsibility. Slim remained disregarded in the wings.

When his advice was offered it was ignored. At the beginning of February Irwin ordered yet another attack on Donbaik. To deal with the bunkers he summoned Valentines from Slim's 50 Tank Brigade. But only one troop was demanded. Slim supported his armoured brigadier's protest at the futility of employing a mere handful of tanks, for the inexpediency of 'penny packets', so often demonstrated in the Western Desert, had been revealed to him both in the Middle East and from observing the problems of 7 Armoured Brigade during the Retreat. His maxim was, 'The more you use, the fewer you lose'. But his representations were overruled, on the ground that only one troop could be moved forward in time and properly deployed on arrival. When his few Valentines did arrive they were rushed into action and wasted without profit.

As days passed, and further attacks failed, both Lloyd and Irwin began to have doubts. But Wavell, who, unlike Slim, had not actually *fought* the Japanese, still underestimated their military qualities. In any

---

* Before the end of 1942 the brilliant bunker-techniques of the Japanese had already been disclosed in the fighting round Buna in New Guinea, and counter-methods—the use of tank-guns, and explosive charges—were being developed. It was too early in the war for such information to be circulated between one theatre and another.

case, he was distracted by constant pressure from London, since ANAKIM and the prize of Rangoon, though now a mirage, continued to dazzle the Prime Minister. (As late as 22 March, when Wavell signalled a proposal that Rangoon should be abandoned for alternative targets such as the Andamans or Sumatra, Churchill 'scrawled in scornful red ink, "A poor tale!" '*) At a Delhi conference on 26 February, therefore, Wavell instructed Irwin to overwhelm Donbaik by weight of numbers, and Irwin, in spite of his and Lloyd's reservations, gave orders a week later for a highly concentrated attack on a narrow front—having examined the ground himself. After delay and modifications the final attempt at Donbaik went in on the 18th, and collapsed like its predecessors. Of 14 Division's *débâcle* at this Hill Difficulty none could argue, as *The Times* did about Laing's Nek, that the engagement was not a defeat, for it was evident to all that 'we simply failed to take the position'.

During this period of disillusion Irwin at last called on Slim, but not, as might have been expected, to apply his skill and experience in the direct conduct of the battle. Instead, when Slim reported to Irwin's headquarters at Calcutta and reasonably asked if he was to be so employed, he learned that he was not to be given an operational command, since a Corps headquarters was unnecessary—with the equivalent of three divisions in the field! He was merely to go down to Arakan on Irwin's behalf, survey the scene and report back. A few weeks earlier, after the catastrophe at Kasserine Pass in Tunisia, Eisenhower had sent Omar Bradley as his personal emissary, but without command functions, to examine and report on the disarray of the American army. Like Slim, Bradley felt uncomfortable. As he wrote in *A Soldier's Story*, 'Mine was not altogether an enviable position, for many people thought of me as Eisenhower's agent on the front carrying tales home to the boss outside the chain of command.' But there was this difference—unlike Slim, Bradley enjoyed the complete confidence of his master, who accepted and endorsed his findings.

When he reached the front Slim soon confirmed at first hand what he had already appreciated from a distance, that Lloyd's command was far too large for a single divisional headquarters to control and administer. Bitter experience had taught him the symptoms of waning morale, and these he detected in abundance. Moreover, the tactics repeatedly employed by Lloyd and his brigadiers seemed to him suspect;

* Michael Howard, *Grand Strategy*, Vol. IV, p. 400.

there was too much fear of the jungle, too much reluctance to use a flank, too little subtlety of manoeuvre. He conveyed all these criticisms to Irwin in Calcutta. Unlike Bradley, he was ignored. His presence at this critical stage of the campaign was not, he gathered, required. He departed on ten days' leave to visit Aileen and Una in Simla. However . . .

> At four o'clock in the morning of the 5th April at Gaya, I was awakened by a banging on the door of the railway carriage in which my wife and I were returning from Simla to Ranchi. I was told by a railway official that I was wanted urgently on the telephone and the train would be held up for me. In my pyjamas I staggered over the recumbent figures that invariably litter every Indian platform at night to the station-master's office. Here I heard Tony Scott speaking from Ranchi. Dramatically he proclaimed, 'The woodcock are flighting!' 'Woodcock' was the code name for the move of Corps Headquarters to Arakan. . . . At dawn on a dismal station platform I said good-bye to my wife. . . . We had had too many partings of this kind in the last twenty years, but this was, I think she would agree, one of our most hurried and most miserable.*

All the same, it was only the prelude to even greater anxieties. When Slim once again reported to Irwin in Calcutta, he was ordered to move his headquarters, less the administrative staff, to Chittagong, where he would assume operational control in the Arakan *only after he had been instructed to do so*—and even then, not administrative control. On the latter point Irwin was adamant. Alice came across nothing more extraordinary in Wonderland; it was a Mad Hatter's contrivance. But there was nothing comical about the situation at the front.

Since January the Japanese had been reinforcing in Arakan with Koga's efficient 55 Division. Switching their pressure from one side of the Mayu to the other, they were now tearing the British apart. On the very day that Slim reached the forward area, 6 April, it emerged that during the previous night the headquarters of 6 Brigade had been overrun and the brigadier and staff killed or captured, while 47 Brigade had apparently disintegrated. 'I was in a strange position, which was new to me, and which I did not like. Things had gone wrong, terribly wrong, and we should be hard put to it to avoid worse. Yet I had no

---

* *Defeat into Victory*, p. 155.

operational control and, even if I had, no troops in hand with whom I
could influence events; Lomax already commanded everything.'

Lomax, not Lloyd. For Lloyd—the tip of a line of pressure that
stretched from Churchill through Wavell to Irwin—had now lost his
Army Commander's confidence. Irwin had already countermanded a
plan of Lloyd's at Donbaik, and when on 29 April, under Japanese
pressure, Lloyd ordered one of his brigades to withdraw, Irwin removed
him, taking command of 14 Division himself until Lomax of 26
Division arrived as a replacement. A conscientious but unlucky
general, Lloyd had done well in Syria;* in Arakan, however, he was
unfortunate in finding a commander whose obsession with the frontal
attack he was unable, until the last, to resist.† Slim had the wisdom and
the strength for resistance. In the meantime, it was an embarrassment,
on his arrival, to find that Lomax and his staff knew as little about the
immediate situation as he did himself. The front was crumbling. What
should he do?

His first and natural instinct was to take over the operational
command, in spite of Irwin's curious restriction. Irwin, after all, had
exercised an imperious personal control of the battle in less critical
circumstances. But there was always something unflurried about Slim.
Allowing himself time to study Lomax, he observed that this officer,
so far unknown to him, was cool, competent, and carrying out a
sensible re-grouping of his shaken brigades. Slim therefore let Lomax
continue to take the strain, without regret, and thereafter they worked
contentedly in tandem. This rapid establishment of a mutual confidence was opportune, for a few days later, on 14 April, the operational
control of all troops in Arakan, from Chittagong southwards, finally
passed from Irwin to Slim. He was in the business of battle again, for
the first time since he retreated down the Palel road to the plain of
Imphal.

The events of the next month may be summarized by saying that
Slim and Lomax co-operated in making sense out of nonsense against

---

* In Bernard Fergusson's memoir of Wavell he is even described as 'a fire-eater'
in Syria.
† Lloyd was too straightforward a soldier to turn against the orders of a superior,
though it is true that his final dismissal followed an attempt to withdraw which
Irwin countermanded. When Slim dined with him in the Bengal Club in Calcutta
on the night of 5 April he found Lloyd 'quite without bitterness'. His later death
in the Middle East was much regretted by Slim, who knew that the Arakan
disaster was due to others as well as to Lloyd.

the wishes of Irwin. After an ingenious attempt to trap the advancing Japanese had failed because of the moral and physical exhaustion of certain units, Slim finally extricated the Arakan brigades on the ground that 'the troops had been in action for the past weeks, were fought out and many of them could not be relied on to hold anything'. For these reasons he opposed Irwin's attempt to retain Maungdaw, well down the peninsula, and even to counter-attack. He explained his policy at the time:

> The surest way of quick success in Burma is not to hammer our way with small forces through jungle when the Japanese has every advantage, but to make him occupy as much area as possible, string himself out until he is weak, and then, when we have got him stretched, come in at him from the sea and air. By luring him northwards into the Chittagong and Cox's Bazar districts we get a better chance to get in behind his forward troops.*

This offensive/defensive concept of withdrawal *pour mieux sauter* foreshadowed Slim's strategy at Imphal in 1944. He now carried it out—not entirely, for Irwin insisted on holding the line somewhat further south. But by the end of May all his troops were back in positions they could safely occupy throughout the monsoon—back, unfortunately, where they had started from with such great expectations.

To be obviously right rarely endears one to the man who is obviously wrong. Irwin had a powerful intellect and an aggressive personality, yet he had failed both to diagnose the realities of the set-back at Donbaik and, when defeat turned into retreat, to present Delhi and London with the naked, uncomfortable facts. Slim, by contrast, had made the correct analysis and insisted on the proper course of action. The result was a tragi-comedy. On 26 May Nigel Bruce, Slim's ADC at 15 Corps, had the painful task of conveying to his general two signals—one ordering him to report to Delhi, and one from Irwin which, after severely criticizing Slim's conduct of the battle, intimated that he would be relieved of his command. After reading them Slim remarked to Bruce, 'I suppose that means I've got the sack. I shall join the Home Guard in England. I wonder if I shall find Irwin there!' They then strolled back together towards Slim's bungalow. As they approached

---

* Churchill put this idea more vividly in his famous memo to the Chiefs of Staff on 8 May, at the Washington Conference: 'Going into swampy jungle to fight the Japanese is like going into the water to fight a shark. It is better to entice him into a trap or catch him on a hook and then demolish him with axes after hauling him out onto dry land.'

they saw a figure on the verandah, clad only in a towel, who was executing a dervish dance and waving a piece of paper. It was Tony Scott, and when they drew nearer they could hear him shouting, 'God is good! God is good!' The paper was in fact a message which should have preceded the instruction to Slim to report to Delhi. It informed him that General Giffard had now replaced Irwin at Eastern Army and wanted him for urgent consultations. His own signal of dismissal reached Irwin while he was visiting Scoones's 4 Corps at Imphal. Ouvry Roberts, Scoones's chief staff officer, received the signal from his cypher office and handed it to Irwin, who forthwith composed a classic telegram for immediate despatch to Slim. It said (as Roberts recalled the text), 'You're not sacked, I am.'*

In *Defeat into Victory* Slim wrote an appraisal of Giffard which indicates the great affinity that grew up between them. Qualities of each were mirrored in the other—courtesy, consideration, unselfishness, lack of show. Giffard, in Slim's view, 'understood the fundamentals of war— that soldiers must be trained before they can fight, fed before they can march, and relieved before they are worn out'.† He might have added that as a young Lieut-Colonel in the First World War Giffard had served a hard apprenticeship in bush fighting, during the East African campaigns against the brilliant von Lettow-Vorbeck. Imagination, strategic insight, sparkle—these were lacking, and a steadiness which seemed like stolidity proved too much for Mountbatten's patience after he became Supreme Commander. But Slim always rode comfortably to Giffard's anchor.

Morale was now low. Disillusion is quick to infect the blood-stream of an army, and difficult to neutralize once the poison has taken hold. Slim thought Giffard's impact restorative, but the new Army Commander's flair with troops was less than his own. More immediately stimulating was the news of Wingate's first raid, from which 2,300 of his 3,000 Chindits returned during the latter stages of the Arakan battle. The only effect of this foray on the Japanese was to sow in the mind of their High Command the idea that it might be feasible for them too to penetrate the mountain bastions of India. There were few specific military results, except an endorsement of the practicability of air supply, which was already familiar to Slim and which he was ready to apply as soon as resources became available.

---

* Letter to author, 16 May, 1975.
† Giffard did not set the troops on fire, but they liked him. They called him 'Pop'.

In the realm of the spirit, however, the contribution of Wingate and his long-suffering columns was considerable. It did not matter that few Japanese troops had been engaged, still less killed, or that most of Wingate's casualties were due to disease. The salient fact, magnified by the instant propaganda of the time, was that soldiers as average as those in Arakan had struck deep into Japanese territory, manoeuvred, fought, survived and returned. The myth of the super-Jap, born at Singapore, developed during the Retreat, and amplified in Arakan was partially deflated. The deflation was more in the imagination of the British and American public than among the troops of Eastern Army, and it was not until 1944 that the myth was conclusively destroyed. Nevertheless, in the battle for the hearts and minds of his soldiers this operation was a 'plus', and Slim concluded that 'for this reason alone, Wingate's raid was worth all the hardship and sacrifice his men endured'.

But more than this was necessary for a resurrection. At the Washington TRIDENT conference in early May Churchill had been infuriated by the death-knell of what he dismissed as one of the most discouraging and discreditable campaigns of the war. He required new commanders and severe disciplines for the demoralized troops. On his return to Delhi from the conference Wavell more sensibly formed an energetic committee to examine with speed 'the present standard of readiness for war of British and Indian Infantry Battalions in India, and to make recommendations for their improvement'. The new plans for increasing the status and quality of the infantry, and in particular the institution of training divisions, were a significant advance on the arrangements made after the 1942 retreat; as they were set in motion they produced, at last, an efficient machinery for manufacturing cadres of battle-worthy reinforcements. Slim's old friend Reginald Savory, whose 23 Division had absorbed months of front-line experience around Imphal, was an ideal Director of Infantry at this critical time.

But Slim himself was planning an offensive. During the next few months a number of large-scale operations would be deeply studied by his seniors, and finally abandoned—on an arc ranging from an advance by the Chinese Yunnan armies to an amphibious assault on the Andaman Islands. Amid the changing fortunes of these enterprises one proposition remained firm—a new push by 15 Corps down Arakan, to regain the Buthidaung-Maungdaw line and exploit towards Akyab. For this post-monsoon operation Slim received two divisions of high quality. 7 Indian, though not yet blooded, had already impressed Slim and was, moreover, commanded by Frank Messervy, whose

cavalier dash at the head of his Gazelle Force in East Africa, at the time
when Slim was fighting at Gallabat, had been legendary. The other
formation, 5 Indian Division, the 'Ball of Fire', had of course been
Slim's own family in Eritrea, and its reputation had increased in the
Western Desert. Its General, Briggs, was well known to Slim and
deeply trusted by him. With these two in front, and a re-animated 26
Division in reserve, he felt a growing confidence.

The confidence spread. It was a new and important factor. Lomax
had stopped the rot, but if Slim was to launch a successful offensive he
must generate a belief that in spite of a sad sequence of reverses it *could*
succeed. 5 Indian Division, for example, after its arrival from the
Middle East in June, spent some months of intensive training in Bihar,
carrying out mock attacks over country chosen for its likeness to
Arakan, adopting ferocious anti-malaria precautions, studying Japanese
methods, etc. The future historian of the Division, Anthony Brett-
James,* was a young officer at the time. He attended a prolonged
discussion of the forthcoming operation at Ranchi, over a huge scale-
model of the terrain, and was profoundly impressed by the way that
Slim, at the end of the exercise, gathered together in a comprehensive
and lucid manner all the main points that had emerged, speaking
fluently, forcefully, and with a complete command of his subject.
Apart from his performance in battle, there is probably no more effective
means for a commander of imposing his will and his personality than by
addressing his assembled subordinates about the battle that lies ahead
and winning them over to his way of thinking by manifestly talking
sense. The techniques of Slim and Montgomery differed, but each, in
his way, was a master of the art of inspiring while informing.

A new attitude was emerging. This was directly reflected in the Five
Commandments which, on General Briggs's orders, were learned by
every member of his division. The second read: 'Be determined not to
let the Jap frighten you with ruses and induce you to disclose your
positions and waste ammunition. Ambush him and do unto him as he
would unto you.' The third instructed: 'Be determined to hold fast
when ordered, whatever happens. The Jap will then have to give you
the target you want, whilst our reserves are on the way to help you.'
These principles, which were to be applied in practice so profitably
during the next twelve months, carried to every soldier the basic ideas

---

* Anthony Brett-James, *Ball of Fire*.

which Slim had evolved during and since the Retreat, and which he was now enunciating as a doctrine throughout his command.

These ideas were bold but simple. They were devised to counter an enemy whose reaction, made instinctive by training, was to by-pass or to infiltrate. In countries where forces are small and areas vast positions can always be turned. If the defender (who may of course be the attacker unexpectedly thrown on the defensive), holds well-stocked pivots of manoeuvre on approaches to vital areas the enemy will be forced to attack, to establish lines of communication to his infiltrating or outflanking forces. The pivots must then stand firm, supplied if necessary by air, and when the supply line of the infiltrators has been cut they can be destroyed by reserves; then a counter-offensive can be launched. It had been Slim's intention to apply those ideas during the last phase of the Arakan disaster, and their unorthodox character had been a main cause of his conflict with Irwin. When the year turned, and the mis-named Japanese 'March on Delhi' began, it would be seen both that they were correctly judged and that a renovated Army had effectively digested them.

But Slim had scarcely moved the headquarters of his Corps down to Arakan, into a more suitable position for controlling the offensive, when he was required elsewhere. On 16 October he received an unexpected summons to report to Calcutta and replace Giffard.* As he drove away from Dum Dum airport to his new command post at Barrackpore the flag of an Army Commander fluttered for the first time on the bonnet of his car.

---

* Sir George Giffard had not been sacked from Eastern Command but promoted to C-in-C of the new 11th Army Group which was a by-product of the establishment of SEAC under Mountbatten. (See next chapter.)

CHAPTER NINE

ON THE EVE

'For now sits Expectation in the air.'
Shakespeare, *King Henry V*

SLIM'S DESTINY had already been shaped by many chance events. None, however, was more momentous than the decisions taken by the Anglo-American High Command during their conference at Quebec in August, 1943. The two allies diverged in their Far Eastern policies—America looking up the Burma Road to China, the British over the sea to Singapore—but they then united in establishing a South East Asia Command with a British Supremo, an American Deputy, and joint air, sea and land commanders. Moreover, they agreed on a strategy for the Command which, though it was not implemented in full detail, ultimately threw the main weight of effort on to the Indo-Burmese frontiers which were about to become Slim's responsibility. His future was born at Quebec.

This may be seen most vividly if it be asked how Slim's fortunes might have varied if Mountbatten had not been appointed Supreme Commander. During the Field-Marshal's last days the Admiral, with considerate understanding, called on Slim before going on to some ceremonial, perhaps the Burma Star Reunion, which the dying man was too ill to attend. As Aileen quietly entered the bedroom to warn the visitor that it was time to leave, she saw Mountbatten leaning over her husband and heard Slim saying, 'We did it together, old boy.' In the shadow of death plain words are spoken. 'We did it together.' There can be no doubt that, from the end of 1943, the whole of the Far Eastern campaign revolved around the Mountbatten-Slim axis, and that the contribution of others, however great, was known and seen to be subsidiary.* Mountbatten could not have defeated the Japanese without Slim's military skills; during the great crises of 14th Army Slim could scarcely have survived without Mountbatten's imperious energy and intimate acquaintance with the Anglo-American corridors of power. They were complementary. Yet there might have been no Mountbatten.

The odds were four to one against. In retrospect the arrival of Mountbatten at SEAC, leading as it did to his appointment as Viceroy and the events of 1947, seems to fit into an inevitable pattern. But an early name proposed by the British for the post of Supreme Commander was that of Air Chief Marshal Sir Sholto Douglas, the AOC Middle East. He was rejected by the Americans as inexperienced in Allied commands. Two other British suggestions also proved unsuccessful—Air Chief Marshal Sir Arthur Tedder, because he was irreplaceable at Eisenhower's right hand in the Mediterranean, and Admiral Sir Andrew Cunningham, because he sensibly refused. It was only then that Churchill, who had privately approved of Mountbatten as a candidate even before he reached Quebec, obtained the conference's agreement to the appointment of a man who, as he signalled to the War Cabinet, was 'young, enthusiastic and triphibious'.†

Douglas, Cunningham and Tedder were all unsuited to the post of Supreme Commander—the first two because of obvious limitations. Tedder, a magnificent and inventive organizer of air power in the support of armies, was also limited, as his wartime record and his autobiography reveal, by an erroneous belief that he knew more than the generals about the actual conduct of the war on land. This was not a wholesome attitude for the director of campaigns against the Japanese.‡ Slim would have been ill-assorted as the subordinate of any of these men.

Mountbatten reached India at the beginning of October. In the

---

* 'I thought him absolutely splendid in every way and never changed my point of view from beginning to end. I have reason to believe he liked me too from the beginning. Nothing could ever come between us. I saw Bill Slim whenever I possibly could and never missed a chance of seeing him on any visit to the Front. We talked over everything with the utmost candour and he and I saw eye to eye all the way through.' Lord Mountbatten, letter to author, 6 May, 1975.

† See Michael Howard, *Grand Strategy*, vol. 111, p. 578.

‡ Moreover, Wavell's *Journal* for 24 June notes: 'I was also quite certain that the Air Force were trying hard behind the scenes either to get complete independence from the control of a soldier or to get an Airman appointed as Supreme Commander.'

account that follows he describes the pessimistic atmosphere he entered, the bases of his new policy as Supreme Commander, and the circumstances in which he personally selected Slim to command the 14th Army.

I arrived in Delhi with a small personal staff on 7 October, 1943. I was impatient to get a move on and left the remainder of my staff to follow me as soon as they could. On arrival I was met by C-in-C India (General Auchinleck) and stayed with him. I was also met by my own three Cs-in-C (Admiral Somerville, General Giffard and Air Chief Marshal Peirse). I had a number of informal discussions with them mainly to let them brief me.

They explained:

(a) They could not stop the Japanese infiltration through the jungle cutting our lines of communication which meant our forward forces had to fall back to re-establish their supply lines.

(b) Air supply was impossible through lack of transport aircraft and we were forbidden by President Roosevelt to divert US Transport Aircraft off the 'Over the Hump' supply to China.

(c) All fighting and even movement and flying in Burma became virtually impossible for 5 months in every year on account of the South-West Monsoon. Giffard and Peirse considered it would be suicidal to pursue an offensive under these conditions.

(d) Tropical diseases caused 120 times more hospitalizations than battle casualties. This was an inhibiting factor which lowered morale.

(e) The attempt to advance on the Arakan Front a few weeks ago had ended in disaster and still further lowered morale.

(f) All were perturbed to hear of the backing the Prime Minister, President and Combined Chiefs of Staff were giving to Wingate, though they were delighted that I had succeeded in getting General Arnold (Chief of US Army Air Force Staff) to set up a special Unit to support operations behind the Japanese lines, which he had named No. 1 Air Commando as a compliment to my recent Command.

(g) The Assam lines of communication were utterly inadequate to support any form of offensive. When I said I had the offer of an American Railway Regiment to come to our help at once, Auchinleck rejected this out of hand and got the Viceroy to support him. Only when I threatened immediate resignation over this did they give in and make an offensive possible.

(h) Giffard and Peirse declined my suggestion that they should go round the front line units and talk to them to raise their morale but would welcome my doing so.

(i) Lack of adequate publicity in the Press at home helped to lower morale. They were glad to hear that the Editor of the *Sunday Dispatch* (Charles Eade) was being attached to my staff to deal with this and welcomed my creating a daily inter-service newspaper 'SEAC' to be run by Frank Owen (former Editor of the *Evening Standard*).

(j) They assumed I would deal only through them (as Chairman of the Committee) and expressed surprise to hear that my power of command really was supreme and I intended to talk freely to senior officers direct, though I would let them know what I said.

I wished to make contact with my brother Supreme Commander of the China Theatre, Generalissimo Chiang Kai-shek, before starting work with my staff. I visited him at Chungking from 16 to 20 October. I also met my new Deputy Supreme Allied Commander SEA, the American General Stilwell (Vinegar Joe) who told me he had just been fired by the Generalissimo and to everyone's stupefaction I got him reinstated. I did this by saying I would not allow any of the Chinese under my command to participate in fighting under any other Commanding General.

On my way back I refuelled at Dum Dum Air Station near Calcutta on 22 October and visited the Joint Headquarters of the Eastern Army and 3rd Tactical Air Force at the Viceroy's House, Belvedere. At Barrackpore I was received by the Acting Army Commander, Lt-General Slim, and Air Marshal Baldwin. They introduced me to about 80 of the most senior members of their staff. Slim surprised me by asking me to address them. Although unprepared I felt the opportunity was too good to miss and did so. I mentioned my talk in my typed diary and on the vital question of keeping up the offensive in the monsoon I had written this:

'I staggered them by saying that I understood that it was the custom to stop fighting during the monsoon in Burma, but that I was against this custom, and hoped that they would support me and keep the battle going to the best of their ability, whatever the weather conditions were. I hope that this policy spoken on the spur of the moment may perhaps yield good results later on, but that remains to be seen.'

I said there was to be no more retreat. If our lines of communication were cut I would arrange for the cut-off troops to be supplied by air.

I mentioned the fearful toll tropical disease took of the men in Burma and said I had set up a Medical Advisory Division of Tropical Disease experts to cut their effect drastically.

The only staff officer who accompanied me was Brigadier Eddie Cobb, the Army Group Director of Plans, whom I had borrowed from Giffard. Cobb checked my memory and told me that although it had been a stirring and inspiring talk it had been criticized by those he spoke to afterwards on the grounds that I did not understand the situation properly and would soon find out that the monsoon made an offensive out of the question during the five months it prevailed. Further they could not see how troops could be ordered to stand fast and face the infiltrating Japanese if they were cut off from their supplies and no transport aircraft were available. They thought it would be a long while before the new Tropical Disease Medical Advisory Division controlled malaria, dysentery and scrub typhus. In fact, to be brutally frank they thought it revealed enthusiastic ignorance and though the rank and file might feel encouraged, they themselves were shaken by my quick decision based on inadequate understanding of the conditions in Burma.

While Cobb was being assailed by the audience I was having a very different sort of talk with Slim and Baldwin. They both liked my ideas and both said they would do all in their power to help me carry them out. Slim made the point that he was really only the Commander of 15 Corps, and had in fact been fired for the recent Arakan disaster by the then Army Commander (General Noel Irwin). He had only been saved by a dramatic telegram to say that his firing was cancelled as Irwin himself had been fired. He was very surprised at being translated from a 'Corps Commander under notice' to acting replacement of the Army Commander who had fired him. Slim had no idea what would happen now that Giffard had been appointed as Commander of 11 Army Group.

I had taken an immediate liking to Slim and offered him the Command of the new Army we were going to create for the Burma Campaign under a new name (soon to become the 14th Army). Slim was obviously delighted but said 'Won't you have to ask General Giffard first?' I said 'No' as I was the Supreme Commander and Giffard was my subordinate. In any case he had given me an encouraging report on Slim and I felt sure he would make no difficulties. Incidentally I was wrong for when I told Giffard on return to Delhi I had given Slim Command of the new Army he demurred and said he would have to think it over.* I suggested he should telegraph to the CIGS asking whether he had to obey my orders or was permitted to protest. At that he gave in and I maintained my ascendancy over him from that moment though I don't suppose he liked it.

Anyway once Slim had accepted we got down to discussing details. He agreed at once to issue orders that there would be no

---

* The presumption must be not that Giffard disapproved of Slim as Army Commander but that he resented the appointment of his chief subordinate by a new young Admiral.

more retreat and that I had undertaken to supply cut off forces by air.*

Slim, ten years older than Mountbatten, sagacious, unhurried, sceptical, took up his command with confidence because he too had suddenly found a man he could trust. 'We began to feel that we belonged to an efficient show, or what was going to be one, and that feeling spread.' It was a novel experience in 1943.

Trust was indeed essential, for it is a curious irony that the victories which Slim's 14th Army was to achieve never represented the true strategic purpose of either Churchill, the British Chiefs of Staff or Mountbatten himself. Their main objectives were always elsewhere, and the method by which it was hoped to attain them was always amphibious, whether the target was Rangoon, or the Andamans, or Sumatra or Singapore. Thus the main direction of Mountbatten's thought and the main weight of SEAC's planning lay along the seaward flank of Asia.† The plans dissolved one by one. The great amphibious assaults never occurred, for the Mediterranean, the Pacific and the German war devoured the resources with which they might have been mounted.‡ But Slim's theatre was always low on the list—low in terms of planning effort at SEAC, low in terms of equipment—and had it not been for a sustained American pressure to support China it might have fallen lower still. In such a situation Slim might well have turned sour. If he never did so, it was partly because, for all his other preoccupations, Mountbatten never betrayed their mutual trust.

The irony in their relationship and in Slim's situation was well illustrated at their first meeting. The Quebec conference had ended, under American pressure, in a decision to recover north Burma by a triple advance—Chiang Kai-shek's Yunnan divisions moving in from

---

* Private communication to author.
† SEAC's attitude during these months is mirrored in the diary of Lieut-General Sir Henry Pownall, Mountbatten's Chief of Staff. On 6 January, 1944, for example, he noted: 'Our minds are now very much moving on the lines that we do not want a big Burmese commitment forced on us and want to be free a year hence to do something that may be more fruitful, e.g. Sumatra. If we get entangled in the jungles of Burma it may very well force us to go on plunging deeper.'
‡ A substantial assault fleet was of course assembled in SEAC until its main elements were withdrawn to the west as a result of the Teheran and second Cairo Conferences in latter 1943, leaving Mountbatten, as he wrote to the author on 10 July, 1975, 'with the odd landing craft which had no ships to lift them back,' (to the west), 'and landing craft under repair.'

the east, Stilwell and his India-trained Chinese down the Ledo Road, and 4 Corps emerging from Assam to cross the Chindwin in the west. Wingate's Long Range Penetration force, which had been enthusiastically adopted at Quebec, was to support all these operations, while a subsidiary offensive would occur in Arakan. Over and above all this a considerable amphibious operation was to be prepared, and when Mountbatten saw Slim at Barrackpore he appears to have stressed, in Slim's words, that 'the main offensive was now to come from a landing in the south'. When Slim asked if there would be enough shipping Mountbatten replied, 'We're getting so many ships that the harbours of India and Ceylon won't be big enough to hold 'em!' And Mountbatten was right to be optimistic; when he got back to Delhi he found awaiting him Churchill's Directive of 21 October,* in which the Prime Minister promised him, four weeks before his first major amphibious operation, 'a battle fleet based on Ceylon', with 10 escort carriers, armoured carriers, etc, and ordered him to assemble all the paraphernalia for a seaborne assault—a Combined Striking Force, an Inshore Squadron, artificial harbours.

Yet nothing happened. The need for craft to support the D Day landings in Normandy and southern France meant that by mid-January any idea of major amphibious operations was abandoned;† Chiang Kai-shek seized his opportunity to cancel the Chinese advance from Yunnan; there remained only Arakan, a limited thrust by 4 Corps plus Wingate's Long Range enterprise, and a push from the north by Stilwell, of uncertain power. Such were the parameters of confusion within which Slim had to work. A grand scheme evolved in the stratosphere, which offered his Army a subsidiary role, had evaporated to leave his two Corps, 4 in the north and 15 in Arakan, at the centre of a picture whose frame had noticeably contracted. Thanks to the Japanese they would remain there until the end of the war.

However, if it was not always clear to Slim exactly where or why he was going to fight, at least he knew that a fight lay ahead—and early in 1944 the pattern began to clarify. At most he had only a few months, after taking over 14th Army in mid-October, 1943, before the battle began. His chapter entitled 'The Foundations', in *Defeat into Victory*,

---

* See *The War against Japan*, Vol. III, Appendix 3, for full text.
† Instead of receiving naval reinforcements, in December SEAC had to send to the West one flotilla of Landing Craft Infantry and 26 miscellaneous landing vessels.

eloquently describes his urgent efforts to improve the organization and administration of his command; to examine it paragraph by paragraph is to see that few generals have been more acute in identifying the immense variety of small essential matters which, if overlooked at the stage of preparation, can rarely be rectified after the guns start firing. The fundamental problem was that of morale, which in one form or another had dogged the Army of the East ever since the fall of Singapore. It was a problem with two faces. Slim had to inject into the individual soldier a will to victory; at the same time he had to attempt the more subtle task of creating for 14th Army a sense of identity. This is a rare feat of generalship, achieved in the western theatres only by Montgomery with 8th Army and Rommel with the Afrika Korps— though Patton went a limited distance with his American 3rd Army. None of these commanders faced equivalent difficulties. Their armies were compact; their theatre of war was homogeneous. 14th Army was scattered over vast distances in a variety of terrains; its structure was polyglot, with the greater proportion of its troops drawn from the infinite racial variety of India. Yet the historic fact remains—that living, self-aware organism which is a true army (as compared with the usual *ad hoc* agglomeration of units) emerged under Slim's hands. How did the improbable occur?

A comparison of techniques is instructive. Montgomery converted the difficult into the simple and then, by an extraordinary feat of calculated showmanship, made his Army believe in the simplicities and thus overcome the difficulties. Rommel gave his Afrika Korps unity by rallying it round himself on the battlefield—the *Feldherr* of the Front Line. Patton worked by braggadocio and a ruthless dynamism—Old Blood and Guts. Slim's methods were gentler, but no less pervasive or effective. His weapon was words.

> There was nothing new in this; my corps and divisional commanders and others right down the scale were already doing it. It was the way we had held the troops together in the worst days of the 1942 retreat; we remained an army then only because the men saw and knew their commanders. All I did now was to encourage my commanders to increase these activities, unite them in a common approach to the problem, in the points that they would stress, and in the action they would take to see that principles became action not merely words. Yet they began, as most things do, in words. We, my commanders and I, talked to units, to collections of officers, to headquarters, to little groups of men, to individual soldiers casually met as we moved around.

And we all talked the same stuff with the same object. Whenever I could get away from my headquarters, and that throughout the campaign was about a third of the time, I was in these first few months more like a parliamentary candidate than a general—except that I never made a promise.*

But words would have remained words, without the man. Soldiers are sceptical of mere words. It was during these peregrinations, however, that his Army began to think of Lieut-General Slim as Uncle Bill. His technique—it was less a contrivance than a natural response— contrasted effectively with that of Mountbatten, who in his own idiosyncratic way contributed enormously to the restoration of confidence by his talks and speeches. The carefully planned casualness of Mountbatten's appearances was invigorating, but from the soldier's point of view this was the Supreme Commander descending to announce that 'God's in his Heaven. All's right with the world,' before returning to the clouds. Uncle Bill, they came to see, was theirs and they were his, linked in the brotherhood of battle. His evident grasp of the present offered them hope for the future. His message was that enshrined in the famous motto of the Royal Tank Regiment: 'From mud through blood to the green fields beyond.'

The core of his success was his concern for his troops as individual human beings, as persons. 8th Army relished Montgomery, but while he could inspire he rarely gave the ordinary soldier a sense that they were both made of the same clay. 'Uncle Monty' is inconceivable; 'Uncle Bill' was a natural endearment. There are many first-hand stories of how, by an instinctive rightness of touch, Slim achieved this sense of togetherness; one suffices. At some point during the advance from Imphal a young Indian artillery officer called Gupta (later Master-General of the Ordnance, Indian Army) was in the command post on his gun position. He looked round to find it occupied by a large unfamiliar figure. At that moment there came on the radio the most insistent of all signals, for a regimental shoot: 'Mike Target, Mike Target, Mike Target.' Gupta brushed the figure on one side and carried out the fire-plan. When it was finished the figure had disappeared, but as he emerged from his command post to get some air Gupta saw to his horror the red hat and unmistakable presence of his Army Commander. He began to stutter apologies, but Slim interrupted. 'Don't bother about

* *Defeat into Victory*, p. 184.

that, my boy. If everybody worked like you we'd get to Rangoon a lot sooner!' Gupta was deeply moved by the instant humanity of Slim's reaction. What is more to the point, he was astonished to discover, some time later, that after this episode he was soldiering far better than he had ever thought it possible for him to do. The essence of Slim's achievement with 14th Army was precisely this—to communicate the faith that moves mountains.*

Between the British and the Indian troops his mode of communication differed. A shared language, shared traditions and attitudes, a shared sense of humour, a shared remoteness from home, a joint membership of a Forgotten Army made Slim's appeal to the British private direct and personal. Roughly speaking they had the same war aims. Through *SEAC* (the paper which Mountbatten wisely created for all the troops, airmen and sailors in his theatre by snatching from his tank in England the brilliant young ex-editor of the *Evening Standard*, Frank Owen), Slim and his Army were kept in close if not always reverent contact. But the Indian element posed a far more complicated problem.

With Gurkha or Mussulman, Dogra or Jat, Slim might converse amicably—often in their own tongue—and they would respond with warmth, but between them and the Scot, the East Anglian or the man of Kent there was a profound distinction. The Army Commander and his British soldiers had a Cause in common—however ill-defined or dimly seen. 'If ever an army fought in a just cause, we did,' Slim wrote in *Defeat into Victory*. 'We fought for the clean, the decent, the free things of life . . . we fought only because the power of evil had attacked these things.' But it is doubtful whether this was the motivation of the Indians. Yet they were all volunteers; they fought, almost to a man, with an absolute loyalty.† Of the 29 Victoria Crosses awarded in Burma

---

* He already had the confidence of the officer corps. His long years of service in the Indian Army meant that he was known to, and trusted by, a high proportion of the divisional, brigade and even battalion commanders. Many were his friends.
† If Slim had to command a Forgotten Army it was, in part, because his Prime Minister was blind to this important fact. When Wavell was sailing in the *Queen Mary* in June to the Washington Conference, he noted in his *Journal* that Churchill had 'the impression that the Indian Army was liable to rise at any moment; and he accused me of creating a Frankenstein by putting modern weapons in the hands of sepoys, spoke of 1857, and was really almost childlike about it. I tried to reassure him, both verbally and by a written note, but he has a curious complex about India and is always loth to hear good of it and apt to believe the worst.'

20 were won by the Indian Army. And in spite of nationalist propaganda
at home, and a so-called Indian National Army in the enemy's ranks,
there were virtually no defections—some Sikhs in Burma, a picket
of Gwalior Lancers in Arakan, localized and insignificant episodes.
They were as integral a part of 14th Army as the British—for other
reasons.

In 1975 the author discussed this question with a substantial number
of generals in the Indian Army, serving and retired, who had fought
as young officers under Slim and whose experiences spanned most of
the divisions in his army—General Bewoor, the Chief of Army Staff;
Lieut-General Rawlley, his Vice-Chief (who won the MC at Kohima);
Major-General Korla (who served throughout with 17 Division);
General Chaudhuri (who served in the Middle East and Burma with
5 Division); Lieut-General Jacob (C-in-C Eastern Army), and others.
They were unanimous in doubting whether their ordinary soldiers,
largely peasants from the villages, had any very clear idea of the 14th
Army as such, or any very strong awareness of Slim. What they would
do—and this was perhaps their chief motivation in battle—was to
follow their officers, *if* they trusted them. What Philip Mason, in his
fine book on the Indian Army, has called 'a matter of honour' would
sweep them to death behind a platoon commander in whom they had
faith. It thus seems that Slim's achievement (with the immense assistance of Mountbatten and Auchinleck) was to create, after all the de-
moralization of 1942 and 1943, an atmosphere—an atmosphere of
credibility, enhanced by success—which filtered steadily downward
from the top until it reached the lowest rank and furthest corner of the
Army.

There was perhaps one other factor, comprehensible only in terms
of Indian mentality and Indian history. During the long years of the
East India Company a phrase was in constant use—'The *Iqbāl* of the
Company Bahadur', the aura of continuing success, what someone
called 'the opinion of our invincibility'. 'Seen from the Indian angle',
Philip Mason observes, 'it was less an opinion, a matter of calculation,
than a matter of destiny and the favour of heaven. It was unquestionably
one reason why men came to the colours and stayed faithful to their
oath.' After a disaster like the First Afghan War the Company's
Iqbāl would decline in potency. So after Singapore, and the Retreat,
and First Arakan the *Iqbāl* of the army, indeed of the British, had a
diminished aura. Slim, it might be said, was in the great tradition of
Clive and the heroes of the Mutiny. By restoring 'the *Iqbāl* of the

Company Bahadur' he ensured that those who came to the colours of his Army stayed faithful to their oath.*

His immediate subordinates, the instruments of his policies, needed no indoctrination. They were all either old and trusted friends or new men whom he soon accepted. Always opposed to the practice of making sweeping changes on taking up a fresh appointment, he did use the opportunity presented by the formation of 14th Army and Eastern Command out of the old Eastern Army to introduce as his Chief Administrative Officer Alf Snelling, whose qualities he had severely tested in Iraq and Syria. Bowen, his Chief Signals Officer, had been with him during the Retreat. The Brigadier General Staff, Steve Irwin, soon won his confidence. In the south his successor at 15 Corps, Philip Christison, had been a fellow instructor with him at the Staff College, while the three divisional commanders, Messervy, Briggs and Lomax, had already been assessed and approved. The Commander of 4 Corps in the north, Geoffry Scoones, was a Gurkha whose shrewd intellect and prudent disposition gave no cause for concern, while at 17 Division there was 'Punch' Cowan, a close friend in peace and a companion in the Retreat; at 23 Division was Ouvry Roberts, Slim's right-hand-man in the days of Habbaniyah and Deir-ez-Zor; at 20 Division was Douglas Gracey, another Gurkha well known to Slim both before the war and during the Syrian campaign. The roll-call of these names was heartening. But two other stars had now entered Slim's orbit whose presence caused him some disquiet. The first was General Joseph Stilwell.

Though Mountbatten had been in the theatre for over a month, the SEAC organization only began its formal existence at midnight on 15 November. Stilwell simultaneously became Deputy Allied Supreme Commander. He was also Chief of Staff to Chiang Kai-shek and Commanding General of all United States forces, both air and army, in the China-Burma-India Theatre, Commander of the Chinese divisions now being trained in India, and therefore, *ex-officio*, Commanding General of the Northern Combat Area which was to be their operational zone. Thus Stilwell, besides being a phenomenally difficult man, was also a phenomenally busy one. Not that he failed to profit from his

---

* For the Indian troops Mountbatten, with his royal connections and his regal style, was a powerful enhancement of the *Iqbāl*, reflecting the aura of a Raj which their fathers and forefathers had served in so many campaigns. Their different impact is a good example of the fruitful Mountbatten-Slim partnership.

proliferations. 'To watch Stilwell, when hard pressed, shift his op-position from one of the several strong-points he held by virtue of his numerous Allied, American, and Chinese offices, to another, was a lesson in the mobile offensive-defensive.'* Nevertheless, his many responsibilities raised an awkward question in November, for under the post-Quebec plan he would control not only the troops moving down the Ledo road but also the considerable Chinese forces which, theoretically, were to advance from Yunnan. How was he to be linked, under Mountbatten's supreme authority, with the operations of 14th Army? The obvious answer was for both Stilwell and Slim to function under the orders of Giffard, who as C-in-C 11 Army Group was the senior land commander in SEAC.

Stilwell stubbornly refused, ranging skilfully over the whole gamut of excuses which his conflicting appointments presented. The real reason was simple—he loathed Giffard; and Stilwell was a man in whom distaste became obsessive. Since the antipathy was mutual it is fortunate that an arrangement which seemed logical on paper was never made, for under the stress of the coming battles it would certainly have collapsed. However, when discussions had reached a deadlock the unpredictable American suddenly declared, 'I am prepared to come under General Slim's operational control until I get to Kamaing.' (Kamaing represent-ing the point at which the advance down the Ledo road would debouch into the more open country of N. Burma.) Though this proposal meant that Slim would be responsible to Giffard for 14th Army and to the Supreme Commander for Stilwell, both he and Mountbatten accepted it, since only an extraordinary command structure, it seemed, could accommodate an extraordinary man.

This offer of Stilwell's was a measure of the respect his anglophobe mind had formed for Slim during the Retreat† and consolidated during its aftermath, when 13,000 troops were flown out of China (a notable early instance of air trooping), to be trained by American instructors at Ramgarh in India.‡ Slim gave careful attention to this training, and

---

* *Defeat into Victory*, p. 205.
† In Stilwell's notes made during the Retreat one remark shines like a good deed in a naughty world. 29 March, 1942: 'Good old Slim. Maybe he's all right after all.' General Fuller, in his introduction to *The Stilwell Papers*, observes that 'the only Englishman he seems to have got on with was General Slim'.
‡ The respect was shared by the Chinese. When one of their divisions was due to return to the Ledo front Slim paid it a farewell visit. The divisional commander

he and Stilwell drew closer together. They had the same sardonic sense of humour. Years after the war, at one of the Burma Star Reunions in the Albert Hall, Slim described to his veterans with great gusto how, one day during the hopelessness of the Retreat, he and Stilwell were sitting on a hill together in some dejection. Stilwell suddenly burst out, 'Well, at least you and I have an ancestor in common!' 'Who?' asked Slim. 'Ethelred the Unready.'

The Yunnan offensive never effectively materialized, but the march from Ledo went ahead in the following spring, and Stilwell's subordination to Slim was faithfully and almost harmoniously maintained. Though his military operations were not of the first importance, and though he ultimately fell out with Chiang Kai-shek and was recalled by Roosevelt, this should not disguise the fact that for many months he was a focus of great authority and a potential creator of large embarrassments. Slim's friendly liaison was therefore invaluable—to himself, to Mountbatten, and to the Allied cause. He was probably the only man in SEAC, including the Supreme Commander, who could talk turkey with Vinegar Joe—and this was perhaps because Stilwell believed that Slim was the only Englishman in the Far East who wanted to fight!

Slim's considered view of Stilwell is on public record in *Defeat into Victory*. A less inhibited private view provides a useful comparison. In the latter fifties, while he was Governor-General of Australia, Slim became involved in a long correspondence with an American in the Philippines, John H. Hart, a former Army officer and student of Sino-American relations who was preparing a book on Stilwell. On 9 November, 1959, referring to *The Stilwell Papers*, Slim wrote to Hart:

> It was a pity that book was published as it was. Such papers, written in the heat and the exasperation of the moment, in spite of their salty humour, did not do him justice. He was much more than the bad-tempered, prejudiced, often not very well informed and quarrelsome old man they showed him to be. He was all that, but in addition he was a first-class battle leader up to, I should say, Corps level and an excellent tactician, but a poor administrator. At higher levels he had neither the temperament nor the strategic background or judgement to be effective. Even in the tactical field he hampered himself by, I believe,

---

responded with a Shakespearian touch aptly devised for his well-read superior. 'Sir,' he said, 'parting is such sweet sorrow'

deliberately employing only mediocre American subordinate commanders* and a good deal of nepotism on his staff. His dislike, openly
expressed and shown, of all 'Limeys', which at times did not make for
co-operation, was, I always found, if not taken too seriously more
amusing than dangerous. I used to tease him about it and he took it
very well. Yet his distrust of the British was deeply rooted, and on
what grounds I could not discover.
P.S. I ought to add that Stilwell served under my operational command
from the end of November 1943 to the latter part of June 1944, i.e.
throughout the most important part of his operations, and I never
found him anything but an exemplary subordinate. I won't guarantee,
however, that he didn't sometimes say hard things about me to his
staff!

A year before he wrote to Hart, in October, 1958, Slim had been in
correspondence with Major-General Kirby, the chief author of the
Official History's *The War Against Japan* series. In a letter written on
the 22nd he commented: 'Wingate was one of the only two picturesque
and puzzling figures in Burma. (Stilwell was the other.)' As 1943 drew
to a close both these enigmatic and self-willed characters became Slim's
direct responsibility, for as Wingate's greatly expanded LRP group†
completed its training in India and moved to the forward zone it fell
under the operational control of 14th Army—and there, until and for
some time after Wingate's death, it remained.

Slim's life-pattern was founded on the concepts of trust, integrity,
loyalty. To dismiss this as an old-fashioned attitude is simply to ignore
the common ethic of all the main religions. In any case, it is fundamental to an understanding of his views about Wingate, since they
derived from a barely qualified distrust—distrust of the man and
distrust of his policies. As to the man, *Defeat into Victory* speaks
eloquently of the consequences of Wingate's death, praising his
magnetism, his dynamic power, his vivid imagination. But Slim had
there reserved his more private thoughts. When he sent to Giffard a
copy of the letter to General Kirby mentioned in the previous paragraph he remarked, in his covering note: 'In my opinion Wingate was

---

* Slim is less than just. The best Americans were in the Pacific or the Mediter-
ranean. Stilwell had to make bricks out of what was sometimes straw.
† Named, as a cover, 3 Indian Division, but more conveniently called Special
Force.

deliberately untruthful in some of his statements, and most disloyal in the method he frequently pursued of passing such statements behind the backs of some commanders to others.' (Giffard replied, simply, 'I never trusted him.') Elsewhere in Slim's papers there is clear evidence that in *Defeat into Victory* he spoke with an intentionally muted voice.

When he wrote to Kirby he was commenting on a draft of the relevant section in the *Official History*, and his careful scrutiny of the text led him to set down for the historian an appreciation which bluntly and honestly summarized an uneasy relationship.

I had a good deal of talk with Wingate on his theories of the role of LRP. His original conception was that his columns should be auxiliary to the main force and avoiding serious clashes would help them by cutting the enemy's communications, etc. Gradually, but more and more rapidly, he changed to picturing the LRP columns themselves as the main force and the normal corps and divisions as playing a subsidiary role on the perimeter. This entailed a much larger LRP force—several divisions in fact—and a heavier scale of equipment. This change in his ideas came before he had considered a 'stronghold' technique, but not as the result of it. The more this idea of a massive new model LRP force gained on Wingate, the more he demanded and schemed to increase his command, to raise the scale of its armament and enlarge its own air force. I think that unless this is clearly put much of his attitude towards Mountbatten, Giffard and in a lesser degree towards me will not be understandable.

At the time of his second expedition, he realized that such grandiose ideas were not practical as we had not the aircraft they would require, and he accepted, though with reluctance and not very genuinely, the role I gave him of 'Strategic Cavalry'. But he worked and schemed unceasingly to build up a great LRP force which would absorb a large part of the standard formations and would be very different from the original LRP columns. It would, in effect, have become a large but normal airborne, air-minded force. I had no objection to this idea—when aircraft were available for it—except that I believed that our ordinary divisions could be adapted—as later they were—by minor changes in equipment, to this airborne role, without all the complications and expense of raising new types of formations, which were less suitable to meet the Japanese in battle.

Soberly considered, I do not believe that the contribution of Special Force was either great in effect, or commensurate with the resources it absorbed. It was, I consider, surpassed by that of many of the normal divisions. Nor do I think, judging by what happened when the Japanese, even with inferior forces, made serious efforts against it, that

Wingate's ambitious visions of his columns as the main force could ever have been translated into reality.

This credo cannot but distress survivors of the Chindits, who joined in a form of crusade led by Wingate—in Slim's words—like a Peter the Hermit. Such a reaction is understandable, for many of them developed a total conviction as they undertook and endured their terrible ordeals; the fanatic is not easily shaken out of his faith—though even among the Chindits there were those who, in retrospect, questioned the capacities of their leader and the validity of their role. Moreover, a biography is not the place to analyse, with the minute attention to detail that would be necessary, the objective truth of Slim's appreciation. That it broadly conforms with the estimates of detached military observers, in the light of all the evidence available since the war, is probably the case, though Wingate has had impassioned apologists. His chief staff officer, the late Major-General Derek Tulloch, produced a powerful argument in defence of his leader which is weakened by its special pleading.* One of the most distinguished of the Chindit commanders, Brigadier Michael Calvert, has never faltered in his panegyric.

If one sets aside the issue of Wingate's personal integrity—as to which one can only say that Slim was not given to lying or to traducing a subordinate—the central fact, ignored by Wingate's defenders, still remains indisputable: he and his Army Commander were thinking about entirely different battles. Wingate was entitled to his ideas, and to the belief that they had been endorsed by Quebec—though that endorsement, as has been seen, was in relation to a scenario which subsequently dissolved.† He was entitled to believe that he had Churchill, Roosevelt and the Combined Chiefs of Staff behind him, for he had been told so in Canada. But the trump cards he thought he held in his hand were all played in favour of penetration—penetration ever further, ever deeper, involving larger and larger resources. During the winter of 1943 Slim formulated a very different conception.

Since Mountbatten first met him Slim had always accepted that the ideal plan for an offensive would be to concentrate on an amphibious operation. But when what he himself called 'the correct strategy of a

---

* Derek Tulloch, *Wingate in Peace and War.*
† Wingate was taken by Churchill to the Quebec Conference in August, 1943, where Wingate's proposals for an extensive Long Range Penetration project in 1944 were accepted by the Americans after endorsement by Churchill and the British Chiefs of Staff.

landing in *Southern Burma*'* was abandoned (as a project, but not as a possibility, for it still remained alive in the minds of Churchill and Mountbatten), he examined with greater attention his own commitment to advance with 4 Corps from Assam up to, and possibly beyond, the banks of the Chindwin. On this, the decisive central front, he now began to wonder whether he could effectively assemble and supply a sufficient number of divisions to overwhelm the forces they would have to meet, particularly as intelligence indicated that the Japanese in mid-Burma were reinforcing. At the same time a new and more positive concept came to dominate his thoughts.

> If we could somehow seriously weaken the Japanese Army *before* we plunged into Burma, the whole picture would be changed. The only way this could be done was, at an early stage, to entice the enemy into a major battle in circumstances so favourable to us that we could smash three or four of his divisions. The thought of how to do this constantly nagged at my mind, but my generalship was not enough to provoke such a battle.

Here, on a larger scale, was the offensive/defensive technique he had sought to apply in Arakan. There he had been thwarted because the Japanese, instead of advancing further north, had settled down for the monsoon season on the Maungdaw-Buthidaung line. This time, as he gradually came to see, the Japanese would not need to be enticed forward; they would come of their own accord. But the relevant point is that with ideas of this nature moving across his mind Slim was entirely justified in his caution over Wingate's ambitious propositions. His concept would require his main strength to be at the key point, not scattered over Burma. It makes more intelligible, for example, his anger at the breaking up of a trained and tested British division, the 70th, to provide columns for Special Force. He believed he had a better role for it.†

---

* In *Defeat into Victory*, written for the general reader, Slim sometimes used general expressions. 'Southern Burma' is probably shorthand for 'the seaward flank of the Japanese facing SEAC'.

† After Bernard Fergusson, a column commander in the first Wingate expedition, had returned and convalesced from his hardships, he was interrogated by the Commander-in-Chief, Auchinleck, about this proposal. Fergusson had advocated the transfer of a few battalions from 70 Division to Special Force. When he was told the whole division was to be transferred he quoted the Scotch minister whose prayer for rain during a drought was interrupted by a cloudburst: 'O Lord, I ken fine I was praying for rain, but this is fair ridiculous!'

In all the contorted relationship between Wingate and his Army Commander nothing was more surprising than its finale. Writing to General Kirby on 5 February, 1958, Slim mentioned Wingate's last visit to his headquarters and added, 'A remark made by Wingate at this meeting may interest you, as perhaps showing on what mutual terms this strange man and I stood. I originally put this remark into the draft of my book but cut it out as better not published. It was the last remark he ever made to me. I said good-bye to him in my office on 22 March and shook hands with him. As he went to the door he turned towards me again and said, apropos of nothing in particular, "You are the only senior officer in South East Asia who doesn't wish me dead!" '

CHAPTER TEN

THE RISING SUN

'The Army has now reached the stage of invincibility, and the day when the Rising Sun will proclaim our definite victory in India is not far off.'

General Mutaguchi

THE AMBITIOUS plans of the Anglo-American High Command for the Burma Theatre during the winter of 1943/44 underestimated the enemy. Their emphasis throughout was on the offensive—on converging attacks in the north (to recover Burma as a highway for the reinforcement of China by land and by air) and on a substantial amphibious assault in the south. For the various operations proposed as a result of the Quebec conference in August, and the summit meetings in Cairo and Teheran during November and December, the keynote was always 'Advance!' It is true that many of these schemes withered as a result of Chiang Kai-shek's intransigence, of the knowledge acquired at Teheran that Russia would declare war on Japan when Germany was defeated, and of soaring indents on landing craft for the invasion of France. By January, 1944, indeed:

All major amphibious operations were abandoned and instead of the seven major related operations there were to be only four smaller operations: the overland advance in Arakan, a limited advance and exploitation by 4 Corps, an advance on the Northern front and operations by LRP groups.*

It is to be noted, however, that even in this summary the *leitmotive* is

---

* *The War against Japan*, Vol. III., p. 66.

still 'advance' and 'exploitation'. At no time, in fact, does significant consideration appear to have been given at the Combined Chiefs of Staff level to the possibility of a major new Japanese offensive in SE Asia.

Nor is this surprising. The world-picture in all map-rooms now suggested an inescapable conclusion—that Japan, since Pearl Harbor, had stretched her resources too far. Indeed, decisions had already been taken in Tokyo to reduce an over-extended perimeter. The Allies were right to feel optimistic. But the Japanese object was to diminish strain on manpower and material, which meant holding the perimeter by the most economical method. Though elsewhere this might require a withdrawal, a contraction of front, it so happened that in western Burma the best answer was to advance. There were not enough divisions to guard the long line of the Chindwin in sufficient strength to repulse a British attack (which was anticipated) while fending off threats from Stilwell in the north and the uncertain menace of the Chinese armies beyond the Salween. But if the great plain of Imphal could be seized, at one stroke the base and supplies for a British offensive would be in Japanese hands and, since only three passes feed Imphal (and only the one via Kohima had a good road) the Japanese would have secured a strong forward bastion defensible with far greater economy against any future attack from India. To seize and grip the passes—that was the critical step.

Ever since a conference in Rangoon on 14 June, 1943, at the head-quarters of Lieut-General Kawabe, commander of Burma Area Army, the Japanese had been busily planning to this end. The two offensives that emerged were superficially distinct, but in fact united within a single strategic scheme. In Arakan 28th Army would attack early in 1944—Operation *Ha-Go*—apparently threatening India's southern approaches but actually aiming to tie down Slim's local divisions and Army reserves. Then, a few weeks later, while the British were well entangled in Arakan, Mutaguchi's 15th Army would launch Operation *U-Go* in the north. *U-Go* was intended to be an *attaque brusquée*, with the specific object of capturing Imphal's plain and passes so swiftly that the monsoon would have arrived before Slim could re-group his reserves and counter-attack. By the next dry season the Imphal bastion would be solid and secure. The Japanese could sit there comfortably or, theoretically, use it as a launching-pad for a later advance into India. But no 'March on Delhi' was seriously envisaged as a consequence of *U-Go*, though the siren voice of Subhas Chandra Bose, commander of the renegade Indian National Army, suggested plausibly that a successful Japanese offensive would set a combustible India alight.*

As commander of 14th Army Slim had a direct responsibility in the field for all the residual operations which, as the *Official History* records, had survived in January, 1944, from the Allies' more ambitious plans. Arakan and 4 Corps at Imphal were obviously under his direction, as were Wingate and Special Force once they moved into action from India, while Stilwell's advance in the Hukawng valley also fell within Slim's ambit as a result of the American's refusal to accept Giffard's authority. Logic, as has been seen, argued against a Japanese general offensive. Nevertheless, while Slim and his subordinates prepared during the winter of 1943/44 for the limited advances which they themselves were committed to undertake, according to the directives of the Allied High Command, they sensed with an increasing aware-ness that something was stirring. There were many low-level indica-tions—patrol reports, the results of air reconnaissance, etc. An ambush by 4 Corps troops on the Chindwin, on 27 January, produced clinching evidence; for prisoner-identification revealed the presence there of elements of the Japanese 15 Division (still, in fact, filtering slowly northward from Siam). This new division on the central front could only mean trouble for 4 Corps.† As for Arakan, both Slim and Christison were well aware that the Japanese had recently introduced an Army headquarters—28th Army—and that this could only presage an offensive.

By the end of January, in fact, Slim possessed the broad details of his enemy's strength, though not of his strategic or tactical intentions. Like Montgomery, who tried to deduce his opponents' mentality from their portraits in his caravan, Slim pinned to his office wall a photo-graph of Kawabe: 'The bullet head, the thick glasses, and the prominent teeth were all there.' But this taught him little more than his own reflections on the Russo-Japanese war, and his knowledge that the enemy facing him had been imbued with the spirit of their fathers who 'were prepared to throw in every man, and more than once tipped the scales of victory with their very last reserves'. If this suggested a fight *à outrance*, the scale of Japanese reinforcement certainly implied that

---

* A 'March on Delhi' is one thing, by-products from *Ha-Go* and *U-Go* another, and there is no doubt that, while invasion of India was not their purpose, the Japanese did anticipate widespread disorders in Bengal and Bihar, both critically sensitive areas for SEAC.

† An appreciation issued by Scoones on 3 February distilled these suspicions.

conflict was not far distant. Apart from 56 and 18 Divisions opposing the Chinese in Yunnan and on the Ledo Road, and the developments in Arakan, on the central front Mutaguchi's 15th Army now contained 31 and 33 Divisions, reinforced, as was now known, by the inflowing units of 15 Division.

Slim's situation was ambivalent and dangerous. An army attacked when it is itself deploying for attack is in the worst posture for defence, both practically and psychologically. When Rommel moved against the Gazala Line in the summer of 1942 the British were caught disastrously in just such a dilemma, holding positions which were primarily start-lines for their own offensive and inhibited in their freedom of manoeuvre by the great dumps of supplies which had been accumulated close behind their front in anticipation of a certain advance. Similarly 14th Army, preparing to re-enter Burma (if only modestly), had made an immense administrative effort to stock-pile in the forward zone, particularly at Dimapur and Imphal, the infrastructure necessary to maintain the dynamism of an attack. 'The whole layout of 4 Corps area', Slim wrote, 'and the dispositions of its fighting formations were designed with the idea of our taking the offensive.' Nevertheless, the ultimate defeat of the enemy on both his endangered fronts would owe much of its success to his use of the Japanese technique of *ju-jitsu*— the conversion of this weakness to an advantage.

A pattern gradually formed in his mind. He must continue to prepare for the operations which he had been instructed to undertake. In the north this meant a move to the Chindwin by 4 Corps in conjunction with Stilwell's thrust on Myitkyina from Ledo, while Special Force disrupted the Japanese rear. In Arakan 15 Corps must advance down the peninsula to capture or at least neutralize Akyab, whose airfields were a perpetual menace to Calcutta. But if a Japanese offensive, which he expected, forestalled either or both of these operations then his 'anti-infiltration strategy', to which he had devoted so much thought in the past year, would immediately be applied. In Arakan forward troops would stand fast, supplied by air, and cut off the retreat of the infiltrating Japanese while his reserves moved up to destroy them. At Imphal, by contrast, his forward divisions (widely dispersed in preparation for an advance to the Chindwin) would have to retire at the outset to the perimeter of the Imphal plain and there hold the entry-points. Meanwhile any infiltrating Japanese would have their retreat blocked while Slim's reserves of infantry and armour destroyed them on the killing-ground of Imphal. The scenario was bold, simple and intelligible. Would it work? At least it was a plan which, unlike those of previous British generals, was based on a realistic estimate of Japanese methods and an assessment of how the Allies' material advantages could be used to counter the enemy's skills.

As Slim calmly calculated the answers to his problems, shuttling between Giffard, Scoones and Christison, there was one outstanding question whose dimensions increased as its relevance to the approaching battle diminished—Wingate. The employment of Special Force was mandatory on Slim. Ever since Wingate's remarkable success at Quebec, there was an inescapable commitment to the Americans for its use in the North Burma Theatre, a commitment emphasized by the presence there of No. 1 Air Commando.* Slim was the first to recognize that this combat unit, enthusiastically supplied by the Americans for LRP purposes, must be used in support of Wingate, and Wingate alone; he resisted all attempts to divert it in other directions. Mountbatten, conscious of the political implications and naturally responsive to the unorthodox, was even more anxious that the commitment should be honoured. The President, the Prime Minister, the Combined Chiefs of Staff and the Supreme Commander were a formidable combination.

Though he questioned the military value of many of Wingate's ideas and suspected him of megalomania, Slim did not oppose the commitment. As a sensible soldier he recognized that he was 'landed' with it and concentrated on finding for Special Force a viable role which would be not too demanding on manpower and equipment. (This was not easy, for already Special Force had absorbed one complete division, 70, and the equivalent of another by way of eight battalions and a West African brigade.) But there was a fundamental difficulty. As men, Slim and Wingate retained sufficient respect for each other's qualities to be able to work together, if only in an atmosphere of armed neutrality. As soldiers, they differed absolutely in their appreciation of the military reality, whose character gradually altered during the darkening eve of the Japanese offensive.

Once the great concentric thrust from Yunnan, the Ledo Road and Assam, Operation TARZAN, was abandoned, the dramatic potentialities for Long Range Penetration which Wingate had brilliantly expounded at Quebec were reduced in scale. Not a single Chinese soldier was

---

* Under Colonel Cochrane of the USAAF, this was a unique force of 30 fighter-bombers, 12 medium bombers, 25 transport planes, 100 light aircraft, 6 helicopters and 225 gliders.

likely to advance from Yunnan. In view of the Japanese build-up, even if 4 Corps advanced it was unlikely to get far beyond the Chindwin, and it seemed more probable (indeed, this was what Slim now wanted) that the next battle would be at Imphal and not in Burma. Thus Stilwell's march on Myitkyina became the operation most likely to benefit from an LRP disruption of Japanese communications, and it was to this end that thinking about Special Force was directed. Since Slim had a responsibility for Stilwell (and since, indeed, any success on that front must be indirectly beneficial for his own) he took the common-sense line of supporting practically and helpfully a project of which he did not, in his heart, approve—but, so far as lay within his power, *not* to the point of weakening dangerously the resources on which he relied for the great battle he anticipated at Imphal. Long Range Penetration was tangential to his policy of defending offensively the *enceinte*. The employment of Special Force therefore involved long and animated discussions.

Although he was in almost continuous orbit between his own head-quarters, Arakan, Imphal, Stilwell's front and the headquarters of Mountbatten and Giffard in Delhi, Slim conferred with Wingate twice in November, four times in December, and eight times in January—at first in Delhi and later in Comilla, that faded and dispiriting Bengali town where 14th Army HQ had come to roost, and Slim's office in the Courts of Justice looked out on walls 'peppered with plaques com-memorating civil and police officers who had been killed by Bengali terrorists'.* Slim took a sardonic interest in this *memento mori*.

Since Wingate was incapable of appreciating any view but his own, discussions were difficult. As soon as TARZAN seemed in danger, he looked for other ways of extending the scope of Special Force, to which end, on 3 December at Comilla, he demanded from Slim the use of 26 Division. But this was the only reserve formation in 14th Army. Since a major battle was looming, Slim promptly refused. Wingate played his ace—the instruction Churchill gave him at Quebec to com-municate with the Prime Minister direct, if necessary. Slim trumped the ace. 'I pushed a signal pad across my desk to him, and told him to go and write his message. He did not take the pad but he left the room.

---

* See Ralph Arnold, *A Very Quiet War*, p. 104. Arnold was Assistant Director of Public Relations, 14th Army. (200 miles east of Calcutta, and 200, as the crow flies, from Imphal, Comilla was in fact far more convenient as a command post than Barrackpore).

Whether he ever sent the message I do not know, nor did I inquire. Anyhow that was the last I heard of his demand for 26 Division.'

With dedicated pertinacity Wingate continued to argue his case, and Slim to surrender nothing he considered vital for the main battle, until the final plan was shaped for Operation THURSDAY—the fly-in of the Chindit brigades (with one, Fergusson's 16th, marching south from Stilwell's country), the concept of the strongholds, etc, all with the object of dominating the Mandalay–Myitkyina railway within an area of 40 miles radius from Indaw. Cutting the communications of the Japanese 18 Division, Special Force would thus aid Stilwell's advance southwards. (The assumption also was that some supply-routes to the Japanese opposite 4 Corps would be interrupted.) Detailed operational orders were not finally issued until 28 February, nor were they achieved without occasional offers to resign on Wingate's part, and passionate proposals that THURSDAY should be abandoned. Mountbatten and Slim tactfully contrived to smooth over these demonstrations which, disproportionate though they may have been, were dangerous in the sense that an emotional signal from Wingate to Churchill was always capable of causing the Prime Minister to erupt. Pownall noted the risk in his diary for 28 January: 'This will bring the PM straight down on to Giffard and Slim, for he has already expressed his doubts as to the quality of the military advice that Mountbatten has been receiving. He will jump at any chance of breaking another general or two and will then push very hard, and maybe successfully, to get Wingate installed in command of 14th Army—which would be a most dangerous affair.'

Indeed! For, in spite of his outstanding gifts of imagination, invention, exposition and leadership, Wingate, who had no staff training, was unsure in his control of forces in the field and too liable, having made his own picture, to read a tactical or strategical situation in its light. His continuing resentment at Slim's refusal to unleash 14th Army in support of his Chindit penetration revealed a profound misinterpretation of the likely state of affairs when the Japanese attack, which he claimed to have foreseen, finally occurred; a profound misinterpretation, also, of Slim's pugnacity, for in a memorandum to Mountbatten of 10 February Wingate referred contemptuously to 14th Army: 'which can hardly be expecting ever to operate beyond the mountain barrier with its present establishment after the experience of the past two years.' He could not grasp that Slim sought a *coup de grâce* before and not after he advanced from the Imphal Plain. Lacking in empathy, he was also unaware that the man who had led the Retreat was committed in his heart to leading the Return.

Fanatics command sympathy by the quality of their conviction, and Wingate's was absolute. Reservations about the validity of his projects do not prevent respect for his ardour and his dedication. But it is equally impossible to withhold sympathy from Slim. Faced with problems on every side, he had also to treat with not only the most dynamic, but also the most contumacious, subordinate of his career. It was a tragedy that Wingate and he could not come together, *bras dessus bras dessous*, and explore in rational discourse the new ideas which Slim was evolving for the destruction of Mutaguchi's army. There was a failure of communication; but it is doubtful whether any commander senior to Wingate—except perhaps Wavell—achieved a sufficient *rapport* with him to talk in these terms. The creator of Special Force was a man apart.

As Army Commander Slim was now concerned with the hundreds of essentially short-range problems presented by the prospect of an imminent battle. But a battle on a considerable scale only gains point and relevance if it fits into a larger, long-term strategical purpose. It is worth remembering, therefore, that while the victories which Slim was about to achieve in Arakan and at Imphal seem to lead effortlessly and inevitably into his reconquest of Burma, alternative strategies were being promoted in London and Washington, at the same time as the *Ha-Go/U-Go* offensive, which would have produced a very different result.

The decisions of the Cairo and Teheran conferences left Mountbatten dissatisfied. If, as the Combined Chiefs of Staff informed him, Germany would probably be defeated before the end of 1944, he envisaged a huge influx into SEAC of landing craft and other equipment with which major amphibious operations could be mounted. His planners agreed, recommending that 'the Japanese in Burma should therefore be contained by the minimum air and land forces required to deny them freedom of action, and the forces available to SEAC should be used to launch a major offensive elsewhere'. The 'elsewhere' proposed was northern Sumatra, whose seizure, Operation CULVERIN, was to be followed by moves against Malaya or in the area of the Sunda Strait. Had this policy been adopted,* Slim and 14th Army might have

---

* If the plan for CULVERIN had been accepted, it is still, of course, an open question whether Germany's refusal to admit defeat before the end of 1944 would not have

become the residuary legatees of SEAC, bequeathed a disregarded portion of the estate. There might have been no triumphant return through the heart of Burma for the man who had conducted the Retreat. Without the enhancement of his brilliant stroke at Meiktila, and the race for Rangoon, Slim's subsequent reputation would then have lacked the full, rounded quality that derives from absolute victory.

On 5 February Mountbatten despatched a team of senior staff officers, the AXIOM Mission, to lay his views before the British and American Chiefs in London and Washington. They carried with them also a dissenting statement from Stilwell, who naturally demanded a forward policy in north Burma rather than dissipation of effort, as he saw it, in Sumatran sideshows. It soon became evident, moreover, that, without informing his Supreme Commander, Stilwell had sent his own mission to Washington, prepared to use every method—the press, radio, political lobbies—to block Mountbatten's proposals. Many factors entered into the prolonged debates in both capitals, which, to the Supreme Commander's disappointment, culminated in the rejection of the Sumatra scheme. A critical one was the discovery, about the end of February, that the Japanese main fleet was lying at Singapore; its significance for CULVERIN was obvious. And on 25 February Roosevelt, certainly influenced by Stilwell's envoys, signalled to Churchill: 'I most urgently hope that you back to the maximum a vigorous and immediate campaign in Upper Burma.' This is not the place to analyse in further detail the AXIOM Mission, for it is abundantly clear that amid the controversies it aroused during those spring months of 1944 the future of Slim and his 14th Army was temporarily in the balance.

Yet Slim himself, however much he may have been aware of these high-level discussions, could waste no time on the future. He now had a battle on his hands and was preoccupied by the demands of the insistent present. During the winter Christison had edged forward his two Indian divisions in Arakan, 5 and 7, so that by the end of January they were in general contact with the road which runs westward from Buthidaung and reaches Maungdaw by the famous tunnels beneath the central Mayu range. Slightly to the north, lateral communications had been established over the Ngakyedauk Pass, at whose eastern exit a considerable maintenance area had been laid out—the Administrative

---

proved an insuperable barrier. Could the necessary resources have been released to the East? The history of DRACULA (see next chapter) is instructive.

Box at Sinzweya—where large stocks of war stores had been established.
Christison was now deploying for a further thrust. In a flash, during the
early hours of 4 February, it seemed as though once again the British
in Arakan were in disarray. A Japanese out-flanking force had sprung
a surprise and started to cut ruthlessly into the rearward areas of the
Corps. Was the old pattern to be repeated?

A Japanese offensive in Arakan, as has been seen, was not unexpected.
But the shock caused by *Sakurai force*, as it filtered through the early
morning mists past British posts in the Kalapanzin valley, would have
been less if certain last-minute indicators had been correctly interpreted.
Brigadier Michael Roberts, with his 114 Brigade of 7 Indian Division,
was away to the east of the Kalapanzin River. (It was through his
troops that the main column of *Sakurai force* slipped, but they destroyed
the Japanese supply section and rearguard.)

> On 21 Jan. one of my battalions infiltrating through the Arakan Hills
> to get into position to envelop Buthidaung caught a large party of
> Japs digging in. The Japs were surprised and fled, leaving three dead
> (and much equipment and rifles) behind. The three dead were all of
> 112 Regt. I told 7 Div HQ at once and in view of the steadily increas-
> ing activity my patrols had reported I said that there was at least a
> battalion of 112 Regt in the area. Corps intelligence said that they knew
> there were some 112 Regt recce patrols in the area, but that was all.
> Two intelligence staff officers from Corps came to see me and more or
> less told me I had got the wind up.
>
> At the end of January a commando raid on the Arakan coast south
> of Maungdaw found elements of 144 Regt, the missing regiment of
> 55th Division last heard of in the Pacific. Soon afterwards the blow
> fell. Corps 'I' hadn't even had time to tell me that my guess about 112
> Regt was right!! I apologised to Christison later that I had only
> suspected one bn of 112 Regt instead of all three. He replied that my
> wisecrack was well justified.*

Since the battalion of 112 Regiment constituted the main element in
Sakurai force, a more alert reaction to this front line evidence might have
been critical in averting surprise.

---

* Private communication. The raid was actually carried out by 81 (West African)
Reconnaissance Regiment. The special significance of 144 Regt was that it appeared to have relieved 112 Regt, which had been holding that strip of coast,
and this fitted with the identification of 112 Regt unexpectedly north of Buthidaung.

But the Japanese were behind his lines. Slim now had his first experience of fighting a considerable battle in conditions of crisis-management.* And he was ill. When the first obscure message reached him at Comilla on the morning of the 4th he had just had his ninth daily emetine injection for dysentery. But as *Ha-Go* developed, and *U-Go* followed, those who watched him observed that as in the crises of the Retreat he continued to display the qualities noted by Voltaire in Marlborough, 'That calm courage in the midst of tumult, that serenity of soul in danger, which the English call a cool head.'

For imposing his will on the violent battle now raging in Arakan Slim had substantial resources, even though he had undoubtedly been caught at a disadvantage. To begin with, the Japanese offensives, both *Ha-Go* and the later *U-Go*, were based on contempt; all their previous experience of the British suggested to Kawabe and Mutaguchi that once again their troops would have a partridge-drive. But training and indoctrination had moulded 14th Army into a skilful and confident adversary, and if Slim had found Kawabe inscrutable, Kawabe had certainly not taken the measure of Slim or realized that this British commander was not one to be rushed off balance. Secondly, though the opening moves in *Ha-Go* had not been precisely anticipated, Giffard, Slim and Christison had all deduced from the available evidence that an offensive was imminent. Indeed, the key to victory was already in Slim's hand, for he had warned Snelling to bring to the highest pitch of readiness the air supply units at Comilla and Agartala.† As soon as the Japanese attacked pre-arranged packing programmes were put into effect; 'the complete maintenance of over a division for several days, everything that it would require, from pills to projectiles, from bully beef to boots, was laid out, packed for dropping, at the airstrips.' And so, when 7 Division's communications were cut and its Administrative Box surrounded, air supply was turned on automatically. In spite of some initial interruptions by Japanese fighters, it was sustained so that

---

* Of course there were many engagements during the Retreat, but no individual battle on the scale of Second Arakan and the opening phase of *U-Go*.
† Throughout the operation Slim and Snelling worked in close co-operation with General Old and his US Combat Cargo Force. With Old, as with Air Marshal Sir John Baldwin of 3 Tactical Air Force, and indeed with all the senior airmen Slim maintained consistently good relations. Their crews, in consequence, drove themselves and their aircraft beyond the accepted limits on behalf of 14th Army. Baldwin and Air Marshal Vincent, of 221 Group, whose fighters and fighter-bombers defended Imphal, both told the author that they simply felt part of the Army. Vincent shared Slim's mess until Rangoon was reached.

in the course of the battle 714 sorties were flown and some 2,300 tons of supplies dropped. Besides the routine requirements of war—food, ammunition, fuel, fodder for animals, water—the packing lists were flexible enough to be able to include mail, plasma, drugs, outsize boots, the *SEAC* newspaper, typewriter ribbons, socks, spectacles, razors and tooth brushes.

This facility of supply would have been of far less value if the doctrine Slim had been preaching so consistently had failed to find an attentive congregation—if the troops of 15 Corps had lacked the spirit, when cut off or surrounded, to stand fast and fight.* The oft-told story of the defence of the Administrative Box, and many another episode during the three weeks' battle, show how new leadership had bred a new self-confidence. It was here that the Japanese miscalculated. Without air supply or armour. Hanaya threw the main burden of the attack on some 8,000 men from his 55 Division—an outflanking force under Major-General Sakurai Tohutaro, and sundry smaller infiltration units. In earlier days speed, surprise and shock would have succeeded even with so diminutive a spearhead; there was a fair chance that the British would have collapsed. Now Slim's old Corps stood firm. During the defence of the Administrative Box even such unwarlike units as an Officers' Shop, a Mule Company and a Field Supply Depot manned the perimeter and furnished fighting patrols. The steadiness of his forward troops provided an anvil against which Slim could destroy the Japanese with the sledge-hammer of his reserves.

That these were copious and ready was due to the foresight of Slim and Giffard. On the eve of the attack Slim had warned Lomax at Chittagong that his 26 Division must be prepared to move at short notice from reserve into battle. Giffard also told Festing, commanding 36 Division, that he too must be alert for a move from Army Group reserve in India to replace Lomax. As the Japanese met with resistance instead of collapse, and started to run out of supplies, both these divisions were fed in smoothly, and by 24 February Hanaya had accepted defeat, with a loss of 5,000 out of his 8,000 invaders.

Almost without a pause, 15 Corps reverted to the offensive. In *Defeat into Victory* Slim asserted that Second Arakan represented 'one

---

* This is an important point. It was only as the battle developed that the air-supply so carefully pre-planned by Slim and Snelling paid full dividends. Had the troops of 15 Corps not stood up to the first shock of *Ha-Go*, and had Japanese infiltration got out of control in the early stages, the picture might have been very different.

of the historic successes of British arms. It was the turning-point of the Burma campaign.' In one sense this was so, for Slim could justifiably claim that he had smashed the legend of Japanese invincibility in the jungle, and thus incalculably reinforced the morale of his army. But it is sometimes maintained that in spite of a tactical success he had been brought within measurable distance of a strategic defeat.

In his conscientious and self-questioning way Slim did not dismiss such criticisms. Many years later, in 1959, General Kirby interrogated him bluntly, suggesting that by the beginning of March, 1944, Slim had committed six of twelve divisions in South East Asia Command to the Arakan front, while '4 Corps was left with its original three divisions to meet the enemy offensive which it was confidently expected would begin within a very few weeks'. Could Slim explain?

Slim replied to the Official Historian on 24 April, 1959, with characteristic honesty, humility and clarity:

> The question raised in your letter—why did I not move divisions from Arakan to Imphal earlier than I did—is a fair one. Obviously in view of what happened, I ought to have done so, and if you say I made a mistake, I shall not contradict you. Looking back it was an obvious error on my part—no one else had any responsibility for it. But in the time between repulse of the Japanese Arakan Offensive and their invasion of Assam, things were neither so clear-cut nor so obvious.
>
> I am not trying to explain away a mistake but certain factors influenced me to delay the move:
>
> a. I heavily reinforced Arakan—probably too heavily—because
>
> (i) This was to be our first major test against the Japanese in our come-back, and I was not prepared at that stage to undertake it on equal terms. I wanted the greatest superiority I could get. Completely to destroy a Japanese offensive would, I thought, have the greatest moral effect on our troops.
>
> (ii) I expected before the battle was over to have to meet the best part of two Japanese Divisions.
>
> (iii) I was not altogether happy about the firmness of the local command. They had allowed themselves to be surprised, their Headquarters had (with my approval) been pulled back, and, while the troops were steady enough, it was necessary quickly to restore confidence in the command.
>
> b. The Administrative Staffs behind Fourteenth Army were insistent that no more troops could be maintained in Imphal until the ration strength (largely non-combatant) in that area was reduced. However, these non-combatant forces were required to re-adjust the Imphal

layout and build defences before being withdrawn. I should have evacuated them at this time more rapidly than I did and in any case I ought to have paid less attention to the fears of Administrative Staffs.
c. I kept the 5th, 7th and 36th Divisions for the follow-up offensive against the Japanese because I hoped to keep them on the run and rapidly to exploit our success. When resistance around Razabil, etc. proved more determined than I expected, I allowed the more experienced divisions to remain to overcome it.
d. I calculated I could use all available divisions to smash the Japanese in Arakan and still have time to move by rail and air at least one to Imphal before Japanese pressure there became intense.
e. As regards 25 Div, it was new and untried. I wanted to use it to relieve 5 or 7 Div in Arakan and use the battle-tried Divisions in whom I had confidence as reinforcements for Imphal. I should no doubt have been wiser as things turned out to have started the relief in Arakan as soon as 25 Div began to arrive.
f. My basic error was that I was too optimistic about the way the Imphal battle would go. . . .
I am afraid this letter has been rather long but it is hard to describe how different things look in the midst of a battle from what they do afterwards, and how hard it is—or was at least to me—to pick out which factors were sure and which uncertain.

Here is a classic illustration by one general of a dictum by another—that observation of General Wolfe which was a favourite of Wavell: 'War is an option of difficulties.' Slim was also putting to Kirby in another form the truth once stated by that shrewd historian F. W. Maitland: 'It is difficult to remember that events now far in the past were once in the future.'

Too much was made of this matter by General Kirby, who seemed to suggest that Slim in Arakan had done what the Japanese wanted him to do, i.e. get his front line divisions into so disastrous a posture that he would have to send in reserve formations which would themselves become inextricably involved. Nothing like this happened. Only 7 Division suffered significantly—of the 3,506 casualties in 15 Corps over half were from 7 Division and its associated troops. Slim could have relieved 5 and/or 7 Division earlier than he did, but his case is strong for retaining them to ensure and exploit his victory. 25, 26 and 36 Divisions were not 'committed' in the sense that, after the short sharp quelling of *Ha-Go*, they were immovably pinned to the ground. The deeper truth is that while Slim was right about *Ha-Go* he was wrong about the initial phase of *U-Go*. It was miscalculation about what would happen when Mutaguchi attacked, as will be seen, that created a need for reinforcements from Arakan more urgently than had been anticipated. Even so, the divisions were available.

Before he became immersed in 'the way the Imphal battle would go' Slim had to see to the dispatch of Wingate's THURSDAY force and to explain its implications to Stilwell. With his two American-trained Chinese divisions, 22 and 38, and his American equivalent of the Chindits, the Long Range Penetration Regiment (better known as Merrill's Marauders) Stilwell had been moving steadily southward during the winter, drawing the Ledo Road behind him. On 3 March Slim flew to his headquarters, where Stilwell was poised to thrust the Japanese 18 Division down the Hukawng Valley towards his strategic objective—as laid down by the Combined Chiefs of Staff—of Myitkyina, whose airfield would so greatly facilitate the supply route to China.

Stilwell's sense of insecurity and his confidence in Slim were curiously demonstrated during this meeting, when he confided the news that he had a secret plan for taking Myitkyina by a surprise *coup*, involving the Marauders in a stiff out-flanking march through the mountains. 'He asked me very solemnly', Slim wrote, 'not to speak of it to *anyone*, and made it quite clear that that included not only my staff but my superior commanders.' Nothing could better illustrate their anomalous relationship than this curious revelation of Stilwell's plans for attaining what was, after all, his prescribed objective. Slim accepted with good humour the explanation that, if the plan reached Delhi, there might be leaks—ignoring Stilwell's implicit aspersion on Mountbatten and Giffard, and the fact that Slim, too, had important projects which were shared with SEAC and 11 Army Group!

Of more immediate significance was Slim's ability to convince Stilwell that THURSDAY, whose fly-in was due to begin in two days' time, had a direct bearing on the drive to Myitkyina, since the rear areas of the Japanese 18 Division would be disrupted by Wingate's brigades. Stilwell was dubious. 'At last he grinned at me over his glasses and said, "That'll be fine if Wingate does it and stays there; if he goes in for real fighting and not shadow boxing like last time".' To this reasonable comment Slim replied, in effect, that THURSDAY was not going to be a perambulation. Indeed, the danger, as proved to be the case, was that Wingate's new technique of 'strongholds' might well lead to his columns being pinned down in death-grapples with the Japanese.

The two generals parted on good terms, and a further essay in amity occurred on the 6th, when Mountbatten arrived, on a visit designed to bridge the breach in relations caused by Stilwell sending to Washington his secret embassy to argue against the amphibious policy presented by the Axiom Mission. Stilwell now made a request which, had it produced a quick result, would have benefited Slim as well as himself. He asked Mountbatten to get the Combined Chiefs of Staff to persuade Chiang Kai-shek that his Yunnan armies should at last attack, thus taking some of the strain off Stilwell, off Wingate's columns, and off 4 Corps at Imphal. The next day, however, a bamboo stem, springing up from beneath the front of his jeep, damaged Mountbatten's left eye and confined him in the American hospital at Ledo, heavily bandaged, until the 14th. The request to Washington was not despatched until the 17th, and though Roosevelt wrote vigorously to Chiang Kai-shek on the 19th the Generalissimo had already signalled his inability to move from Yunnan across the Salween because the Japanese were about to start operations in China. The old pattern of *non possumus* was repeated. Slim could therefore expect no relief from the east for Stilwell, for Scoones, or for Wingate.

The first of Wingate's brigades, 16, under Bernard Fergusson, had already been on the move for nearly a month. Leaving Ledo on 8 February, it struggled southwards through intolerable country until, by 5 March, it had reached and crossed the Chindwin. Fergusson's weary troops were now making for the area of Indaw, to set up a stronghold, ABERDEEN, and interfere with enemy reinforcement. That same day, the 5th, THURSDAY began in strength with the glider-borne fly-in of 77 Brigade under Michael Calvert. Slim, who had rushed back to Comilla from seeing Stilwell, returned to Lalaghat airfield in Assam, where 80 gliders stood waiting in pairs for the take-off, due to begin at 5 pm. On that Sunday afternoon there were assembled, at what was truly an historic moment, Slim, General Old, Baldwin, Cochrane and, of course, Wingate. At 4.30 pm tension was high, though the Chindits were laudably calm. A light aircraft from the Air Commando suddenly arrived and Colonel Gaty, USAAF, produced for an astonished company photographs taken with a hand camera, a few hours previously, of the three landing strips, PICCADILLY, BROADWAY and CHOWRINGHEE, on which 77 and thereafter 111 Brigades were to descend.

The truth about the next few minutes can never be absolutely known, since the evidence of responsible eye witnesses is conflicting. Some say that Wingate kept his head. Some say that he took the decision to proceed with THURSDAY. Others disagree. What is certain is that the photographs showed PICCADILLY to be covered with obstacles,* and raised the possibility that the Japanese had been alerted, though BROADWAY and CHOWRINGHEE were clear.

Slim's own account in *Defeat into Victory* was based on notes he made nearer to the event. Wingate, he observed, was in an emotional state, maintaining that it would be murder to send his men on to the unobstructed landing-strips, as these were probably surrounded by Japanese. When Slim took him on one side and persuaded him that this was unlikely, Wingate declared: 'The responsibility is yours.'

> I knew it was. Not for the first time I felt the weight of decision crushing in on me with an almost physical pressure. . . . I knew that if I cancelled the fly-in or even postponed it, when the men were keyed to the highest pitch, there would be a terrible reaction; we would never get their morale to the same peak again. The whole plan of campaign, too, would be thrown out. I had promised Stilwell we would cut the communications of the enemy opposing him, and he was relying on our doing it. I had to consider also that one Chindit brigade had already marched into the area. . . . 'The operation will go on,' I said.†

This statement has an inherent probability. It is buttressed by the fact that Slim was incapable of telling a lie, whether in his own defence or to harm another. He was human, and he could forget. But his memory of this traumatic episode was too specific to suggest that its details had faded in his mind. It had certainly not faded before the end of the war. While he was still in command of 14th Army he issued for limited circulation within the Army a personal account, marked 'Secret', of its campaigns. Describing the scene at Lalaghat he wrote: 'General Wingate was convinced that the whole plan of operations had been betrayed and at first wished to postpone it. I was most averse to postponing the operation.' It was not in character for Slim to try to mislead his own Army on a matter of this kind. Moreover, he carefully went over the ground again in 1958, when commenting on drafts of the *Official History*. 'I am quite certain', he wrote to General Kirby on 22 October, 'that when PICCADILLY was found to be obstructed,

---

* In fact these were not obstructions laid by the Japanese, but felled trees left in a normal way by foresters.
† *Defeat into Victory*, p. 261–2.

Wingate's own immediate reaction to me was to stop the fly-in. .... It was not a case of my "allowing it (the fly-in) to be carried out"; I *ordered* it to go on if Baldwin agreed on the air side ... it was not up to Wingate to *"confirm"* my decision, which was an order.'

It is therefore interesting that two days after the shock of Lalaghat Wingate should have composed a report in which he presented himself as responsible for the decision to continue with THURSDAY.* He was highly wrought, almost manic in his oscillations between euphoria and pessimism. To one capable, like Wingate, of attempting suicide, the dark side of things can seem impenetrably blank. When he re-crossed the Chindwin after his first expedition he was met by General Savory; his first words were, 'I expect they'll court martial me.' Yet after a meal and a long sleep he woke to find that the Press had made him a hero, and adopted the role. Slim, by contrast, was calm in this as in many other crises. Even Tulloch, the disciple to whom Wingate was *guru*, wrote: 'I admired Slim tremendously on that occasion. He had, of course, a poker face—useful for any commander—which enabled him to appear completely unruffled, indeed almost unconcerned. Yet the final decision to go on with the operation rested squarely on his shoulders, and in the event of disaster he would carry a major share of the blame.'

As the gliders flew off to BROADWAY—the first only 70 minutes late on take-off, in spite of the changes of plan—Slim remained for a while in the control tent, refreshed with hot sweet tea by Tulloch's batman, gay in a red American jockey cap. But there was little gaiety among those who waited—Old, Baldwin, the Chindit staff. Reports and rumours of gliders crashed or astray were followed, in the early hours of the morning, by a signal from Calvert at BROADWAY—'Soya Link'—indicating that things had gone wrong. 'So the Japanese *had* ambushed BROADWAY! Wingate was right and I had been wrong. He gave me a bitter look and walked away. I had no answer for him.'†

But it was Slim who had been right. At daylight the code-words 'Pork Sausage' confirmed that all was well, and by 10 March 9,000

---

* For the full report see Derek Tulloch, *op cit*, p. 198.
† Calvert's second-in-command, Colonel Rome, was among them. 'Claud', Brigadier Calvert recalled in *Prisoners of Hope*, 'told me Slim was a tower of strength—absolutely calm, absolutely in the picture and worth a guinea a minute to the staff whose nerves became badly shaken as they realized how badly astray some of the gliders were going.' In sending 'Soya Link' Calvert had not himself panicked; it was a justifiable situation report in the light of the casualties and confusion before dawn brought reassurance.

troops and 1,100 animals had already been deposited in the rear of Mutaguchi's 15 Army. The initial reaction of the Japanese was that they were of no consequence. In any case, they had other preoccupations. On the 7th, as Calvert's men furiously converted BROADWAY into a stronghold, columns of the Japanese 33 Division began to move westwards by jungle tracks across the mountains in a march which would carry them to the rim of Imphal. It was the opening gambit in the game called *U-Go*.

CHAPTER ELEVEN

THE PLAIN OF KNIGHTS

'It was a glorious victory, wasn't it?' said the White Knight, as
he came up panting.

Lewis Carroll, *Alice in Wonderland*

SHORTLY BEFORE Christmas Day, 1944, the Viceroy of India flew
up to Imphal to take part in a unique and memorable ceremony. It
was on 15 December that Slim paraded himself and his three Corps
Commanders, Scoones, Christison and Stopford, to be dubbed as
knights by Wavell in the plain to whose victorious defence all four, in
different measure, had made their distinctive contribution—Slim by
direction of a whole Army, Scoones by his conduct of the siege,
Stopford by the relief of Kohima and Imphal itself, and Christison by
preventing an initial disaster in Arakan. In sight of the mountains where
the Japanese had crept so close Slim was heard to issue one of the most
unorthodox orders of his career: 'Lieutenant-Generals, by the right,
quick march!'

It is a curious human fact that these seasoned commanders, who had
endured so many shocks and strains, were now uneasy. Slim was
certainly on edge. His Chief Engineer, Major-General Hasted, borrowed
a couple of scrapers from a local airfield construction unit to make a
parade ground for the occasion. When he asked his Army Commander
whether it was satisfactory, Slim grunted nervously, 'There's more
than enough room for me to make a fool of myself!' And several
witnesses observed how Stopford, that redoubtable Rifleman, was
petrified with apprehension. Still, all proceeded with 'good order and
military discipline', and as Aileen watched with Mountbatten the proud
moment when a touch of Wavell's sword raised her husband to a
Knight Commander of the Bath she, and all present, were part of a

ceremony unequalled in the history of the British and Indian Armies.*
But a few months earlier, in the spring of the same year, there were
times when such an event must have seemed almost beyond belief.

Even as late as the end of February, 1944, the dispositions and
activities of the divisions in Scoones's 4 Corps implied that they, rather
than the Japanese, were preparing for an offensive; and such, indeed,
was their mission. The shades of Quebec still lay heavily over the
Burma Theatre. But there was a general awareness that the Japanese
might 'have another go', and Slim, in conjunction with Scoones and
after discussion with Mountbatten, had prepared his strategy in the
event of the enemy forestalling 14th Army's offensive. Withdraw
forward units and formations on to stable 'pivots of manoeuvre', be
unconcerned if Japanese infiltration develops, cut off the enemy's
advance troops from their lines of communication and destroy them
ad lib with your mobile forces and such reserves as you need to introduce. Yet, however clear the principles, their application presented
delicate problems of timing if, on the indications of a Japanese move,
Slim's front line troops were to disengage smoothly.

His difficulties may be discerned in the lay-out of 4 Corps. If the
Plain of Imphal be envisaged as the hub of a wheel, five spokes extended
from its centre. First was the life-line, the supply route climbing and
descending via Kohima to Dimapur—now, after great efforts, a road
with a good surface and excellent traffic control. Next, to the north-
east, ran a route of indifferent quality to Ukhrul. Directly to the south-
east there was the better road running via Palel to Tamu; from here,
through the vile Kabaw Valley, the Chindwin could be reached via
Kalemyo. (This, of course, was the main escape-route for Burcorps in
1942.) Kalemyo was also accessible along the fourth of the spokes, the
road or track which, often degenerating into a muddy slough, passed
southwards out of the Plain through Bishenpur and beyond the Burma
frontier to the high points, amid the Chin Hills, of Tiddim, Kennedy
Peak and Fort White, before linking with the Palel–Tamu route at
Kalemyo. Finally there was the track, undeveloped and of lesser
importance,† which wound for 50 miles westward over the hills from

---

* The King granted special permission for the exceptional arrangements. (Slim
was gazetted KCB and the three corps commanders KBE on 28 September.)
John Slim was staying with his father at the time, and Una accompanied her
mother. When last had a commander's wife and family watched him receive the
accolade on the field of battle?
† It was, in any case, effectively cut on 15 April, when in a suicide effort three

Bishenpur to Silchar in Assam. These were the radii along which the
battle for Imphal was decided.

Throughout February Scoones's forward divisions were still
deployed offensively around the extremities of the two most threatened
spokes—threatened, in particular, because communications along them
ran at right angles to a Japanese advance. Cowan's 17 Division was in
the Kennedy Peak—Tiddim area; Gracey's 20 Division was feeling its
way ahead towards the crossings of the Chindwin from Tamu. Yet as
the month passed indications of a Japanese offensive multiplied—
captured documents, accumulations of boats, rafts and power craft,
increased evidence of motor transport and even, far in the rear, employment again of the famous Sittang Bridge which had been blown in the
early days of the Retreat. Slim was in regular touch with Scoones as
the picture developed, by telephone and in person. It was during one of
his visits to Imphal that he addressed a conference of officers from the
Corps, among whom was Macdonald da Silva,* then serving in a
battalion of the Bombay Grenadiers. He was impressed by Slim's
arrival, which was late, for the Army Commander had been sadly
misled by his escort. He stumped on to the platform and sternly
addressed the assembly. 'I know you think the Military Police are
bloody awful,' he said. 'Now I know why!'

Such a shaft of his wry humour may have delighted his officers, but
it reflected, perhaps, the pressures on Slim's mind. After the presence
of the Japanese 15 Division was discovered,† Scoones, on 3 February,
had made proposals for a limited withdrawal of 20 Division and certain
arrangements for counter-attack, appreciating that this new enemy
formation was intended to make an enveloping attack on 20 Division
while elements of the Japanese 33 Division kept 17 Division busy in
the Tiddim area. During the month, therefore, Slim, in consultation
with Giffard, ordered a modest scale of reinforcement for 4 Corps. But
their growing apprehension took final shape in a far more drastic
scheme which reflected more completely the ideas Slim had been
maturing. Embodied in the Appreciation which Scoones issued on 29
February—the blue-print for the Imphal battle—it crystallized those
ideas in an operational plan. The argument was simple. By the 29th, it

---

Japanese succeeded in blowing up the suspension bridge over a gorge 80 feet
deep. None of the intruders survived.
* In 1975 Mr da Silva was head of the Administrative Training College at Kohima
† See p. 149.

had become evident that a large Japanese reinforcement had occurred on Cowan's front. Scoones now assessed, correctly, that the enemy's main object was to isolate and destroy 17 Division which, out on a limb, hung on a vulnerable line of communications. If these were cut the Division would be prevented from withdrawing to the vital 'pivots of manoeuvre' covering the approaches to Imphal. (For 17 Division these were located in Bishenpur.) The whole Corps was spread over a front of 200 miles; in the absence of lateral communications, to get from 17 to 20 Division meant a roundabout 250-mile journey via Imphal. '4 Corps', Scoones declared, 'cannot meet a major offensive in its present dispersed state and runs a risk of defeat in detail. It must concentrate to fight a battle.'

At the first sign of a definite threat ('which', the Appreciation stated, 'will be interpreted as the first crossing of the Chindwin by more than one battalion') 17 Division would be ordered to withdraw, unassisted, towards the Imphal Plain while 20 Division would be similarly ordered to fight a delaying action from Tamu up the Palel road as far as the commanding feature of Shenam. Here it was to hold to the last. One brigade of 17 Division would remain as a block some distance up the Tiddim road; the residue, together with 23 Division, 50 Parachute Brigade and the two armoured regiments of 254 Tank Brigade, would constitute a mobile reserve. Such was the gist of a paper which set out in detail all the courses open to the enemy and to 4 Corps with luminous clarity. It was immediately accepted by Slim and Giffard, who passed it in early March to Mountbatten—just as the Supreme Commander was about to visit Ledo and sustain the untimely accident to his eye. But Slim's acceptance had been conditioned by one critical assumption: he intended, as he wrote to Kirby in his letter of 24 April, 1959, that 'there would be an orderly withdrawal into the Imphal Plain by the two forward divisions unhampered by the Japanese advance'.

In the event one division was cut off, and only escaped through the steadiness and skill of its commanders and troops. Slim always maintained subsequently that this was due to a major misjudgement on his part, and others who admired him—Ouvry Roberts, for example, who was commanding 23 Division at the time—felt that here he made his biggest mistake of the campaign. He was by now convinced that a Japanese offensive would open about 15 March. On the 7th he met Scoones at Imphal, having supervised the departure of the Chindits at Lalaghat and reviewed the defensive plan. That day he authorized the withdrawal of 17 and 20 Divisions, but not until their commanders

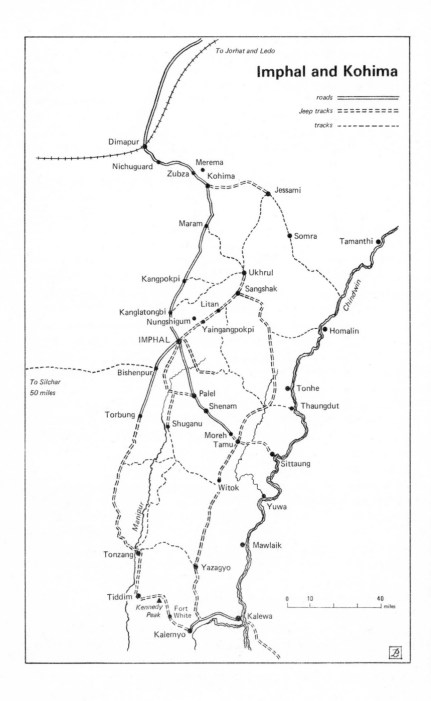

To Jorhat and Ledo

Imphal and Kohima

roads
Jeep tracks
tracks

Dimapur
Nichuguard
Zubza
Merema
Kohima
Jessami
Maram
Somra
Tamanthi
Kangpokpi
Ukhrul
Sangshak
Litan
Kanglatongbi
Nungshigum
Yaingangpokpi
Homalin
IMPHAL
Bishenpur
To Silchar
50 miles
Tonhe
Palel
Shenam
Thaungdut
Torbung
Shuganu
Moreh
Tamu
Sittaung
Witok
Yuwa
Manipur
Mawlaik
Tonzang
Yazagyo
Tiddim
Kennedy
Peak
Fort
White
Kalewa
Kalemyo
Chindwin

0   10   40
                     miles

received orders from Scoones *personally* when he was satisfied beyond all reasonable doubt that a major offensive had started.

Evidence of this came in on the 9th, when a two-man patrol of 1/10th Gurkhas reported that 2,000 Japanese, with animals and guns, had crossed the Manipur River south of Tiddim. As there was no further confirmation this report was discounted (Scoones's yardstick of 'a battalion west of the Chindwin' referred to 20 Division's front).* By the 13th however, the Japanese were vigorously active along the Tiddim road, setting up road-blocks in 17 Division's rear, and also thrusting menacingly along the front of 20 Division. On the morning of the 13th, therefore, Scoones instructed Cowan to withdraw. By the evening he had reported his action to Slim at Comilla and also told him that he had pushed a brigade of 23 Division up the Tiddim road in Cowan's support. A general verdict on the Imphal battle must be that Scoones was not always as rapid in decision as he was sound in judgement, and here is a good instance, for the relieving brigade from 23 Division only arrived in the nick of time, Ouvry Roberts having jumped the gun and sent it forward 12 hours before Scoones had ordered him to do so. Those hours were critical. But, this meant that, as one brigade of 23 Division was still forward in the Kabaw Valley, Scoones was already reduced to its third brigade, and some armour, as his sole Corps reserve at the very outset of the battle.

Cowan's division was slow off the mark.† Whereas Gracey had briefed his immediate subordinates and given them the code-word WELLINGTON, which he would use to set withdrawal in motion, 17 Division seems to have been taken by surprise. It was at best a complicated matter to manoeuvre 2,500 vehicles, 3,500 animals and thousands of men down a bad, single road in mountainous country. The consequence was that the Japanese stranglehold on Cowan's communications tightened, there was fierce and continuous fighting,

---

* This information reached 4 Corps HQ on the 9th. It was not corroborated till the 11th, when a further report indicated that 3,000 Japanese were moving north past the right flank of 17 Division. On the division's left flank Japanese thrusts had in fact been occurring for several days. But the country was close, accurate reconnaissance by air was difficult, and it is perhaps not surprising that near-fatal delays occurred in reaching an assessment of the true situation.
† Withdrawal did not start until 1700 hrs on the 14th.

and when he visited Imphal again on the 15th Slim discovered that the last reserve brigade of 23 Division had also been committed as a relieving force. It was not, in fact, until 5 April that 17 Division, after falling back slowly, was re-deployed in the Plain. In effect, therefore, the opening stages of *U-Go* caused all three of Slim's divisions at Imphal to be committed, and almost succeeded in eliminating one of them. The basis of a strong force for immediate counter-attack, a critical element in his planning, had ceased—at least temporarily—to exist. Who was to blame?

An Army Commander far behind his front—and Comilla was considerably more than a crow-flight from Tiddim—may have wider sources of information than his divisional or corps commander, but can scarcely be expected to have the fingertip feel of an obscure and rapidly developing situation. Slim had calculated that 15 March would be D Day for Mutaguchi's attack, but in fact the opening moves against 17 Division in *U-Go* began several days earlier. If he had done what he reproached himself for not doing, and reserved to himself the responsibility for issuing from Army Headquarters a fixed date for the withdrawal, he would have had to have named a day well ahead of the 15th, if he was to meet the criterion he mentioned to Kirby, that his two forward divisions should *make an orderly retirement unhampered by the Japanese advance*. And what would then have been the effect on morale? In making his arrangements for the withdrawal Slim had surely followed the sound and normal practice in respect of retirements which have to be put off to the last minute—namely, to leave the final decision to the local commander. It seems therefore that his instructions to Scoones were sensible—except that they failed to work.

But the reason for that failure lay with the men on the spot and not with Slim. There was obviously confusion; its source seems to lie somewhere amid the communications between Scoones and Cowan. Gracey, as has been seen, was poised, adequately informed and able to brief his subordinates.* Scoones felt that he had fully warned Cowan, yet Cowan was convinced that he had not been put properly in the picture and that the early indications of activity on his front were

---

* Lieut-Colonel J. H. Williams, ('Elephant Bill') received a Top Secret warning from Scoones and Gracey in person to prepare in five days' time to move his invaluable elephants out of the Kabaw valley. When he received the code word on 16 March he was organized for the withdrawal. And he had to organize elephants!

unreasonably overlooked at Corps.* (They might, nevertheless, have caused him so to alert his Division that it was not surprised when the order to move was given. 'Withdrawal', however, was not a word encouraged by Cowan.) Whatever its origin, the consequences of this confusion were immediate and daunting as *U-Go* expanded its thrust down the other spokes of the wheel.

A biographer, even an official biographer, lacks the amplitude of an Official Historian, and it is impossible to describe briefly the intricate battle for Imphal, which, as Slim wrote, 'swayed back and forth through great stretches of wild country; one day its focal-point was a hill named on no map, the next a miserable, unpronounceable village a hundred miles away. Columns, brigades, divisions marched and counter-marched, met in bloody clashes, and reeled apart, weaving a confused pattern hard to unravel.' Yet the main threads in the tangle are easily identified.

The attack from the south on Imphal was carried out by the Japanese 33 Division, reinforced by armour and heavy artillery, along the Tiddim and Kabaw valley roads directed on Bishenpur and Palel. Its right column closely followed up 20 Division's withdrawal to the Shenam Pass, where it was stopped and never got any further. Its main thrust along the Tiddim road, after an initial success which nearly inflicted a disastrous defeat on 17 Division, was stopped at Torbung gap through which the Tiddim road entered the Imphal Plain. Further north the Japanese 15 Division thrust eastwards from the Chindwin with its right flank moving just south of Ukhrul, but on this boundary line between 15 and its neighbour 31 Division (whose objective, as will be seen, was Kohima), another invaluable delaying action was fought by 50 Indian Parachute Brigade at Sangshak. Here, until 26 March, the Japanese were prevented from gaining further ground to the west.

During this opening phase, therefore, the perimeter of Imphal was contracting as planned in the south and east, though under greater pressure than Slim and Scoones had intended, and their divisions, fighting tenaciously, were retaining cohesion. But once 17 Division was cut off and 23 Division committed, the shortage of reserves and reinforcements became an instant danger. Before the main impact of

---

* This sentence is based on discussions with the late General Scoones and Major-General Cowan. Though the earliest indications reached 4 Corps on the 9th, they presumably were not forwarded to Army as 'A1'. Could Slim have based an order to withdraw on them, supposing that he had reserved the responsibility for himself.

Mutaguchi's attack Slim and Giffard had already made preparations—allotting 50 Parachute Brigade and 23 Brigade of Wingate's Special Force to the Assam front and alerting 5 Division for a move north from Arakan. But by 14 March this was evidently insufficient. Fortunately Mountbatten left the Ledo hospital that day and flew back to Delhi via Comilla, where Slim asked him for extra aircraft from the sacred Hump route to China.* Mountbatten said he would do what he could. On his return to Delhi he also ordered Giffard to expedite a move to the Central front from India of Stopford's 33 Corps HQ and 2 British Division, which Giffard and Slim had already initiated.†

The problem in SEAC was not so much numbers of men, but getting the right men to the right place at the right time. The next day, at Imphal, Slim heard from Scoones that his last infantry reserves had been committed, and realized that to move 5 Division by the cumbrous methods of road and train might fail to meet the emergency. He therefore signalled to Mountbatten that he needed 25 to 30 Dakotas from 18 March to 20 April. Mountbatten replied the same evening that he could have the aircraft at once. Between 19 and 30 March, with the transport aircraft ferrying non-stop, the whole of 5 Division was switched to the northern battlefront.

Mountbatten had already borrowed and returned a group of Hump transports to make possible both air-supply to Arakan during *Ha-Go* and the fly-in of THURSDAY, but it had taken ten days to extract permission from Stilwell and the Combined Chiefs of Staff. On that occasion he had relied on the right granted to him at the Cairo conference 'to divert up to an average of 1,100 tons a month from the airlift over a period of six months to meet the requirements of the Burma campaign'. This time he acted first and let permission follow—in fact authority was not granted from Washington until the 17th. (After the previous diversion of Hump aircraft Roosevelt had actually told Mountbatten not to ask again.) Since every hour was vital to Slim—for the result of the battle largely turned on preventing Mutaguchi from taking Imphal on the run—this decision of Mountbatten's, absolutely

---

* Sir John Baldwin used to call this critical meeting at Comilla 'The Eye Conference'. Mountbatten had taken a considerable risk in leaving Ledo prematurely. The American eye specialist who removed his bandages there told him, years afterwards, that he was sure that this would cause the loss of Mountbatten's left eye.

† The same evening Slim reiterated his need by signal. 'Press most urgently for these aircraft in view of the present situation.'

correct but involving a high degree of moral courage, perfectly illustrates how one man complemented the other.* The function of a commander is to make the big decisions correctly; his minor errors then fall into place. Mountbatten was not free from error, but here he is to be seen making the big, right judgement and thus enabling Slim to concentrate on the battle, confident in the timely arrival of his reinforcements.

Concentration of thought was indeed paramount, for all his divisions in 4 Corps were now fighting hard, 17 for its life. As yet there was no counter-attack force. And Mountbatten's acquisition of aircraft from the Hump route was an uncovenanted blessing; certainly it had not been a factor in Slim's plans. 5 Division, shuttled from the south, had a hectic arrival.

> So critical was the situation when the division arrived, the nearest Japanese being only a little over thirty miles away from the airstrip, that some units were sent straight into battle as soon as they touched ground. One brigadier found, on landing, that one of his battalions had gone into action at Litan, while another was on its way to Kohima, two entirely opposite directions—while a battalion commander who arrived after two of his companies was amazed to find them both on their way up to the front up different roads!†

Yet the division's airlift was in fact a brilliant and successful improvisation which again demonstrated the confident flexibility of Slim's staffs and the determination of the air-crews. Two brigades arrived at Imphal, while the third, 161, flew to Dimapur and shared in the most famous episode in the battle—the siege and relief of Kohima. For here too Slim's—and Scoones's—original calculations were astray. Correct in their estimate of the main course of the offensive, they had also forecast a Japanese thrust at Kohima and perhaps Dimapur, to interdict the Dimapur–Imphal lifeline—but not with more than one regiment, the equivalent of a British brigade.‡ Instead, by the end of March, when

---

* In *Defeat into Victory* Slim made an unintentional slip in placing his meeting with Mountbatten at Comilla on the 13th and not the 14th. The implications of a meeting on the 13th would have been that Mountbatten delayed 48 hours before providing the vital aircraft, which was not the case.
† Geoffrey Evans and Anthony Brett-James, *Imphal*, p. 157.
‡ The calculation was that no more than one Japanese regiment could be *maintained* at Kohima because of the exiguous communications on this front. In the end, of course, it did prove impossible to maintain Sato's 31 Division there.

161 Brigade completed its flight, the whole of the Japanese 31 Division
was drawing close to Kohima. In discounting the likelihood of so large
a threat Slim and Scoones had forgotten the words of the fairy story.
'Impossible?' said the Ogre. 'We'll see, presently.'

During these tumultuous days Slim's tensile strength was tested to
the limit, by strain beneath which most men's metal would have
snapped. The mere physical stress was enormous—shuttling in uncomfortable aircraft between his widespread commands (his back a
constant source of pain) and keeping track of developments not only
at Kohima and Imphal, but in Arakan, on Stilwell's line of march, and
in the distant jungles where the Chindits manoeuvred. Then there was
the moral effort, exacted by the constant need to appear calm and unconcerned among staffs and troops only too aware that things were
going wrong.* Remarkable in his ability to carry these two burdens,
Slim also revealed one of the commander's highest gifts—the capacity
to grip a battle which is manifestly running his enemy's way, and by
fresh dispositions so to alter the pattern of the conflict that the enemy,
in the end, is dancing to his own tune.

He was not unaided, for the Japanese—and Mutaguchi in particular
—made miscalculations which radically weakened their operations from
the start. In order to forestall an offensive by 15 Corps, *Ha-Go* was
launched earlier than had been intended, thus increasing the gap before
the start of *U-Go* and allowing Slim longer to recover balance. When
U-Go began on the planned date, moreover, 15 Division was still
incomplete. Having assumed that *Ha-Go* would imprison Slim's
reserves in Arakan, they also took it for granted that even if there were
troops going spare in the south they could only reach the Imphal
theatre slowly and painfully by the normal routes of rail, road or river.
The flexibility of air power was under-rated, though by now there was
abundant evidence available. Moreover, the fatal mistake of despising
one's enemy which had ruined *Ha-Go* was taking its toll down all
U-Go's avenues of approach. Instead of retreating in panic, 4 Corps
and its reinforcements were either standing fast or bitterly contesting
any ground surrendered—and nowhere more so than around the
District Commissioner's bungalow at Kohima.

Round this historic little demesne Slim's 14th and Mutaguchi's 15th
Armies interlocked. The defence of the Kohima ridge by Colonel

---

* Slim had a favourite saying: 'Those who matter don't worry, and those who
worry don't matter.'

Slim's birthplace in Bristol.

2. Edwardian Summer.

With the Birmingham University OTC.

4. Slim's Lambs.

5. With the 9th Bn. Royal Warwickshire Regt, Blackdown, 1915.

6. 'My Fiery Steed'.

7. Sergeant Philip Pratt, Warwickshire Yeomanry.

8. The Adjutant.

9. With John and Una.

10. The Buglers, 1/6th Gurkha Rifles.

11 and 12. Meeting with the Russians, Persia, 1941.

13. After the Retreat: the Bad Days

14. Wavell dubs Slim on the Plain of Knights.

15. Una with Sir William.

16. Into Mandalay; Rees drives Slim, Stopford and Vincent.

17. Mandalay—Giving the Good News.

18. Aileen, Deputy Commissioner, the Indian Red Cross.

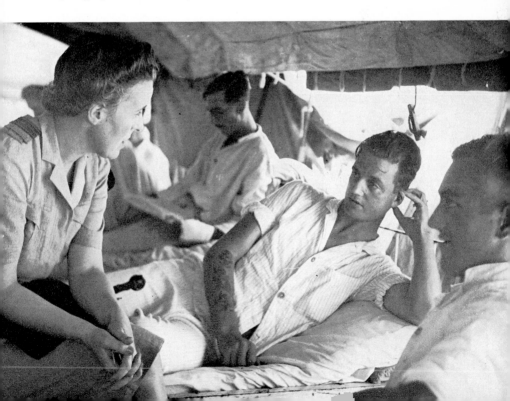

19. The Spirit of the 14th Army.

20. Rangoon at Last: Slim with Chambers of 26 Division and Air Vice-Marshal Vincent.

21. The Drive to the Guildhall.

"Wonderful news -- we're going to get Slim, dear!"

3. Prime Minister and Governor-General—Menzies and Slim.

24. The Family.

25. 'We did it together.'

26. Aileen, Viscountess Slim.

27. Uncle Bill.

Richards, 4th Royal West Kents and the rest of the meagre, miscellaneous garrison was epic. Yet the Kohima battle is an interesting example of how a commander, by failing to do the obvious thing, can lead his opponent, through insuring against the obvious, to misjudge the true situation. Sato, of 31 Division, had strict instructions to take and hold Kohima—no more. This fitted in with the essential purpose of *U-Go*, which was merely to occupy the Imphal Plain and dominate its exits.* Yet Slim and his subordinates were bound to reflect that the obvious move for Sato seemed to be to mask Kohima and make at full speed for the railway and supply depots at Dimapur.†

As the menace of 31 Division became more immediate the counter-moves which caused its ultimate defeat were already occurring. On 27 March 161 Brigade of 5 Division began to arrive at Dimapur, while from India 2 Division, 23 LRP Brigade and HQ 33 Corps were also on their way to Assam. That same day Slim himself flew to Dimapur and temporarily put the whole Dimapur–Kohima zone under the command of Major-General Ranking of 202 Lines of Communication Area. With Slim's approval, 161 Brigade was covering Kohima and keeping open lines of retreat for the Assam Regiment's outposts further east. But on 30 March Ranking received from 14 Army a directive which set his priorities as 1. The defence of Dimapur; 2. The protection of the railway, the retention of a firm base and mobile striking force at Dimapur; and *only* 3. The defence of Kohima. Stopford, who was about to take over operational control with his 33 Corps HQ, handed Ranking this directive himself and instructed him to withdraw 161 Brigade from Kohima as soon as possible. Though Ranking, on the night of the 31st, telephoned Slim to ask that he might retain one battalion of 161 Brigade at Kohima, the Army Commander upheld Stopford's ruling. And thus it was not until the last minute, at dawn on 5 April, as the Japanese were attacking, that after a further change of plan 4th Royal West Kents slipped into Kohima and the siege began.

---

* This was certainly the limited objective of *U-Go*. It is also worth noting that in their construction of the British Order of Battle the Japanese had erroneously placed 'two or three divisions' in the Shillong-Dimapur area—perhaps a result of the deceptive activities of Lieut-Colonel Peter Fleming's D Division. See Duff Hart-Davis, *Peter Fleming*, Ch. XII. This misinformation may also have served as a deterrent to any idea of exploiting beyond Kohima.

† They were aware that Mutaguchi had a contingent of the Indian National Army. This was some 7,000 strong and in the event of a successful Japanese advance could have stimulated sabotage and uprising in NE India. It was a damp squib, whose military inadequacy was revealed in the course of the fighting.

But even if, during the opening phase at Kohima, Slim's touch was uncertain, this was also his last important miscalculation. By now he was reading the battle with accuracy and assurance. Mutaguchi had fully declared his hand. Slim knew the scope, weight and direction of the Japanese offensive. It had created for him the opportunity he had wished to devise himself—the presence of large enemy forces, at the end of bad communications, on a killing-ground where his armour and mobile reserves would enable him to annihilate them. Scoones had handled the withdrawal to the pre-arranged positions, covering the entrances to the Imphal Plain, with cool dexterity. Reserves were arriving from Arakan and India. All over the broad front 14th Army was fighting steadfastly and efficiently. In the battle of attrition that lay ahead, as in all such battles, the commander's strength of will and nerve would be decisive—and if it was later on, at the battle of Meiktila, that Slim revealed his highest qualities as a creative strategist, it was at Imphal that these moral powers predominated.

His poise was illustrated on the morning of 3 April, when he met a worried Stilwell at Jorhat. The possibility that the Japanese might cut his supply-line via Dimapur to Ledo threatened the American with the loss of his private dream, the capture of Myitkyina before the monsoon. He therefore made what for Stilwell was a large gesture, offering to detach from his advance Slim's old friend, 38 Chinese Division, and send it back to protect the endangered railway. Slim firmly refused, telling Stilwell that he was confident of winning the decisive battle now looming, that at worst he would not allow Japanese interference with Stilwell's communications to continue for more than 10 days (they were never in fact cut), and that the drive on Myitkyina must proceed unchecked.* These orders were ratified by Mountbatten at a conference in Jorhat the same afternoon.

Slim was a realist; he was not simply making a dramatic gesture to Stilwell, for in spite of the bitter struggle at Kohima his situation improved so markedly during the next few days that he was able to order Scoones, on 10 April, to switch to the offensive on both his central and northern fronts. In most battles there is a moment when the swaying pendulum decides to swing positively in one direction. For Slim that moment occurred during the first part of April. There

---

* See *The Stilwell Papers*, p. 267, where Stilwell's diary for 3 April notes: 'Much to my surprise, no question of help from us. On contrary, Slim and Supreme Commander said to go ahead.'

were only six weeks left before the breaking of the monsoon.* 17 Division was safely back, two brigades of 5 Division were on the Ukhrul approaches, 20 Division was like an iron peg driven into the heights of Shenam, and 23 Division was more readily available as a mobile reserve. Counter-attack now seemed feasible, particularly after the last serious threat to the security of the *enceinte* had been removed. This was the Japanese seizure on 6 April of Nungshigum, the conspicuous feature which towers over the north-east corner of the Plain and offered observation over the most important airstrip. Its loss would have been a disaster, but, as Slim recalled, 'On the 13th, while Hurri-bombers, their guns blazing, dived almost into tree-tops, and tanks, winched up incredible slopes, fired point-blank into bunker loop-holes, our infantry stormed both peaks—and held them.'

An assessment of the aid directly supplied by Wingate's Special Force to Slim's effective defence of Imphal is difficult to formulate. That Stilwell's front was substantially assisted is not in doubt, but in spite of the many optimistic generalizations that have been published about the Chindits 'cutting the communications of Mutaguchi's army', to quantify the results involves a delicate calculation—partly because of the lack of hard information. Yet justice to Wingate requires one to make the attempt, since Slim's disapproval of the Chindits' leader, at the time and after the war, was based not so much on the idiosyncrasies of his personality as on the conviction that his operations were not cost-effective. Slim resented, in fact, having to supply precious men and aircraft for Special Force when he believed he could have used them far more profitably himself. So what, in the event, was the profit for 14th Army?

The balance in manpower is not impressive. Some twenty Chindit battalions, with one field and one anti-aircraft battery, occupied the attention, at first, of about eleven battalions brought together under the Japanese 24th Independent Mixed Brigade, only one of which was withdrawn from Mutaguchi's 15th Army.† As the operations around Indaw increased, and Stilwell's threat to Myitkyina intensified, elements of the reserve 53 Division were also fed into the fighting which might

---

* A main reason why Slim had awaited Mutaguchi's offensive with satisfaction was his feeling that if the Japanese could be halted and hammered at Imphal the monsoon would ruin their communications and create the conditions for a decisive counter-stroke.

† Two were summoned from Bassein, two from Moulmein, and two from Siam. The battalion from 15th Army was returned to it at the end of March.

otherwise have reinforced at Imphal—but it is to be noted that by May, when 53 Division began to arrive at Indaw, Mutaguchi was already finding it hard enough to supply his existing force at Imphal. As to interdiction of supplies, we know that in the rear of 31 Division a supply train was cut off by bridge-blowing. We know that Fergusson's 16 Brigade identified the dump in the Indaw area where several days' supplies had been accumulated for 15th Army, and was able to direct the RAF to its destruction. We know that 111 Brigade, in *two weeks'* operations, destroyed the insignificant amount of 'nearly 200 tons of stores and 20 vehicles, and inflicted 430 casualties'.*

That all three Japanese divisions at Imphal and Kohima grew progressively and in the end critically short of supplies is indisputable. But the sort of interdiction described above—even though other concrete examples may be quoted—was hardly at a rate to imperil an army, and Slim, looking back, was reasonably entitled to ask whether his opponent had not been hamstrung by his own incapacity rather than by the intervention of Special Force. Mutaguchi had sent his divisions trudging into battle over some of the worst lines of communication in the world, carrying with them their own supplies for 20 days. This wild administrative risk was based, of course, on contempt, and an assumption that Imphal's dumps would be captured. Once that assumption was effectively challenged, the Japanese had created their own logistic nightmare.

In forming and revising his judgements on his campaigns Slim was consistently honest and self-critical. He warmed to the courage of the Chindits—their four VCs, Calvert's great fight at White City and then at Mogaung, the gallant march of Fergusson's brigade. But even in retrospect he could not budge from the conviction that the greatly enlarged Special Force had been an expensive mistake, and he certainly was not persuaded that its efforts had made a significant contribution to the Imphal battle.† Indeed, to him its mission was to help Stilwell—

---

* John Masters, *op cit* p. 219.
† This is not to say that Slim did not later believe that Special Force might have been of greater help to him, or that he did not blame himself for preventing this. In *Defeat into Victory* (p. 268) he states flatly that he was wrong in making Special Force, under Wingate and then under Lentaigne, concentrate on supporting Stilwell. At the time of writing he believed he should have moved the Force into 'direct tactical co-ordination with the main battle'. It is difficult, however, to believe that Slim would have broken his word to Stilwell. During March Brigadier Roberts spent a day at 14th Army HQ at Comilla. 'I had one official

this is what he had promised Vinegar Joe—and at the time he neither sought nor expected much relief for his own front. He made his attitude abundantly clear on 21 March.

On that day Wingate visited Comilla to make two requests. He asked for his reserve 14 Brigade which, it will be recalled, had been earmarked for the Kohima front—and this Slim granted. But by now Wingate had decided that Special Force, in addition to dominating the Indaw region, could also decisively cut the lines of communication of Mutaguchi's divisions around Imphal. He therefore asked Slim to be allowed to use 14 Brigade for this purpose, although he had just set Fergusson the task of attacking Indaw with 16 Brigade during the night of the 24th/25th, on the definite undertaking that he could count on support from 14 Brigade. Slim refused; yet in spite of this refusal, and without informing Fergusson, on 23 March Wingate gave Brigadier Brodie of 14 Brigade written orders to move south immediately after flying into Burma that night, and begin to interfere with the communications of Mutaguchi's 15th Army. Slim never discovered this disobedience until after he had written *Defeat Into Victory*. Had he done so, his comment would have been caustic; apart from the contempt for his own orders, he could hardly have overlooked the fact that the attack of Fergusson's exhausted brigade on Indaw, launched without the expected support, was a predictable failure in which good men uselessly died. Slim did not believe in futile death.

Nor could he tolerate sharp practice. Yet this would not be an excessive description of Wingate's next act at Comilla on 21 March. When Slim refused to supply him with more aircraft, so that 14 Brigade could be flown into Burma more rapidly, Wingate threatened to send a telegram to Churchill. Slim told him to go ahead, if he so desired. But the signal that Wingate passed to Mountbatten for transmission to London (without showing it to Slim), read '. . . Get Special Force four transport squadrons now and you have all Burma north of twenty-fourth parallel plus a decisive Japanese defeat. . . . *General Slim gives me his full backing.*'* The Supreme Commander forwarded the telegram,

---

session with Bill and one private one in his room with a whisky and soda. There he told me he was under very high power pressure to change the role of Special Force (which, he had told Stilwell, would help him) to let it go south to disrupt Jap 15th Army communications. He went on with a grin, "Don't you attempt to answer that question. I'm paid to do that and I shall probably make the wrong decision and they will end up like Grouchy." ' (Letter to author, 13 August, 1975.)
* Author's italics.

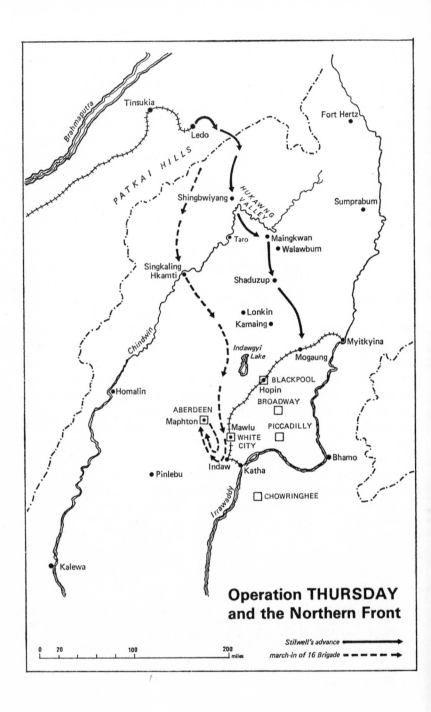

**Operation THURSDAY
and the Northern Front**

0	20		100		200

miles

Stilwell's advance ━━━▶

march-in of 16 Brigade ━━━▶

as he was bound to do, but with a significant covering note which declared 'While we all agree that we cannot have too many transport aircraft in this theatre particularly at this juncture neither Peirse, Giffard nor I know exactly why Wingate requires these extra squadrons.' Slim's own reactions were described by him to General Kirby in his letter of 5 February, 1958. 'When I saw Wingate on the 22nd I had a row with him on the grounds that he had taken my name in vain, knowing as he did that I regarded the Imphal operations as the decisive ones and that any increase in transport aircraft I should use for the main front.' Thanks to valiant struggles with the Americans by Mountbatten and the British Chiefs of Staff such an increase was achieved, and maintained—for the main front.

In spite of the shining devotion and gallantry of the Chindits, and the wayward brilliance of their leader, Slim had thus some reason for considering Wingate's demands inordinate. Yet when on the evening of the 25th Wingate's aircraft crashed into a mountainside to the west of Imphal, Slim immediately and generously recognized that 'there could be no question of our loss. Without his presence to animate it, Special Force would no longer be the same to others or to itself. He had created, inspired, defended it, and given it confidence; it was the offspring of his vivid imagination and ruthless energy. It had no other parent. Now it was orphaned.' Wingate, characteristically, had told at least three of his subordinates that in the event of his death they would succeed him, but Slim chose another, Brigadier Lentaigne, then commanding 111 Brigade west of Indaw, a Gurkha who had served under him during the Retreat.

The succession to his command was only one of the unresolved issues bequeathed by Wingate to Slim. Uppermost was the question of THURSDAY's role. Wingate had been on the verge of dissipating the Chindits' limited strength by operating them in two directions. Was support of Stilwell their objective, or were Mutaguchi's communications to be given priority? At first Slim appeared to accept Wingate's change of front, and indeed at the Jorhat conference on 3 April Mountbatten himself endorsed his Army Commander's agreement that part of Special Force (14 and 111 Brigades) should be turned south and west against 15 Army's rear.*

---

* As the situation was in the melting pot Slim, characteristically, was not prepared to countermand orders issued to Special Force, although they were contrary to his wishes, until the newly appointed Lentaigne had had a chance to take hold.

But some of Lentaigne's own officers, particularly Calvert and Fergusson, argued strongly against moving back again towards the Chindwin; nor, on examination, did it seem that accessible Japanese lines of communication existed which could profitably be attacked. On 9 April, therefore, at a meeting between Mountbatten, Slim and Lentaigne, the Jorhat decision was reversed, and Special Force was firmly and finally committed to assisting Stilwell's advance from the north. At the precise point, in fact, when Slim was beginning to sense that the tide of the battle for Imphal was on the turn, Special Force disappeared into another part of the forest. But Mountbatten and Slim had sent it there—its inevitable destination, in fact, ever since the Quebec Conference.

Though Imphal and Kohima have often been dramatized as separate battles by authors of memoirs and military studies, Slim himself, at the time and subsequently, insisted on considering them as one, an Army battle, a 14th Army battle. In his correspondence with General Kirby he was emphatic in making the point—which, indeed, is obvious enough; for *U-Go*, though complex in its unfolding, was a unified operation with a single objective, and could only be countered by centralized control. But in a conflict on so considerable a scale, fought in so many sectors by so many major and minor units, the results of a reversion from the defensive to the offensive are less immediately visible than, say, amid the clearly defined battle-lines of the Somme. So the effect of that new impetus which began to flow through 14th Army in early April (after the initial shocks had been absorbed, and reinforcement and re-grouping put in train) can best be measured not by the events of a single day, but by a broad contrast between the position then and that of six weeks later, when the monsoon arrived to seal off the Japanese for the final weeks of destruction. Slim's own summary cannot be bettered:

> By the middle of May, 1944, therefore, my worst anxieties were over. At Kohima the Japanese had been thrown definitely on the defensive; on the Imphal–Kohima road the advance had begun; around Imphal, Scoones could feel assured that, unless the enemy were greatly reinforced, danger from the north and east was unlikely. The Japanese 15th Division had been well hammered and was losing cohesion. To the south and west, where the redoubtable 33rd Japanese Division was being reinforced from both their 53rd and 54th Divisions, there was still the prospect of a last attempt by the enemy. Our command of the air over the whole battlefield was virtually unchallenged and, thanks

to this and to the daring of our patrols, the enemy system was falling into confusion. Most significant, too, the monsoon was almost upon us. The more satisfactory turn that events had taken did not pass unnoticed in other circles than Fourteenth Army. The number of visitors at my headquarters notably increased.*

So confident, indeed, was Slim by the middle of May that he was already living comfortably with a bold concept: the relief of Imphal was not *in itself* so important or urgent as the destruction of 15th Army *in situ*. (This was as difficult for Asia-watchers in Whitehall and Washington to comprehend as, after D Day, was Montgomery's policy not of breaking out at Caen but of drawing the German armour on to his front and away from the Americans.) Slim's private date for the opening of the Imphal–Kohima–Dimapur road was the third week in June, and he had no doubt that the siege could be withstood even beyond that point. All the same, as long as the Japanese could be blocked and held along all the other spokes leading into the central hub of Imphal, the spoke running through Kohima was the one where they must be not merely held, but wiped out of the way. In April and May, therefore, this was the radius along which attention was inevitably focused.

The best of generals need luck, and Slim was certainly fortunate in the turn of events at Kohima, for of the three factors critical for his success only one lay within his direct control. He could cope, and cope energetically, with the question of reinforcements. But he had no rational ground for expecting that Sato would concentrate the whole of his effort, day after day, against the defenders of Kohima, instead of making some effort to reach Dimapur,† or that Colonel Richards and his scratch command around the Bungalow would hold on so long.‡

---

* *Defeat into Victory*, p. 332.
† Sato did in fact make one sortie against the Dimapur road and cut it for a short time some 10 miles south of Kohima.
‡ The scale and intensity of the fighting in and around Kohima was, of course, even greater after the relief of the garrison than before. 2 Division's War Memorial at Kohima marks the fact with its famous inscription:

> When you go home
> Tell them of us and say
> For your tomorrow
> We gave our today.

When Slim unveiled a temporary memorial in 1944 the third line had been incorrectly carved. In 1963 a bronze panel was substituted, reading 'your' for 'their'.

Yet so it was: and it was characteristic of the garrison's spirit that when 2 Division relieved its survivors on the 18th, and Colonel Richards thereafter submitted a report to Giffard, he should have ended, after that terrible fortnight, with the words, 'Thank you very much for sending me to Kohima.'

Both then and subsequently Slim felt that Sato was lacking in enterprise. 'It is true', he once wrote to Kirby, 'that lack of flexibility was a major Japanese fault but it was, I think, not so much a case of their commanders "following their orders to the letter" as a lack of moral courage which prevented any subordinate from telling his superior that his orders were unsuited to the situation or indeed impossible.' But 'lack of moral courage' begs many questions about the Japanese mentality. Sato doggedly followed his orders 'to the letter'—to capture Kohima. Yet when the counter-attacks of 33 Corps and the interdiction of his supply lines thwarted his effort and disintegrated his division, he did have the moral courage to disobey Mutaguchi's orders to send part of it down to Imphal. Moreover, after further protests about the impossibility of his situation he signalled on 1 June his intention to withdraw. When Mutaguchi replied, 'Retreat and I will court martial you,' Sato answered 'Do as you please. I will bring you down with me.' He was finally relieved of his command on 27 June and placed on the Reserve, a medical certificate having been issued declaring that he was suffering from a nervous breakdown at Kohima. (Mutaguchi lasted until December at the head of 15th Army, when he too was removed under a cloud.) If Sato lacked enterprise he was scarcely short of moral courage.

Around the Plain itself, meanwhile, the increased pressure from 4 Corps was most effective in the north, along the line between Ukhrul and the point where 15 Division had cut the Kohima–Imphal road at Kanglatongbi. On the more southerly spokes, passing through Shenam and, on the Tiddim road, through Bishenpur, most bitter fighting produced a situation of stalemate—yet this was enough, for time and reinforcement were on Slim's side, while Mutaguchi could only strengthen one of his fronts by reducing another.

This became satisfactorily evident when 15th Army's commander, pursuing his original battle plan, instructed Sato, as has been seen, to detach a regimental group from 31 Division at Kohima and send it to 15 Division's aid. Fortunately a copy of this order was captured at Imphal on 20 April, and the next day, at Kohima, 'an officer of the Cameron Highlanders came face to face with a Japanese cyclist on a track near Merema and shot him dead'. Papers on the man's body included a confirmation of Mutaguchi's order and full details of Sato's plan for continuing operations at Kohima. Thus Slim, on the 21st, was able to instruct Stopford so to increase pressure at Kohima that no important Japanese force could be detached for Imphal, and Stopford was able to do so in full knowledge of Sato's intentions. During the next few days, in consequence, the Kohima battle raged even more savagely and on the 25th Sato decided to disobey his orders and hold back the reinforcements Mutaguchi had instructed him to send south. In the Japanese view, this disobedience substantially affected the ultimate failure of 15 Division to break into the Imphal Plain. It certainly slowed up the advance of 33 Corps at Kohima; but that, since it also speeded up the annihilation of Sato's division, fitted in well with Slim's general policy. The episode is thus a good instance of what Slim meant by insisting that he was fighting 'an Army battle'.

His policy, unaltered since the start of the battle, was steadily but inexorably executed. While his divisions inched forward from north and south along the Imphal road, and around Shenam and Bishenpur the death-lock continued, Mutaguchi's army was withering away— exactly as Slim had planned, far to the west of the Chindwin. The stubborn refusal of his enemy to admit or contemplate defeat was a great assistance. Even as the end approached, the indomitable 33 Division at Bishenpur received from its new commander, Major-General Tanaka, an order seriously intended to spur it to greater efforts. 'Now is the time to capture Imphal . . . it must be expected that the division will be almost annihilated . . . in order to keep the honour of his unit bright, a commander may have to use his sword as a weapon of punishment.'

But it was a world war. Imphal was only one piece in the total jig-saw, and Slim was not immune from those demands and pressures from far-distant theatres to which all Allied commanders, in the West as well as in the East, were exposed. Though the battle ran his way, therefore, it was not without shocks from distant sources. At the beginning of May, for example, Scoones calculated that the airlift of stores into Imphal was so far below the required level that if the road were not re-opened by mid-June desperate measures would be necessary. Slim received the message on 4 May, and simultaneously was informed that Mountbatten had been instructed by the Chiefs of Staff to return to the Middle East by 8 May the seventy-nine transport aircraft which had been loaned to SEAC during the first hectic days of

U-Go. 'Simultaneous receipt of two such messages at a critical moment in a battle which had to be won at all costs was sufficient to dismay any but the most determined commander. Slim was, as usual, imperturbable.'* Through Giffard he informed Mountbatten that if the aircraft were removed without substitution he could not be responsible for the consequences.

If the demand of the Chiefs of Staff had been met it is difficult to see how victory could have been achieved at Imphal. Neither Giffard nor Slim had the status, *vis-à-vis* London, to ignore it, and in any case the matter did not lie within their scope. But once again Mountbatten exercised that imperious and self-confident authority which, like a core of high quality steel, strengthened the SEAC command. Once again he acted on his own responsibility, ordering that the aircraft must not be released without his permission. Stirred by the struggle at Imphal, Churchill warmed to this gesture, signalling to Mountbatten: 'Let nothing go from the battle that you need for victory. I will not accept denial of this from any quarter, and will back you to the full.' In fact denial continued, and it was not until mid-May, after a stubborn fight with the Chiefs of Staff, that Mountbatten was able to ensure a sufficiently stable airlift. But as soon as Slim heard, on the 5th, that Mountbatten had refused to release the precious transports he went confidently ahead with the policy of pressure and attrition.

It is understandable that the Chiefs of Staff were not accommodating. They had never sought a major action in the area on the scale of the Imphal battle. Their minds were now filled with the imminent Normandy invasion and its uncertainties.† Not surprisingly, another distraction for Slim occurred on 27 May, when Pownall, who was in London, signalled to Mountbatten that the Chiefs of Staff were criticizing the lack of offensive action by 4 Corps up the Kohima road. The Supreme Commander immediately tackled Giffard: 'I know . . . that you realize the vital need for opening the Kohima–Imphal road as quickly as possible but really must ask you when you can start your offensive to the north.' In the circumstances Mountbatten's question was understandable, but it was unnecessary, put 'for the record', because Slim had never faltered in making it clear that 'it was not the task of 4 Corps to fight its way out but of 33 Corps to fight its way in'.

---

* *The War against Japan*, Vol. III, p. 341.
† Yet as late as D Day, 6 June, Alanbrooke was talking about 'a possible disaster at Imphal'; so Pownall noted in his diary.

This pattern continued. Forcing their way through some of the most defensible country in the world 2 and 7 Divisions of 33 Corps fulfilled their mission within the time-limit Slim had set for himself—destroying 31 Division in the process. 'The Chief of Staff of the Army', a Japanese noted, 'was astonished at the amazing and, in the Japanese Army, unprecedented spectacle of headlong retreat.' At 10.30 am on 22 June tanks and infantry of 2 Division met their opposite numbers from 5 Division, edging up from the south; the road at last was clear, and that evening, with blazing headlights, lorries of the first supply convoy ran through to Imphal.

It would be some weeks yet before the Plain became a safe sanctuary, but the process was now inevitable. The Knights had earned their reward.

——————★★★★★——————

CHAPTER TWELVE

A HEAVEN-BORN CAPTAIN

'He who can alter his tactics in relation to his opponent and thus
succeed in winning may be called a Heaven-born Captain.'

Sun Tzu

THE JAPANESE *U-Go* offensive had imposed on the Allied High
Command the necessity of fighting a major battle amid the
mountains of Assam during the first half of 1944. However welcome
in Washington, this was not a development relished in London, and
for far too long there was no evidence of a mutually acceptable strategy
for the future. Month after month Mountbatten awaited a clear-cut
directive from the Combined Chiefs of Staff. Though instructions had
been promised, and often requested with urgency by the Supreme
Commander, it was not until 3 June that they finally arrived in SEAC.*
Their absence had hardly inhibited Slim while he was absorbed in a
defensive battle, but with victory at Imphal in sight it was essential that
he received from above the orders on which his forward planning
could be based. Fortunately the Combined Chiefs made up their minds
in sufficient time for the operations of 14th Army to continue in a
coherent and logical fashion.

Mountbatten's directive, a mere six months late, ordered him to give
first priority to maintenance and expansion of the air lift to China, and
then 'so far as is consistent with the above to press advantages against
the enemy by exerting maximum effort, ground and air particularly,

---

* Mountbatten stressed to the author, however, that during this period when
South East Asia seemed to be in the pending tray he maintained many lines of
intelligence with London and Washington, both official and private, which kept
him abreast of the movement of thought.

during the current monsoon season and, in pressing such advantages, to be prepared to exploit the development of overland communications to China. All these operations must be dictated by the forces at present available or firmly allocated to SEAC.' *Particularly during the current monsoon* was a bold phrase, and it might seem surprising that Mountbatten and Slim found themselves able to accept it, for during the first six months of the year the losses throughout SEAC in killed and wounded were 40,000, but wastage from sickness and disease accounted for no less than another 282,000. Yet this was the joint policy which Slim and the Supreme Commander had resolutely adopted from the beginning of their co-operation. Emphatic notes in Slim's papers indicate that he never caused his men to fight in insalubrious conditions as a matter of choice, but even before he became Army Commander he had recognized that readiness to continue operations during the monsoon was a necessity for the defeat of the Japanese.* His willingness to drive his Army onward during the present monsoon, when malaria and other ills were at a peak, was fortified by a growing confidence in the benefits flowing from the new drugs, the new forms of treatment, and the vastly improved preventive measures which Mountbatten and he had caused to be introduced.†

Slim himself was not immune—or guiltless. At the moment when the success of his Army and the arrival of new orders enabled him to start planning positively for the future, a severe attack of malaria cooped him up in Shillong hospital. And it was a self-inflicted wound. 'Troops were forbidden to bathe after sunset and I had disobeyed my own orders. Returning very muddy and late one evening I had washed in the open and been well and deservedly bitten by mosquitoes.' *Quis custodiet ipsos custodes?* (Wingate's typhoid, which interfered with the planning of THURSDAY, was ascribed to a thirsty but thoughtless draught of water from a vase of flowers.) In the hospital at Shillong was a young Australian artillery officer, Lieut-Colonel Crichton-Brown. He was bored by being restricted to his private room and yearned to be transferred to the society of a general ward. A martinet

---

* The words 'particularly during the current monsoon' were in fact inserted in Mountbatten's brief by Ismay, with Alanbrooke's approval, as a deliberate support of the policy which Mountbatten was advocating, which Slim endorsed, but which Giffard, as was known in London, rejected.

† When Slim took command of 14th Army in October, 1943, the malaria rate was 84 per cent of its total strength. By 1945 it had fallen to one per 1,000 per day.

Matron refused. Single rooms for Colonels. Hearing that the Army Commander was in the hospital Crichton-Brown asked that his permission should be sought for a transfer. The answer from Slim came back: 'No. But does this officer play chess?' Army Commander and gunner colonel then met in battle across the board; and a decade later, when Slim was Governor-General of Australia, he was able to renew his links with one of the Commonwealth's leading citizens, Sir Robert Crichton-Brown.

By the directive of the Combined Chiefs of Staff Mountbatten was specifically committed to a land campaign in upper Burma, to develop the air and land links with China. There was no word about amphibious operations. The directive thus nakedly revealed the disproportionate influence of the two Allies in mid-1944, since the Americans had got what they wanted and the British were unable to resist—even though in London and at Mountbatten's headquarters the seaward flank of the Japanese still seemed the desirable objective. But Slim was harbouring more ambitious thoughts. 15th Army was disintegrating, as he had dreamed it might; for him the most logical step was to exploit his victory—to Rangoon? 'I believed, more firmly than ever, in spite of the doubts of so many, that, if we were to regain Burma, it must be by an overland advance from the north. For the first time this now seemed a practical proposition.' On 9 June Mountbatten issued his own directive, to Giffard at 11 Army Group, of which the section primarily affecting Slim laid down: 1. Opening of communications between Dimapur and Imphal (which, as has been seen, was achieved on the 22nd); 2. Removal of the Japanese from the Imphal Plain and down to the line of the Chindwin; 3. Preparations to exploit across the Chindwin on a 130-mile front due east of Imphal. This was permissive—but not permissive enough for Slim, who visualized already a second, decisive battle in the very heart of Burma, after which, having reached the shattered core of the Japanese strength, he could turn southwards for the sea.

From June, 1944, this distant objective, so triumphantly attained, was always in his mind. In retrospect the great curve of operations from the repulse of *Ha-Go* in Arakan, through Imphal and Kohima to the crossings of the Chindwin and the Irrawaddy, and south again to the threshold of Rangoon, has a beautiful consistency. But the aesthetic quality of the curve was not a casual effect. No other senior commander in South-East Asia envisaged it; Slim was the artist whose inner eye conceived it and whose master hand gave it a visible form.

As the Imphal battle waned* an immense effort of reorganization, administrative preparation and operational planning was necessary if 14th Army was to be ready, after the monsoon, to take advantage of the dry campaigning season and strike into the heart of Burma. Nor, as Slim pointed out, were doubters lacking. After Bernard Fergusson had brought back his 16 Brigade from its THURSDAY adventures he was summoned to a conference at Dehra Dun.

> It was an enormous affair convened by Slim, whom I now met for the first time (though a year before, recovering in a convalescent home in Simla from my wound, malaria and malnutrition, I had been looked after wonderfully by his wife, who was running it). I think all the Corps Commanders and Divisional Commanders of 14th Army were there; Brigadiers were six a penny. . . . There was a lot of talk, much of which sounded to me almost defeatist. I remember but will not reveal the identity of a divisional commander who said—and not without support from others—that to prevent the Japanese cutting the road behind one a force of at least a brigade would be needed every X miles; there were only Y brigades in the 14th Army; it was Z hundred miles to Rangoon—*ergo*, it would be impossible to capture Rangoon overland . . . this was frankly too much for me. . . . Something like a brainstorm broke over me; I got to my feet, and I gave them an earful . . . in the hush that followed a tall, languid, fair-haired Brigadier whom I had never seen before got up on one of the terraces opposite. . . . 'I don't quite know who the last speaker was,' he drawled, 'but obviously he was talking sense. I mean, it's obvious, isn't it? I mean, it's obvious to anyone who uses his brains, and has been for a long time'. . . . We might well have gone on like this, but for a dry interruption from Slim at his table. 'Brigadiers West and Fergusson having left us in no doubt as to their views, they will now kindly keep their mouths shut for the rest of the conference.' But it was nicely and jocularly said. . . .'†

What irked Fergusson, after his experience of two Chindit operations, was an apparent failure to appreciate that air supply had released armies from the tyranny of the road as an umbilical cord between the base and the front line. But 'before the conference ended I was cross-

---

* Though the Japanese withdrawal started earlier, it was not until 10 July that Mutaguchi reluctantly issued a formal order for a general retreat.
† Bernard Fergusson, *The Trumpet in the Hall*, p. 190. The languid Brigadier later became General Sir Michael West, GCB, DSO and two bars, Commander, *inter alios*, of the Commonwealth Division in Korea.

examined at length by Slim about certain details of our methods. He and his staff, at any rate, were fully alive to the potential of air supply.' Had Fergusson met Slim earlier he would have been aware of how deeply rooted this concept was in his Army Commander's thoughts. But for all that the episode was typical of Slim's planning technique. He was neither Napoleonic nor egocentric in his approach. Disapproving of 'soviets', or any hint of 'government by committee', he was nevertheless a natural democrat, sparing no pains to elicit from his subordinates a full spectrum of opinion about any important problem. Because he treated the views of others with respect, they gave them freely—and sometimes unfavourably. But in Slim's entourage there was no room for sycophants. He rated the integrity of an adverse argument more highly than self-seeking flattery. The atmosphere surrounding him is well captured by his Chief Engineer, Brigadier (and subsequently Major-General) Hasted:

> The senior Mess, of which I think I am the only survivor, was extremely close-knit, with absolutely no rivalries. In it 'Uncle Bill' was just what his affectionate nickname implied. We all spoke freely what was in our minds. We had no secrets from one another, and Uncle Bill joined wholeheartedly in the conversation on whatever subject. His presence commanded a natural respect born of our knowledge of the greatness of the man himself, but there was no ghastly hush as so often happens in senior messes when the commander enters. His quick-witted and penetrating mind was more than a match for anyone round the table, and woe betide the speaker who knew little of his subject or facts. He was a great judge of character and very quickly put his finger on weaknesses. I think this enabled him to get the best out of everyone who served under him; although he didn't suffer fools gladly, he accepted those posted or serving under him and knew whether to ride on a curb, or a snaffle, or when to use the whip, which was in fact seldom necessary. Of all his many attributes I never cease to admire his calmness and courtesy when the strain of a 'touch and go' situation for long periods on end must have been wellnigh unbearable. His imperturbability did not stem from insensitivity, but rather from a superhuman self-discipline.*

A commander preparing a new offensive naturally considers the security of his flanks. On the right wing of his enormous front, in

---

* Letter to author, 16 May, 1974.

Arakan, there was nothing to cause Slim concern. Coming events in central and northern Burma would be a sufficient preoccupation for the enemy, and (as proved to be the case) there was little likelihood of a strong new Japanese initiative disturbing the equipoise which Christison and 15 Corps had established and maintained since their successful defeat of *Ha-Go*.* After the arrival of the monsoon in mid-June brought operations on both sides to a halt, the obvious policy—hard though it was on 15 Corps—became one of maintaining a minimum strength in Arakan and transferring resources to support Slim's exploitation eastwards from Imphal.

On Slim's left wing, or Stilwell's sector—the region of NCAC, Northern Combat Area Command—for a time the situation was less tranquil. Reassured by Slim at Jorhat that his communications were safe, while those of the Japanese 18 Division opposing him would continue to be disrupted by Special Force, Stilwell had brilliantly impelled his Chinese down the Hukawng valley, and, by the arduous outflanking march of Merrill's Marauders, captured on 17 May the airfield at Myitkyina. He seemed within an inch of realizing his dream and fulfilling his mission. 'WILL THIS BURN UP THE LIMEYS?', his diary for that day triumphantly demands. But the triumph was premature. Though no less than 30,000 Chinese were drawn in to buttress the exhausted rump of Merrill's force (whose commander collapsed soon after reaching the airfield), the fighting round Myitkyina, as Slim put it, 'settled down into an untidy, uninspired, ill-directed siege' during which Stilwell drove the increasingly rebellious Americans with merciless indifference. The town itself, fanatically defended by Major-General Mizukami and a miscellany of a mere 3,500 men, was not taken until 3 August. From Washington's viewpoint this now meant that aircraft carrying supplies to China would have an easier route via Myitkyina than via the Hump. For Slim it meant that when the British 36 Division had joined Stilwell from India (and assuming that the Chinese armies in Yunnan began to exercise effective pressure on Burma's eastern border), he could anticipate that as his own advance developed the Japanese on his left flank would be fully preoccupied.

Unfortunately, however, Stilwell's disappointment maimed not only the Marauders but also Special Force. In a sense this was not now Slim's personal concern, since from 17 May the Force had been placed directly under Stilwell's orders. However, as Myitkyina held out and Stilwell's

---

* In fact the Japanese never attacked again in Arakan with more than a regiment.

frustration intensified, his complaints about the alleged pusillanimity and disobedience of the exhausted Chindits became extravagant.* (It is fair to say that his own staff tended to conceal the truth from him.) Lentaigne's infuriated explanation that Special Force had now been pushed beyond the limit was brushed aside; Stilwell contemptuously asked to be relieved of its command. Once again, therefore, Slim was interposed between SEAC and Stilwell. Early in June Mountbatten sent him up to the headquarters of NCAC in an attempt to make peace between an unreasonably irascible American and a justifiably indignant Irishman—and Slim succeeded. Lentaigne agreed to fight on until the fall of Myitkyina and for the moment Stilwell became less overbearing. Then, shortly afterwards, Kamaing, to the west of Myitkyina, was captured, the point at which, it will be recalled, Stilwell's formal responsibility to Slim came to an end. The tribulations of the surviving Chindits did not end, however, and it finally required Mountbatten's personal intervention to extricate them before Stilwell allowed disease and attrition to wipe them out.

It was well for Slim that he had a robust temperament and a clear vision of the correct strategy for his army. A less tenacious mind might at this point have been discouraged or confused, for in mid-July there broke out on the higher levels of the Anglo-American command a debate about policy in the South-East Asia theatre which, if one strongly supported course of action had been adopted, might (as in the case of CULVERIN) have left 14th Army with an undistinguished role. Slim was fully aware of the main issue involved, and it must have been strange, as he moved among the troops in which he took such pride, to feel that decisions being taken in London and Washington might deny them the ultimate fruits of their recent victories.

Yet this was possible. On 23 July Mountbatten submitted to the Chiefs of Staff two new and alternative plans. The first, CAPITAL, would bring 14th Army in the spring of 1945, by three phases, to the line Mandalay–Pakokku on the Irrawaddy. A fourth phase would later involve 'exploitation southwards towards Rangoon'. But the other plan, DRACULA, was for an amphibious and airborne assault on Rangoon itself, starting in January, 1945—with the inevitable con-

---

* The strictures were unjustified. The Chindits fought on and fought hard. In the final phase, before 111 Brigade was evacuated it had been reduced to the strength of a company and Major Blaker of the Highland Light Infantry had been awarded a posthumous Victoria Cross.

sequence that 14th Army would be restricted to a holding role, containing the Japanese forces in the general area of the Chindwin. In early August Mountbatten visited London where he found DRACULA was welcomed, and, indeed, on 12 August the Chiefs of Staff sent a vigorous signal to Washington recommending its acceptance by the Combined Chiefs.

Meanwhile Giffard, Slim and Stilwell had been asked by Mountbatten for their comments on the unaggressive role proposed under DRACULA for the Allied forces in North Burma. Among the possibilities they were asked to review was the suggestion that, if the Japanese attempted another offensive (even though that seemed unlikely), 14th Army should in this event fall back to the plain of Imphal! They reacted unanimously and forcibly, pointing out that the shattered Japanese must be kept on the run—according to the classic principles of war. Their arguments had weight, for on 17 August Mountbatten signalled that the first two phases of CAPITAL—taking 14th Army over the Chindwin to the area of Ye-u in the Shwebo plain—should be put in hand immediately while DRACULA would be launched in the spring of 1945 with resources transferred from Europe. Such was the general situation when Churchill and his Chiefs of Staff sailed on 1 September for the OCTAGON conference in Quebec.

While this second summit conference was proceeding in the Canadian city Mountbatten again signalled, to say that after further discussions with his Commanders-in-Chief he was anxious to maintain the dynamism of operations in North Burma, and ready to review the degree of risk involved in mounting DRACULA with reduced forces from his own theatre, should reinforcements from the west prove unavailable. Since the OCTAGON discussions clearly revealed that the end of the war in Europe was by no means imminent, and reinforcements for the East unlikely, and since the Americans, of course, strongly supported a concentration of effort in North Burma, the conference resulted in a directive sent to Mountbatten on 16 September which, though this was not obvious at the time, contained the charter for Slim's final triumphs. 'Your object is the recapture of all Burma at the earliest date,' the directive began. But, after adding that the Combined Chiefs approved the stages of CAPITAL 'necessary to the security of the air route, and the attainment of overland communications with China', to whose 'vigorous prosectuion they attached great importance', and after agreeing to DRACULA *if* it could be carried out before 1945 monsoon, the directive ended:

3. If DRACULA has to be postponed until after the monsoon of 1945, you will continue to exploit Operation CAPITAL as far as may be possible without prejudice to preparations for the execution of Operation DRACULA in November, 1945.

This final paragraph of the Quebec directive, it can now be seen, was the covenant for Slim's historic pursuit from Meiktila to Rangoon.

But though these discussions, until they were resolved, had disturbing implications, Slim was too balanced a personality to be distracted by them, and in any case he had received sufficiently clear instructions to enable him to proceed with forward planning in such a way that if, from his point of view, the worst failed to happen, and DRACULA were cancelled or postponed, he would be well poised to proceed with a march to the sea.* On 24 July Giffard ordered him to start making preparations for CAPITAL on the *assumption* that it would be launched during December, though they would not know about the future of DRACULA at least until September—latter September, as has been seen. This in effect meant that, whatever the measure of uncertainty, Slim could develop plans in detail for the re-occupation of central Burma up to the Mandalay–Pakokku line. In this advance the first bound was clearly the line of the Chindwin.

There was much to be done and done immediately. Apart from deciding the precise shape of the major battle which must be fought beyond the Chindwin, the routes to the river itself had to be cleared of Japanese rearguards, during the worst climatic conditions conceivable, and then built up from mud and ooze into a roadway for an army. Tired divisions must be given leave and rest. Immense administrative arrangements would be necessary for a march through the mountains, across a great river, and into the Burma plain. Air-supply and air-cover would be critical, and had to be devised.

Slim stream-lined. By early August Scoones and his 4 Corps HQ withdrew to India and all operations forward of Imphal were placed under Stopford and 33 Corps. To India, also, or to tranquil rest-and-rehabilitation areas at Kohima or Imphal the bulk of 14th Army's divisions were temporarily pulled back, making their maintenance

---

* 'From his point of view' only in the sense that, *in the military circumstances of 1944,* he believed that his was the correct strategy for recovering Burma. But Slim was no Patton, seeking personal glory. If a viable DRACULA could have been mounted, promising genuine success, he was too good a soldier and too dedicated to his country's interests not to have welcomed it.

easier during the monsoon and allowing some opportunity for refreshment, training and reinforcement.* The advance to the Chindwin was therefore conducted by Stopford, under orders issued by Slim on 6 August, with a mere two divisions, 11 East African working from Tamu eastwards to the Chindwin at Sittaung and southwards down the Kabaw valley to Kalewa, while 5 Indian on the right made for Kalewa along the equally unfriendly Tiddim road.†

Their battles were indeed more with nature and the elements than with the Japanese—though the veteran 33 Division was still a dour adversary. Conditions in the Kabaw valley during the monsoon were so liquid that 11 E.A. Division was fully maintained by air (the pilots flying through tempest, turbulence and minimal visibility), as was 5 Indian after it was realized that less effort was involved in simply allowing the Tiddim road to collapse behind the division as it struggled ahead.‡ In the Kabaw valley the situation was such that the chief staff officers of 14th Army and 33 Corps were unable to get closer to the East Africans than Tamu; beyond Tamu they would have had to be parachuted into the Valley. Once dropped, they would have been unable to return! Malaria and the accompanying diseases of the monsoon were rife, even the 'salted' East Africans suffering heavily, while for the Tiddim road the figures are eloquent. In its operations 9 Brigade of 5 Division lost in 26 days 9 killed, 85 wounded and 507 from sickness.

By mid-December bridgeheads over the Chindwin were secure. On the 10th, indeed, a Bailey bridge—the longest, at that moment, in the world—had been completed at Kalewa. The retiring Japanese, though still tenacious fighters, had not been the chief opposition. Valley mud, the torrential rain, the constant debilitation, the miseries of the Chocolate Staircase, the raging bridgeless Manipur River—these had chiefly sapped and tested the spirit of Slim's Army. Nothing had cracked. It was an achievement which would have been un-

---

* 17 and 23 to India, 2 and 7 to the north and 20 to the south of Imphal. (The officers and men of 2, 7 and 20 all had some leave.)
† In the wild country south of the Tiddim road the irregular Lushai Brigade operated with brilliant success against the flank and communications of the retreating Japanese.
‡ The immense administrative problems which Slim and his staff had to overcome in their forward planning for the advance into Burma are dramatically illustrated by the fact that at an early stage an inescapable truth emerged—engineering resources made it impossible to convert more than a *single* route (down the Kabaw valley from Tamu to Kalewa) into a roadway for the Army's communications. An all-weather road through the valley was started soon after the Imphal victory.

imaginable two years or perhaps even one year previously—the achievement of an army whose commander had inspired it to feel at home with the impossible.

A cross that all commanders bear is that while they are preoccupied with the current battle their minds must be calmly contemplating the next. For months Slim had been reflecting, both privately and in discussion with his staff, about the right way to engage the Japanese beyond the Chindwin, but speculation is one thing, an operational plan another. During the monsoon months, as his divisions painfully inched their way south through the torrents and landslides of the mountainous Tiddim road and the mud and floods of the Kabaw valley, it was an operational plan that his headquarters had now to prepare. For this logistics were a critical factor, since a scheme for battle must inevitably turn on the number of troops, guns and tanks he could advance and maintain by routes of a daunting inadequacy. It would be a severe test of staff-work, but his weapon was strong. Snelling and Hasted, his chief quartermaster and engineer, were epitomes of experience and resourcefulness, nor had he suffered, as he might have done, from the departure of his trusted chief of staff, Steve Irwin, who became Commandant of the Staff College, Quetta. Irwin's replacement, 'Tubby' Lethbridge, fitted the niche precisely. A shrewd, robust, good-humoured Sapper, he headed the Lethbridge Mission which had recently made a comprehensive tour of war theatres to learn lessons applicable to South-East Asia.* Here was a fertile addition to what Slim called 'the partnership'.

What he sought was another killing-ground. The destruction of the Japanese army was his target, not places, even places with evocative names like Mandalay, so telling in a communiqué. Like Berlin to Eisenhower in the last stage of the advance from the Rhine, to Slim, for the moment, Mandalay was merely 'a geographical expression'. His problem therefore was how and where to bring the Japanese to battle—and with what? Protracted staff studies revealed that the maximum force supportable beyond the Chindwin—at 400 miles from the Dimapur railhead and 200 or more from air-supply bases—was four complete

---

* See Alanbrooke's diary for 13 April, 1944: 'A long Chiefs of Staff meeting at which the Lethbridge Committee attended. They have just been touring the world: Washington, Canada, Honolulu, Fiji, New Zealand, Australia, New Guinea, India, Burma, etc., studying the requirements of the war against Japan. Their report is very good and provides much food for thought and progress.' Arthur Bryant, *Triumph in the West*, p. 181.

divisions, two infantry and two tank brigades. Though the losses of the Japanese during recent operations amounted, even in their own estimation, to 65,000 out of 115,000, Slim reckoned that he still might be faced on the central front by five and a third enemy divisions, as well as substantial miscellaneous troops—even allowing for the two divisions which would probably be retained in the north, and another two to three divisions in Arakan and the south. The margins were adverse.

Nevertheless, Slim proceeded undeterred with his planning, in the knowledge that Allied air-power gave him many advantages denied to the enemy; that east of the Chindwin he would reach open country where his superiority in armour must tell; and, above all, that a high proportion of his officers and men had been hardened into professionals. Their skills, however, had been specifically developed to fit them for jungle and mountain. But beyond the Chindwin loomed the certainty of swift mobile warfare—a world where tanks would operate in quantities instead of by twos or threes, where guns must be capable of fire-and-movement, where infantry must manoeuvre fast and far. Imaginative and intensive re-training were necessary if 14th Army was not to emerge into the open mentally and physically unprepared. Such things happen. After years of trench warfare troops of the Allied armies in 1918 were often found to be slow in mind and movement as the Germans retreated and advances were measured not in yards, but in miles.

In his customary way, Slim spent as much time as he could spare observing and encouraging the retraining throughout his Army, as well as visiting where possible the units still engaged in action. It was on such a day that he found himself back at Shwegyin.* His reactions recall the remark of General Lee to his Military Secretary when, in 1864, Grant was threatening him on the Rappahanock. 'Colonel, we have got to whip them; we must whip them—and it has already made me better to think of it.' Slim wrote, in the same spirit:

> 'There, still lying in the amphitheatre of hills on the river bank, were the burnt-out and rusted tanks that I had so reluctantly destroyed and abandoned in the Retreat, two and a half years before. As I walked among them, resavouring in imagination the bitter taste of defeat, I could raise my head. Much had happened since then. Some of what we

---

* see p. 102.

owed we had paid back. Now we were going on to pay back the rest—
with interest.'*

But where? After running due south from the Kachin Hills the
Irrawaddy turns sharply westward at Mandalay, to link up, after some
50 miles, with the Chindwin, whose converging course has taken it
steadily to the south-east ever since it left Kalewa. A glance at the map
indicates how the conjunction of these two great rivers forms a loop or
sack, in the centre of which lie the flat lands around Shwebo. The
Japanese, Slim calculated, would fight desperately to defend Mandalay,
and at Shwebo they must make their stand. He had found his killing
ground. But before the main battle occurred he visualized some tough
fighting to gain the few gaps in the Zibyu Taungdan, that extensive
range of high, broken country which provides a strong flank guard to
the eastern bank of the Chindwin from Kalewa northwards to Homalin
and beyond. It was a natural assumption that on this line the Japanese
would make a considerable effort to block the northern entries into the
Shwebo plain. Two hundred miles of sheer cliff 2,000 feet high, with a
maze of ravines and crossed by a mere three tracks unsuitable for
vehicles, constitute a formidable bulwark.

These assumptions were flawed by ignorance of Kimura's real
intentions, as will be seen, but they were founded on the best information available to Slim at the time. It was on this basis, therefore, that an
operational plan was devised for sending 14th Army across the
Chindwin, starting on 3 December, in an offensive which was intended
to culminate in a second climacteric battle, the strategic fruits of victory
at Imphal.

In the weeks before it started, as the final arrangements were being
perfected, an earthquake occurred in the structure of South-East Asia
Command which, after the dust had settled, left Slim free at last from all
responsibilities other than his own army and the conduct of the battle.
The trace on a seismograph recording the development of the shock
would run right back to 1943 and the time of Mountbatten's arrival,
for it was then that the limitations of Giffard as senior commander of
the British land forces became evident. This inadequacy was the direct
cause of what now happened. The story, which has never been fully
told, is of the greatest importance for an understanding of the context
in which Slim had to operate. He himself is partly to blame for obscur-

---

* *Defeat into Victory*, p. 369.

ing the facts in *Defeat into Victory*. The truth is that Giffard lacked elasticity of mind; though he stoutly shielded Slim from interference, and though Slim was never insubordinate to Giffard as he later was to Leese, Giffard was never in tune with Mountbatten or capable of 'thinking big' like Slim. A good man misplaced. One would have to use the cliché 'a great gentleman' to describe Giffard, whom the troops called Pop, and Slim, who felt a deep affection for him, was too loyal to analyse in print those defects of intellect and imagination which in fact made Giffard a brake rather than a propellant.

The three-tier system of a Supreme Theatre Commander, beneath whom an overall Land Forces Commander exercises authority over the generals actually fighting the battle, is a cumbrous and delicate instrument almost entirely dependent on the quality of the personalities involved. During the last phase of the African campaign Alexander, in the middle role of Land Forces Commander, succeeded because he was trusted by his superior, Eisenhower, and because he effectively dominated his subordinates, Montgomery and Patton. While Montgomery exercised overall command of the allied land forces in Normandy he too was effective because his steely will enabled him to impose (in spite of many questionings) a correct strategy on both his Supremo, Eisenhower, and his American colleagues in the field. In each case, though for different reasons, the system worked. But in South-East Asia, so long as Giffard was the layer between Mountbatten and Slim, the system never worked as it should have done. And the difficulty was that while the upper and lower layers, Mountbatten and Slim, were in tune, Giffard was discordant.

This was clear from the beginning. When Mountbatten enunciated his policy of fighting through the monsoon Giffard deprecated it and Slim welcomed it. When Mountbatten said that the low state of the troops' morale must be improved by personal visits and talks by their leaders, Giffard opted out, leaving the job to be successfully carried out by Mountbatten and Slim. In the running struggle for authority between the Supreme Commander and the three Service Commanders-in-Chief Giffard sided consistently with Admiral Somerville and Air Chief Marshal Sir Richard Peirse. He openly resented his subordination to a young and junior naval officer, and was much inclined to block Mountbatten's proposals not because he had examined them on their merits but because Mountbatten had made them. It will be recalled that he was stiff about Mountbatten's appointment of Slim to 14th Army—not, surely, because he disapproved of Slim, but because he felt the appointment was his prerogative. Mountbatten and Slim were men in a hurry; the Japanese could not be defeated by the dragging of feet.

A major issue arose at the beginning of the Imphal battle. It related to the initial movement of reserves, particularly from Arakan. Mountbatten considered that Giffard and his staff had not sufficiently alerted himself and SEAC, and was furious at having to insist on moving 5 Indian Division from Arakan by air at the cost of switching aircraft off the Hump and then reporting what he had done to Washington. Pownall's diary for 18 March, 1944, tells the story from first hand. When, as Mountbatten's Chief of Staff, he explored the situation with Giffard he found him complacent. 'He said that Slim had plenty of troops and could move them as he wanted. It was clear he didn't propose to intervene himself . . . and he made it plain that he would regard intervention by Mountbatten as being unwelcome.' Giffard even objected to Pownall's sending to Mountbatten (still in hospital at Ledo with his bandaged eye) a report about the possibilities of transferring reinforcements from Arakan to Imphal. This is a damning entry. Pownall, as all readers of his diary become aware, was in no sense 'a Mountbatten man'. He was simply an able if conventional staff officer of high quality. The upshot was a cutting letter from Mountbatten to Giffard and, subsequently, an angry meeting between two incompatible personalities. The *Official History*, which is inclined to dust over this episode, misses the point. The affair was in fact the culmination of months of incalcitrance by Giffard, who held himself aloof in Delhi and never attempted that meeting of minds with his Supreme Commander which was essential, since he lacked the brilliance and *timbre* to go it alone, like Montgomery in Normandy, and could only function effectively if he was at one with his Supremo, like Alexander with Eisenhower in North Africa.

However much Slim might like and defend Giffard, such episodes and attitudes were good neither for him nor for his army. Then, in May, things came to a head. Mountbatten and Slim were determined to carry on operations through the monsoon. Giffard protested that he would not be able to make sufficient divisions available for both monsoon and post-monsoon operations, as too much relief and rehabilitation was needed after the recent battle. Mountbatten asked to see his programme of rehabilitation. 'He replied in so many words that it was his business to tell me what divisions he could make available, and that he could not agree to my checking over his programme to see if I could extract more from him.'* Hence, as Pownall put it in his diary, 'the painful necessity to give George Giffard his *congé*'. Mountbatten told Giffard that he had lost confidence in him. He must be replaced by a younger, more aggressive and more co-operative Commander-in-Chief. Giffard accepted the news with grace, and agreed with slight modification to the official letter which Mountbatten now despatched in Pownall's hands to the CIGS in London.

Giffard's misfortune opened up a wide field, for it was always a major limitation that all Americans (and Stilwell in particular) disliked him with varying degrees of animosity. Thus until his post fell open it was impossible to propose the logical next step and create a commander responsible for all Allied Land Forces, South-East Asia. Stilwell, who tolerated Slim as a superior, would have rejected Giffard out of hand. But now Mountbatten could empower Pownall to seek the approval of the Chiefs of Staff in London for this new post and to discuss with them possible candidates. The prime favourite was Oliver Leese, though there is no doubt, in the light of Leese's performance after he was ultimately appointed, that the other possibility, General Sir Richard O'Connor, would have fitted more harmoniously into the command structure of SEAC.

In the event Pownall returned empty-handed, and it took six months before Whitehall and Washington could reach agreement about a commander for ALFSEA. Giffard remained at his post, and though elaborate precautions were observed to conceal the fact that he was 'under notice' his anomalous position must have caused him an inner anguish which he never revealed. Indeed, the paradox was that once he and Mountbatten had shared the moment of truth he became co-operative and constructive. 'I wish to place on record', Mountbatten recorded in his papers, 'that Giffard behaved, throughout his time with me, in a perfectly courteous and loyal manner. . . . Taking risks which I know went greatly against the grain, he now made formations available for further operations when his whole inclination was to take them out and rest them, and he agreed to reduce periods of rehabilitation to a minimum. If he could have behaved in this way earlier, I might never have had to ask for his relief.'

Slim was always generous in his praise for the support he had received from Giffard, but this is to gloss over the fact that his immediate

---

* Mountbatten to author.

superior, remote in the headquarters which he insisted on retaining in Delhi, was as far away in spirit as he was on the ground. It was time for him to go.

Suddenly the log-jam broke. Chiang Kai-shek's tolerance of a man who understood him too well, and despised what he understood, ended with a demand for Stilwell's recall, to which Roosevelt submitted on 18 October.Three Americans replaced one—Sultan taking over NCAC, Wedemeyer becoming Chiang's adviser and the brilliant Wheeler Deputy Supreme Commander. All were men of whom Slim approved and with whom he could work without friction. But the main significance of Stilwell's departure was the fact that it made politically possible the introduction of an overall commander for the Allied Land Forces. On 12 November Sir Oliver Leese, who till then had commanded 8th Army as Montgomery's successor in Italy, took up the ALFSEA post. Since this involved the abolition of 11th Army Group, the peaceful removal of Giffard could also be effected. But though the post of ALFSEA was necessary as a co-ordinating centre, the arrival of a newcomer from Italy had no real effect on the Mountbatten–Slim axis and perhaps strengthened it.* By now Supremo and General had learned to trust each other with a confidence founded on experience.

The institution of ALFSEA did, however, have one immediate practical advantage for Slim. By a logical move 15 Corps in Arakan ceased to be his responsibility. The great rearward administrative areas behind 14th Army were grouped under a new Lines of Communication Command. The airfields, depots and staffs on which the air supply organization depended were also removed from Slim, and integrated as the Combined Army Air Transport Organization. 15 Corps and the two new formations were all placed under the umbrella of Leese, as ALFSEA; and since NCAC, long before Stilwell's departure, had also ceased to be Slim's responsibility he was able, just before his next battle started, to devote himself to it without these considerable distractions. And it was well this was so.

The scheme Slim initially devised was for a crossing of the Chindwin by two Corps. The more southerly thrust, by Stopford's 33 Corps, was to break out of the Kalewa bridgehead with 20 Indian and 2 British Divisions, and 254 Tank Brigade. 2 Division would aim for Ye-u, and 20 Division for Monywa. Further north a re-formed 4 Corps

---

* In simple terms, Mountbatten's confidence in Leese diminished rather than increased, as the months passed, while his trust in Slim never wavered.

was to emerge from the bridgehead at Sittaung, penetrate the Zibyu Taungdan obstacle, and then make for Shwebo and a link-up with 33 Corps. Originally an airborne operation around Shwebo was contemplated, but Slim had a distaste for such ventures and their diversion of precious aircraft from the vital function of supply. Suspecting also that the Japanese knew that his airborne resources were small, he reckoned they were more valuable as a threat than a weapon. In any case, the idea proved unnecessary, since 4 Corps fulfilled its mission successfully on foot and wheel and track.

It was a Corps with a new look. Early in August, while still at Ranchi, Scoones had started planning for its move across the Chindwin and by 11 October had moved his headquarters back to Imphal, where the Corps was already concentrating. 7 Indian Division at Kohima was battle-hardened, but the other formation, 19 Indian, was still virgin— an innocence well balanced by its high morale and the calculated dynamism of its commander, Major-General 'Pete' Rees, who brought to the battlefield that restless energy and impetuous leadership-from-the-front which characterized Rommel. And these qualities in Rees were soon supported by the cavalier dash of a new Corps commander, for in early December Scoones returned to India as C in-C Central Command, to be succeeded on the 8th by Frank Messervy from 7 Division—Messervy who, Slim wrote, 'had the temperament, sanguine, inspiring, and not too calculating of odds, that I thought would be required for the tasks I designed for 4 Corps'. Slim had urgently requested Messervy's appointment, but he was not blind to his limitations, and realized that the Corps Commander's drive must be stabilized by a steady chief of staff. He chose, therefore, a sound and sensible Sapper, Brigadier Cobb, who had been Director of Plans to Giffard and for a time to Mountbatten. Messervy, well aware that a brake was being applied, protested to his Army Commander. He didn't know Cobb. Cobb didn't fit. 'Very well,' Slim replied, 'no Cobb, no Corps.' Messervy accepted defeat, and admitted Cobb into what he was the first to recognize as a fruitful alliance.

Messervy had not actually taken over when 19 Division set off on 4 December, the spearhead of the Corps, pushing over the Chindwin to the north of Sittaung with its first objective 60 miles away at Pinlebu. (At the same time a brigade of 20 Division from 33 Corps was advancing through difficult going, having crossed the Chindwin on the 3rd at Mawlaik, some 30 miles north of Kalewa.) But the operation orders Messervy received from Slim on the 7th, as he took up his new command, were specific and stimulating. By mid-February he must have concentrated his Corps in the Ye-u/Shwebo area, having broken *en route* through the 200-mile barrier of the precipitous Zibyu Taungdan, made contact with 36 Division coming down from NCAC, tidied away any Japanese resistance and wheeled south to the heart of the Irrawaddy loop.* In words which both Messervy and Rees could relish the order added: 'You will realize that the Japanese opposing you are neither in great strength nor in good shape. It is therefore legitimate for you to take certain risks, which in other circumstances would not be justified.' Was there a conscious or unconscious echo here of the exhortation issued to his advancing armies by Haig on 22 August, 1918? 'Risks, which a month ago would have been criminal to incur, ought now to be incurred as a duty.'

Suddenly, however, suspicions which had been growing in Slim's mind since early December became a certainty. By comparison with their normal capability, the resistance of the Japanese now had a merely token quality, even along the easily defensible tracks and defiles of the Zibyu. Short of transport and engineers, with no artillery, 19 Division nevertheless was allowed to move so fast that by 12 December Rees was 45 miles from Sittaung; on the 14th he entered Pinlebu, and on the 16th made personal contact with a staff officer from 36 Division and symbolically united the central and northern theatres. Each day strengthened Slim's conviction. Air reconnaissance revealed that Japanese movement across the Irrawaddy was eastward and not towards the 14th Army. Captured papers, liberated Burmese, the absence of prepared defences all told the same story—the Japanese had no intention of making a stand within the Irrawaddy loop, but were going to hold Mandalay with the great river before and not behind them. Slim was on the verge of pouring his army into a vast sack void of the Japanese. If he continued with his current arrangements the only course open would be to carry by storm a wide and strongly defended waterway before the decisive battle for central Burma could even begin. Since he had at no time entertained so profitless an idea, his immediate aim must be to issue new instructions to his Army. It is no wonder that some observers at Imphal on 14 December, when Slim and his corps commanders were knighted, felt that he seemed on edge. He was in the midst of one of the greatest crises of his career.

---

* The object of the wheel being to catch the Japanese between the pincer-claws of 4 Corps and 33 Corps advancing from the west.

In retrospect—in *Defeat into Victory*, for example—Slim ascribed the Japanese withdrawal beyond the line of the Irrawaddy partly to the speed with which 14th Army had attacked across the Chindwin and partly to the military judgement of Kimura, who had replaced the discredited Kawabe as Commander-in-Chief. In latter 1944 Slim knew of Kimura's arrival, but not of his qualities. His firm assumption that the Japanese would hold out west of the Irrawaddy had been based to a considerable degree on the belief that Kimura would act with the conventional rigidity of Kawabe; the withdrawal east of the river he later ascribed to an unexpected and laudable flexibility of mind on the part of his new opponent. But what he did not know at the time, and appears not to have appreciated when writing his book in the fifties, was that after the summer defeats Imperial General Headquarters in Tokyo decided that Burma Area Army was too weak for its commitments. As early as 19 September instructions were issued to Field-Marshal Count Terauchi, whose far-ranging responsibilities as C-in-C Southern Command included Burma, to ensure the security of strategic areas of *Southern* Burma at all costs, but to consider a severance by the enemy of communications to China as of secondary importance. From the Japanese point of view, therefore, the territory within the Irrawaddy loop had become expendable even before Slim crossed the Chindwin,* and Kimura in withdrawing was doing no more than carry out effectively a pre-determined strategy.

Whatever the origins of the enemy withdrawal, Slim had now to deal with a *fait accompli*. Within a matter of days his decision was taken. To attack the Japanese around Mandalay frontally across the Irrawaddy would be suicidal, and never entered Slim's mind. To wheel his army so as to cross the river and come in on their northern flank would be an administrative nightmare, if not an impossibility. In any case, such an operation offered none of the rich strategic rewards promised by the more daring plan which Slim in fact adopted—and christened EX-TENDED CAPITAL. On 16 December a short signal informed ALFSEA that the Japanese were withdrawing, that the original CAPITAL plan was scrapped, and that Slim's new intentions would follow shortly. On the 17th he sent Leese a summary of the revised EXTENDED CAPITAL plan, a full, elaborated statement not being despatched until the 20th.† But

---

* Not, of course, without resistance. The Japanese left sizeable rearguards between the Chindwin and the Irrawaddy.
† After stating in this signal that his prime object was the destruction of all

meanwhile on the 18th he summoned his two Corps commanders to Messervy's headquarters at Tamu and, entirely on his own initiative, gave them his verbal orders for the radically different offensive they were now to undertake, with instructions to start the necessary moves immediately. Within hours these were put in train, and on 19 December Slim issued a 14th Army Operation Instruction setting out the details of his plan. That he took these decisions wholly on his own responsibility was understood by his subordinates at the time and confirmed by him in retrospect. 'This I considered to be something I should do myself without asking for approval from ALFSEA or SEAC,' he wrote to Brigadier Roberts on 22 October, 1959. 'So I did not ask for sanction.'

No doubt this behaviour was high-handed and reprehensible. Still, what Slim had in fact done was to initiate at short notice the most subtle, audacious and complex operation of his whole career. Its execution revealed—if the revelation was by now necessary—that Slim was a complete general, since every element of the military art was requisite if EXTENDED CAPITAL were not to fail. Deception and surprise, flexibility, concentration on the objective, calculated risks, the solution of grave administrative problems, imagination, sang-froid, invigorating leadership—all the clichés of the military textbooks were simultaneously and harmoniously brought to life as Slim, with an absolute assurance, conceived and accomplished his masterpiece.

EXTENDED CAPITAL was an exquisite example of the dictum of Clausewitz: 'Everything is very simple in war, but the simplest thing is very difficult. These difficulties accumulate and produce a friction which no man can imagine exactly who has not seen war.' For the essence of the plan was simplicity itself. The Japanese were evidently nervous about Mandalay. With a whole Corps, therefore, Slim decided to convince them that his main assault would come over the Irrawaddy in this sector. Meanwhile, blanketed by this deception, a second Corps would assemble further south, strike unexpectedly across the river and make at headlong speed for Meiktila, the ganglion or nerve-centre of Japanese operations in Central and Northern Burma.* That critical

---

Japanese forces in Burma, Slim formally declared his hand for the first time by adding that his ultimate aim, for administrative reasons, must be the capture of a south Burma port between March and May. He had already given his Corps Commanders a port as their target—verbally on the 18th and in writing on the 19th. ALFSEA does not appear to have raised any objections.

* Meiktila was an important centre of communications by road and rail as well as a region of supply-bases, hospitals, depots, etc.

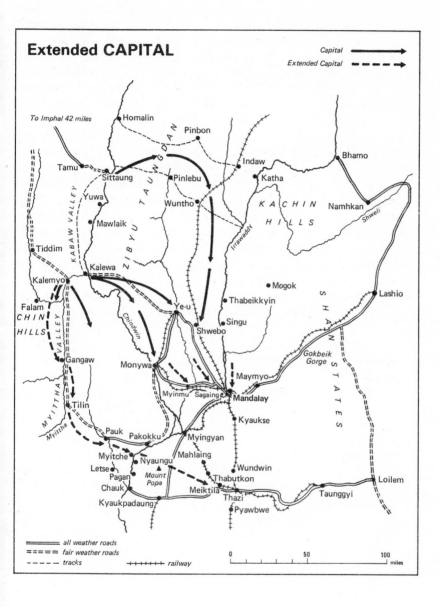

Extended CAPITAL

Capital ➤
Extended Capital ➤

To Imphal 42 miles
Homalin
Pinbon
Tamu
Sittaung
Pinlebu
Indaw
Bhamo
Katha
Yuwa
Wuntho
KACHIN
Namhkan
Mawlaik
HILLS
Shweli
KABAW VALLEY
ZIBYU TAUNGDAN
Irrawaddy
Tiddim
Kalewa
Kalemyo
Mogok
Lashio
Falam
Ye-u
Thabeikkyin
CHIN
HILLS
Chindwin
Singu
Shwebo
Gangaw
Monywa
Gokbeik
Gorge
MYITTHA VALLEY
Tilin
Myinmu Sagaing Mandalay
Maymyo
Myittha
Kyaukse
Pauk
Pakokku
Myingyan
SHAN STATES
Myitche
Nyaungu
Mahlaing
Letse
Pagan
Mount
Popa
Wundwin
Loilem
Chauk
Thabutkon
Kyaukpadaung
Meiktila
Thazi
Taunggyi
Pyawbwe

═══ all weather roads
≡≡≡ fair weather roads
--- tracks
+++++ railway

0   50   100
miles

area secured, all enemy resistance along the upper Irrawaddy must crumble, and 14th Army would be poised for EXTENDED CAPITAL'S second phase—the race for the sea to capture a port in Southern Burma, Rangoon or perhaps Moulmein, before the arrival of the monsoon in May threw Slim's extended communications into chaos. This was the ambitious project (cherished by the senior staff of 14th Army as the SOB or 'Sea or Bust' plan) which was first presented by Slim to his Corps Commanders at the Tamu meeting on the 18th, and then embodied formally in the Army Operation Instruction circulated on the following day.

The responsibility, and therefore the credit, for undertaking EXTENDED CAPITAL are Slim's. He alone would have carried the stigma of failure. But it would be wrong to maintain that the concept of the operation was uniquely his. As Brigadier Hasted observed, the atmosphere at Slim's headquarters was one of collaborative discussion. He and his staff tossed ideas about, and in this particular case there is no doubt that alternatives to the CAPITAL plan were under review—however theoretically—long before the Japanese withdrawal became evident. 'In a casual conversation', Brigadier Roberts recalled,[*] 'I once asked Bill when he first thought of Meiktila as an alternative to Ye-u/Shwebo. His answer was that he didn't think he did think of it first: the whole 14th Army staff was continually thinking about it and he didn't know who first said Meiktila. The result of their joint thinking and discussions was EXTENDED CAPITAL.' An ideal relationship, of course, between a general and his staff, the virtue in this case being that when, in early December, a complicated new plan was put into effect at great speed, the preliminary discussions had been so relevant that 14th Army could be given a new orientation almost overnight, without confusion or misunderstanding.

Still, the plans for most great battles, on analysis, can be seen to have a simple structure. Once the commander's intuition, imagination, *coup d'oeil* has revealed that structure to him, it is in the overcoming of difficulties as they accumulate, and in the tolerance of the mental and physical strains imposed on himself and his forces—the friction—that he displays his qualities. The difficulties inherent in EXTENDED CAPITAL began to accumulate immediately,

> 'not single spies,
> But in battalions'.

---

* Letter to author, 8 September, 1975.

As the plan was put into action, however, none proved to be insuperable by Slim's steady, fertile mind, the constructive support of Mountbatten, the unimaginable endurance of the air-crews, the dexterity of the engineers and, above all, the *élan* of the front line soldier. Kimura was deceived by a man who had contrived to 'alter his tactics in relation to his opponent', and his army was irremediably shattered. In so defeating the Japanese Slim earned a Chinese accolade, for Sun Tzu would surely have recognized him as a Heaven-born Captain.

CHAPTER THIRTEEN

SEA OR BUST

'Wars are a dialogue between one plan and another.'
General Ahmed Ismail,
C-in-C of the Egyptian Army in the Yom Kippur War

IT WAS Kimura who used the phrase 'the battle of the Irrawaddy shore', which aptly summarizes his mis-reading of the aim of EXTENDED CAPITAL. Once Slim had outlined this new plan on 18 December the immediate priority for Stopford and Messervy was to re-arrange their respective commands, for here lay the secret key to an effective crossing of the river. Aware of Japanese nervousness about the Mandalay front, and aware, too, that Kimura had identified the aggressive 19 Division as part of 4 Corps, Slim had decided to add Rees's Division to Stopford's existing formations in 33 Corps, 2 and 20 Divisions,* and then, by setting up a dummy Corps headquarters and by careful manipulation of wireless traffic, to persuade the enemy that 19 Division's activities represented the operations of a genuine 4 Corps still trying to link up with 33 Corps in the Shwebo plain for a joint, direct assault on Mandalay. In this way Kimura's main strength should be distracted and pinned down by Stopford. Many other ruses were employed to further this deception. In the weeks to come the Japanese were so completely misled that the way Slim mystified Kimura, the concealment of 6 Panzer Army's location before the Ardennes offensive, and the persuasion of the Germans at the time of D Day that a phantom Army truly existed in S.E. England may perhaps be accounted the

---

* 33 Corps also included 254 Tank Brigade and the independent 268 Infantry Brigade.

three most interesting examples of military deception in the Second World War.

But this was only half the secret key. By concentrating all operations between Chindwin and Irrawaddy in Stopford's hands, Slim released Messervy and his 4 Corps HQ to direct that part of 14th Army's offensive which was intended to deliver an unsuspected but mortal blow. Slim and his staff had long been aware that, after traversing the Kabaw valley and reaching Kalemyo, it was possible, instead of taking the short cut to the Chindwin at Kalewa, to proceed due south on the difficult route via the Myittha valley, hitting the Irrawaddy at Pakokku.* If a force could be secretly assembled and successfully launched across the river at this point, Meiktila, the critical target, lay only some 80 miles away. This was Messervy's mission. Its essence consisted in moving a whole Corps unobserved down the Kabaw and Myittha valleys, a march of 300 miles, establishing a bridgehead across the Irrawaddy, and then hurling a fast striking force over the good going to Meiktila, all *before* the Japanese could realize that 4 Corps was no longer somewhere far to the north, within the Irrawaddy loop, and effectively re-deploy their forces.

Clausewitz's remark about the difficult simplicities of war is here most apt, for on paper the plan looks uncomplicated, yet the problems it involved were enormous. They must be emphasized, because Slim's ultimate triumph at Meiktila was not merely the result of devising a skilful plan of attack; it entailed—since the decision to implement EXTENDED CAPITAL was his alone—an immense confidence not only in his own judgement but also in the resourceful dynamism of his Army and the readiness of those in his rear, right down the line to Mountbatten, to provide the extra logistic support his operations would require—particularly if he was to be able to advance southwards to the sea. When he called Stopford and Messervy to that meeting at Tamu on 18 December and gave them their new orders, Slim was committing an act of faith, for all the factors in which he trusted for the success of his new plan were interlinked. The failure of a single link could destroy the whole.

The first difficulty was to secure the route to the Irrawaddy without giving the game away. Ahead of his main force, therefore, Messervy sent up the Myittha valley 28 East African Brigade, the hope being that

---

* The potentialities of the Myittha valley by-pass had been familiar to Slim since 1942, when it was used by 2 Burma Brigade during the Retreat.

the latter would be taken for units of 11 East African Division, which, as has been seen, was recently active in the Kabaw valley. Security was strict. Slim ordered a virtually complete wireless silence south of Kalemyo. Behind this cover moved the first element of the striking force, 7 Indian Division, whose prime task was to secure a bridgehead beyond the Irrawaddy. All these forward moves proceeded smoothly and without arousing the enemy's suspicions*—even when stiff opposition at Gangaw in the Myittha valley had to be overcome on 10 January with impressive aid from the RAF. But the difficulties stand out if it be appreciated that when Slim gave Messervy orders on 18 December virtually none of 4 Corps was yet deployed forward—the Africans, for example, were at Imphal and most of 7 Indian Division at Kohima.

Everything was urgent, if Slim was to reach a southern port before the May monsoon. Yet to carry the immense weight of 4 Corps transport, wheeled and tracked, for fighting and supply, there was only the one viable land-route up the Kabaw and Myittha valleys. Analysis discloses four main ways in which the inventive fertility and determination of his Army, powerfully supported from the rear, were able to overcome this grave and frustrating limitation.

The first step was to extend through the deliquescent Kabaw valley a road capable of functioning in all weathers. The solution had already been found by Hasted, whose earlier work on the great airfield construction programme in the Brahmaputra valley had introduced him to the properties of *bithess*—strips of hessian coated with bitumen, which, when laid with correct technique on a flat surface (and correctly maintained) could provide a strong and waterproof highway. Since no alternative possibilities existed—the vast quantities of stone that would be necessary were unavailable, as was the transport to lift them— Hasted proposed the *bithess* method to Slim although, as he made clear, he had no experience of its durability for roads carrying a heavy volume of traffic. Slim took the risk, the idea succeeded,

---

* The unobserved assembly of the striking force was helped by the fact that Japanese intelligence appears to have 'lost' 7 and 17 Indian Divisions, assuming that they had been so battered as to prevent them appearing at the front for some time. The events in the Myittha valley were therefore interpreted as being no more than a Long Range Penetration operation which could be handled by the troops on the spot. So unworried were the Japanese that Count Terauchi committed a supreme error by ordering the enemy's 2 Division to transfer from Meiktila to Indo-China.

and within 120 days 123 miles of allweather communications were laid.*

But the decision to use the Myittha valley raised further problems. Hasted had long thought that the Nyaungu area, some 15 miles south-west of Pakokku, would make an ideal crossing-place, and had indeed discussed this means of passing over the Irrawaddy with his fellow-Sapper, Brigadier Cobb, even before the latter had joined 14th Army or the advance down to the Chindwin was being planned. Then the project had seemed theoretical. Now, suddenly, Slim told Hasted about his intentions for 4 Corps and asked him how soon he could construct an adequate route up the Myittha valley.

> An impossible question to answer at the time. So I asked for a couple of days to have a look and rake up what information and data I could. I flew the course in a fighter, but with the thickness of the jungle and the difficulty of tracing streams and what existed of a jungle track† I was little the wiser at the end of my investigation. We therefore conjured up a 'by guess and by God' answer, which came to about 42 days. I didn't quite know what Uncle Bill would say when I had to confess it was very much a shot in the dark. His reply was character-istic: 'God help you, Bill if it takes more than 50!'‡

The third achievement is particularly significant, since it demonstra-ted how, for all his generalship in the field, Slim's operations might have been slowed down and even halted had it not been for the co-operation of the air forces, the authority of Mountbatten and the staff of ALFSEA. It is evident that the nature of the terrain, the great dis-tances and the lack of land communications all placed air supply at a premium if EXTENDED CAPITAL was to succeed. Put simply, the require-ments by air lift for 14th Army were calculated at 705 long tons a day from 16 December, rising steadily to a peak of some 1,200 daily tons from the beginning of March onwards. Yet even before Slim had announced his new plan on 10 December the means for this vital

---

* Apart from forward delivery of mile upon mile of hessian, this method consumed immense amounts of precious fuel. For laying one yard of *bithess* track, it was reckoned, a gallon of petrol and a gallon of diesel were needed to 'gum up the works'.

† The 230 miles from Kalemyo to Pakokku are described in the *Official History*: 'for the most part unmetalled, narrow and tortuous, with many steep hills, hair-pin bends and bridges too weak to carry the necessary loads'.

‡ Letter to author, 25 March, 1974.

sustenance were unexpectedly narrowed. Early that day, as Slim vividly recalled in *Defeat into Victory*, 'I was awakened in my headquarters at Imphal* by the roar of engines as a large number of aircraft took off in succession and passed low overhead. I knew loaded aircraft were due to leave for 33 Corps later in the morning, but I was surprised at this early start. . . . To my consternation, I learnt that, without warning, three squadrons of American Dakotas (75 aircraft), allotted to Fourteenth Army maintenance, had been suddenly ordered to China. . . . It was a crisis.' Since 14th Army needed a minimum of some 7,000 sorties a day from mid-December, the loss without warning of 75 aircraft sharply underlines the narrowness of the margin within which Slim had to work, the unpredictability of his American allies, and, indeed, his courage in proceeding with a daring operation like EXTENDED CAPITAL when the unreliability of his reserves had been revealed on its very eve.

Yet the obstacles were overcome. By careful pressure on the American and British High Commands. Mountbatten contrived to maintain at least the minimal number of aircraft required. Their productivity, it is true, was often the result of using crews and planes far beyond the danger-point for metal and man—a sacrificial service which emphasizes once again the spirit of co-operation engendered between Mountbatten, Slim and their airmen, a spirit which irradiates the pages of the transport squadrons' histories. But supplies must be delivered as well as carried. As the divisions moved forward, therefore, tremendous efforts were made to hack out and level airstrips every 50 miles. 'As things turned out', Brigadier Hasted recalled, 'we did just as Bill foresaw, and forward units soon cottoned on, so much so that the reports of airfields ready to receive supplies became almost embarrassing! It was a standing joke at 14th Army HQ. The sight of one in operation had to be seen to be believed. On one occasion I was flying with Uncle Bill on a visit to one such field. Unfortunately we arrived just as supply had started. Each time we made an approach run an American D.C. would cut in in front. We circled for half an hour before we could get in. Even so, he never lost his temper.'

By a paradox the fourth difficulty to be overcome by 14th Army, deep in the land-locked heart of Burma, was naval. At the outset, even before CAPITAL was extended, Slim and his planners appreciated that Chindwin and Irrawaddy must be converted into conveyors if all the

---

* Where since mid-July Slim had established first a Tactical, then a Main Head-quarters.

thousands of tons of supplies required for the advance were to be reliably delivered in the forward areas.* Commendable foresight at the War Office in London and GHQ in India set in train during 1944 the pre-fabrication of shallow-draft tugs, barges and lighters, the first of which, lifted experimentally by rail to Dimapur and onward by road, actually reached Sittaung on the Chindwin by 28 November and was used by 19 Division in its crossing of the river. Thereafter, by road or air, large numbers of these craft reached 14th Army.

But after Slim decided on EXTENDED CAPITAL it was clear that as his troops raced southward through Burma the volume of water-borne supplies would have to be drastically increased, and so:

> One hot day at the beginning of the advance I took Bill Hasted, my quiet-spoken Chief Engineer, a little upstream of Kalewa and said 'Billy, there's the river and there are the trees,' pointing to the great forests within half a mile of the bank. 'In two months I want five hundred tons of supplies a day down the river.' He looked thought-fully at the river and the trees, and then at me. 'The difficult we will do at once; the impossible will take a little longer,' he quoted from a saying in frequent use in Fourteenth Army, and added with a grin, 'For miracles we like a month's notice!' 'You're lucky,' I answered, 'you've got two!'†

Rich stands of teak were there for the cutting. Forestry units and Colonel Williams's invaluable Elephant Company were soon delivering timber in bulk. A former furniture manufacturer, Lieut-Colonel Layton, improved the existing design for locally manufactured 'Eastern Army boats' which had been evolved as early as 1942. By the end of the campaign no less than 541 of those craft were shaped from the trees and launched on the river. With a certain panache Commander Holt of the Royal Navy, working in a tent beside the Chindwin, also produced drawings for a battle fleet. 'They were two wooden, punt-like vessels, with lightly armoured bridges, which steamed twelve knots, and were armed with one Bofors gun, two Oerlikons, and a couple of Browning light automatics mounted for anti-aircraft fire. I claimed to be the only general who had designed, built, christened, launched and

---

* The difficulty was also geographical. The advance would have to be made against the grain of the country, through regions where the river communications ran at right angles to the advance.
† *Defeat into Victory*, p. 398.

commissioned warships for the Royal Navy.'* On the day of the
launching, when the gunboats were named *Una* and *Pamela* after the
daughters of Slim and Mountbatten, Uncle Bill was fortunate in avoiding perhaps serious injury. As he cruised up the Chindwin towards the
construction yards he noticed some Sappers building a pier and, typically, drew in to talk to them. The pier was incomplete, and the plank-
ing loose. Slim leapt off the launch unconcerned, landed on a free plank,
and disappeared into the pontoon below, to emerge sound but shaken.

Some chronological compression is inevitable in an account of these
many and varied logistical preparations, a part only of what constituted
a continuous and increasingly complicated background to the actual
fighting. For a time the fighting itself assisted the logistics. As 33
Corps steadily obtained a stranglehold on the Irrawaddy loop it was
seizing ground essential for the maintenance of the Army in the
Meiktila area. When 19 Division swept south, for example, and met 2
Division at Shwebo,† airstrips were acquired vital for supplying the
advance, while 20 Division, by reaching down the Chindwin to
Monywa, helped to prepare the way for the boat-yard's output at
Kalewa. And all these operations, of course, were simultaneously
succeeding in their prime purpose of confusing Kimura and persuading
him that the target of 14th Army was Mandalay.

By 1 February Slim's two Corps Commanders had laudably executed
the first part of the orders issued to them at Tamu only six weeks
previously, since their troops had already reached or were in sight of
the Irrawaddy along a front of no less than 200 miles—from 20 miles
south-west of Pakokku to Thabeikkyin, due north of Mandalay,
where 19 Division had already established a bridgehead, profitably
repelled the counter-attack of 15 and 53 Divisions, and made itself
secure. Continuing evidence of Japanese nervousness about the
Mandalay front, and relative disregard of the area further south, confirmed that 14th Army's simple yet subtle deception plan was working
perfectly. Slim now held the strategic initiative in the palm of his hand.
His air umbrella, which had prevented the enemy from observing the
secret deployment of 4 Corps, was unpierced, and the Irrawaddy itself

---

* Both craft sank next day, due to leaking nail holes in the timber. This remained
a problem after they were refloated and fitted out.
† Shwebo was ear-marked for 2 Division, but the van of the ardent 19th arrived
first. This was the occasion when Pete Rees was congratulated for kicking a
goal while the referee was not looking.

was a massive guard against Japanese reconnaissance on more than a minor, local scale. All that remained was to cross the river.

Yet this, so simple-sounding, was fraught with difficulty. 'Like most large rivers in the East, the Irrawaddy bore little resemblance to the course shown on the map.'* Each monsoon altered the sandbanks and deep water channels along which the river would flow during the dry season. Moreover, accurate information about these shifting channels and variable shores could only be obtained, particularly in the area selected for the main crossing, at the last minute as the antennae of 4 Corps probed down to the western shore without attracting the enemy's attention across the water. The emergence of new sandbanks extended and complicated the assault crafts' route. And the craft themselves, the most that could be assembled at the end of 14th Army's long and overcrowded lines of communication, were at best enough to carry and build up one attack division per Corps. Many were in poor shape or obsolete, and something like 50 per cent reliability of the outboard engines seemed a prudent estimate.† The course for the leading waves of the assault would be some 2,000 yards.

In breaching the Irrawaddy line Slim was thus undertaking the longest river-crossing of the Second World War in a context of improvisation, deficient equipment and last-minute intelligence. Comparisons between great battles are usually unsatisfactory, but it serves to emphasize his achievement if one draws a contrast with Montgomery's advantage at the Rhine crossing. Behind his 21st Army Group lay the vast and efficient road and rail network of N.W. Europe. He had airborne divisions to drop on his immediate front. His technical equipment—the continuous smoke-screen, amphibious vehicles etc.— was lavish and up-to-date. An enormous artillery park, rich in ammunition, gave him unlimited support. Compared with the Irrawaddy, the Rhine is narrow and its behaviour readily calculable. (On the other

---

* Michael Roberts, *Golden Arrow: the Story of the 7th Indian Division in the Second World War*, p. 176.

† Though the last minute intelligence was more or less adequate, one great difficulty was that, owing to the shortage of craft, the assault crossings had to be timed and launched in such a way that craft could be switched from one crossing-site to another.

‡ An earlier example suffices. Movement forward of the vast amount of material required for bridging the Chindwin demanded great quantities of efficient lorries. The discovery that one type was inadequate for the difficult haul onwards from Tamu meant that the engines of 200 lorries had to be changed in two days by scratch teams of mainly inexperienced men.

hand, Montgomery was attacking where the Germans expected him to cross, whereas Slim had deceived his enemy. Consequently each commander could assume a very different ferocity of opposition.)

Still, Slim's problems were real, they were daunting—and they were overcome. The method was that of orchestration—of careful, de-synchronized crossings each planned to achieve a specific effect along the whole 200-mile front. In the north Rees, throughout latter January, ably distracted Kimura with 19 Division's Thabeikkyin bridgehead. Then, on 13 February, Gracey's 20 Division, having captured Monywa, crossed the Irrawaddy at Myinmu and, for the next fortnight, diverted on to its positions large forces of Japanese infantry and tanks which continued to counter-attack in wave after wave of suicidal and fruitless effort. Bull-dozers were needed to bury their corpses. By this noisy overture Kimura's pre-conceptions were, it seemed, confirmed. The target was Mandalay.

But the main part of Slim's grand design* followed immediately and elsewhere, so unexpected that his point of lodgement on the far bank of the Irrawaddy was the weakest in the Japanese line—the boundary between 15th and 28th Armies, traditionally the most vulnerable link. It was guarded, moreover, by little more than a contingent of the Indian National Army. And here too deception was effectively applied within the orchestrated plan. Slim had properly left the arrangements for the crossing to Messervy and Evans, whose 7 Division was to establish a bridgehead from which the mobile force could debouch on Meiktila. Pakokku they dismissed as a convenient but too obvious spring-board. Instead Nyaungu was selected, 20 miles downstream, and it was here that during the night of 13/14 February, less than two days after Gracey's diversion at Myinmu, there began what Slim called 'this all-important crossing . . . on which the whole fabric of my battleplan rested'. Aided by feints to the north and south of Nyaungu, impeded by blunders and mechanical failures, rescued by its own determination, 7 Division firmly established itself east of the river within a bridgehead several miles in extent.

---

* The *design* must be emphasized. The de-synchronized crossings of the Rhine by the Americans and then the British were not the product of an overall plan. The de-sychronized crossings of the Irrawaddy were the product of calculation and foresight. In conversations with Mountbatten Slim had drawn deeply on his experience as Chief of Combined Operations in the development of techniques for assault landings and their follow-up. On 16 February Mountbatten himself crossed to Nyaungu to watch the work in the bridgehead.

On its southern fringe loomed the ruined city of Pagan. 'Its twelve hundred temples, madder red or ghostly white, rise, some like fantastic pyramids or turreted fairy castles, others in tapering pagoda spires, from the sage green mass of trees against the changing pastel blues, reds and golds of sunrise.'* For General Evans it was more to the point that the I.N.A. defenders of Pagan had offered the white flag and surrendered without a fight. 'This incident,' Slim mordantly observed, 'was, I think, the chief contribution the Indian National Army made to either side in the Burma War.'

Anxious to secure Meiktila before the Japanese could react effectively, Messervy abandoned his plan of concentrating his striking force within the bridgehead before unleashing it. Instead, as soon as it could be ferried over it was pushed outward beyond the 7 Division perimeter. Commanding the force was General Cowan, whose veteran 17 Division, after its rest in India, had moved back to Imphal, where by the end of January it had been reorganized, with two brigades fully motorized for mobile operations, while the third was lightly equipped and air-portable. (Soon afterwards 5 Division was similarly transformed, with 'Sea or Bust' in Slim's mind.)† In February 17 Division had been brought up to the forward zone, dropping off its air-portable brigade at Palel. Through Nyaungu, therefore, Cowan fed his two mobile infantry brigades, two regiments of 255 Tank Brigade, armoured cars and a battery of self-propelled guns, all on wheels or tracks, a sight customary in Africa and Europe but then unique in the Burma theatre.

By 4 March Cowan had advanced 80 miles, occupied Meiktila and destroyed its garrison, after receiving his airborne brigade, 99, which was able to fly in at Thabutkon airfield, west of the town. Yet this genuine success was not absolute, for Slim and his subordinates well understood that it was in the Japanese character, as soon as the real enemy thrust had been identified, to counter-attack with every man available, whole, halt or maimed. 'The Burma Army had been dealt a crippling blow,' the *Official History* rightly observes, 'but the fight to retain Meiktila was to be long and bitter since the Japanese concentrated every unit and formation they could to break 14th Army's stranglehold on their main line of communication, a stranglehold which threatened the destruction of all their forces in North Burma.' This is exactly what Slim wanted; it provides a classic example of the 'battle of destruction',

---

* *Defeat into Victory*, p. 429.
† The proposal for these changes was made by Messervy, and welcomed by Slim.

in which the commander seizes ground his enemy must recover at all costs and destroys him in the course of his counter-attacks.

Slim was on the scene before Meiktila had been subdued. On 1 March,* having flown back the previous day from the Mandalay front where he had co-ordinated with Stopford the moves of 33 and 4 Corps, he wished to visit Cowan. The reports he had received on his return to his headquarters at Monywa suggested that 17 Division's attack at Meiktila was losing impetus and 'we could not risk another Myitkyina'. The RAF, however, stubbornly refused to fly him, as the Thabutkon airfield was still unsafe. Anyone else, but not the Army Commander. Flattered but furious, Slim seized the opportunity offered by a visiting American general with his own B.25 bomber. Would he like to see the Meiktila battle? This admirable example of 14th Army improvisation succeeded. They picked up Messervy at Pagan and were soon at Cowan's command post. It was the worst day of the battle. Describing it, Slim was moved to write a memorable description of his old friend, whose conduct of a conflict so different from those of the mountain and jungle had much impressed him. This was a confusion of tank versus gun, road-blocks, snipers, bunkers in fortified houses, constantly changing its pattern and pressures. Cowan, Slim saw,

> was very short of sleep and remained so for several days. Yet throughout he was alert to every change in the situation on any sector, and swung his air and artillery support to meet and take advantage of it. His firm grip on his own formations and on the enemy never faltered. To watch a highly skilled, experienced, and resolute commander controlling a hard-fought battle is to see, not only a man triumphing over the highest mental and physical stresses, but an artist producing his effects in the most complicated and difficult of all the arts.†

One feels the pride and contentment with which Slim wrote of this high-quality performance by a man with whom he had shared so much—1/6th Gurkhas and Abbottabad, the 1942 Retreat, close family affections. For he wrote in sympathy also. A few weeks earlier, visiting

---

* In *Defeat into Victory* Slim refers to 1 March, whereas the *Official History* places these events on the 2nd. But Slim's personal diary for 1 March reads: ' . . . pick up Messervy—go Meiktila. See 1/7th clear bunkers. Back to Monywa.' For the 2nd his only entry is 'R.A.F. Concert'!
† *Defeat into Victory*, p. 447.

19 Division's bridgehead, he had called on his old battalion, the 1/6th Gurkha Rifles, and among those whom he had known so long—since they were raw recruits from Nepal, or the babies of his fellow-officers— he was able to meet Cowan's son, an officer of fire and promise in his father's pattern. But a few days after Slim's flight to Meiktila, as Cowan was fighting desperately to retain the town, news came that his Gurkha son had died of wounds at Mandalay. Years after the war, as he was working on his book, this bitter coincidence was still an unhealed wound in Slim's memory.

Fortunately he had more agreeable recollections. Every Great Captain has his personal style. One recurrent characteristic of Slim's, as powerful in the Army Commander as it had been at Gallipoli, is his natural and instinctive affinity for the front line. This is a matter of *nuance*. Some commanders properly feel that in spite or perhaps because of their seniority they must 'get up front' as a duty—this was a compulsion very strong in commanders of the Second World War who had served as young men in the First and remembered the contempt, on the Western Front, for the Brass Hats in their safe châteaux. But Slim always made for the front as if he was returning home. Nowhere is this more evident than in his wonderfully vivid account, in *Defeat into Victory*, of how, leaving Cowan to conduct 'his grim orchestra', he took his party off to see 'how it was being handled lower down'.

For Slim this meant penetrating on foot into the heat of the battle, where one of Cowan's brigades was assaulting the northern outskirts of Meiktila. Here his party watched a tank-and-infantry clearance of Japanese bunkers only a few hundred yards away. Moving even further forward, Slim suddenly discovered that they were in the direct line of fire from a Sherman tank shooting from the far side of the bunkers. 'One army commander, one corps commander, an American general, and several less distinguished individuals adopted the prone position with remarkable unanimity.' But to understand fully this aspect of Slim—who certainly had no right to be involved in a company operation—it is necessary to read his own complete account, and then ask whether anything comparable can be found in the memoirs of his peers. This was not, for example, the style of Omar Bradley or Montgomery.

The capture of Meiktila by Cowan precipitated the full-scale Army battle, in favourable conditions, which had been the object of Slim's drive into Central Burma, enabling him so to shatter the Japanese that a race against time to the sea would be practicable. Kimura, as was anticipated, assisted him. Once the commander of Burma Area Army grasped the realities at Meiktila he was appalled but not stunned. Instead, with desperate energy he summoned reinforcements from every quarter, placing all operations under Honda, of 33 Army, with the aim of eliminating the Nyaungu crossing (over which, in the five weeks after a vehicle ferry opened on 15 February, no less than 10,000 vehicles, tanks and guns were transported), destroying the troops of 4 Corps east of the Irrawaddy, relieving Meiktila and thus keeping open a corridor to the south for the inevitable Japanese withdrawal.

The widespread fighting that followed was savage in its intensity, but Slim held all the cards. Though battalions, regiments, artillery units hurried to Honda from 18 Division in the north, from Mandalay, and from Pegu in the deep south, the urgent needs of a crumbling situation caused them to be fed into the attack piecemeal as they arrived, and piece by piece they disintegrated. A highly efficient wireless intercept service at Monywa gave Slim the means of directing air-strikes on the various Japanese headquarters as they changed position, and gradually the enemy's signals failed and died, thus increasing the confusion and lack of control which, with absolute air superiority, the bombers and fighters of the Tactical Air Force ruthlessly imposed. As usual in a crisis, the *kamikaze* spirit flowered and the Japanese fought with a suicidal fanaticism. It was at Meiktila, indeed, that the phenomenon of the 'human mine' was first observed—a soldier crouched in a foxhole, with an aircraft bomb between his legs, prepared to drop a heavy stone on its fuse as a tank passed over him. But fanaticism was no longer enough against the *élan* and well-tempered efficiency of 14th Army.

The epicentre of the conflict was at Meiktila. The Japanese made a supreme effort to recover the airfield just east of the town, through which all Cowan's supplies had to pass until 7 Division, following up, had cleared the road back to the Irrawaddy. To hold the field 5 Division's airborne brigade was flown in, amid shell bursts and bullets, but the enemy, dug into broken ground which was an obstacle to armour, used copious mines and boldly handled field guns to neutralize 255 Brigade's Sherman tanks. It took to the end of March to eradicate the last Japanese. Cowan's capture and defence of this critical centre, round which the whole of Slim's grand strategy revolved, make one of the brightest stars in 14th Army's galaxy.

Before March was over the emergency had passed, for 7 Division threw back all Japanese attempts to reach the Nyaungu crossing and firmly controlled the vital road from the Irrawaddy to Meiktila. Moreover, by capturing the river-port of Myingyan General Evans gave Slim the wharves to which his new-built transport craft could ply down the Chindwin from Kalewa. These were developments of critical importance for Slim as ground-work for his drive to Rangoon, and the military student is unlikely to let them, mundane as they seem, be overshadowed by another event which occurred in March, dramatic though its overtones may be. The British were back in Mandalay.

A month earlier, on 27 February, Leese had issued an ALFSEA Operation Instruction in which 14th Army was ordered to:

1. Destroy the Japanese forces in the Mandalay area.
2. Seize Rangoon before the monsoon.

Slim was a loyal and sensible subordinate who was careful, when writing *Defeat into Victory*, to soften or omit his disapproval of some of the acts and instructions of his superiors. This time, however, he could not conceal his feelings. For once, his pen dipped in acid. 'As orders, based on the Fourteenth Army Operation Instruction of 19 December, 1944, to achieve these objects had already been given to corps two months previously, no changes in our plans or dispositions were necessary. Operations continued at an increasing tempo.'*

The tempo, indeed, was such that only three weeks later, at 1.30 pm on 20 March, a British artilleryman in Mandalay nailed a Union Jack to the flagstaff of Fort Dufferin, the last point of Japanese resistance in the historic city. Stopford's 33 Corps had both distracted the enemy north of besieged Meiktila, and captured Mandalay itself, in rapid moves starting from its three bridgeheads across the Irrawaddy. 19 Division swept down on Mandalay from 40 miles upstream. 2 Division, already well across the river, thrust towards the city from the south, while 20 Division—'I had never seen troops who carried their tails more vertically', Slim recalled—shot south-eastwards out of their much-battered lodgement at Myinmu to quarter the area between Kyaukse and Wundwin in the Meiktila–Mandalay road-rail corridor. As for Mandalay itself, the inch-by-inch withdrawal of the Japanese into the central fort has often been described—the medium guns firing over

---

* Slim considered that his operations were never creatively advanced by ideas or orders from Leese and his ALFSEA staff. It would be unjust, however, to suggest that Leese was merely an absentee landlord. During EXTENDED CAPITAL Slim's little private diary shows that Leese frequently visited his 14th Army HQ for conferences, sometimes at Slim's own request.

open sights to breach the walls, the aircraft skip-bombing, the enemy
destroyed in hole and cranny by flame or grenade. It was a challenge
welcomed by the dynamic 19 (Dagger) Division, and no one who has
read it could forget Slim's vignette of its inimitable commander. The
setting is Mandalay shortly before the final day.

> Through all this noise and the clatter of men clearing a battlefield
> came a strange sound—singing. I followed it. There was General
> Rees, his uniform sweat-soaked and dirty, his distinguishing red scarf
> rumpled round his neck, his bush hat at a jaunty angle, his arm beating
> time, surrounded by a group of Assamese soldiers whom he was
> vigorously leading in the singing of Welsh missionary hymns. The
> fact that he sang in Welsh and they in Khasi only added to the har-
> mony. I looked on admiringly. My generals had character.*

During the operations for and around Meiktila and Mandalay 14th
Army's total battle casualties amounted to 10,500. Considered objec-
tively, the cost was low, in view of the scale and bitterness of the
fighting. In any case, a moment may sometimes be discerned in the
history of an Army when its determination to achieve final victory
changes to certainty that victory is already within its grasp. It is a mood
of exultation and absolute confidence, diffused by the mysterious bush-
telegraphy of a soldier's world. Those who raced forward with 8th
Army's divisions from Alamein were caught in its spell. In 14th Army's
case the assurance which had gathered steadily during the last year now
acquired this extra dimension. They *knew* they had won.

Yet it was by no means a case of all being over bar the fighting.
While stiff fighting indeed lay ahead, the battle for supplies would be
at least as formidable if Slim was to fulfil his own intentions, and Leese's
instructions, by capturing Rangoon before the rains. The reason was
geometrical. Since the average working radius for a transport aircraft
was about 250 miles from its base, the curve within which planes from
Agartala could operate only ran to the south of Kalewa, while those
loading at Imphal could just make Mandalay and Myingyan. From
Chittagong, aircraft reached a line well to the west of Meiktila. In
effect, none of Slim's air bases could maintain his army during the final
phase of EXTENDED CAPITAL. The problem was anticipated and its

---

* *Defeat into Victory*, p. 468.

resolution was perhaps the main contribution of Leese and his ALFSEA staff to the Burma campaign.

If 14th Army was not to be starved of all necessities as it sought to take Rangoon before the monsoon broke, its southward march must be fed from the flank. Good planning by Leese and Christison had secured the islands of Akyab at the beginning of January (helped by a Japanese withdrawal) and Ramree by mid-February (delayed by enemy resistance). Here were the flanking airfields. But an immense administrative effort was required to shift the squadrons, stockpiles, technicians and communications, to create, while the battle still raged, an entirely new network of supply. The staffs and the engineers succeeded. On 20 March Akyab began to function, supplying the first stage of the advance south; on 15 April Ramree started to operate, and now Slim had a base from which aircraft could range far beyond Rangoon. Mountbatten was tireless in maintaining a minimum number of squadrons, and ruthless, with an inevitability whose justice the crews recognized, in driving men and machines beyond the conventional limits.* 14th Army never lived on fat. There would be incidental shortages, and sometimes tightened belts. But though terrain, climate or the enemy might hold up the fighting man, it is fair to say that the 'Sea or Bust' advance was never significantly impeded by lack of supplies.

As Slim contemplated his prospects about the middle of March, he could of course do no more than hope that manna would continue to fall from heaven; and the time factor was terrifying. By mid-May the south-west monsoon would be flooding South Burma. Suppose his army were to be bogged down. Supplies both by air and by road would wither. In any case he had grave doubts about the reliability of his transport lorries, worn out by many months and many miles of hard going. His armour, too, could only be described as venerable. Slim talked to the crews and extolled their efforts. He warned them that every tank must cross the start line in the final race and all must be in at the finish. Then, if they wanted, the crews could push them into the

---

* The situation, comparable in some ways with that of the fighters in the Battle of Britain or during the 'bloody April' of 1917, was unique for transport squadrons who were asked to fly at double sustained rates for months on end. There was immense resistance from the senior airmen, but Mountbatten, who personally visited squadrons to explain the need, had his way. 'It was the most difficult order I ever had to give, and without it Bill and I would have lost.' Letter to author, 22 December, 1975.

sea! Even morale-raising, however, could not overcome another of his problems: the war in the West meant that British reinforcements for the East no longer arrived, yet great numbers of 14th Army's men with long service overseas were now due to be sent home. It was likely—and indeed proved to be the case—that the experienced 2 and 36 British Divisions would be withdrawn from his Army, as would most of the British battalions in his Indian formations.

Yet over-riding all was his faith in himself and his men. Slim was too balanced to become obsessed by vainglory. He made plans by calculating to the last nut and bolt rather than by disregarding facts for the sake of a fantasy. Even his most desperate ventures were governed by a strong sense of realism. His hazardous drive to the south was therefore based on a fine, hard-headed calculation of the possible; was rational rather than emotional conviction which persuaded him that his troops could out-run the rains. Though he was indeed defining a cherished dream, he was also announcing the result of long, shrewd thought when he gave as the main intention in his Operation Instruction of 18 March 'the capture of Rangoon at all costs and as soon as possible before the monsoon'.

How often, however, does a commander find himself, after winning a victory, compelled to fight yet another battle before he can reap the full reward—to clear his start line before he can launch the pursuit! This was now Slim's situation, for Kimura's calculations also turned on the coming of the monsoon—'his with hope', Slim confessed, 'mine with dread'. Though the 15th and 33rd Armies were in fragments, it seemed just possible to harass and hold back their enemy until the rains stopped him in his tracks. With customary fanaticism, therefore, the Japanese fought bitter but disconnected rearguard actions from south of Meiktila right across to the far western side of the Irrawaddy. At Thazi, Mount Popa, Pyawbwe, Chauk and many other points the struggle was hard and, more critically, time-consuming. Above all, the prolonged struggle at Meiktila imposed such considerable delays that 14th Army's advance, when it at last started, would have to be headlong if Rangoon was to be reached before the rains.

Slim had, in fact, taken out insurance. In February Leese had proposed an amphibious capture of Rangoon, but Slim then convinced Mountbatten with his case for concentrating everything on the destruction of the Japanese army in mid-Burma, which, he argued, ought to bring Rangoon as an automatic gift. Now, however, delays were postponing his advance, though nothing could postpone the

monsoon. At a meeting with Leese at Monywa on 19 March he therefore recommended that a modified DRACULA should be launched against
Rangoon in early May. The urgency was obvious—the factors of space
and time spoke for themselves. Yet for some unaccountable reason
Leese procrastinated, taking eleven days to propose a specific plan—
and even then it was as late as 10 April that Mountbatten, alert to the
seriousness of the situation, had to fly to Calcutta and personally
countermand a refusal by Leese for the use in the operation of essential
airborne troops. Contingent arrangements then went ahead quickly
for an assault on Rangoon by 15 Corps from Arakan, and for developing its port facilities rapidly, irrespective of whether 14th Army or 15
Corps was the actual captor.

Yet even if an amphibious attack on Rangoon proved to be necessary
and successful, Slim would still have to link up with 15 Corps. It would
still be disastrous if 14th Army were held up somewhere in the wilderness when the monsoon broke. Speed was mandatory,* and it was with
relief as well as pride that on 11 April the Army Commander stood
by the roadside to watch 5 Indian Division (in which he had started
the war as a brigadier) spearhead his pursuit force, *en route* for the sea
as they chased the remnants of Honda's force which had been finally
shattered only the day before by 17 Division and its supporting armour
at Pyawbwe. But how could pride be withheld? John Masters, now the
chief staff officer in Pete Rees's 19 Division, was an eyewitness.

> I had not seen him close to since Persia, three and a half years
> earlier, but he said 'How's it going, Jack? Pete driving you mad?'—
> and then I stood back, wishing I had a camera, as Slim, 4 Corps
> Commander, (Frank Messervy), and three divisional commanders
> watched the leading division crash past the start point. The dust
> thickened under the trees lining the road until the column was motoring
> into a thunderous yellow tunnel, first the tanks, infantry all over
> them, then trucks filled with men, then more tanks going fast, nose to
> tail, guns, more trucks, more guns—British, Sikhs, Gurkhas, Madras-
> sis, Pathans, Americans†. . . this was the old Indian Army going down
> to the attack, for the last time in history, exactly two hundred years

---

* There was a further need for speed. If an amphibious operation was launched
against Rangoon it would be essential for 14th Army to capture airfields north of
the city, at Prome and Toungoo, before the assault's D Day. The fields were
required to provide fighter cover for the parachute attack at Victoria Point. (See
below.)
† The men of the American Field Ambulance were admired in 14th Army for
their selfless dedication.

after the Honourable East India Company had enlisted its first ten
sepoys on the Coromandel Coast.*

As Slim stood in the dust-clouds (encouraging his men towards an
enterprise which, if it was to succeed, must take them 300 miles in some
30 days, whatever the enemy's resistance), he could certainly feel that
compared with that phase of ebbing morale in 1943 the *Iqbāl* of the
Company Bahadur had now been fully restored.†

A map instantly reveals the obvious routes for Slim to select. Due
south from Meiktila to Rangoon the main road and railway of Burma
run side by side. To the west, separated from this 'railway corridor' by
the hill-complex of the Pegu Yomas, the Irrawaddy also flows due
south to Prome; thereafter its spreading fingers grope south-westwards
into the delta, but from Prome a road and railway strike directly for
Rangoon. The 'corridor' was the natural centre-line for a mobile
thrust, and the natural participants had been conveniently assembled
at its head—Messervy with his 4 Corps, consisting of the motorized
5 and 17 Divisions and 255 Tank Brigade. To Stopford and 33
Corps was remitted the less spectacular but still onerous task of pressing
down the Irrawaddy, guarding Messervy's flank, and cutting off for
ultimate destruction the Japanese 28th Army in Arakan and south-west
Burma.

Nothing, indeed, was easy, for the advance drew 14th Army out of
the 'dry belt' which had suited so well its operations in the Irrawaddy
loop and around Meiktila. Now, on the eve of the monsoon, every mile
southward took it into regions of intense humidity, stifling heat, and
savage pre-monsoon storms. The urge to press on was diminished by
overwhelming exhaustion and the atmosphere of a Turkish bath. For
airmen, on whose regular delivery of supplies the advance depended,
the climate brought their customary purgatory—particularly in the
form of those mountainous cumulus clouds, so familiar from previous
sorties, within which an aircraft could be hurled about to the point
of disintegration.‡ As Americans would say, the advance was the end-

---

* John Masters, *op cit*, p. 312.
† It is relevant to note that 29 Victoria Crosses were awarded during the Burma
campaigns, compared with 27 for North Africa, 22 for North-West Europe, and
20 for Italy.
‡ It is impossible to over-dramatize the appalling conditions in which the air forces
continually operated behind and above the battlefields of South-East Asia. Deeply
conscious of the crews' courage and endurance, Slim fought hard — as a soldier —

run, but from the men on the ground and in the air it exacted no less fortitude than their earlier trials.

Since time was his chief enemy Slim lived from day to day, under continual strain. The Japanese were always most dogged when they were doomed. Nevertheless 4 Corps moved fast, using *blitzkrieg* techniques which were certainly novel in the eastern theatre. Racing from bound to bound, one division in the lead at a time, the spearheads would seize an airstrip, an airborne battalion would fly in after the engineers had done their work, (airfield engineers were put to travel with the foremost tanks), and then the pattern would repeat, every 50 miles or less. Where well-defended strong-points could be by-passed by the advancing armour, they were left for the following infantry to subdue. The emphasis throughout was on unbroken forward movement.

One event, minor in retrospect but major at the time, added to Slim's sense of strain. The entry in his personal diary for 28 April reads: 'Fly to Pagan and back. Warn Stopford about talk. Order him to cancel Admin. paper. Tell Principal Staff Officers about Stopford.' The previous day there had come into Slim's hands an insubordinate paper written by one of Stopford's administrative staff officers which complained about denial of supplies by 14th Army to Stopford's Corps, and alleged that only local initiative and representations to SEAC had kept it going. Slim, assuming that the paper had been circulated with Stopford's authority, was furious. He summoned his own 'Q' Brigadier, Walsh, and told him they were leaving at dawn on the 28th in a Dakota 'with room for one returning Corps Commander and his baggage'. Slim and Stopford retired into the headquarters office at Pagan while Walsh paced up and down outside, awaiting the result with interest. They emerged smiling, for Stopford was able to convince Slim that he had neither authorized circulation of the document nor even seen it. But his neck had been on the block.

2 May having been set as D Day for DRACULA, Slim was haunted by his calculation of time and distance. As 4 Corps swept on past Pyinmana (taken on the 20th—and General Honda was nearly taken as well) he had 11 days to get to Rangoon, with over 200 miles to go. At Toungoo on the 22nd Honda just escaped again—the vulnerability of its com-

---

to obtain for his airmen the recognition and decorations which, he believed, were bestowed in a niggardly manner by the responsible senior officers in the RAF.

mander symbolizing the disarray of his retreating 33 Army. Here, where the figures were 160 miles and 8 days, the betting was three to one on 4 Corps beating 15 Corps to Rangoon. And hopes continued to run high until, at the end of April, Cowan's 17 Division, now in the van, was brought to a halt and compelled to deploy by the defended town of Pegu.

What might have been an event of high symbolism turned to anticlimax. Not only Cowan, but five of the battalions in his 17 Division now clearing Pegu had been driven off the same ground three years earlier by the Japanese. The town was under control, and the division concentrated, by the evening of 1 May; Rangoon was 50 miles away. But any remaining hopes that Slim's old friend might lead his battle-scarred force triumphantly into the city were immediately dashed. Within 24 hours heavy rain thickened into continuous torrents; the monsoon had arrived prematurely and, as waterways flooded, bridging was protracted or impossible. What should have been a swift and final thrust became a miserable crawl through mud and minefields by Cowan's sodden infantry. Still, the advance continued, in spite of floods and demolitions, so that by 6 May a company of 1/7th Gurkhas with some light armour had entered Hlegu, just 28 miles from Rangoon. But at 4.30 in the afternoon these men (from the battalion Slim had commanded in 1938, and which, he remembered with pride, 'in January, 1942, had fired the first shots of the Burma war') linked up with a column of Lincolns, moving north from 26 Division's landing at Rangoon. DRACULA had beaten EXTENDED CAPITAL by a short head.

Yet from one point of view DRACULA was the greater anticlimax. Preceded by intensive planning, the amphibious operation was masked by a fleet containing two battleships, four cruisers, two aircraft carriers and five destroyers; no Japanese warships were encountered. After a parachute battalion* had secured the key outpost of Victoria Point on 1 May it became clear that Rangoon was empty of the enemy; aircraft had observed the famous 'Extract Digit' message painted by British prisoners-of-war on the roof of Rangoon gaol. Nevertheless on 2 May the convoys of 26 Division were sent in under air cover and supported by bombardment—to take over a city occupied only by welcoming inhabitants. In a sense Slim had already made a token entry, for it was

---

* This was the only parachute attack in the Burma campaign. Had the Japanese resisted at Rangoon, its success would have been critical, since the batteries at Elephant Point commanded the Rangoon River.

during the afternoon of the 2nd that Wing Commander Saunders (commanding 110 Squadron of 221 Group, which under Vincent had been so intimately interwoven with all 14th Army's operations) appreciated the realities and landed his Mosquito on Mingaladon airfield. Having confirmed the true situation at the gaol, he set off down river in a sampan bearing for Assault Force headquarters the message pinned on the main gate of the gaol by the chief Japanese officer as early as 29 April: 'We hereby give you liberty to leave this place at your will.'

But it would be foolish to smile at DRACULA. Though hindsight makes the operation seem over-cautious, the insurance policy which Slim took out when he asked that contingency plans for an assault should be prepared had matured profitably. The early arrival of the monsoon so hampered his advance and so threatened his supplies that even if his Army had reached Rangoon without DRACULA, it must nevertheless have been in grave if temporary difficulties. The estimate of the *Official History* is that the administrative benefits justified the landings. Slim recognized this truth.

There was one possibility which might have removed every element of anticlimax. During 1 May Slim and Messervy received reports that Rangoon had been evacuated by the Japanese. They therefore set off together in Slim's Dakota with two American officers on 14th Army's staff, and flew along the Pegu-Rangoon road at 2,000 feet. They were coming within sight of Rangoon when they ran into anti-aircraft fire, 'like somebody dropping a tray on the kitchen floor', as Messervy put it. 'Bill Slim,' he recalled, 'was in front, a few feet from the wireless which was hit, and two or possibly three more projectiles came through the under-side of the fuselage. None did any damage except one which got poor Fullerton in the leg.' Fortunately a dressing station had been set up beside the airfield on which they landed near Pegu, and there by chance was the consulting surgeon of 14th Army, John Bruce,[*] on a visit to one of his forward teams. His skill saved Colonel Robert Fullerton's life, if not his leg.

The measure of Slim's sense of guilt is indicated by his remarks in *Defeat into Victory*, written a decade later. He knew the jaunt was indefensible—for an Army and a Corps commander, at this stage of the battle—even though Japanese anti-aircraft fire was hardly a major

---

[*] Later Sir John Bruce, Emeritus Professor of Clinical Surgery, Edinburgh University, whose gifts won him international distinction.

threat. Nevertheless, he should not have been there and he knew it. However, granted that he was there, the possibility arises which would certainly have provided a fitting climax to the Burma campaigns—an event more dramatic, say, than MacArthur stepping ashore in the Philippines or Mark Clark driving into Rome. Messervy wrote: 'I often wonder what we would have done had we got to Rangoon. I feel that if we had found the airfield clear and possible for landing we would probably have done so and Bill Slim could have personally occupied Rangoon.'

★★★★★

CHAPTER FOURTEEN

A LITTLE LOCAL DISTURBANCE

'Who loses, and who wins; who's in, who's out.'
Shakespeare, *King Lear*

ON 10 May, 1945, Slim unexpectedly flew up to visit his wife at Shillong, where Una was at school. They had spent halcyon days there in 1937, when Slim at last obtained his Gurkha command. Now, during the privacy of a picnic on the hills, he tossed a bomb-shell. 'I've always told you', he said to Aileen, 'that you'd be the first to know, if I was sacked. You know now.'

For days he was in a state of shock. How could it be the victorious commander of 14th Army, who had just conquered the Japanese in Burma after surmounting unexampled difficulties, should now receive his *congé*? Yet this is what appeared to have happened, and the explanation lies in a sorry story of mismanagement and misunderstanding. The chief cause was the appointment of Oliver Leese to ALFSEA; the proximate cause was the fact that, though Burma had been freed, a major amphibious operation, ZIPPER, had still to be planned and implemented for the invasion of Malaya. At this stage the atom bomb was not a factor, (Slim first heard about it when he was in London in June), and everybody in SEAC assumed that a great struggle still lay ahead.

On 5 May Leese visited Kandy for an interview with Mountbatten, during which he proposed an alteration in the structure of command. The planning for ZIPPER had been remitted to HQ 14th Army, and a new 12th Army HQ was envisaged to control the final, but relatively trivial, mopping-up and garrisoning of Burma. Leese's remarkable proposal to the Supreme Commander was that Slim, since he was tired by years of continuous action, and inexperienced in amphibious warfare, should be shunted to 12th Army while Christison be promoted from 15 Corps to 14th Army.* Christison's greater knowledge of amphibious operations, amplified by the work of his Corps in Arakan, seemed to Leese a sufficient recommendation for the command of ZIPPER.

Mountbatten profoundly disagreed. Unless Slim was desperately fatigued and really in need of a rest there could be no question of removing him; even if that were the case, Mountbatten recommended that leave and a temporary appointment would be appropriate. Though he accepted that Slim was obviously tired, he had taken the full measure of his resilience and fortitude. There was nothing wrong with 14th Army's Commander that rest and refreshment would not rectify. He therefore gave Leese a limited permission to sound out Slim about his ideas for the future, but emphasized that no positive steps should be taken without Sir William's complete and willing concurrence and Mountbatten's own approval. In retrospect Leese confirmed that this was his instruction. 'I would like to make it quite clear that Mountbatten told me to go and see Slim, and see what he thought about the idea that he should command the Army in Burma. On no account do I want you to think that I am blaming Mountbatten for what happened. He certainly gave me no authority to sack Slim. I therefore went over to see Slim with a view to getting his reactions to the idea. Naturally I hoped he would agree to it.'†

The sad fact is that at the root of Leese's proposition lay a sound idea. To have formed a new 12th Army headquarters which could plan and launch ZIPPER undistracted and unwearied by the current operations in Burma, and to have left 14th Army to rest on its laurels, would have made sense militarily and would have caused no affront. To hand over ZIPPER to a 14th Army headquarters from which Slim had been removed was psychologically and militarily clumsy.

The course of events is difficult to comprehend. On the same day

---

* It is ironic to note that as far back as 1928 *The Army Quarterly* published the text of the winning entry in that year's competition for the Bertrand Stewart Military Prize Essay. The theme was: 'Amphibious warfare. Refer briefly to its prevalence in past wars; discuss its probability in the future, and the best methods of meeting our requirements in this form of warfare.' The winner was Captain W. J. Slim, MC, 6th Gurkha Rifles.
† Letter to author, 25 April, 1973.

as his meeting with Mountbatten Leese sent off a private signal to Alanbrooke, the CIGS in London, formulating his proposals and requesting approval; he received a non-commital acknowledgement. Possibly because he was impatient about delay over what he considered a vital appointment, or possibly because he was inexplicably confused about the extent of his authority to make it, Leese then flew down to Christison's Advanced HQ at Akyab. His first words to Christison, as Sir Philip recalled them, were: 'Dickie considers Bill a tired man and I agree, but he's been through a lot. I have been told to ease him out gently and you are to take over 14th Army at once. As a matter of fact Bill is on his way home already.'* If these are not the precise words, their gist was clear to Christison at the time. He naturally assumed that he was Army-Commander-designate. In good faith he informed the staff of 15 Corps that he was to be promoted, and was given by them a traditional farewell and congratulatory dinner.

Thus when Leese flew up to Meiktila, on 7 May, to confront Slim himself, the auguries were not propitious. Slim was stunned and wounded by ALFSEA's proposal that he should leave his beloved 14th Army, which he had directed and inspired, for a makeshift army with a minor role and the certainty of attrition, as its troops returned to England or were diverted to ZIPPER. The wound was not salved by the news that he was to be replaced by a Corps Commander whose achievement in Arakan, however successful, was scarcely comparable with his own. (His pencilled diary for 7 May contains just two curt entries: 'Meiktila airstrip still out. Sack 1530.') But, in typical fashion, he made no attempt to argue his case. Without acrimony he explained that if his superior officer had lost confidence in him, Leese was fully entitled to remove him. He could not, however, accept the transfer to 12th Army and proposed to send in his papers. Leese was taken aback. It is a measure of his failure to grasp the realities of the situation he himself had devised. He therefore urgently requested Slim to take time and reconsider his decision. Slim replied that it was impossible for him to change his mind.

A fatal musinderstanding had occured. Slim, not surprisingly, was under the impression that he was *limogé*—sacked.† Leese had been too ambivalent—wanting to replace Slim but trying to ease him out with his own connivance. He forgot that he was dealing with a man not

---

* Letter to author 13 November, 1972.
† The French sent their discredited generals to command at Limoges.

easily duped. However, 'I quite see that the evidence you have gives
the impression that I sacked Slim. This too was obviously the opinion
of Mountbatten, Alanbrooke and Slim. I respect these opinions, and I
only want to repeat to you that I went to see Slim with no intention to
sack him. I thought, before I left him, that he accepted my idea. . . .
In retrospect, I should obviously have gone back to see Slim in the
morning to confirm my opinion of the outcome of our meeting, but I
had arranged to fly off that morning to Quetta to talk about our
operations to the Staff College.'*

The period that followed was the most painful in Slim's life. Something had occurred that cut across all his codes of behaviour. There
was honour—was it honourable to demote a commander at the peak of
victory? Demotion was for the deficient. And loyalty—surely there
was something disloyal in the abrupt dismissal of a man so recently
trusted over such large issues? And justice? He did not suffer, like
Churchill after leaving the Admiralty in 1915, from the thwarting
of a fiery ego, but he knew his worth. Then came the corroding doubt,
inevitable in so self-questioning a man as Slim: had he really been
inadequate, and if so, how? The misery was intensified by the fact that
he must keep it to himself.

All allegations that Slim took direct action in his own defence are
incorrect, and based on a total misunderstanding of his character. He
did not, as is sometimes stated, appeal to Auchinleck, Commander-in-
Chief, India (his titular superior in the Indian Army), nor did he send a
protestation to the Army Council. Apart from some trusted friends,
and the necessary few among his staff and subordinates, nobody heard
a word from Slim himself. He was too hurt to beat his breast in public,
and in any case such demonstrations were foreign to his sense of dignity
and duty. On 8 May, the day after the 'sacking', he had to fly to Rangoon
for a conference. With great self-control he gave away no hint of his
distress (as Messervy confirmed to the author)—not even to his staff
officer, Colonel Godwin, who travelled with him in his aircraft.

Auchinleck received not an appeal but a straightforward request.†
The circumstances, and some of Slim's feelings, are set out plainly in a
letter he wrote on 16 May to his old comrade-at-arms, Sir Reginald

---

* Letter to author, 25 April 1973.
† Slim's letter to Auchinleck was sent on the 14th, together with a letter to Leese
confirming his intention to retire. He wrote these letters after attending the local
celebration for VE Day!

Savory. (Savory took the trouble to visit Mhow, where John Slim was an officer cadet, to warn him confidentially about his father's maltreatment and to assure him that all would be well.)*

One paragraph of the letter reads:

> I received a very nasty shock last week when Oliver Leese sent for me and informed me that he was removing me from command of the Army. He gave as his reason his opinion that I was not capable of planning or carrying out the forthcoming operations of the Army. I have always said that commanders should have a very considerable right of selecting their own subordinates, and if that is how he feels his action in removing me is perfectly proper. All the same, you will realize how I feel about leaving the Fourteenth Army, which has been my baby and has always treated me so exceedingly well. Leese offered me command of the Burma Army (or garrison) after Fourteenth Army has left it but I did not feel in the circumstances that there would be enough confidence between us to justify my accepting the offer. I have therefore written to the C-in-C suggesting that I go on leave pending retirement. As a matter of fact, any other job that is likely to be offered me, if I am offered one at all, would be rather a flop after the Fourteenth Army, and anyway there are dozens of Lieut-Generals with the highest reputations in Europe elbowing one another for jobs in this theatre.

He had written in similar vein two days earlier to Donald MacDonald, for whose priestly integrity he had so deep a respect. 'It is appropriate that you should mention your hopes that I should acquire a bowler.† Your prayers are answered: I have done so. I was suddenly told by Oliver Leese that he was removing me from command of the Fourteenth Army. It was a bit of a jar as I thought the Fourteenth Army had done rather well. However, he is the man to decide. I have had to sack a number of chaps in my time, and those I liked best were the ones who did not squeal. I have applied for my bowler and am awaiting the result. Aileen, I may say, is delighted.'

---

* 'He also gave me a letter from my father, setting out the position in simple terms, with no rancour.' John Slim, letter to author, 22 December, 1975.
† In military slang to 'acquire a bowler' normally implies dismissal. MacDonald, of course, like a good Cameronian was simply recommending Slim the procedure advocated in the Scottish Psalter.

> *No longer hosts encountering hosts*
> *Shall crowds of slain deplore:*
> *They hang the trumpet in the hall*
> *And study war no more.*

But if Aileen had adjusted to the idea of her husband's retirement—understandably, since they had been so little together since 1939—Slim was in torment, aggravated by the fact that, as the days drifted by, he found his position more and more anomalous. When was Christison coming to take over? On 9 May,* as his diary records, he thought it imperative to put the senior staff officers at Army HQ in the picture, under pledge of secrecy, and simply, directly, firmly, without self-pity or complaint he instructed them to transfer their loyalty to the new man. That was all; but night after night he could be heard in his room overhead, tramping mechanically up and down, up and down, the condemned man in his cell.

The effect on his staff was traumatic. On the day Slim addressed them Colonel Denis O'Connor,† one of the 14th Army planners, had been sent by the BGS, Brigadier 'Tubby' Lethbridge, on a mission to the commander of 2 Division, Major-General Nicholson. It was a long journey, and he did not return until the evening. When he went to Lethbridge's hut to make a routine report he found, to his astonishment, that the Brigadier was in tears. He asked what was wrong and Lethbridge replied, 'But don't you know? Of course you can't, you've been away all day. Uncle Bill's been sacked!' A little later O'Connor ran into Slim himself. Embarrassed, he blurted out how sorry he was. Slim was stirred, perhaps by the unexpected solicitude. He put his hand on O'Connor's shoulder, thrust out the famous jaw and said, 'Don't worry, my boy. This happened to me once before and I bloody well took the job of the chap that sacked me. I'll bloody well do it again.'

That was a temporary animosity. Rumours inevitably spread, for an army is an extraordinarily rapid conductor, and inevitably divisional commanders and others who had fought under Slim rushed to him and threatened to resign. At least one senior RAF officer reacted similarly. But in each case Slim's response was deflating. He told them not to be fools, and reminded them of their duty. All witnesses agree, however, that during these tense days anger and revulsion were beginning to permeate 14th Army. Far away in India a medical officer, Lieut-Colonel Murray Pheils of the East African Division, heard a report on the bush telegraph and noted the consternation of his colleagues. Down

---

* He was in Shillong with Aileen from the 10th to the 12th, when he returned to Meiktila. The next day he assembled his Corps Commanders, as his diary puts it, to 'tell them I am going'.
† Lieut-General Sir Denis O'Connor, KBE, CB.

in Arakan and far north in Delhi, amid the Lutyens palaces, rumour fed on rumour.

Panic was unnecessary, since the depth-charge fused by Leese had now exploded. On 14 May Mountbatten received a blunt signal from the CIGS, in which Alanbrooke described his astonishment at receiving a cable from Leese reporting that (*without the approval he had previously requested from London*) he had taken the positive steps which had led to Slim's discomfiture. Adding that he had every confidence in Slim's outstandingly successful record, the CIGS pointed out forcefully that no changes of this order could be made without a personal recommendation from Mountbatten to London. Meanwhile, he declared, he had expressed his extreme displeasure to Leese that he should even have discussed the matter with Slim.

If Mountbatten's situation was not so grave as that of Eisenhower in December, 1944, when that other Supreme Commander came within a hair's breadth of recommending the removal of Montgomery for insubordination, it was nevertheless extremely delicate. An angry Alanbrooke was as dangerous as a wounded buffalo. Though Mountbatten's conscience was clear in respect of the actual orders he had issued to Leese, he must, as any commander should, have felt some responsibility for the way they had been interpreted. It was not as though he had absolute confidence in Leese's judgement. Over a number of matters, personal and military—the Rangoon landings, for example—he had been openly dissatisfied; on 6 May, in fact, the day after Leese first made his proposals, the Supreme Commander had sent to the CIGS a letter setting out the grounds for his discontent.

However that may be, the crunch had come. Mountbatten acted with surgical speed. He immediately interviewed Leese at Kandy, informed him that he had acted without authority, and made it clear that the unacceptable changes he had initiated must be reversed.* Leese, with disarming contrition, made no excuses but readily admitted that he had blundered. On the 17th he sent his Chief of Staff, Brigadier Walsh, up to Meiktila to try to persuade Slim to abandon the idea of retiring and accept the 12th Army appointment. Had Slim willingly agreed the crisis might have been resolved, but his rejection was still absolute, as

---

* In disentangling the complications Mountbatten found himself actually inhibited by the fact that he wanted Slim rather than Leese at ALFSEA. 'I think it was this desire which made me rather more cautious than I should have been in talking to Oliver himself.' (Letter to author, 26 April, 1975).

the contemptuous entry in his diary reveals. 'Visit from Walsh and Kimmins. Suggest I take Burma Army until [they] find [a] better man.' The visit, incidentally, illustrates how little even the senior staff officers in South East Asia were aware of what exactly was happening. During their flight to Meiktila Kimmins,* the Director of Plans at SEAC, noticed that Walsh was preoccupied and asked, in complete ignorance, what was on his mind. Walsh simply replied, mysteriously, that 'he was afraid Oliver was about to do something stupid'. Edric Bastyan,† who had come from Italy with Leese as his Chief Administrative Officer and was wholly loyal to him, has also informed the author that, though he had an obscure sense of unease, he knew nothing specific about these critical developments.

The climax came with a telegram on 23 May from Leese to Slim, telling him that it had been decided to send Stopford to 12th Army and to retain Slim, at the head of 14th Army, to conduct ZIPPER. Colonel Godwin witnessed the telegram's arrival.

> The sound of a jeep was heard and Michael Oldman the Assistant Military Secretary came round the corner grinning hard and asking where the Army Commander was. As his footsteps creaked up the rickety staircase, Bill Bowen gripped my arm saying 'Jimmy, is this it?' We heard the knock on the door and Bill Slim's deep-throated 'Hullo.' We then heard Michael say 'I have a signal for you, Sir, which I think will interest you' . . . and then an unbearable pause. At long last an enormous deep chuckle or two. . . . 'Ha-ha-ha' . . . and we were up the stairs almost before they could finish, nearly knocking Michael over in our eagerness and sudden embarrassment at behaving like kids. One look at Bill Slim's face creased with smiles was enough; things had come right, thank God.

But things had not come right for others. Christison had been astonished, though naturally delighted at his apparent elevation. Now he found himself embarrassingly left in the air—holding the baby of the make-shift 12th Army in Burma, which Slim handed over to him on the same day that he heard he had been re-instated. But Christison was soon to be rescued from this awkward posture by receiving temporary command of 14th Army (until Sir Miles Dempsey could arrive from England), while Slim took a well-earned holiday.

---

* Lieut-General Sir Brian Kimmins, KBE, CB.
† Lieut-General Sir Edric Bastyan, KCMG, KCVO, KBE, CB.

For Leese everything had gone wrong. Questioned by Mountbatten, Slim stated that he was prepared to continue to serve under
him—with reservations. Aware that he had already disposed of one
exalted commander, Giffard, Mountbatten therefore made a case for
retaining Leese—under his supervision at Kandy. But Alanbrooke was
adamant, and at the beginning of July a letter passed from the Supreme
Commander to Leese, now on leave in Kashmir, informing him that
he would be replaced at ALFSEA by Sir William Slim. Auchinleck,
Sir Keith Park for the RAF, Admiral Power for the Navy, and the
American General Wheeler, the stalwart of SEAC, all volunteered
their approval of the change.

But Slim knew nothing of the mechanism by which it was effected.
He had not been party to the signals traffic between Kandy and Whitehall. He had not fought to defend his interests, and he expected no
prize. As he and Aileen set off during the afternoon of 9 June (after
presenting a Samurai sword to the Viceroy, Wavell, and lunching
with Auchinleck), for their first visit to England since the beginning
of the war, he did so on the assumption that it would merely be a
refresher before he, now restored to 14th Army, led it in the last
bloody but triumphant assault on the Japanese. It happened that his
old friend General Sir Richard Gale, then commanding the British
Airborne Corps, was in the SEAC theatre to discuss airborne aspects of
ZIPPER. The Slims travelled back to England in his aircraft. During the
journey Slim passed to Gale a fat typescript—his Despatches—and
suggested that Gale might look at it. Gale did so with fascination.
'Yes', said Slim, 'you wouldn't think they'd sack a chap for doing
that.'

It was Leese himself who proposed, after the *status quo ante* had
been re-established, that Slim should be granted a month's leave in
England. Reporting this to Mountbatten, his Chief of Staff, Lieut-
General Sir Frederick Browning, observed that it was a pity security
had to be very tight because Slim would be denied the great ovation
he deserved. As another great Field-Marshal, 'Wully' Robertson,
remarked on a famous occasion, 'I've 'eard different.' It was of course
impossible, even if the home authorities had so desired it, to conceal
the formidable presence of Uncle Bill. He was fêted in traditional style
at the Mansion House. There was a civic reception in Edinburgh. He
was naturally invited to broadcast. Birmingham did honour to its most
distinguished living soldier with a Lord Mayor's luncheon at the
Council House, and he visited the two schools of his childhood, St

Philip's and King Edward's. The past, ever present in his mind, walked alongside him. At St Philip's Leighton was there to greet him, the master from whom, 40 years ago, he had learned a memorable lesson. And it was surely a memory of his early manhood among the iron-workers of Stewarts and Lloyds that made him say, in his address at the Council House: 'I think in some ways the 14th Army has very much of what I believe to be the Birmingham spirit—resilience, adaptability and a cheerful refusal to lie down in the face of difficulties.'

He attended meetings of the War Cabinet and the Chiefs of Staff, flew over to Germany for a brief visit to his fellow-victor, Montgomery, and shared with Aileen a precious week of private peace in the Cotswolds. But there was one ceremonial occasion of deeper significance. Bill and Aileen were invited down to Chequers. Neither had the least inkling that Churchill, to whom Slim was a stranger, might be assessing his personality before ratifying his promotion to the senior military post in SEAC. The best evidence for this is a statement of Slim's during a conversation after lunch, when they were discussing Churchill's preoccupation, the forthcoming election. The Prime Minister orated optimistically about his chances, till Mrs Churchill coolly pointed out that the Forces' ballot was uncertain. 'Well, Prime Minister,' said Slim, 'I know one thing. *My* Army won't be voting for you.' Nevertheless Churchill formed a judgement which persisted. Years later, in 1952, Lord Moran recorded him saying: 'When a man cannot distinguish a great from a small event he is no use. Now Slim is quite different. I can work with him.'

And so it proved. Shortly afterwards Aileen was sitting in their room at the Savoy Hotel when Slim entered. He had been summoned to Whitehall. Usually, when he returned from such sessions, he would sit down and quietly give Aileen the gist of them. But this time he remained silent, bemused. His air was so disconcerting that Aileen asked him if anything was wrong. Something astonishing had happened, he said. 'They've made me the Commander-in-Chief.'

★★★★★

CHAPTER FIFTEEN

AFTERMATH

'Over all the mountain tops is peace.'

Goethe

WHEN SLIM returned to take over the land forces in South-East Asia as Commander-in-Chief the Second World War had come to a halt. They had told him in London about the atom bomb and its intended use. Hiroshima and Nagasaki were thus no surprise, and as he and Aileen were passing through Rome on their return flight they heard the news of Japan's unconditional surrender. It was ironical that Slim had reached what now looked like being the peak of his military career on the eve, as it seemed, of peace—for he well knew that in the post-war world there would be more officers of high competence available than could be accommodated in his profession.* Nevertheless, when on 16 August he entered his new headquarters at Kandy in Ceylon, near to Mountbatten's extensive power-house for SEAC, he found that his hands were full.

During his absence the Japanese remnants in Burma—mainly the troops of 28th Army trying to break out eastwards through the Pegu Yomas and across the Sittang—had been eliminated in a brilliant finale which destroyed some 14,000 enemy at a cost of under 2,000 casualties. Much mopping-up and pacification remained, not least among the Burmese themselves. But throughout the famous hunting-grounds of 14th Army the residual problems were essentially minor. It was in the vast new territories for which he was about to become responsible that Slim was required to find answers to grave and urgent questions. From Malaya to the Dutch East Indies, through Siam, Indo-China and

---

* He had been promoted General on 1 July.

Borneo, Singapore and Hong Kong, the pressing need was to establish
law and order. This was not war as he had recently known it, but the
challenge was formidable.*

Mountbatten who, as Supreme Commander, carried even wider
responsibilities, has defined the legacy he inherited from the Japanese
'Greater East Asia Co-Prosperity Sphere' in one word—chaos. At the
time of Japan's collapse the regions which he and Slim had to re-
habilitate contained 128 million people, among whom 750,000 of the
enemy were still at large. Dominating all was the knowledge that some
125,000 Allied prisoners, many near to death, must be rescued before
disease, starvation or revenge cut short their suffering. And throughout
this immense theatre the turbulent forces of Asian nationalism, pent
up under the Japanese occupation, were now coming vigorously and
often viciously into play. With so many problems demanding simultaneous solution Slim was soon as heavily involved as during the days
of battle.

For South East Asia Command the prisoners—about 250 camps of
them—were a natural first priority. Where exactly were they? What
were their most urgent needs? How could they be recovered? A decision
by the Combined Chiefs of Staff led to inexcusable delay in answering
these questions, for inevitably they appointed an American to take
overall control of the Japanese surrender, and, as inevitably, the task
fell to MacArthur. The Supreme Commander in the Pacific decreed,
however, not only that a formal surrender in his own theatre must
precede one in South-East Asia, but also that no landings or re-entry
into territory held by the Japanese must occur until he, MacArthur,
had received in person the definitive surrender of Hirohito's Empire.

For prisoners in their foetid camps the implications were incalculable.
Admiral Mountbatten therefore turned a Nelson's blind eye on his
instructions, and from Slim's command small teams were swiftly
organized to be parachuted into the camps with the minimum necessities and at least the promise of more—though full relief was impossible

---

* It is exemplified in the first Directive Slim issued as ALFSEA, on 23 August,
which set out the phases for occupation of the liberated areas and covered re-
entry into Singapore, the return to Malaya, recovery of complete control over
Burma, developments at Bangkok and Saigon, occupation of Siam and French
Indo-China, re-organization of the large forces under his command and, not
least, preliminary arrangements for handling the explosive situation in the
Netherlands East Indies.

until MacArthur had personally accepted the full Japanese surrender aboard the battleship *Missouri* in Tokyo Bay on 2 September.

But as the prisoners gradually emerged, and as the precise nature of the conditions in which they had lived became plain to him, Slim's spirit revolted. He had learned to live with death, but, as men felt at the sight of Belsen or Auschwitz, this was of a different order, a deed of gratuitous bestiality. Tolerant, slow to condemn, habitually charitable, towards the Japanese Slim nevertheless remained implacable. 'There can be no excuse for a nation which as a matter of policy treats its prisoners of war in this way,' he wrote a decade later in *Defeat into Victory*, 'and no honour for an army, however brave, which willingly makes itself the instrument of such inhumanity to the helpless.'

Once MacArthur had had his day, regional surrenders could be formalized. On 3 September, at Singapore, Christison* took the submission of the Japanese Seventh Area Army and the South Seas Fleet— a moment of great personal significance, for it was Christison whose 15 Corps had executed DRACULA and re-entered Rangoon, where his only son was killed in action in 1942 and his father, ninety years previously, had performed the first surgery ever carried out under anaesthetic in the field—on an Ensign who was later called Field-Marshal Lord Wolseley. There then followed, on 12 September, the ceremony of unconditional surrender by all Japanese forces in South-East Asia, again at Singapore, beneath the Union Jack hauled down by the vanquished garrison in 1942.† Slim sat beside Mountbatten, studying intently the blank masks of his opponents. They showed no emotion, and he felt none, though in other places he had watched with a stir of sympathy the acceptance of defeat by men of other nations. 'They sat there', he recalled, 'apart from the rest of humanity.'

For Slim the Samurai sword was a potent symbol. He himself acquired Kimura's weapon, which was prominently displayed thereafter wherever he lived—at once a trophy and a constant reminder. His own code had imbued him with a keen sense of personal honour, and he appreciated the meaning for a Japanese officer—and his men—if a victor compelled him to hand over in public the sword which encapsulated all his loyalties. He would be defiled. No legend of an

---

* Between 6 July, when Leese vacated the post, and 16 August when Slim officially occupied it, Christison acted as Commander-in-Chief, ALFSEA. He then returned to 15 Corps and took over control at Singapore.
† It had been concealed and preserved in the notorious Changi gaol.

unconquered army could flourish, as happened in Germany after 1918, if the Japanese themselves watched their military leaders accepting the ultimate shame. Though MacArthur ruled that the surrender of swords was an archaic practice not to be enforced (particularly as officers might be unable to control their men after losing face), Mountbatten decided that loss of face was the prime consideration, and with his benediction Slim carried out the policy ruthlessly. All Japanese officers in the area of his command surrendered their swords to British officers, and the more senior, divisional or army commanders, did so in front of large parades of their own men.

Naturally, there were attempts at evasion. Sir Denis O'Connor, then still a staff Colonel, was sent by Slim on a tour of Malaya to visit Japanese units and recover ceremonial swords—no easy task, as the location and strength of units was often still unknown. At one point a major tried to hand over a sword which O'Connor knew should be surrendered by a General. He was told that the General regretted he was ill. After threats of 'within five minutes—or else!' a car drew up, from which a Major-General emerged on the run—until he remembered and began to limp. The episode produced a letter of crawling apology from the Japanese 7 Area Army which, after announcing that the delinquent General had been 'confined' for 15 days by no less a person than the Commander of the Southern Malay Army, continued, under the heading:

Punishment of Maj.-General Oko

Maj.-Gen. Oko has been suffering from the sprained foot for some time, which disables him but to walk a very short distance. On that occasion Maj. Gen. of course had full mind to go to greet your officers, but due to lack of car he was waiting in his camp. He was finnaly had the chance to go when the Japanese officer, who was acting as an usher, came to give lift to Maj. Gen. Oko. Thus he could at last present himself to greet the British officers.

This mild explanation, however, was rendered less credible both by the General's 'confinement' and by 7 Area Army's declaration that 'we at once have taken the necessary steps in warning the whole force against an incident of this nature, which should never be repeated once again in the future'. O'Connor's report on the affair gave Slim the greatest satisfaction.

His pleasures could only be infrequent, however, for his general condition was low. Throughout the journey to and from England he had suffered much pain and had been physically weakened by haemorrhoids. This drain on his resources continued when he returned to Kandy and a life of great pressure and much journeying. The doctors and his staff were uneasy about him; as an instance, in one letter Slim described the discomfort, particularly at take-off and landing, of a flight he had to make in a Sunderland flying-boat. At last he had to admit defeat and enter hospital for a taxing operation. During the short remainder of his service in South-East Asia he was still recovering from this set-back. It was not a good time, for Aileen, up in Simla to close her wartime flat and settle her affairs, had also been in hospital and was in no proper state when she flew to his side.

His military family, moreover—the old, intimate, tested brotherhood of 14th Army—was no longer around him. He was surrounded by new faces, for in his usual way he had only brought to the ALFSEA command a few personal aides, retaining, to their astonishment, the senior staff officers, many of whom Leese had imported from 8th Army and who, aware that they had caused the ejection of their predecessors, expected to be displaced in their turn. (Their knowledge of some, though not all, of the events described in the previous chapter cannot have diminished their forebodings.) Lieut-General Sir Edric Bastyan, then Principal Administrative Officer to ALFSEA, whose loyalty to Leese was firm, told the author what a profound impression Slim's lack of prejudice had created, and how swiftly he himself developed an equal attachment to his new commander. But these reorientations could hardly happen overnight.

There was one on his staff, however, who was soon linked to Slim for the most private of reasons. After the victory in Europe a young Guards officer, Lord Brabourne, decided to apply for transfer to the Far East. His efforts led to his appointment as ADC to Oliver Leese, but at that moment the change in the ALFSEA command occurred. He was astonished to find that Slim, unwilling to let a junior officer suffer because of his senior's demotion, had decided to retain him as his own ADC. They travelled back on the same aircraft to Kandy. One day in Ceylon Aileen told him that the Supremo and his family (including a daughter) were coming to tea, and insisted (much against Brabourne's will) that he should be present to help with their entertainment. At the tea-party he fell instantly and finally in love with Patricia Mountbatten, whom he married in the following year. If Slim's quarters in Kandy were a less fertile source of engagements than his Government House in Canberra proved to be, he and Aileen were never, as benign match-makers, to surpass this alliance with the daughter of a Supreme Commander.

Slim's disability did not prevent him from attending the Singapore surrender, nor had it withheld him, on its eve, from what was in effect the first major amphibious operation of the post-war period. In his address at the surrender Mountbatten spoke of the ships anchored off the Malayan coast and how 'a large force started disembarking from them at daylight on 9 September.... As I speak there are 100,000 men ashore.' This was ZIPPER, the operation against a Malaya assumed to be held by the Japanese which had been in active preparation ever since Joint Force Commanders were appointed early in May. Many difficulties beset those preparations, most notably the insistence in London on a vigorous fulfilment of PYTHON, the scheme for repatriation of men who had served a minimum of three years and four months in the Far East. Then came the Japanese collapse. For many reasons it was nevertheless felt to be most practical to proceed with the landings as planned, though the most feasible date could not be earlier than that envisaged for ZIPPER as an operation of war—9 September.

When the landings actually occurred it became immediately evident that there had been grave deficiencies in planning, particularly in the selection of beaches for touch-down, and that determined opposition from even a few Japanese battalions might have been disastrous. Though the *Official History* considers that if a genuine invasion had been launched it would ultimately have been successful, in view of the known weakness of the enemy, it quotes startling descriptions of the unopposed landings to support the view that the opening phase of a true assault would have been a nightmare. 'Conditions on the beaches were chaotic,' one account states, 'vehicles drowned in scores as there were no decent exits from the beaches, and roads became choked with ditched tanks which tore up the road surfaces and verges.'

Commenting on ZIPPER in his short book on Slim, Brigadier Calvert observes: 'The schemings and musical chairs of the high command in South-East Asia, from which Slim does not emerge unmuddied, must have been partly to blame for this bad planning.' This is demonstrably unjust to Slim, who had indulged in no scheming. Though Brigadier Calvert declares that when Leese attempted to displace him 'Slim appealed in person to the Army Council as was now his right', this is fiction. As for the planning of ZIPPER, it is evident that Slim was in England for most of the operative period and after his return to ALFSEA in mid-August had certainly no time, amid the plethora of his commitments, to discover, for example, that those responsible were at fault in such elementary matters as the selection of suitable beaches. Thus when he and Mountbatten arrived on the scene on 11 September, the initial confusion having been disentangled, he was witnessing an affair which was none of his making and in which he can have taken little pride. His comments on ZIPPER in *Defeat into Victory* are significant for their brevity and reserve.

There were many knots in the vast dishevelled skein of South-East Asia. One which had a personal significance for Slim, and in whose loosening he certainly played a notable part, was the difficulty of restoring orderly government in Burma. A brief flash-back is now necessary. Since 1942 many Burmese, particularly the hill-men—Karens, Chins, Kachins—had given substantial assistance to 14th Army. (The Karens alone supplied an efficient force of 12,000 tribesmen armed and organized under British officers.) But there was another factor—the Burma National Army (or Patriotic Burmese Forces). Under its able leader Aung San, who had been trained in Japan and returned to his country with the invaders in 1942, the BNA had taken a positive, if not dramatic, part in the operations of its new overlords. As the tide turned, however, intelligence reports indicated that the BNA was ripening for a change of allegiance and matters came to a head at the end of March, 1945, when, convinced that the Japanese were facing defeat, the BNA rose against its masters.

The implications of this *volte-face* were anxiously weighed at as high a level as that of the Chiefs of Staff and the War Cabinet in London. There was serious concern that the aftermath of war in Burma might result, for example, in a situation analogous to that of Greece, where the Communist-ridden resistance movement had thrown up in EAM and ELAS a hard, recalcitrant core which impeded peacetime settlement. Many old hands of the pre-war civil administration in Burma strongly opposed any pandering to the 'patriots'. It was here that Slim and Mountbatten (for his was the prime responsibility) were instrumental in gradually de-fusing a potentially explosive affair.

They had independently reached the conclusion that the BNA would be of considerable value for irregular harassment of the Japanese, and should therefore, in spite of the inherent risks, be fostered and supported. This was Slim's recommendation, endorsed by the Supreme Commander. The question was, on what terms? Slim, while still commanding 14th Army, had decided on a confrontation with Aung San, who on 16 May was conveyed to Meiktila, dressed in a local version of the uniform of a Japanese Major-General. They quickly established a mutual regard. Though subsequent negotiations were to take a long and tortuous course it is clear that the firm but liberal and uncensorious manner with which Slim handled the meeting was of a critical value. Each recognized in the other his own qualities of realism, courage and—as Slim frankly declared about Aung San—honesty.

Nevertheless, Aung San was sitting on an ant-heap, furiously active with conflicting political activities and aspirations.* It is not surprising, therefore, that in spite of further meetings with the military authorities and Mountbatten himself the terms under which members of the BNA could be incorporated in the post-war regular army of Burma had not been fully agreed when Slim returned in mid-August to the post of ALFSEA. At the request of the Burmese themselves Mountbatten assembled at Rangoon on 6 September a large joint conference of British and Burmese military and political representatives. To Slim was given the task of opening the meeting with a long speech in which, by surveying the record of events since 1942, he clarified the present British attitude towards Burma by bluntly assessing the pro- and anti-Japanese activities of the Burmese people. In spite of the record (in spite, too, of their political advisers' doubts) Mountbatten and he were prepared to do business on the basis of the balance-sheet, but in strictly realistic terms.

Thereafter a structure for peacetime Burma was gradually—though only temporarily—erected. The dual processes went ahead in tandem of disbanding and (where suitable) re-enrolling the BNA, and of apprehending the considerable number of Japanese troops who had still not accepted defeat. By 16 October it had become possible for Sir Reginald Dorman-Smith, the Governor of Burma in 1942, to return to Rangoon and restore the civil authority, under which preservation of law and order reverted to the police. Yet the continuing presence of the Japanese, whose repatriation was inevitably slow, and the disruptive effect of their occupation on Burmese society left the military with many delicate responsibilities, and meant that the end of the emergency could not be finally declared by Dorman-Smith until 19 April, 1946. Then 'in theory anyhow Burma had achieved internal as well as external peace.'†

---

* He was assassinated in 1947, along with half the Burmese Cabinet. U Saw, who was responsible, was later hanged.
† *The War against Japan*, Vol. V., p. 264.

During these and his myriad other preoccupations Slim had a firm base in Kandy. For a while Aileen and Una were able to be with him, and the family was re-united when John arrived on leave from Japan, where he was appropriately serving as ADC to General Cowan, now commanding the British-Indian Division in the Allied Occupation Force. It was even more appropriate—looking back to Abbottabad in the twenties—that having been commissioned in his father's regiment, 1/6th Gurkhas, he should be at the side of Slim's old friend and fellow-officer in the capital of their enemy.

Slim's transport at this time was regal—or worthy of the cream of Chicago's gangsters. That is to say, the Cadillac company had produced a small number of prototypes of an armoured saloon car, and shipped one or two to South-East Asia for trial. The car was 21 feet long, weighed three tons and cost £23,000. Two technicians were sent out to maintain each vehicle. Slim's driver was Bill Richardson, whose varied war had included several trips to Dunkirk in 1940 aboard *Crested Eagle*, and driving a gun-tower in Arakan during *Ha-Go*.* A man of great perception and humanity, what Richardson particularly noticed in his high-ranking master was a natural and instinctive sympathy. When they returned from a night journey, for example, it was Slim, never even an ADC, who went personally to rouse the cooks and ensure that his driver had a meal. Once, when they were out driving, Slim asked Richardson if he was comfortable in 'those hobbledehoys'— his Army issue boots; thereafter he drove in soft shoes. And particularly Richardson remembered how one day they passed two soldiers tramping along in the heat and dust. Slim ordered them to come aboard, and afterwards instructed Richardson that he should always give a lift in such circumstances, as it was unfair to let men exhaust themselves in that climate unnecessarily. Some time afterwards Richardson was driving one of Slim's staff, a rather pompous Colonel, who was furious when Richardson obeyed standing orders and picked up some foot-sloggers. The Colonel refused to accept that such were the C-in-C's explicit instructions. On his return he reported to Slim's office and complained that good order and military discipline had been breached by stopping the Commander's car to give a lift to Other Ranks. 'And did you?' said Slim, menacingly.

And now Slim's life-pattern was suddenly switched in a new direction.

---

* In 1975, when the author consulted Mr Richardson, he was driving Lord Boyd-Carpenter, Chairman of the Civil Aviation Authority.

For over a quarter of a century his main preoccupation had been the Indian Army and the frontiers of the Raj. Now the Raj itself was on the verge of dissolution. Just in time, it might be said, he received an un-expected summons—to become the Commandant of a revived Imperial Defence College in London—and not merely to take command but to start up again from scratch an organization which had inevitably been out of commission for the last six years. The call was unexpected precisely because, even at this high point of his military career, Slim's persistent humility made him dubious about his chances of another appointment after that of ALFSEA, and during his time at Kandy the uncertainties of civilian life seemed disturbingly close. Acceptance, nevertheless, was not automatic. 'Slim came to me with the letter offering him the IDC in an unusual state of agitation. He said he had to show me the letter but had already decided to refuse. After all my support and finally replacing the sacked Leese by himself he could not let me down by deserting me. He added that he found the post-war problems fascinating and he saw eye to eye with me over my not over-popular policy towards the colonial peoples, and had decided to stay and support me.'* Mountbatten, however, insisted that he must accept—without disclosing his immediate reason, which was that he feared Slim's health, already impaired, might be undermined by the pressure and conditions of work in the vast realm for which they were respons-ible. But he did disclose his long-term objective. 'I said that the British Army was going to go through the most appalling difficulties, adjusting to peacetime conditions, and that I knew of no one else who could deal with them as efficiently, sensibly and with real leadership as himself.' An Indian Army man would need a couple of years in England to learn his way round Whitehall, get known by the Army at home, and become universally acceptable for the job. So Slim must go to the IDC.

In December he sailed away with Aileen and Una from the lands where he had turned defeat into victory, aboard a troopship whose passengers were much edified by the presence of Uncle Bill, and on Christmas Day, 1945, he entered a new world—through the docks at Liverpool.

There was probably no better man in the Army than Slim to com-mand the IDC at this particular time. He had done the pre-war course, and 'knew the form'. But post-war staff courses have a special character.

---

* Mountbatten, letter to author, 22 December, 1975.

Obviously the students will be of the highest quality, hand-picked from a wide range of men already tested in war and likely to go far in their respective Services—a glance at the post-1918 Staff College lists confirms this platitude. They are also, however, bound to be men jaded by years of action, responsibility and absence from home. Moreover, from the point of view of the intra-Service and military-political questions which grace the curriculum of the IDC, an immediately post-war phase presents peculiar difficulties both to the directing staff and to students. There is so much to digest and re-assess in the wartime experience; doctrine is fluid and unsettled, prejudices are strong, hardened warriors think they know best—while in 1946 huge new factors such as the atom bomb, the descending Iron Curtain and the growing realization of Britain's exhaustion called many preconceived ideas into question.

Sane, stable and shrewd, Slim diagnosed the problem and possessed the resources of character and understanding required for its solution. He saw that this was no time for putting students under steam-pressure. In their individual ways they would want to reflect, they would *need* to reflect, and he could understand this with empathy because he himself had always been a ruminant. The atmosphere must be easy-going within proper limits, relaxed but stimulating. But before anything else could be done a suitable building was necessary, since the first task with which Slim was charged was to find a new centre for the resurgent Imperial Defence College. Like eager estate-agents he and his ADC quartered the heart of London, working fast, since his days of entitlement to an aide were running out. The mansion of an American heiress in Regent's Park seemed possible but remote. In the end they found and settled for Seaford House in Belgrave Square, to the general satisfaction of successive decades.

When the 1946 course of the IDC opened under General Sir William Slim, GBE, KCB, DSO, MC, the commandant found himself among friends. The senior naval instructor was Guy Russell, his fellow-student in 1937 and now a Rear-Admiral with the CBE and DSO. Edric Bastyan from ALFSEA was among the Army Brigadiers on the student list, and Lentaigne was there from the Indian Army. An Air Commodore called Dermot Boyle would later become Marshal of the RAF and Chief of the Air Staff: another, Hudleston, had commanded the Tactical Air Force in NW Europe during the invasion in 1944, and Group Captain Bufton had been an organizing brain behind the Bomber Offensive. There was a good clutch of naval Captains, and in

Lieut-General Simonds Canada had sent one of her most brilliant and forward-looking field commanders of the war.

Slim's successor at Seaford House, Sir John Slessor, has recorded one of his remarks at this time which reflects his style as Commandant: 'A faulty strategic decision in an exercise at the IDC involves no unnecessary widows.'* (Their portraits, appropriately, now face one another in Belgrave Square.) The 1947 course contained two men who were to become High Commissioners in Australia during Slim's Governor-Generalship—one, Brigadier (later General) Cariappa for India, and the other Brigadier (later Lieut-General Sir William) Oliver for the United Kingdom. Oliver's recollections also recapture the tone of Slim's relaxed régime!

> He created an atmosphere not unlike that at a university, with the students as post-graduates who could make as much or as little of it as they wished. The day would start at a reasonable hour and there was a pleasant lack of formality. There was a lecture or discussion most mornings. In the afternoon there was a syndicate discussion, or one could read in the library—or just go home. The tone was set by the Commandant, who played us with a very loose rein. It was the stature of the man himself that impressed us. Here was a great commander who obviously thought the course worth while. So we got on with it.†

One visitor also rated Slim's capacities highly—but in a different sense. Characteristically, he decided that a lecture by a leading Communist would be good for the students—and perhaps for the Communist. He therefore invited Arthur Horner to the IDC. When Slim and Guy Russell were saying farewell to him at Seaford House Horner suddenly remarked, no doubt courteously, 'Well, there's one thing. When the revolution comes *you'll* be the first to be strung up to the lamp-posts. You're too dangerous.'

There was no lack of extramural activities. Like his students, Slim relished the return to civilization after the strains and austerities of war. He and Aileen had a convenient house in Trevor Place, Knightsbridge. There were old friendships to burnish and new friendships to explore. In England he was still rather a legend than a familiar figure, and the least known of the great war leaders was therefore much in demand for

---

* Marshal of the RAF Sir John Slessor, *These Remain* (Michael Joseph, 1969), p. 14.
† Letter to author, 21 October, 1975.

speech-making, prize-giving and similar ceremonies. But there was one medium which, with astonishing speed and effect, brought home— literally, home—to the British public that the hero of the Forgotten Army had qualities not to be overlooked in days of peace. This was the BBC.

The broadcast on 'Courage' which Slim delivered during 'the bitter winter of 1946'* created a profound impression—not least, perhaps, on Slim himself. The reactions revealed to him—though he would certainly not have admitted the fact so specifically—that through radio, by talking to people in their homes, he could capture the attention of audiences far larger than all the armies he had commanded—capture it by the simplicity of his words, the integrity of his thought, and some indefinable quality of voice which lifted him immediately into the class of 'star' broadcasters. The author, who joined the Talks Department of the BBC at this time, vividly remembers how for years that hyper-critical community referred to Slim's 'Courage' broadcast as a model. He became *persona grata* to the professionals.

This was partly because his talks had an uncommonly persuasive authority. In England, and later in Australia, his themes were always those about which he knew that he and his audience shared a common concern. His 'Courage' broadcast, for example, was not primarily about war, but about the moral and mental qualities which would enable his countrymen, groping for new orientations, to tackle the problems of peace now that the stimulus of a fight for survival had disappeared. Someone was needed to inspire in 1946, as Churchill had done in 1940. No one could repeat a miracle, but of all the voices raised in exhortation during those drab days it was Slim's that seemed to have the Churchillian *timbre*.

His success was also partly due to his own professionalism. He took immense pains to conceal his pains. Just as that other self of his, Mr Anthony Mills, had diagnosed the necessary formula for short stories acceptable in the popular press, and effectively applied it, so Slim appreciated that the essence of broadcasting is the *spoken* word. He would therefore spend many hours working over his drafts and trans- lating the written text into the language of speech, which, he noted, is 'less precise, less meticulously grammatical and more colloquial'. The result was always an apparently effortless conversation-piece, lucid, carefully casual, with humour always at hand to retain the listener's

---

* See *Courage and other broadcasts*, p. 4.

attention for his more serious message. So professional a sensitivity to the nuances of the spoken word is regrettably not the normal characteristic of senior officers.

As the partition of India approached, it was obvious that Slim would probably be sought by one or other of the two new communities. During the summer of 1947 he was in fact wanted by both. First Nehru approached the Viceroy with the proposal that Slim should become Commander-in-Chief in India, informing Mountbatten that he had made up his mind and would not go back on it. The very next day Jinnah called, to tell the Viceroy that he wished for Slim as Governor of East Bengal. Slim refused both offers. Since he envisaged retirement when his time at the IDC ran out at the end of the year, and had no other prospects before him, the Indian proposal in particular must have been tempting. But the counter-arguments were moral, and therefore conclusive.

On 17 July he sent Mountbatten a personal letter of explanation. First, he said, he would be serving two masters, the British and the Indian Governments. Their policies were bound to differ. 'I should thus have to choose either to be loyal to my employers and disregard British policy or to support it against the intentions of the Government that paid me.' Moreover, Slim added, 'I am by no means an ardent believer in the desirability of keeping the two Indian dominions within the Empire. I think there is, from one point of view, a lot to be said for keeping them out. As I understand one of the chief reasons for HMG wanting me to go to India is to do what I could to keep India in the Empire, I don't think I should be a good choice for their purpose.' Mountbatten replied on 28 July to say, 'There is no question of my misunderstanding your motives. I have never doubted your judgement before, and I do not doubt it now.' I have also', the letter ended, 'made no bones about my views that you should be the next CIGS, and have told several important people this in no unmeasured terms.' Much was soon to flow from Mountbatten's commitment.

Meanwhile, as his two-year term at the IDC ran out there was only one other possible billet in the Army for a soldier of Slim's status—and Montgomery was now CIGS. When he turned down the offers from Nehru and Jinnah, Slim had written to Mountbatten: 'I give up command of the IDC in December and then, as far as I know, go on leave pending retirement. Whether I shall get any job in civil life or elsewhere after that I do not know—probably not if I go on refusing ones I am offered like this.' His effective date of retirement (from the *Indian*

Army, as his Record of Service properly registers) was 1 April, 1948. Well before then, however, he had in fact launched into civilian life, for at the beginning of the year he transferred to the Marylebone Hotel, the headquarters of British Railways, to start a new career as Deputy Chairman of the Railway Executive.

In the event, he did not remain long enough with the railways for the public to feel the effects of his presence. Had he stayed, there is little doubt that he would have become Chairman. Though he had extricated an army from Burma, even Slim would have found it difficult fully to reconstitute the shabby, technically out-of-date, under-capitalized system which would have been his inheritance. Still, the situation was analogous to that of 1942—where so many factors were adverse, much might still be saved by clarity of mind, common sense, firmness of purpose and the occasional inspired touch. Above all it was a situation which demanded from those on the Executive unusual skills in their human relations—particularly with the diverse multitude of their employees, who needed a sense of purpose and a very considerable boost to their morale. During the months he spent in their midst it was perhaps in this area of management that Slim, not surprisingly, began to make himself felt.

It was too soon for him to form judgements or express opinions about technical matters, and indeed he felt it to be a weakness in the management structure that he was surrounded by men who were expert precisely in their field, but insufficiently equipped by outlook or experience to diagnose or overcome the human problems of the railways. He himself, because the front line was his preference, had always been in touch with the men at the front. Instinctively, therefore—but also by intent—he turned and talked to the Other Ranks of British Rail. For a boss to come so close produced, at first, a natural suspicion in the unions, but Slim himself had worked on the shop floor in the old days at Stewarts and Lloyds, he had long practised the art of handling puzzled and thwarted men and it is certain that, apart from the general value of his sanity and experience as a member of the Board, his most individual contribution, which would have borne larger fruit had he remained, was in the vague but vital area of personnel management.

To say this is not idle hagiography. In November, 1948, the Prime Minister issued a Minute which was circulated under the title *Management and Men in Socialized Industries*.

The Prime Minister had been talking with General Slim and the conversation had touched on the relationship of officers and men. They had recalled 'from his great and my limited experience' the importance of officers really knowing their men off parade and being regarded by them as natural persons from whom to seek advice. The Prime Minister also recalled that, when Welfare Officers had been introduced, he had warned all concerned of the dangers of officers thinking that the welfare of their men was no longer their job but a job for specialists. . . . *General Slim had stressed the danger in industry of divorcing the management from the workers.**

Attlee went on to warn that 'there was a need for the kind of spirit and leadership which obtained in a good regiment, an *esprit de corps* not only of the regiment but of the company and platoon. It was necessary in, for example, the coal industry to get the *esprit de corps* of the pit . . . the success of socialization largely depended on getting the right spirit.' He asked those of his colleagues concerned with the nationalized industries to give the matter their attention.

The Prime Minister's wisdom fell on barren ground. Token discussions followed—even a proposal that 'the subject of leadership should be stimulated throughout industry generally by a broadcast talk or talks by General Slim which could be reproduced in pamphlet form for distribution in industry . . . with a view to discussion at all levels of joint consultative machinery'. But Ministers took the defeatist view that, as the Boards of the nationalized industries 'might dislike a proposal which seemed to imply that conditions in the socialized industries were worse than those under private enterprise, there might be advantages in broadening the inquiry to cover private industry as well'. Not surprisingly, therefore, it was decided that 'in all the circumstances it seemed better not to proceed with the suggestion of fostering discussion of General Slim's views on leadership, which might give the impression that the Government thought that the military spirit should be introduced into industry'.†

This episode is instructive about Slim—and about Attlee, the Attlee of whom his former Private Secretary, Sir David Hunt, has written: 'He was an outstandingly good regimental officer. . . . He proudly maintained his connection with the South Lancashire Regiment and corresponded frequently from Number 10 with his old batman.' There

---

* Sir Norman Chester, *The Nationalization of British Industries* (HMSO, 1975), p. 851. Author's italics.
† *Ibid.*, p. 852.

were too many adverse factors—social and political prejudice, simple inertia, lack of imagination—but here was a moment when just possibly the principle of man-management which Slim had first learned on the shop floor in the Black Country, and later applied so fruitfully in 14th Army, might have been brought to bear in a great and growing area of Britain's social democracy. Certainly they were principles which had irradiated his work in the Railway Executive, and none can doubt that during the following quarter of a century the collaborative, intimate, sympathetic relationship between management and men which Slim and Attlee saw to be essential has not always distinguished the nationalized industries of Great Britain.

By November, 1948, however, Attlee's profound respect and admiration for Slim had transformed his future. The reason was simple. On 20 September the sitting CIGS, Montgomery, was summoned by the Minister of Defence, A. V. Alexander, and offered the appointment of Chairman of the Commanders-in-Chief of the Western Union. Before Montgomery departed for Fontainebleau at the end of October a successor was required, and in this situation one fact was paramount: the victor of Alamein and D-Day had no wish to be followed by the commander of 14th Army. The superficial arguments, which Montgomery deployed vehemently, were that Slim had spent his life in the Indian Army (a neat touch from one who, like Slim, had first gone to war in the Royal Warwickshire Regiment); that he was unknown and therefore unacceptable to the army at home; and that, anyway, he was no longer serving. But enough is now known of Montgomery's psychology for the guess to be hazarded that in seeking to exclude Slim he was mainly ensuring that his own image would not be diminished by comparisons. It is significant that his personal choice for the succession was Lieut-General Sir John Crocker, an officer who had acquitted himself capably but without the highest distinction in NW Africa and under Montgomery in Europe, and who, though many good judges would have found him tolerable, was simply not of the same order of magnitude as General Sir William Slim. With typical assurance Montgomery made the fatal error of informing Crocker privately that he was to become CIGS.*

---

* This was unfair to Crocker. When he himself became CIGS Montgomery had also been unfair to his old Chief of Staff, Major-General Sir Francis de Guingand, by telling him that he was to be made VCIGS—leaving de Guingand in the air when the appointment was not ratified.

But this was not the case. Attlee was unhappy. Moreover Mount-batten, now back in England, was seriously concerned, for in 1947, as has been seen, he had already been arguing that Slim was the natural replacement for Montgomery. The late Viceroy therefore visited the Prime Minister, on whom his influence was not slight, to insist that Slim must be the new man. Attlee agreed in principle, but emphasized Montgomery's opposition and rehearsed his arguments. Mountbatten brushed them aside, recommending that the Prime Minister should summon the CIGS and simply inform him that Slim would be ap-pointed in his place. As to the question of Slim's retirement, the answer was easy—he should be brought back to the active list as a Field-Marshal.* So fortified, Attlee saw Montgomery and told him what was to happen. After repeating his stock objection to Slim the retiring CIGS ended, 'And anyway, I've told Crocker.' 'Very well', said Attlee, 'untell him.' (Attlee, Mountbatten recalled, 'was obviously rather pleased with this short order.') So it was that by negotiations of which he was unaware the man who before 1914 had dodged the rules to join Birmingham University's Officer Training Corps was nominated to the highest post in the British Army. When the appointment was announced John Slim was on a course at the School of Infantry at Warminster.† As the news came over the wireless the whole mess burst spontaneously into cheers—an immediate sign of what soon became evident to all, that Slim was not merely a 'Sepoy General' but as acceptable at home as he had been east of Suez.

Once Slim's appointment was promulgated—he was to take up his post on 1 November—Montgomery's Military Assistant, Lieutenant-Colonel Richard Craddock,‡ reported to his new master. The MA to the CIGS is the pivot of his office. In view of Slim's withdrawal to civilian life, and his ignorance of the inner workings of Whitehall, there would be practical questions to answer. When Craddock arrived at the headquarters of the Railway Executive in the Marylebone Hotel he found that the questions put to him were indeed of an acute and extreme practicality. Would there be a car? Was there a house for the CIGS in London? There was no official residence. Would Slim be able to continue to live in his own house at Oxted in Surrey? When

---

* Slim was actually promoted Field-Marshal on 4 January, 1949.
† After the partition of India he had transferred, in 1948, from 1/6th Gurkhas to the Argyll and Sutherland Highlanders.
‡ Later Lieut-General Sir Richard Craddock, KBE, CB, DSO.

these matters had been sorted out a further, critical issue arose. What expenses was a CIGS allowed? It happened that in those days the daily expense allowance for each of the three Chiefs of Staff was grotesquely minute.* When Craddock disclosed the sum Slim exploded.

He was already, he explained, losing a good many hundreds of pounds a year by dropping from his present salary to that of CIGS. His present expense allowance, though not enormous, was respectable— but *this* sum! 'You must do something about it'—a substantial assignment for a modest Lieutenant-Colonel. Fortunately Craddock found sympathy in the Treasury from an official who had served under Slim in 14th Army. The new CIGS, he pointed out, was an exceptional case. His distinguished service had kept him overseas for most of his life. As head of the Army it would be his duty to get to know as many of the key officers under his command as swiftly as possible. Only so could he carry out his task efficiently. He would need for the most compelling reasons to entertain regularly. The Chiefs of Staff rate was obviously insufficient. Whatever the magic he used, Craddock extracted a higher rate, personal to Slim alone, on the basis that *the other two Chiefs of Staff were not informed*. It is not surprising that he went far in his profession!

The Western Union beckoned, and Montgomery's mind had crossed the Channel. There was little opportunity or time for handing over. Slim did go down to Whitehall, however, to call on his predecessor. The staff in the office of the CIGS eyed him with a suspicious respect— for how many of them, they reflected, might be left in a few weeks' time? (Had Whitehall been Burma they would have known that Slim never waved new brooms.) As Montgomery and Slim talked in the private room of the CIGS it was evident that the former was expatiating on some unsolved problem which he was bequeathing, of why this and that had kept it unsolved, of how difficult it had all been. One sentence percolated to the outer office. Slim was making his Parthian shot. 'And why', he asked Montgomery, as he moved to the door, 'didn't *you* do something about it?'

---

* To be precise, ten shillings a day!

CHAPTER SIXTEEN

THERE GOES THE ARMY

'I am not worried about the war; it will be difficult but we shall win it; it is after the war that worries me.'

Field-Marshal Smuts

IN 1947 Slim had twice received and resisted a call to arms. 'I accepted neither honour, Hindu or Mohammedan, but became instead a British railwayman.' A third call now brought him to the summit of the British Army, and yet, he wryly reflected, it was doubtful whether he had entered its citadel in Whitehall more than five times during the whole of his professional career.

One chilly November morning in 1948, in black overcoat and Homburg hat, I walked up the main steps of the War Office to be confronted by the tall frock-coated Head Porter in his gold-banded top hat. He looked down at me and I looked up at him; there could be no question which of us was the more impressive figure. He asked me, civilly but without cordiality, what was my business, and was about to direct me to the side entrance for unimportant callers, when I rather hesitantly said: 'As a matter of fact, I'm the new CIGS.' A look of amazed incredulity passed over his face.*

Rescued from this confused watch-dog by an imperturbable ADC, Slim was conducted to the office of the Chief of the Imperial General Staff, where, he was informed, he would be left alone for a little while to take his bearings.

---

* *Memoir.*

I sat at the desk which was now mine. It was bare, except for a heavy, antique silver ink-stand, complete with red and black ink and, in addition, two small receptacles, one for shot to clean quill pens, the other for fine sand to sprinkle over newly written letters. Both of these, long since empty, had been replaced by a more modern and virgin white blotter. I looked curiously round the room. On the walls, so close as to be almost touching, hung oil paintings of 18th and 19th Century commanders-in-chief of the British Army, be-wigged, be-ribboned and be-horsed. They looked down on me, the interloper, with haughty and unanimous disapproval. . . .

Swinging around once more, I noticed opposite my desk, high on the only wall not covered by pictures, a pelmet-like affair obviously housing rolled maps. On either side from it dangled long cords, each with a label. . . . I gave Europe a manful tug. With a startling rattle and crash a huge map came hurtling down. With it, also, came a miniature dust storm, while corpses of long dead moths pattered about my head. When I dared to open my eyes, I found myself at a few inches' range staring at a part of the map.

Across it, printed in the boldest letters, I read:
'Austro-Hungarian Empire' !*

After this exhilarating overture there was a knock on the door, and Gerald Templer† entered from his adjoining office. They were strangers. Templer introduced himself as Slim's Vice-Chief and was asked to sit down. Instead he marched up to the desk of the CIGS and, after formally shaking hands, announced: 'Sir, I am very sorry to tell you that I offered your resignation, on your behalf, last night.'

The background to this extraordinary declaration ought to be fully intelligible from the account supplied by Montgomery in his *Memoirs*. It is not, because the combination of *suppressio veri* and *suggestio falsi* which Montgomery, like Churchill, so often wielded in his reminiscences invalidates his narrative. The true facts are different. They are supported not only by Slim's unpublished memoir but also by the testimony of Field-Marshal Sir Gerald Templer and General Sir James Steele.

The issue was simple but fundamental. Following the run-down of wartime conditions of service it was evident that a system of limited conscription for the armed forces would be essential if minimal efficiency

---

* *Memoir*.
† Field-Marshal Sir Gerald Templer, KG, GCB, GCMG, KBE, DSO.

was to be preserved. Under the National Service Act of 1947, due to come into operation at the beginning of 1949, men would be called up for one year with the colours and six years on the Reserve. But commitments were already expanding—the blockade of West Berlin, for example, started in June, 1948. In any case the Army Council continued to dispute the cost-effectiveness of a single year's service. Many troops were still required in the East. Yet by the time a man had been called up, trained, shipped to the East (for air-trooping was impossible), and returned to England so that he could be discharged, as the law required, at the end of a year, his effective term in an operational theatre would be little more than five months. The Royal Navy and the RAF did not feel that they were substantially affected, but those responsible for the Army were desperately concerned, particularly since the wastage of regular, professional soldiers in the training of short-term recruits would be enormous. The Army Council therefore sought a two-year term, was prepared to settle unwillingly for 18 months, but contemplated resignation over anything less. The atmosphere was not sweetened by the existence of a powerful anti-militarist lobby within the ruling Labour Party.

Montgomery stated in his *Memoirs* that he fought this issue through to the end of his period as CIGS. In fact Sir James Steele, then Adjutant-General and responsible for manpower, was summoned from lunch at his club to attend a War Office meeting at which Montgomery announced to a stunned group of officers that he had personally settled with the Minister of Defence, A. V. Alexander, for a 12-month term. Steele, an Ulsterman, exploded, nor did the then Colonel of the Royal Irish Fusiliers, Gerald Templer, find it easy to restrain himself when in his master's absence it fell to him to expound Montgomery's policy to the Army Council. Though he did not know Slim personally, he knew his character, and therefore made it plain that the incoming CIGS would find the proposal unacceptable to the point of being prepared to resign. These critical events immediately preceded Slim's arrival at the War Office. He naturally knew nothing of them, but Templer was correct in his assumption that a man of inviolable integrity would rather retire than accept conditions likely to wreck the Army for which he was responsible. Now, surrounded by portraits of the haughty past, by the wigs, the chargers, the mothy map of a defunct Empire, he explained to his new Chief the urgency and the delicacy of this unforeseen dilemma.

Slim kept calm. He was accustomed to the loneliness of what

Americans call command decision. First he must assemble and assess
the facts. He summoned the Adjutant-General, as the staff officer most
directly involved; moreover, Templer was a stranger but Steele and
Slim had been fellow-students at Quetta in 1926. After confirming the
details of the Vice-Chief's report, Steele repeated Templer's contention
that a one-year term of service would break up the Army. Unwilling to
accept immediately their irrefutable logic, Slim spent a day or two in
confidential reconnaissance. After he had spoken to the other Chiefs
of Staff, Admiral of the Fleet Lord Fraser and Marshal of the RAF
Lord Tedder, and found that they were firmly behind the Army
Council, his mind was clear and he saw what he must do.

In 1942 he had extricated an army from Burma; now he had to
extricate the British Army. There was a single condition on which the
one-year term might have been accepted, and this did not exist.
Montgomery gives the impression that he had obtained from A. V.
Alexander an assurance that military commitments in the Far East
would be cut, thus making the one-year proposal more viable. But
Alexander never admitted that he had made such a promise, and
certainly neither Templer nor Steele was aware of it. Nor, in his
memoir, does Slim himself mention this as a factor. Indeed, the battle
he now knew he must fight was precisely over the issue that twelve
months was useless for men who must serve in Hong Kong or Malaya.
After only a few days in his chair, therefore, he went to see his Prime
Minister with a resignation in his pocket.

> Resignation would mean throwing away a post which must be the
> ambition of every professional soldier almost before I had assumed it.
> I should never be able to attempt any of the things I was already
> thinking should be done and had hoped to do. I was, I am ashamed to
> say, under pressure from less worthy motives. I would have to go
> back to civil life, but my railway job was already filled and other pros-
> pects not inviting. I even got to the stage of arguing with myself that
> the responsibility was not mine; all I had to do was to carry it out with
> as little damage as I could. Perhaps I was exaggerating its possible
> effects; I was new, maybe there were factors of which I was ignorant.
> My moral courage was, I thought, beginning to look a little brittle. I
> had better take action to goad myself to sticking to a resolve which I
> knew in my heart was right.*

---

* *Memoir.*

It is characteristic that neither at the time nor in his reminiscences did Slim show any consciousness of his strength vis-à-vis the Government. Had a CIGS of his stature and reputation resigned, a few days after he had been summoned back from civilian life to become head of the Army, the political consequences must have been enormous and possibly disastrous for the party in power.* Would Labour have been prepared to risk the loss of office for the sake of a six-months' addition to the term of National Service? In the event such a drama was avoided by Attlee, who respected Slim as much as Slim respected the Prime Minister—they had served at Gallipoli in the same division—and now listened to his CIGS, as Slim put it, 'with alert attention, showing a well-founded appreciation of the defence considerations involved, and, as always, a sympathetic knowledge of how high-level decisions affected officers and men in units'. After asking a few pertinent questions Attlee quickly told Slim to take no further action until he had heard from him. The Government then accepted the recommendation of the now united Chiefs of Staff, and reverted to an 18-month term of National Service. The *res publica* had been preserved; the Praetorian Guard had not defected.

This episode revealed to Slim the truth about his inheritance. As CIGS Montgomery was divisive and irritant. His grasp of strategy, his personal knowledge of foreign commanders (including the Russians), his vast experience and unquenched energy were indisputable. But he split the Chiefs of Staff by pursuing his wartime vendetta with Tedder, and sending Templer to represent him at meetings attended by the Chief of Air Staff—just as he used de Guingand at Eisenhower's conferences in 1944. In office he travelled the world, but he left his VCIGS with instructions that allowed no deviation; the consequent rigidity impaired relationships with other departments. It was evident, too, that his thoughts and actions were still those of an overlord of great armies in the field rather than of the military adviser to the Government, while that rapport with the ordinary soldier which he had so notably achieved in the Mediterranean was now diminishing. It would be unjust to imply that he did not usually behave with propriety, but the atmosphere of his régime was uneasy. It is significant that the relevant chapter in his *Memoirs* is entitled: 'I make myself a nuisance in Whitehall.'

---

* Still more so if, as was likely, Fraser, Tedder and the whole of the military members of the Army Council, including Steele and Templer, had followed him.

Histrionics were out of place. Neither Montgomery nor Slim was a 'great' CIGS, because this was not a time for greatness. Alanbrooke flowered in such a time, but the post-war epoch was one of retrenchment, contraction of commitments, loss of Empire, reduction and fusion of famous regiments, uncertainty about roles and organization beneath the mushrooming atom bomb. The Army needed confidence, guidance, protection, reassurance. These were Slim's targets, and he achieved them. When he retired Sir Brian Horrocks noted in the *Sunday Times*, on 3 November, 1952, that he had given stability to the Army, improved the conditions of its pay and service, and raised its status. 'In 1948 no single division was fit for war. Now three infantry and three armoured divisions are ready, plus a division in Hong Kong, the Gurkha Division in Malaya, and the Commonwealth Division in Korea.' A changed international situation and the work of others had brought all this to fruition, but it was Slim who created a climate favourable to wholesome growth.

'After so strenuous an introduction to my War Office desk I felt the need for a little fresh air'—a need, too, to examine at close quarters the modern British Army. A strategic revolution lay just behind him—the loss of India as a base and of the vast reserve of Indian manpower. In his judgement—confirmed in Korea, Africa, Malaya, Indonesia, Ireland —the infantry still remained the bedrock of the British Army, so he naturally began by inspecting the Guards Training Depot at Caterham, accompanied by his old friend of the Eritrean campaign, Sir John Marriott, who was then commanding London District. (With typical subtlety, Slim calculated that because Marriott had led Indian troops in action he would be less likely to look askance at a sepoy CIGS.) When the guard presented arms at the Depot Slim returned their salute, but Marriott pointed out with relish that this honour was not for the CIGS; the guard only turned out for Royalty or for the Commander of Household Troops—himself! Slim bided his time. After an inspection which gave him no opportunity for criticism he made his farewells. When the CO of the Depot asked him for his impressions he replied, with an eye on Marriott, 'Splendid! I haven't seen anything so good— not since the last time I inspected an Indian Training Battalion.' 'Fifteen all, I think', said Marriott, as they got into their car.

He next visited the School of Infantry at Warminster to watch the more sophisticated instruction in technique. While he was there he made one of those gestures which kept his memory green. Looking in on a discussion about patrolling, he happened to notice in the class the future Major-General Korla who, he well knew, had served with extreme distinction in Cowan's 17 Division throughout the retreat in 1942, at Tiddim, Imphal, and in the long drive back through Burma. He had been particularly adept and courageous at leading patrols across the Chindwin and behind the Japanese lines in the early weeks of 1944, when intelligence was at a premium. Now he was on attachment from the Indian Army. As soon as Slim spotted Korla he ordered him to stand up, pointed at him and said to the class, 'Gentlemen, you need discuss no further. This officer knows everything about patrolling you need to know.' That was good for the British infantry officers—and heart-warming for Korla.

As CIGS he never ceased to be himself, endearingly fallible yet unerringly right about the fundamentals. Perhaps only Slim would have attended a meeting at 10 Downing Street without an important file, and then, when it had been rushed over from the War Office, allow himself to be photographed as he emerged from the conference with TOP SECRET screaming from the document in his hands. Certainly only Slim could have failed to turn up at an important meeting in the Prime Minister's room at the House of Commons, which concluded a series of talks for which Malcolm Macdonald and Field-Marshal Lord Harding had flown home from the Far East. The reason was simple. At the House Slim had fallen in with some MPs who had served in 14th Army, and become so absorbed in conversation that he forgot the meeting and later went home. His Military Secretary, Lieut-Colonel Fanshawe, spent agonized hours attempting to locate a vanished CIGS. When he asked Slim next morning if he had made his apologies, Slim replied sweetly, 'Yes. The Prime Minister was very nice to me'! His Military Secretaries, Personal Assistants and ADCs, Craddock, Fanshawe, Harington, Hankinson and the rest, lost their hearts to him as Slim's staff always did, but they knew that he knew he was a master at the old soldiers' game of 'getting away with it'.

In this he felt secure because of his confidence in being able to come up with the right answer. Before a conference he would, as the Guards say, be 'idle' about reading the briefs prepared by his staff, yet it was noticed that in discussion he was rarely faulted. Or intimidated. After Churchill returned as Prime Minister there was a high-level meeting about standardization of equipment at which feelings were running high. Churchill, who opposed the idea, launched out on one of his monologues. 'When I was at Omdurman I rode with a sabre in one hand and a revolver in the other.' Slim interrupted, 'Not much standardization there, Prime Minister.' He diffused confidence and strength. If he had a weakness, it was a tendency to be too soft-hearted about senior officers who had proved to be inadequate. He always loathed sacking. Few things gave him sleepless nights—he never, for example, was troubled by re-living his wartime experiences—but the prospect or memory of a dismissal haunted him. Yet a CIGS has under him a very substantial number of generals, and his ability to select and monitor them is critical for the health of the Army. This limitation of Slim's was small in its effect; none the less, it was a limitation.

All the same, members of the War Office staff who used to watch his unflurried air as he marched along its corridors would say to themselves, 'There goes the Army!' In a precise sense he was its embodiment. Montgomery's thesis, that Slim's service in India would alienate him from the home Army, was never valid. In the First World War he had soldiered and suffered with the Royal Warwicks at Cape Helles, Sari Bair and in Mesopotamia. Ancient and famous regiments had buttressed his 14th Army. Where would he have been during the Retreat without the 7th Hussars and the men of the Royal Tank Regiment in 7 Armoured Brigade? High above Kohima, in Naga Village, stands the memorial to the Cameron Highlanders with its proud lament, 'Lochaber no more'. Beneath it lies the minuscule perimeter defended to the death by The Queen's Own Royal West Kent Regiment, and there, too, is the simple cenotaph of 2 (British) Division with its infinitely moving inscription:

> When you go home
> Tell them of us and say
> For your tomorrow
> We gave our today.

All his strong sense of history and tradition, his memories and, it must be said, his pugnacity impelled Slim to love and fight for the British Army as he had fought with his beloved Indian divisions. The boundaries of Empire were contracting, the economy was weak, the political climate was adverse. There were powerful voices to advocate a root-and-branch rationalization of the infantry regiments. Truncation, amalgamation, extinction were in the air. If the British Army survived, with its regimental core impaired perhaps, but substantially healthy, this was due in great part to Slim's shrewd and patient management. But the most vulnerable of tomorrow's children were the new

National Service soldiers. Slim devoted himself wholeheartedly to
their nurture.

> I spoke to hundreds and hundreds of them, for they interested me
> intensely. They spoke freely even to generals and did not hesitate to
> air grievances when they thought they had them. But they did not com-
> plain that the training was too hard, the hours too long, the conditions
> too rough. . . . The most attractive thing about these National Service-
> men was their eagerness to see active service. As time went on and the
> minor wars so characteristic of the British Army's past increased, it
> frequently happened that his battalion was warned for overseas just as
> the National Serviceman's time was coming to an end. So many of
> them wished to go overseas with their comrades that I managed to get
> introduced a one year voluntary extension of their service to enable them
> to do so.*

By 1951 about half the Army was composed of conscripts. Slim was
not starry-eyed. As he said in a BBC broadcast, it was unfair to blame
the Army for failing to teach these young men in eighteen months what
their families had signally failed to teach them in eighteen years. But
here he was thinking of the problem children who came his way, the
delinquents, the illiterate. In the main, and comparing them with the
volunteer soldiers beside whom he had gone to war in 1914, he rated
their military qualities surprisingly high, and cherished them.†

Youth he was always ready to condone—admiring its enthusiasm
and respecting its innocence. When he had to go down to Sandhurst to
take a passing-out-parade as the Sovereign's Representative, he worked
for hours on the text of his address, closeted in his Whitehall office and
unapproachable. He was on edge; these cadets who would shortly
march away into the future to the sound of 'Auld Lang Syne' must be
given the right message. On his return Templer confirmed that all had
gone splendidly. However, months later Slim came back from observing
an exercise in Germany to tell his VCIGS with great joy how, in the
training area, he had run across an infantry platoon lying very noticeably at ease. He got out of his car and summoned the platoon com-

---

* *Memoir.*
† Lord Head, who became Secretary of State for War in 1951, observed Slim
closely in this context, and was impressed by what he called Slim's 'sociological
awareness', finding in him an intuitive understanding of human problems not
simply in the Army, but among people in general.

mander. The young man saluted this unexpected Field-Marshal with a natural perturbation, and began to explain nervously that they were not shirking. His Company Commander had told him to give the men a break, as the exercise was ending. Slim brushed that on one side. How long had he been an officer? Was he from Sandhurst? 'Oh, you must have been on the passing-out parade I took.' The subaltern agreed. 'What did I say?' After prolonged thought and in much confusion the youngster replied, 'Well, Sir, all I remember is that you said the Japanese were a lot of little yellow baskets.'*

Unfortunately there was always the likelihood, during Slim's term as CIGS, of more than 'the minor wars so characteristic of the British Army's past'. Détente with Russia was still distant, while the forces of Communism in the Far East, soon to erupt over Korea, were visibly active. It would be fair to say that in neither of these politico-military areas was Slim entirely at home. He had the wisdom to understand and assess the advice of men more expert than himself; he lacked the first-hand knowledge that might have enabled him to originate. But since in these fields policy and budgets normally prescribed a limited military initiative, he and his fellow Chiefs of Staff hardly had a chance to perform Alanbrooke's creative role—until the last year of his tenure. Slim's was essentially a caretaker government.

In 1950, nevertheless, he undertook at great personal cost a long and, as it proved, abortive enterprise. The Middle East was a dangerous vacuum. If and when the Egyptians were brought to terms there might be an easement, but until then the British presence was inadequate; there was no Commonwealth support, and the Americans continued to exercise their wartime suspicion of 'imperialism'. Slim was therefore despatched via the Canal Base to Australia in an effort, doomed before it began, to persuade Menzies's Government to undertake military commitments in connection with the Eastern Mediterranean. Slim was in great pain. His back had rebelled. He rejected his doctor's advice that he was unfit to travel and spent the whole expedition in more or less continuous discomfort. Every time his aircraft touched down he needed treatment. And all for nothing. Though Menzies himself—as he showed during the 1956 Suez crisis—had an acute sense of what was at stake in the Middle East, his colleagues and his country were by now firmly orientated towards the Pacific. The Australian Chiefs of Staff (and particularly the CGS, Slim's old friend of IDC days, General Sir

---

* Communication from Field-Marshal Sir Gerald Templer.

Sydney Rowell) were unyielding—though the then Chief of Naval
Staff, Admiral Sir John Collins, confessed to the author that his main
concern in the discussion was to acquire an aircraft carrier for his Fleet!
The CIGS returned empty-handed—but Menzies had measured his
qualities. Two years later the consequences for Slim would be incalculable.

Australia's preoccupation with a Far Eastern strategy seemed justified
by the outbreak, on 25 June, 1950, of war in Korea, and the consequent 'police action' undertaken by the United States. 'Insofar as it
was supposed to be a United Nations action, the United States was
carrying a hugely disproportionate share of the burden of the war and
of the casualties. In the first weeks of the war, and again in November–
December, 1950, our military position had approached desperation.'*
This was true, but how far should Britain go in implementing
Security Council's resolution of 27 June that 'Members of the United
Nations furnish such assistance to the Republic of Korea as may be
necessary to repel the armed attack and to restore international peace
and security in the area'? At the end of November an alarmed House of
Commons decided that a point of no return had been reached, when it
received an incomplete report of a statement made at a press conference
by President Truman. It seemed that at this time of crisis he was about
to furnish General MacArthur with discretion to use the atomic bomb.
Attlee flew to Washington immediately for 'a wide survey of the
problems which face us today'.

Slim was in his train—and Attlee, it may be supposed, was more
comfortable in being supported on this delicate mission by the present
rather than the previous CIGS. The heat had in fact been removed from
the conference before the British arrived, for a 'damage-control party'
at the White House immediately prepared and issued a statement
affirming: 'Consideration of the use of any weapon is always implicit in
the very possession of that weapon. However, it should be emphasized
that, by law, only the President can authorize the use of the atom bomb,
and no such authorization has been given.' As this point was clarified
during the conference, Attlee still continued to press for greater Allied
control of MacArthur's operations and closer consultation over the
potential use of the bomb. He made slight progress. Dean Acheson,
the American Secretary of State, observed that 'he spoke, as John Jay
Chapman said of President Charles W. Eliot of Harvard, with "all the

---

* Professor Bernard Brodie, *War and Politics*, p. 65.

passion of a woodchuck chewing a carrot". His thought impressed me as a long, withdrawing, melancholy sigh.'* Clever, but unjust. As Churchill used to do with Roosevelt, Attlee bravely but firmly laid, as the Americans would say, the case of their British ally 'on the line'. The legend is untrue that he stopped Truman using the bomb, but his personal initiative led to an invaluable clearing of the air before the deeper Anglo-American involvement in the military developments of the fifties. Attlee acted like a porcupine—a prickly, uncomfortable partner in conference. Slim, supported by Tedder, had an emollient but more constructive role. The two chiefs had the dual task of extracting from the Americans exactly what was happening in Korea and of convincing the US Joint Chiefs of Staff that the British were solidly committed to the defence of Europe.

> The first purpose of the British group was to find out what was going on and why in North Korea. The explanation was entrusted to General Bradley, cross-examined by Field-Marshal Sir William Slim, and took up most of our first day. The truth was hard to state and harder to believe. But Omar Bradley's patent integrity was equal to the first task, which he did not attempt to gloss. Before the meetings ended, General Collins had returned from the front and reported to the joint group. . . . The hysteria about evacuation had, temporarily at least, subsided.†

The essential point was that Omar Bradley—now the US Chief of Staff, but once the only American General in the Normandy bridgehead balanced enough to comprehend Montgomery's strategy—found in Slim a counterpart, calm, trustworthy, massive in his integrity. They were at home with one another. Certainly the mutual confidence established in these discussions must be seen as a significant background to that moment in Brussels, during the afternoon of 19 December, when the NATO Council, with the preliminary connivance of the United States, appointed Eisenhower as Supreme Commander, Allied Forces Europe, and America was indissolubly committed in the West.

Churchill's return in October, 1951, carried Slim back to Washington in very different circumstances. At the end of the year he sailed with the

---

* Dean Acheson, *Present at the Creation*, p. 478.
† *Ibid.*, p. 481.

Prime Minister's party on the *Queen Mary* for discussions the main
purpose of which was to acquaint Churchill with Truman's administration and renew, so Churchill hoped, his wartime 'special relationship'.
The topics were largely in Slim's field: 'Almost every aspect of defence
policy, American bases in Britain, the much-mooted European Defence
Community, and the practical implementation of the North Atlantic
Treaty.'* But Churchill was not Attlee. He had not yet made one of
the worst appointments of his career and drafted his beloved Field-
Marshal Lord Alexander as Minister of Defence. This did not occur
until March, 1952, and meanwhile Churchill happily doubled the duties
of Defence Minister and Premier. Slim's main problem, therefore, was
not to negotiate with the Americans so much as to keep abreast of his
chief. In this he might have failed disastrously, for when there was a
question of formalizing the plan to make an American Admiral the
Allied Commander in the Atlantic (as had been informally agreed by
the Attlee government) Churchill lost his temper. 'You have urged me
to do this fake without any explanation to public or Parliament.' And
indeed Slim had so urged him, as had the First Sea Lord, Admiral of the
Fleet Sir Rhoderick McGrigor.† Yet while Churchill turned scornfully
against McGrigor, he emerged from this pother with an enhanced
opinion of Slim. 'Slim is quite different. I can work with him.'

A working relationship was now important, since Slim by his
seniority had become Chairman of the Chiefs of Staff Committee, his
colleagues being McGrigor and Sir John Slessor, who followed Tedder
as Chief of Air Staff. At Churchill's instigation these three, in the spring
of 1952, applied themselves to preparing a paper which, in its final form,
as the Report by the Chiefs of Staff on 'Defence Policy and Global
Strategy', was the most important strategic review since 1945 and set
the tone of British defence doctrine (if not entirely of practice) during
the next decade. For peace and concentration the three Chiefs rusticated
themselves. The most superficial study of their conclusions indicates
that the driving force, in terms of intellect and relevant experience,
was Slessor, yet the Marshal of the RAF has readily admitted‡ that
Slim was an invaluable monitor of their discussions, rarely originating

---

* Sir Ronald Wingate, *Lord Ismay*, p. 189.
† The Atlantic Command, SACLANT, went to Admiral McCormick, USN, on
11 April, 1952.
‡ Private communication.

proposals but intervening at the right moment to eliminate the un-
tenable or ratify the viable. In a way Slim's reputation suffers from the
nature of his qualities. Common sense is neither dramatic nor glam-
orous; it is merely rare. But Slessor, whose peak years had immersed
him in the esoteric problems of policy and command, appreciated the
presence of this reliable touchstone. It was vital that their calculations
were unflawed.

The basic theme of the 1952 Report was that increased effort was
necessary to win the Cold War, that success could be achieved by
deterrence, that Britain should therefore concentrate on complementing
America's nuclear strength, and that this concentration should be
accompanied by improvements in the long-term efficiency of counter-
measures.* (The paper was prepared before the hydrogen bomb had
become a factor.) To compensate for this effort, unnecessary commitments e.g. in Trieste and Austria, should be liquidated; the build-up
of ground troops in Europe should be diminished; the Middle East
should have lower priority than the Far East, and a settlement with
Egypt might lead to a diminution of the Mid-East base. To give increased flexibility, there should be an expansion of the RAF's Transport
Command, offset by a reduction in troopships.

When all these propositions had been hammered out the three Chiefs
of Staff retired to the Royal Naval College, Greenwich, to produce in
purdah their final text. Lieut-General Sir Ian Jacob, who had just been
extracted by Churchill from directing the BBC's Overseas Services to
become the temporary Chief Staff Officer to the Minister of Defence,
received the text when it reached Whitehall. From his immense wartime experience in the military secretariat of the War Cabinet, Jacob
was able to see that the paper was still somewhat inchoate, bearing the
marks of too many hands. He felt embarrassed at putting such a point
to men like Slim and Slessor, both outstandingly articulate writers.
However, he tackled Slim and was deeply struck by the considerate
humility with which the CIGS accepted Jacob's recommendation that
the text should be tidied up by the Secretariat of the Chiefs of Staff.
The result was approved by Churchill, and endorsed by the Cabinet

---

* This chapter was written before the publication of Professor Margaret Gowing's
two volumes, *Independence and Deterrence: Britain and Atomic Energy, 1945–
1952*. These volumes reinforce the view that Attlee's tight security in atomic
matters meant that Slim, like the Chairman of the Defence Research Policy
Committee, and other heads of service committees, were effectively in the dark
about the issues on which they had to decide.

in July. If all its proposals were not immediately implemented, it still stands as a watershed.

On the other side of the world, however, another man had also been impressed by Slim. In *Afternoon Light* Sir Robert Menzies has given a frank account of the situation which faced him, as Prime Minister of Australia, towards the end of 1952. The current Governor-General, Sir William McKell—a former boiler-maker who had risen as a lawyer and politician—was appointed in 1947 by the Labour Premier Ben Chifley. 'Chifley thought that the Governor-Generalship was a well-paid "job" which could usefully be held by a party member, whether the King knew him or not, or liked him or not. There was no discussion with the King. One name only was put before him, and that by cable.' A successor to McKell must be found before the year's end, and all Menzies's revulsion from the practice of his predecessor and the Labour Party now found expression. He decided to call in the Old World to redress the balance of the New; to opt, in traditional style, for another British Governor-General. His choice must be a man of indisputable stature, capable of restoring the dignity of his office—a dignity much diminished by the open disdain with which Chifley and his fellows had treated their place-man. Menzies selected Slim.

With due propriety he raised the matter with the Queen, during a visit to London in December, on the basis that the Australian Prime Minister had the constitutional right to nominate but that the Monarch was entitled to approve. He therefore arranged that while he was staying with Lord Salisbury for the week-end, the Queen, he and his host should each write down the names of three candidates. Two days later he reported again to Buckingham Palace, to compare the lists and discover that the name at the head of each was the same. 'So now, Ma'am,' said Menzies, 'I nominate Slim and you are bound to approve!'

> Armed with this singularly happy conclusion, I got the authority of the Queen to speak to Sir William Slim; drove straight down to the Map Room; got him out of Conference, and on behalf of Her Majesty offered him the post.
>
> It is interesting to recall what happened. I said: 'Sir, I gather that you are about to finish your term as Chief of the Imperial General Staff.' 'That is so,' he said. 'Under these circumstances, I have the authority of the Queen to ask you whether you would care to be Governor-General of Australia.' 'Are you serious?' 'Never more so. We should all be delighted.' 'Could I have a talk with my wife? Of course you have not met my wife. She is very important in this matter.

For, if I accept this post, which I would like to do, you must understand that I have a considerable faculty for dropping bricks. But she has a genius for catching them before they hit the floor!'

Next day, to my pleasure and the immense satisfaction of the Australian people, he accepted.

CHAPTER SEVENTEEN

THE SYMBOL

'The Governor-General of Australia being the King's direct personal representative, the appointment of someone notoriously not chosen either by, or in effective consultation with him, and whose appointment would, by reason of party political convictions, be distasteful to a large section of Australian citizens, must inevitably weaken the symbolism of the Governor-Generalship and, therefore, of the Crown which it represents.'
Sir Robert Menzies, 28 November, 1946

THE ANNOUNCEMENT of Slim's appointment aroused few chauvinist sentiments in Australia. At a stroke Menzies had achieved his first objective—to present his country with a man of stature whose credentials could not conceivably be impugned, who was *au-dessus de la mêlée* of Australian politics, and whose aura was sufficiently strong for him to stand effectively as a symbol of the royal presence. Slim's military achievements made him immediately respected and, in principle, a welcome guest for a society whose own soldiers in two Great Wars had been the embodiment of its national pride. Full judgement was reserved until Australia had taken a closer look at him, but even before he arrived Slim's treatment in the press had been warm. There was a sense of interested anticipation.

Nevertheless, it was part of the pattern of Slim's life that his enterprises had a way of running into troubles at the outset—Gallabat, Kohima, his first week as CIGS. And now the unexpected occurred again. He, Aileen and their staff were due to arrive at Melbourne on the *Himalaya* on 23 March. Suddenly and secretly, however, Churchill obtained from Menzies permission to retain Slim in London for the time being,* because of the tense situation in the Middle East and Slim's special knowledge of the problems. This typically Churchillian improvisation may have brought comfort to the Prime Minister, but it was a torture for his ex-CIGS since secrecy was maintained right up to the end—even to the farce of a farewell luncheon at the Savoy from which the guests emerged to see placards shouting SLIM FOR EGYPT. (John Swinton, the young Guards officer who was now one of Slim's ADCs, then had the wretched task of going down to Tilbury to recover the mountain of luggage which, as a cover, had been loaded on to the *Himalaya*.) In any case, the affair was a storm in a tea-cup, for Slim was soon released from his bonds, and on 30 April he came ashore at Melbourne into a New World.

Of his arrival in Burma in 1942 Slim later wrote: 'Experience had taught me that before rushing into action it is advisable to get quite clearly fixed in mind what the object of it all is.' Ten years later he was absolutely sure about his object. He was the Queen's Representative. From this fact his military mind derived the logical conclusion that to attain the object of representing the Monarch properly he must be a perfectionist. Everything concerned with his office must attain the highest standard. In discussions during the voyage, therefore, the principles of operation emerged—discipline, order, impeccable behaviour, meticulous attention to detail. Though the problems ahead were obscure, these were themes which Aileen—herself facing a formidable new role—could comprehend and later implement, with her natural gift for *décor*, her instinctive social flair, and her strong Presbyterian sense of duty. At his right hand, moreover, Slim had as Military Secretary a Greenjacket of sterling quality and wide experience, Lieut-Colonel Martin Gilliat, an ex-prisoner of war who had already served as Deputy Military Secretary to the Viceroy of India in 1947-8 and, in 1956, would undertake an enduring task as Private Secretary to Queen Elizabeth the Queen Mother. Gilliat understood what had to be done. And Aileen's Private Secretary, Judy Hutchinson, the guardian of the map room at Alexander's headquarters in Italy during the war, was no stranger to the problems and the protocol that surround high office.

When the *Strathnaver* touched in at Fremantle it was boarded by Murray Tyrrell,† the Official Secretary to the Governor-General (or, in

---

* And, in all probability, send him to Egypt, for which plans were far advanced.
† Sir Murray Tyrrell, KCVO, CBE.

Slim

effect, his Chief of Staff), who had served McKell in this capacity and, during a long period of public service, had worked close to many Ministers and Prime Ministers. Australia was his village. With contacts everywhere, and a trained nose for developing situations, he was a dexterous organizer who deeply relished the challenge of a difficulty. A tendency, in those days, to appear sardonic and serious belied a natural *gaminerie* and a bent for the unorthodox. It was in his nature to 'give it a go'. Slim was fortunate beyond all possible calculation in finding such a man awaiting him—but luck with staff had always been pattern in his life.* He—and Aileen—were doubly fortunate in that Tyrrell's wife, Nell, blended with complete harmony and tranquillity into the close-knit circle of Government House.

The Official Secretary is an official of the Federal civil service, and it was Tyrrell's task to convey to the new Governor-General a typewritten departmental document which set out formally the logistic facilities and arrangements for the execution of his duties—in short, the house-keeping accounts. Slim found this no more to his taste than he had found the existing expense allowance for CIGS. Producing a counter-document (which happened to be a scrawl by Menzies on the back of an envelope,) he pointed to the discrepancies between Department and Prime Minister; and, he said, Tyrrell could tell Canberra that he had no intention of coming ashore if *that* was the brief. Recalcitrance was victorious. Tyrrell had to do some rapid unscrambling on the telephone before Slim's ruffles were smoothed; for the time being it confirmed him in the view he had formed during Slim's 1950 visit, when he heard him speak harshly to a late-arriving officer, that—in the Australian vernacular—his boss was a 'pommy bastard'. He did not know, of course, that in 1950 Slim was racked with pain and should never have undertaken the journey; he was not normally offensive to sub-ordinates. Nor did Tyrrell know that, when he had come to understand his Governor-General as a man rather than a figurehead, he would be converted into one of his staunchest admirers.

After touching in at Melbourne the Slims went immediately under-ground for a few days, leaving the press with *bonnes bouches* like 'the Australian infantrymen are among the toughest and most aggressive soldiers ever produced in world history. They were like that at

---

* It is worth noting that from the beginning Slim insisted that in his personal staff the ratio of Australians to British should be about double. This was by no means a tradition at Government House.

Gallipoli and they are just as magnificent in Korea today.' That could do no harm; but the journalists were denied all knowledge of the hideaway. It happened that on a small fruit farm at Croydon near Melbourne lived one of their oldest friends, Kay Hargrave, and careful plans had been laid for them to move straight from the *Strathnaver* to Croydon for a little breathing-space before the rigours of office began. Kay and the Slims had first met when she came to Delhi from Australia in 1930 as the 18-year-old bride of Reg Breadmore, a young staff officer working at Army HQ alongside Slim, Lockhart and Vickers. They shared the same compound, and Aileen taught her inexperienced new friend everything about running an Indian bungalow. Her husband died during the war, and she later married Bill Hargrave.

Inevitably the press smoked them out at Croydon, but the Slims withdrew in good order and sailed round to Sydney, before taking up their official residence at Government House, Yarralumla, Canberra, the old colonial-style mansion standing in dignified seclusion on the rim of that great orbital pattern woven by Frank Lloyd Wright's pupil, Burley Griffin, when he designed for Australia a brand-new capital city. In the early fifties that design had not yet been fully implemented, and the modern Canberra, with its great satellite suburbs, would seem a large excrescence in comparison with the small-scale intimacy of Slim's day. Before they could begin to enjoy their new home, however— indeed, they had hardly crossed its threshold—the imp of the unexpected struck again. Aileen fell suddenly and desperately ill.

A fierce and dangerous haemorrhage was the culmination of troubles that had dogged her over the years, a drain on both physical and mental reserves. Murray Tyrrell was immediately involved in the first of many crash actions in the Slims' service. Fortunately his own doctor was John James, a surgeon of quality. 'I called him in; he examined Aileen; I showed him to a telephone in the ADC's room; he roused the Canberra hospital, the ambulance, oxygen and so on. I then drove this great man at 70 mph through a rain storm to the hospital some five miles away; he had every sister and medico jumping in seconds flat; we loaded the ambulance and raced back to Government House. Much later that night James came to me, about 11.30 pm, and remarked, 'It's all right for the present. Can I have a whisky?'*

---

* Letter to author, 26 June, 1975. Subsequently James was awarded the CBE for the continued distinction of his work, and his memory is perpetuated by the John James Memorial Hospital in Canberra.

Though the first crisis had passed grave dangers remained. Life was literally draining away. 'She had her fifth blood transfusion this morning,' Slim wrote to Philip Pratt. A call was therefore put through to William Morrow in Sydney.* After a distinguished war record, for which he had been awarded the DSO, Morrow had emerged as an outstanding physician within the Australian medical community. But, in short, all that he too could do was give the best advice and ensure the best treatment, and hope. Fortunately, the miracle occurred, and Aileen was left to gather her strength. It was bitter for Slim to have to be sworn in as Governor-General before Parliament on 8 May without Aileen beside him—his true consort, with whom so many of the troubles as well as the triumphs of his life had been shared.

But now Slim had taken the oath. What would be the strategy of his next campaign? Section 2 of the Australian Commonwealth Constitution declares that 'a Governor-General appointed by the Queen shall be Her Majesty's Representative in the Commonwealth, and shall have and may exercise in the Commonwealth during the Queen's pleasure, but subject to this Constitution, such powers and functions of the Queen as Her Majesty may be pleased to assign him'. He is the *personal* representative of the Queen as 'Elizabeth the Second, by the grace of God, of the United Kingdom, Australia and her other Realms and Territories Queen, Head of the Commonwealth, Defender of the Faith.' A High Commissioner acts for the British Government: the Governor-General's status and duties derive entirely from the Crown. But what, in 1953, were his actual 'powers and functions'?

In the Victorian era that fountain of ideas about the monarchy, Walter Bagehot, distinguished between its charismatic or decorative function and its residual positive powers: 'to be consulted, to encourage and to warn'. By 1953 only the former lay effectively within the grasp of the monarch's representative in Australia. The last time that a Governor-General had a substantial role in the actual process of directing affairs was probably 1942, and circumstances then were wholly exceptional. War had suddenly reached the threshold of a naked continent. Curtin, the Prime Minister, a man of undoubted political gifts, was hard pressed to master the problems created by a threat of invasion and the military mobilization of his country's resources. But in the Governor-General, Lord Gowrie VC, he found a tower of strength. Shrewd, experienced, accessible, Gowrie had already made his mark as

---

* Sir William Morrow, DSO, ED, FRCP, FRACP.

a State Governor. As Governor-General he was respected and admired. Curtin turned to him freely for advice and encouragement. But Slim faced a different situation and a different Prime Minister.

The atmosphere of post-war Australia was one of robust and assertive independence. A Governor-General who, 'subject to this Constitution', sought to assert himself was asking for trouble. In his life of Edward VII Sir Philip Magnus described how Queen Victoria used to explore 'a wide and dubious land' beyond the bounds of her constitutional rights. This was a territory the Governor-General could only enter at his peril. Technically he could take decisions. Acts of Parliament generally received Royal Assent at his hands. Financial appropriations could only be made if their purpose 'has in the same session been recommended by message of the Governor-General to the House in which the proposal originated'. He must ratify certain appointments . . . and so on. But in all this he was really acting as a rubber stamp. Over the rare issue of a double dissolution of the Houses of Parliament he retained a certain option, but normally the responsible and proper course was for the Governor-General to follow the written submission of the Prime Minister. 'The Governor-General was entitled to be a political realist.'* Realism meant self-control.†

Nobody, certainly, was more aware of the realities of politics than Menzies. With his lawyer's mind, he appreciated in the minutest detail his constitutional rights as Prime Minister *vis-à-vis* the Queen's Representative, nor would he accept any entrenchment on them. He had always stood four-square to the world, as a proud leader and a powerful antagonist. Between him and Slim the relationship would have to be very different from that between Curtin and Gowrie. It is

---

* L. F. Crisp, *Ben Chifley*, p. 406. Realism was also required in Slim's relations with the six State Governors, each of whom, unlike their equivalents in Canada, has the right of direct communication with the Queen. Thus when the Governor-General emerges from the federal territory of Canberra he, the Queen's representative in Australia, is on the ground of the Queen's representative in a particular State. Delicate questions of protocol, practice and personalities are thus inevitably raised. Slim was painstaking in his diplomacy to avoid contentious relations with his fellow representatives of the Queen.

† All these remarks relate to 1953, when the political scene was different from that of the seventies and the key figures were Slim and Menzies. The dismissal in 1975 of the Prime Minister, Gough Whitlam, by the Governor-General, Sir John Kerr, demonstrates the great power still available to the Queen's Representative in certain circumstances. But it is also a reminder that during Slim's Governor-Generalship these circumstances were hardly conceivable.

doubtful whether Menzies had ever supported himself on another's shoulder.

In his early months, therefore, as Slim sniffed the air, it became clear to him that if he was to lift the Governor-Generalship on to a higher plane it would be a delicate if necessary business. He inherited no precedents from his predecessor, for McKell, loyally and unobtrusively performing the ritual of his office, had avoided uncomfortable initiatives. Slim therefore went into action like a soldier. During his first year he may be observed tapping along the enemy front and establishing a firm base for future operations. It was the phase of reconnaissance.

His first task was to ensure his rights and perquisites. When he presided over the Federal Executive Council, for example, he soon noticed that the explanatory matter on which he was supposed to form a judgement was inadequate. How could he approve what he could not understand? He had come from the post of CIGS, and was accustomed to, had indeed required, accurate and intelligible briefings. Both military training and the dignity of his office were offended by this slipshod behaviour. His protests penetrated the Government departments in a flash, and the briefs improved. He had dug in.

A more fundamental matter was the reorganization of the whole financial system by which the office of Governor-General is supported, and for this his successors owe a substantial debt to the Field-Marshal— and to Aileen. It could hardly have been achieved had not Slim been the man he was—and Menzies's man. The result derived from the process of renovation which Aileen instituted at Yarralumla and Admiralty House in Sydney, a process, incidentally, which bequeathed to Australia two buildings of a style and quality worthy of their vice-regal purpose. The drab war years had taken their toll. Some irreverent lines captured the atmosphere of Government House not long before the Slims' arrival.

> Dixon's hut gone Yarralumla
> Comes greenroofed with double gables
> (Bride-cake Gothic, frostly smugly).
> Ugly porte-cochére. Good stables.
> All rooms tall rooms. Ballroom 'off-white',
> Quite an architectural cocktail.
> Yarralumla! White and static,
> So aesthetically erratic,
> Morally, perhaps, Balmoral. . . .

Half hotel and wholly temple,
Temple, not of Gods or Muses,
But a country's daily uses.*

With imperious energy and creative flair Aileen effected a transformation scene, but the necessity for obtaining departmental approval for each item of expenditure, however trivial, finally exasperated her beyond control. 'I'm not going on with this', she announced, 'if I can't be trusted.'

It happened that Menzies was about to make a call. Observing the cigar smoke flowing from the study—they always kept a good Havana for the Prime Minister—Aileen thought the auguries promising. When Menzies emerged and twitted her light-heartedly about one of her minor efforts at re-decoration she knew she was safe, as Slim confirmed when he said he had mentioned the awkwardness to Menzies and that Menzies had promised 'to do something about it'. The something was a radical alteration in the system of pay and subvention. Henceforth the Governor-General would receive a specific personal salary, from which he would only be expected to be responsible for genuinely private matters—e.g. his personal as opposed to official guests. All other items, upkeep, transport, official entertainment etc, would be charged to the Government's general account—on flexible lines which removed the annoyance of indents over petty matters. Menzies obtained the approval of his political colleagues without difficulty;† thanks to his good will and his commitment to Slim the financial scope of the Governor-Generalship was thus considerably and beneficially en- enlarged.

Friction, nevertheless, was a possibility inherent in their relationship. They were two strong men, and one had his hands tied behind his back. For most of his professional life Slim had been a decision-making animal. He was now in a realm of impotence, and though he relished the charismatic side of his role and the distinction of his position, he yearned for modes of action. Lieut-General Sir Frank Berryman, who observed him closely, described him at this time as 'a caged eagle'. After eight years as Viceroy of India Lord Dalhousie refused to join the Cabinet in London because he found it intolerable to have to sit

---

* From *Sunday at Yarralumla*, by Ethel Anderson (Angus and Robertson, 1947).
† His device was typically adroit. To have amplified Slim's *salary* would have involved constitutional procedure.

among equals. Slim, who had commanded an army in India and enjoyed more actual power than a Victorian Viceroy, was not even on terms of parity with Menzies in the process of decision-making. Some of his early essays into the 'wide and dubious land' of personal initiative were inevitably misjudged or mistimed. This was all part of his learning process. But though at first he occasionally exacerbated the Prime Minister, Menzies never directly reproached him. They paced round one another like two sagacious old hounds, suspicious, alert, but each too full of respect for the other to start a fight.* Indeed, Menzies confessed in his memoirs that 'I never went into his presence without feeling nervous', and Slim would later say the same about Menzies. Respect, however, gradually warmed into a firm friendship.

The explosive possibilities of the situation were well illustrated when Slim, on tour in the north, made a speech in which he criticized the Government's defence policy—appropriate from an ex-CIGS, but dangerous for a Governor-General. Immediately Menzies heard of it he was on to Tyrrell for a text. No copy was available. Tyrrell was sternly ordered to get Slim to ring the Prime Minister. After a struggle the Official Secretary contacted his master in far-distant Darwin, to be told that if the Prime Minister wished to speak to the Governor-General *he* could telephone *him*! Impasse—but not for Tyrrell. He found a competent telephone supervisor, explained the situation to her confidentially, and told her that she *must* bring Ajax and Achilles together. Later she rang to report success, and when Tyrrell asked how the conversation was going she replied, 'Rough at first—but it's OK now.'

Reconnaissance on another front stimulated a more public reaction. On 27 October, 1953, in his opening address to the National Congress of the Returned Services League, Slim took a risk and spoke out bluntly. The time had come, he said in effect, for the war veterans to stop thinking that they were a special case, to stop putting pressure on the Government for special treatment, and to accept that it was reasonable for the Government to resist such pressure. This was daring, for the experience and aftermath of two World Wars had made the RSL something of a sacred cow. Far more than the British Legion or the veterans' organizations in the United States, it formed a compact and powerful

---

* Lord Carrington, who was British High Commissioner in Australia, 1956–1959, found that Menzies would grumble privately to him about Slim, and Slim would grumble privately to him about Menzies.

political lobby. Menzies, for his party's profit, had granted it formal access to the Cabinet committee concerned with repatriation and resettlement. Its voice was not ignored in the corridors of power.

In a sense Slim was saved by an ill-considered outburst on the part of a demagogic RSL activist, Bill Yeo, who accused the Governor-General of speaking for the Government. This was a serious charge, embroiling the Queen's Representative in a purely Australian party conflict. But it revealed to Slim the line along which he could now advance into the 'wide and dubious land'. His position gave him a solid base. If he used it to draw attention to matters of broad concern about which nobody else with the right authority would be willing to speak, he could count on his words being accepted sympathetically and even with a sigh of relief.* This became his policy during the main period of his office. As he impressed himself on Australia, he turned into the kind of father figure from whom home truths are permitted. In this he was carefully circumspect, though he would refer with relish to 'my annual calculated indiscretion'. But he had evolved a new function for the Governor-General.

So it proved in November, 1953. Yeo had gone too far. Both inside and outside the RSL there was a genuine realization that the clamour for bread and circuses for the veterans was inopportune and excessive —realization, too, that Slim had had the courage to state an undeniable truth. Australians admire guts. The RSL, in fact, put its own house in order. At a lively meeting of the Congress speaker after speaker rose to deplore the implications of Yeo's speech, and finally he announced in front of his fellow-members that 'I entirely withdraw and apologize if anything I said can be taken as an expression of disloyalty to Her Majesty the Queen, or to her representative.'

The decorative or ritualistic side of the representative function was developed to a high degree of perfection. Some maintained that the Slims went beyond the bounds of what was necessary for a viceregal organization in a down-to-earth democracy like Australia. The general verdict was different. Most Australians were secretly, if not openly, satisfied to recognize a new sense of style at Government House. The insistent punctilio at dinner parties and receptions, the immaculate *décor*, the precise attention to protocol were more respected than condemned. And what is forgotten is that when the Slims came to

---

* No leading politician would have risked a public criticism of the RSL. The veteran vote was too important.

Australia the only models on which they had to build, from their own experience, were the conduct of The Viceroy's House in Delhi and the effortless efficiency with which a royal occasion would be stage-managed in London. Having witnessed the best, neither Slim nor Aileen could be content with a second-class solution. Painfully, persistently, conscientiously they polished the drill for party-giving and improved the amenities of their establishment. ADCs were exhorted, servants were schooled, the cuisine was civilized. In all this the driving-force was Aileen. Determined that only the highest standards would suffice for Bill, she doubled the parts of *chef de protocol* and *grand hotelier.*

Slim enjoyed the dignity of his office. He had, too, a proper pride in his eminence, in the long climb, by his own efforts, from the days of pupil-teaching and boiler-tube-making. Like his boyhood hero, Sir Cloudesley Shovell KCB, he had made his way to the top. 'Here I am,' he once remarked to his aides, 'a grammar-school boy surrounded by Old Etonians.' But he really undertook and performed these necessary formalities because he had made a military appreciation that this was how the battle should be fought. His heart lay in other places. After the dinner-parties were over he would slip away with some old service friend from England, or a new and accepted acquaintance. Over a glass or two in his study they would talk for hours about the issues of war and peace, totally relaxed and totally happy.*

Often, however, these conversations had a more subtle purpose. Menzies, a past-master at the game, came to be impressed by Slim's shrewd and percipient comprehension of the Australian political scene. This was no rubber-stamp Governor-General; he had taken the measure of the forces active in the society over which he symbolically reigned. Yet a Governor-General, unlike an Army Commander, has no titular intelligence staff. His subordinates are there simply to facilitate his official performance. Slim therefore became his own intelligence centre, garnering and collating information from many sources. Tyrrell, with his private and continent-wide network of contacts, was an invaluable agent. Gilliat, widely welcomed and widely entertained, would bring back useful situation reports. Bill Morrow the physician soon found himself entangled. A *doyen* of the Australian Club in Sydney, which

---

* It is indicative of Slim's wide-ranging sympathies that one friendship established during these man-to-man sessions, and maintained until his death, was with Sir Daryl Lindsay who, as artist and Director of The National Gallery of Victoria, made so profound a contribution to Australia's aesthetic life.

contains perhaps the most representative cross-section of Australia's men of affairs, he would sometimes be summoned up to Canberra for a week-end. He came to know that such a summons invariably entailed a long Sunday morning walk with Slim in the grounds of Government House, during which he would be asked, 'And what does the Australian Club think of *that*?' In the end, if any large public issue cropped up he found himself automatically noting the reactions within the Club, confident that a few days later he would be interrogated.

But there was another commitment, secret, absorbing, and more enduring in the result than any of these private or public preoccupations. It is astonishing to recall that amid all the strains and time-consuming activities of his office Slim wrote the greater part of *Defeat into Victory*. (The strain and the consumption of time entailed may be illustrated graphically. In his flights all over Australia, to New Zealand, New Britain and New Guinea, Slim logged over 1,100 flying hours.) When he left England he had already completed the story up to the end of the 1942 retreat, but it was in Australia, amid hard journeys by air and land, amid the social distractions of Government House and the insistent routine of public duties, that he composed all the main chapters in which his victories over the Japanese are so fully, so honestly and so lucidly described. Anyone who has worked on a military narrative of this nature, infinitely complicated in its subject-matter, knows the need for peace, for continuity of thought, for time to ponder and weigh and analyse. Denied all these amenities by the nature of his office, Slim nevertheless achieved an inner tranquillity which enabled him to produce a balanced and magisterial work, now universally recognized by the general public and the military circles of many countries as unparalleled. His commander's gift of maintaining calm in the chaos of battle stood him in good stead.*

He was far from the files of Whitehall, far from the colleagues and subordinates of his war years. Yet once again his luck held. His old Quetta friend of 10th Gurkhas, now Brigadier Michael Roberts DSO, who had an exemplary record in 14th Army, was a member of the Historical Section of the Cabinet Office, first working on campaign narratives and then as part-author of the 'War against Japan' series in the

---

* While he was writing *Defeat into Victory* he discussed its publication with Menzies, on the basis that what he was writing might be considered controversial and therefore an embarrassment for the Australian Government. Menzies replied that what Slim was writing was for posterity. So far as Australia was concerned, he as Prime Minister would accept all responsibility.

Official History. To Roberts Slim despatched the draft of each of his chapters, with detailed questions, queries about maps, meticulous inquiries about spellings and dates and locations. Roberts, never over-awed by his seniors as a soldier, and indefatigable in the pursuit of truth as a historian, was the touchstone Slim needed. Pages of courteous but ruthless criticism passed continuously from London to Canberra. The files of their correspondence show with what humility and integrity the former Commander-in-Chief accepted, without self-justification or demur, the comments of his junior. In the *va-et-vient* of their letters many significant points emerged. It is clear, for example, that in *Defeat into Victory* Slim throttled his feelings about Wingate and in his generosity was less out-spoken than he might have been. It is clear that the exclusion of the section he wrote on his sacking by Oliver Leese (see Chapter 14) was the result of a careful consideration, a sense of charity, and a genuine inability to grasp the other's motives. The truth is that it was not in Slim's nature to denigrate.

When the book was published in the spring of 1956 the first edition of 20,000 was sold out immediately and within a few weeks a further edition of 20,000 was in hand. After that flying start it has sold continuously, in hardback and paperback, all over the world.* At its publication Slim registered his debt to Roberts in a letter of characteristic self-depreciation and semi-serious humour:

Government House
Canberra
23 March, 1956

My Dear Michael,

Now that DEFEAT INTO VICTORY is launched I feel that the first person I must write to is you! Without all the unselfish help you gave me, not only in checking my accuracy and clarity, but in going to such endless trouble over the maps, the book would either never been finished or, if it had been, would have been much worse than it is from every point of view.

I hope you already realize how grateful I am for everything you have done and for the hours of your leisure you have sacrificed for me. If you don't realize it, I can only say I am really and truly grateful. I have

---

* It was years afterwards, in a speech at a City dinner, that Slim declared: 'We Field-Marshals have learned, in peace as in war, to sell our lives dearly.'

asked Cassells to send you a copy of the book and at the first opportunity I would like to inscribe it as suitably as I can.

One copy of the book has reached me and I think that Cassells, with your help, have made a very good job of it. I have had two comments on it so far. One from a lady: 'It really is a solid volume—just the thing to throw at one's husband! I must get a copy.' The second from son John—who incidentally is at home for a month or two: '*Another* bloody book to read for the Staff College!' So it ought to suit all tastes.

With every good wish and again my thanks.

Yours ever
Bill

In the style of *Defeat into Victory*, masculine, lucid, assured, Slim's voice is unmistakable—that voice which spoke so cogently in his memorable broadcasts: indeed, to few books can *le style, c'est l'homme* be more accurately applied. But the orchestration of so large a theme was a very different matter from the pot-boilers of Mr Anthony Mills. Slim had to evolve a more mature technique for so complicated and extensive a narrative. In this process he sought and accepted keen criticism from Tyrrell, and was greatly indebted to a new friend, Gordon Arthur, who was particularly strict in overcoming Slim's tendency to indulge in over-long sentences. But this friendship went deeper. The Rt Rev. Gordon Arthur, later Bishop of Grafton, was then Rector of the old pioneers' church of St John's, Canberra, a man whose transparent sincerity and spiritual strength brought him closer to Slim than any priest except, perhaps, Donald MacDonald in Burma. He became Slim's unofficial chaplain. From Government House Bill and Aileen would regularly attend services at St John's, as well as those of other denominations—particularly the Presbyterian church of St Andrew whose dedicated Minister, Hector Harrison, was soon linked to them by a mutual regard. (So strong was Slim's impact on Harrison that he would find himself, twenty years afterwards, unconsciously straightening his back while advancing down the aisle of St Andrew's, just as he had done in the presence of the Field-Marshal.)

Arthur, like MacDonald,* took an unabashed view of Slim's spiritual state. He saw that the Governor-General was a man with a genuine but unsophisticated religious instinct, well aware of the limitations of his faith. Though Slim would go to church, for example, as a personal need

---

* See p. 4.

as well as a gubernatorial duty, Arthur noticed that he never took communion. But his attitude was well defined in an address he gave at an Australian university. 'It has been my fortune to deal, for many years, more with men than with theories, and it has always seemed to me that a man's spirit is as separate from his mind as his body is. All these react on one another: yet as you can have a brilliant intellect in a crippled body, so you may have a warped spirit linked to a powerful mind. And how often have I found in a man of no outstanding mental capacity a noble spirit.' Here is the basis of that passionate passage in *Defeat into Victory* which analyses the spiritual basis of morale.

When Slim died Bishop Gordon Arthur, as he now was, spoke at the National Memorial Service in St John's Church on 24 February, 1971. 'He travelled all over Australia', Arthur recalled, 'learning about the country first-hand, seeing things for himself, making contact with all sorts of people, listening to them, talking to them. He soon came to know Australia better than most Australians . . . he was able to speak authentically, *for* us, as well as to us.' It was Aileen who initiated that verbal identification. During the early days, while Slim was feeling his way and speaking a shade aggressively, letters would come in demanding, 'Why is he always telling *us* what to do?' Aileen pointed out that the 'I' and 'you' formula was necessarily divisive, and suggested that 'we' would go down better. While he was still a newcomer Slim felt that this would be presumptuous, but he gradually slipped into the usage, and the letters died away. Such niceties, however, became unnecessary as he travelled further afield, into the outback, to the lonely regions of the coasts, to the mines, the deserts, the sun-baked voids where families of cattlemen and prospectors cling to the rim of life. During those 1,100 flying hours he had sweated, thirsted, been desiccated by dust. He had quartered the continent, and become an Australian.* It was appropriate that when he retired in 1960 he was given the unique tribute of an Australian passport, valid for five years.

In all these expeditions he was simply applying the technique for bridging a communications gap which he had developed during the doldrum months of 1942/3 when he was regenerating the morale of his

---

* This was demonstrated by an extraordinary gesture. During an inland tour in 1958 the aborigines at Fossil Downs took Slim, alone, to their secret burial grounds, and revealed to him the private mysteries of their tribal lore. He was presented with a message-stick which authorized him to communicate new knowledge, but only to senior members of the tribe.

troops. 'We, my commanders and I, talked to units, to collections of officers, to headquarters, to little groups of men, to individual soldiers casually met as we moved around.' How many of the anecdotes still circulating in Australia are about Slim and some individual casually met as he moved around! Into an up-country bar marches the Field-Marshal, clad in his full panoply. 'Christ!', exclaims an astonished cobber. 'No,' says Slim, 'the Governor-General.' This exchange, which is vouched for by members of his staff who were present, became an instant legend. There were many similar occasions when Slim played diamond cut diamond. Deric Thompson was with him in a distant region of the Northern Territory when they stopped at an indifferent inn for a meal. Slim was in uniform. The bar was full of rough drovers. Slim put his Field-Marshal's hat on a hook, and went upstairs to the dining-room. When he returned he found that one of the mob was wearing his hat and looking at him in a challenging way, obviously hoping that he would be outraged. Slim merely picked up a drover's broad-brimmed wideawake, put it on at a jaunty angle and grinned at his audience. 'How's that?' he said.

As these episodes proliferated the bush-telegraph spread over Australia a sense that this Governor-General was a *man*, forthright, sardonically humorous in a way the Australians understand, not easily provoked and readily accessible. Above all, his humanity shone. Whenever he and Aileen flew over the great bare stretches where, for hundreds of miles, the only population is the tiny groups of men and their families around the radio transceiver stations, they would load the plane at their own expense with newspapers for the husbands, magazines for the wives, sweets for the children, and fresh bread— fresh because the only other bread that reached the backblocks was four days stale. As the plane was still touching down the children would run alongside with outstretched arms, shouting 'Uncle Bill, Uncle Bill, Uncle Bill!'

Nor was it only in the outback that casual but memorable meetings occurred. One day Slim was driving outside Canberra with Arthur Fadden. When they stopped for a drink there was, this time, only one man at the bar. Slim was not in uniform, and the three of them had a friendly conversation. When Fadden temporarily retired, the man said to Slim, 'Who's that chap? I know his face.' 'That', said Slim, 'is your Acting Prime Minister.' 'Christ! Fancy him talking to poor bastards like you and me!'

The fact that most of these stories are based on a session in a bar does not imply, of course, that Slim was a tippler.* In fact he was notably abstemious throughout his life; a whisky and soda was his average ration. But anyone who has travelled during the Australian summer knows how the body is dehydrated by heat and dust. A glass of ice-cold beer becomes a physical necessity.

By these methods Slim imposed his personality. The significance of his office was emphasized for Australia by the royal visit of 1954. Slim was fortunate in its timing, for it happened just when he was beginning to consolidate his position. The preparations were a nightmare, since Yarralumla, so modest in scale, was a band-box within which the royal entourage had to be packed and entertained. In May Aileen wrote to Philip Pratt a retrospective letter which vividly catches the flavour of those hectic days:

> At times we had 20 workmen hammering all over the house and through it all guests to dinner, lunch and tea! But Feb. 13th arrived and we opened our doors intact to receive the Queen and Prince Philip. They stayed in our house for five days and I loved every moment of it. They were such fun and so easy and yet so wonderful to watch in all they did. A terrific programme each day. We took in 19 extra bodies of both personal and domestic staff. We never sat down less than 24 to lunch and 50 was *nothing* for dinner—and we had a happy little garden party for 3,800! So it took some thought.

The strain, however, was relaxed by the discovery that off duty their monarch had a gay and even impish sense of humour. Prince Philip was now a Field-Marshal. There was one of those irrecoverable moments when, in the quiet of the long drawing-room, Philip marched up and down practising his baton-drill under Slim's command while the Queen was overwhelmed by laughter. But the most moving scene occurred during a ceremonial march-past. It was pouring with rain and, as the troops strode by the covered royal stand, the white blanco on their webbing was washing off on to their uniforms. The close-packed crowd, and other officers on parade, sheltered under coats or umbrellas.

---

* Nor, unfortunately, does it mean that they are all true! The great oral tradition of Australia happily switches a good story from one context to another. The Slim/Fadden anecdote, for example, is sometimes put in a setting which involves William Hughes, Lord Stonehaven, and a grazier on a train between Sydney and Melbourne. Nor are *soi-disant* eyewitnesses a safeguard. The author met six eyewitnesses of an event in which Slim was the principal character—in six different parts of Australia.

But there beside the royal platform stood the Queen's representative, bolt upright, unprotected, soaked. He was ageing, his wounds caused him frequent pain, it was not what his doctors would have ordered; he knew his duty. Nevertheless, as Aileen wrote to Pratt, 'He is becoming older and has much discomfort from his arthritic neck. So nasty for him, for he gets headaches. His doctors despair of him, for he will NOT do what they tell him!!' However, there is little doubt that the impression he made during this successful visit was another turning-point in Slim's career. The Queen, with Menzies, had selected him for Australia; from Australia he soon proceeded to Windsor Castle as Governor and Constable, a standard-bearer once again.

As an immediate, practical consequence of the visit he was created GCVO, thus achieving the rare distinction of 'the four Gs'. After his return to England in 1946 he had been raised from CBE to GBE. In 1950, while he was CIGS, he outstripped his old hero Cloudesley Shovell by advancing from KCB to GCB, and after his appointment as Governor-General in 1952 he was awarded the GCMG. There remained the Garter, and this too was bestowed on him shortly before his retirement from Australia. Honour in the sense of pursuit of duty was the leitmotiv of Slim's career, but it is certain that none of his actions, as soldier or as proconsul, was affected for a second by the thought of the Honours List. Nevertheless, he took a proper pride in the recognition of his work. There was no cynicism about baubles.* He unashamedly identified himself with the established order, a servant of the state, and he accepted its tribute with modest but unfeigned satisfaction.

The maverick inside him prevented self-complacency—the maverick that caused him to relish the great croquet-battles of Government House because 'this is the only English game you don't have to play like a gentleman'. One day Lieut-General Sir Thomas Daly, who had commanded the Commonwealth Brigade in Korea and from 1966 to 1971 was Chief of the Australian General Staff, had to call at Yarralumla on some business. He asked Slim about a figure he had not seen there before. Slim replied that it was a man from the Treasury who came regularly to audit the accounts. Daly naturally said he assumed they were in good order. The Field-Marshal confessed that this was so, but that when he had put a similar question to one auditor he was told,

---

* Except foreign ones. When he was CIGS his Military Secretary, Colonel Craddock, asked him why he received none during the war. 'They all stopped at Kandy.' (Kandy was the headquarters of SEAC.)

'Yes, Your Excellency; but you are the most expensive Governor-General we have ever had.' The master of the quick counter-attack riposted immediately. 'I know,' he declared. 'But, as the lady said to the sailor, you can't have the Fairy Queen for fourpence.'*

It was partly a sense of what was due to the Queen's Representative, but more his lifelong devotion to 'the right way of doing things' that made him a stickler for perfection. He was never a martinet. A point he often made in his Australian speeches was that liberty can march with discipline—though discipline must accompany liberty. But on any ceremonial occasion he was exacting. He enjoyed inspecting a passing-out parade of the cadets at Duntroon, yet he could be merciless in his comments if their drill went wrong. (At the same time Major-General Dunstan noted that when he came to address the term of cadets that was passing out he had a gift of ignoring all the others on parade, and the huge surrounding circle of parents and guests. When he spoke, he appeared to be advising and encouraging each of the young men about to become officers as though the two of them were locked in a confessional.)

The whip-lash cracked infrequently, but its cut was deadly. After he had arrived in the forecourt of Admiralty House in Sydney with an escort of motor-cyclists from the local police, Tyrrell indicated that it was usual for the men to be inspected. Slim—tired, perhaps, or in pain—was unwilling, but grudgingly agreed. He then gave his verdict. 'When I looked at your uniforms', he said, 'I thought you had been cleaning your motor-cycles with them—until I saw your motor-cycles.'

The truth is that beneath the urbane veneer there still lurked the *grognard*, the old campaigner. When he protested to the Department of the Interior about some ugly power-lines which defaced the view from Government House, and the matter was postponed until the basin of Lake Burley Griffin had been filled, Slim exploded. 'If I had a dozen of my old Sappers and Miners here, I'd have those bloody poles down and that line buried before breakfast.'

His *bête noir* was always inefficiency where competence should be expected. But in peace as in war he was tolerant and sympathetic about the failings of human nature. There was an occasion of extreme embar-

---

* Michael Roberts noted that he also told the auditor that when he took over Government House the carpets were so threadbare that he hadn't enough ADCs to stand over the holes during a reception.

rassment when Sim Bennet, Chairman of the Canberra Jockey Club, invited him to make the presentation to the winner of the Gold Cup. The successful owner was a local farmer. After Slim had presented the Cup—and congratulated the winner—the farmer launched out on an interminable discourse about how he had played football and cricket, been thwarted by injury, taken up tennis, developed tennis elbow, and finally devoted himself to racehorses. Those in the audience who were not amused were markedly bored. At last the farmer turned to his Governor-General and said, 'Thank you very much for presenting me with the Cup, Sir William—er—the name is Slim, isn't it?' In the club-house Bennet wondered whether it was not unusual for a Governor-General to be asked his name in public. 'Not at all,' said Slim, 'I had to ask his name, so why shouldn't he ask mine?'

If tolerance is an uncommon virtue, tolerance under stress is rare. And Slim was frequently under pressure. His wounds nagged. Fragments from the explosive bullet were still lodged in his back, and on long journeys by car or plane he would always unostentatiously slip a pad behind him. The grind of his public duties was incessant. Half-seriously, he imagined the Australians saying, 'Let's have the Governor-General, he's cheaper than a conjuror.'

In one letter Aileen wrote a cadenza on the theme: 'We are quite hectic as usual. I have managed (how I know not!!) to give 6 dinners and 3 lunches within 15 days (the dinners are usually in the thirties!). As well as that we have each opened three affairs, and seen the Melbourne Cup. Yesterday we flew back to Melbourne—Bill was given the Freedom at the Lord Mayor's Banquet. It was memorable and moving for us both. Now we have just flown back. I am doing cards before preparing to go to Sydney tomorrow where Bill opens the Pan-Pacific Rehabilitation Conference. Home for tea to receive 5 Guide State Commissioners who come to stay while attending their Federal Council which I open on Tuesday: and then we attend the Cenotaph ceremony. So there is a brief glimpse into our lives!!'

John, too, was a cause of concern. After serving with his father's old regiment, 1/6th Gurkhas, he transferred in 1948 to the Argyll and Sutherland Highlanders, with whom, as part of the Commonwealth Brigade, he fought in Korea. When Slim went to Australia, the CIGS (without parental prompting) sent him out as a staff officer attached to Army HQ in Melbourne—his service with the Australians in Korea being a recommendation. But then he was drawn into active service again in Malaya, and Slim was too old a soldier to forget the dangers inherent in that stern guerrilla. His concern is implicit in a letter he wrote to Pratt in July, 1957. 'He went back to Malaya for a last special operation. I'm always a bit nervous about "last" operations but he cabled us to say that this one had been "successful", whatever that means, but he had been rather bruised "where Daddy got shot last". So I suppose he landed in the trees with a bit of a bump.'

Because they had an old-fashioned sense of duty and responsibility, in Australia Bill and Aileen drove themselves hard. Inevitably nerves became frayed. No wonder, while Aileen was still subject to haemorrhage, Bill was in frequent discomfort, and the inescapable round of functions and ceremonies persisted. But there was another reason. With the man in the street or the drover in the outback Slim was entirely at home. At his official entertainments, however, if he felt nothing in common with his neighbour he could sit grim, silent and preoccupied, as daunting a companion as Churchill in a similar mood. In these and other ways he could puzzle and perhaps hurt. Aileen admonished: 'You *must* talk to them.' Moreover, Slim had never previously commanded an establishment like Government House, and with a certain indifference to the logistic problems of large-scale housekeeping he expected everything to run like a well-drilled military unit. There were intermittent schisms. To their devoted staff this was an open book, as it was to close, observant friends. Yet these were but passing clouds. The radiant sun was never dimmed for long.

Indeed, one who entered the heart of their circle put the matter in a correct focus. 'It seemed to us that they were two people deeply in love with one another, fretting at the chains which pinioned them to the constant view of the public, when they so often longed just to be alone with each other.' These witnesses were Betty Foott and her mother Ethel Anderson (author of the Betjemanesque lines on Yarralumla), whose husband, Brigadier Anderson, had been Private Secretary to three Governors of New South Wales and then Private Secretary and Comptroller to Lord Gowrie when he was Governor-General. They thus knew the viceregal *ambience* intimately. Soon after the Slims arrived they were, in Mrs Foott's words, 'catapulted into friendship', life-long and life-enhancing.

Ethel Anderson was an exotic in the Australian scene. Like Aileen, she had followed the sound of the drum with her soldier husband in India. A painter—with murals in five English country churches to her credit; author of poems, essays and short stories that were distinguished and distinctive; nourished by Colette and Firbank, by Proust, Joyce and Henry James, she wore in Australia the air of another civilization, and Slim, for whom words and ideas were more important than war, discovered in her a kindred spirit. She and Betty, therefore, felt the true warmth of the radiant sun.

'What *I* remember', wrote Mrs Foott,* 'was the kindness and thoughtfulness shown by Bill and Aileen for us all. There was often someone upstairs in bed—a Bishop's wife; an over-worked mum; a politician—being cherished and rested and cared for—but they weren't on view, and few people knew they were there. I remember Government House chiefly for its happiness. Bill sitting under the famous deodar tree, carrying on a conversation with his year-old granddaughter Sarah in her pram—incomprehensible to both parties but mutually satisfactory. Or the Christmas parties—Aileen in a brown lace dress, dancing a reel with John; the Cassons all collected together at Yarralumla because Aileen discovered Dame Sybil had hardly seen anything of their prisoner-of-war son since 1939, and there were all three teaching us "The Twelve Days of Christmas". My mother and Bill on a pale blue sofa in that long white drawing-room, discussing the Form of The Short Story, or contemporary poetry—she with her long silver ear-trumpet at the ready so that she could easily hear his refusal to comprehend her beloved Auden, Eliot and Dylan Thomas.'

By 1956 they were able to escape for a well-earned leave in England; yet once again, as in 1953, the darkening shadow of Suez overlaid their pleasure. Aileen flew, but Slim came by sea, and his ship had to be diverted from the Canal to the Cape route. After spending their time, as Slim put it, 'dashing about England in an Austin A30',—and also staying with the Queen at Balmoral—on the return journey they passed through Cairo, where Roden Cutler,† the Australian Minister, had been fighting with his British colleague, Humphrey Trevelyan, a doomed rearguard action. When the Slims arrived most Australians had abandoned Egypt. Cutler had a responsibility for the remaining handful. He tried to make suitable arrangements for the Slims at the airport: they were on a scheduled Qantas flight, but the brakes of the aircraft required attention and they were unexpectedly delayed. The VIP lounge was 'unavailable'. Cutler, whose VC had not been lightly earned, restored the situation and conducted the Slims to this haven in

---

* Communication to author, May, 1975.
† Sir Roden Cutler, VC, KCMG, KCVO, CBE, Governor of New South Wales from 1966.

the midst of an indifferent or hostile throng. But the Egyptians were feeling their strength. The lounge soon filled with a mob of Very Unimportant People, including a mother suckling her child. It was too much. The Field-Marshal conducted another of his successful disengagements. There was, perhaps, a bitter relish in his later remark to Menzies: 'If you'd been PM and I'd been CIGS at the time of Suez, we'd have finished the job effectively.'

And the stresses continued. In the summer of 1957 Slim was compelled to enter a Melbourne hospital for a week because of what he termed 'aggravated lumbago'. There was aggravation enough from the damage wrought on Sari Bair and the metal sprayed into him in Eritrea. Then Aileen, in September, was rushed into hospital in Sydney with another haemorrhage, not so severe as the first, but insidiously weakening.

Yet Slim's dry humour survived. In October Cassells published the text of his famous radio talks, *Courage and Other Broadcasts*. 'I don't think it will sell at all,' Slim wrote to Pratt, 'except a few maiden aunts may give it to their reluctant nephews. All "Up St Hilda's!" stuff.'

It was irony, however, rather than humour that characterized his reception of the first post-war Japanese Ambassador to Australia. The man who had attended in Singapore the surrender of all Japanese armed forces was not disposed to charity. 'Their plight moved me not at all,' he had written (while in Australia) at the end of *Defeat into Victory*. 'They sat there apart from the rest of humanity.' In 1957 his views had not changed. The Japanese Ambassador must now present his credentials, but Slim was sour. 'I shall keep the Samurai sword in the hall, anyway.'*

When the Ambassador and his staff arrived at Government House in their formal morning dress they marched past the sword impassively —except for the two secretaries at the end of the column. Lieut-Colonel Ralph Connor, who was on duty as Comptroller of the Household, observed how one of them spotted the sword, winced, and surreptitiously prodded his companion. Slim was not a vindictive man, but during recent years he had been re-living campaigns which the Japanese had precipitated and poisoned; on this issue he was unforgiving.

According to the terms of his original appointment the Governor-General should now have been preparing to retire. But, as the Aus-

---

* Slim had a certain expression which Aileen used to describe as his 'There-are-Japanese-at-the-bottom-of-the-garden face.'

tralians say, he had 'come good'. His popularity and indeed his ascendancy were now unqualified. His speeches and broadcasts were listened to with unfeigned attention, and, as he wrote to Pratt, 'They give me a lot of rope in the things they let me say.' No longer controversial, he had become more of a sage, dwelling on the ancient verities with a simple but authoritative conviction which prevented him from sounding conventionally banal. And he had a way of coining pithy phrases that passed immediately into circulation; when he spoke at some agricultural meeting of 'a grumble of graziers' his words became common currency. In the far-flung quarters of Australia, in Queensland, the Northern Territory and the west, from New Guinea to the wheatlands and vineyards of the south he was better known than any previous Governor-General—and known because he had been there. For all their undeniable qualities, neither his immediate predecessors, Gowrie, Gloucester, McKell, nor his successors, Dunrossil,* de l'Isle, Casey, Hasluck made an impact so great as Slim. If he had wished, and if protocol had allowed, he could have reigned at Government House for ever. As it was, his appointment was renewed for a further two years. Menzies, and Australia, were unwilling to release a pearl of such price.†

Until 26 January, 1960, when the Slims finally embarked at Melbourne, their calendar continued to be crowded. Yet once again, in the midst of the maelstrom, he managed to create a zone of calm within which he was able to prepare his *Unofficial History* for publication. It is true that this engaging book (which one enthusiastic reviewer described as 'The first war memoir ever in which a great soldier admits that now and again he was wrong') is a collection of articles already published in *Blackwood's* or written but not yet printed. Their appearance in book form, however, meant that Slim was speaking 'for the record'. He therefore went through the same meticulous process of cross-checking the most minute details with Michael Roberts in London as he had so fruitfully adopted in the case of *Defeat into Victory*. When

---

* Before he died, after only a year of office, Lord Dunrossil had given clear evidence that he would have been a Governor-General of great distinction, but he hardly commanded Slim's authority or breadth of appeal.
† Slim's decision to soldier on was not automatic. On 10 September, 1958, he wrote to Brigadier Roberts: 'Our time in Australia is drawing to a close. I have stayed an extra year over the orthodox five, and although the kind Australians have asked me to stay longer, I think for many reasons I had better come home— and down to earth again—before I'm too old.'

the book began its unchecked career in 1959, it was as exact and true as the protagonist and the professional historian could make it—except (as in the case of *Defeat into Victory*), in one respect. Slim was scrupulous, unlike certain other commanders (Montgomery and Tedder spring to mind) in avoiding what might cause pain or making allegations where the issue was in doubt. About Gallabat, for example, he wrote to Roberts on 11 August, 1958, 'Is it wrong of me to talk about my British battalion (The Essex) running away? The story doesn't make much sense unless the incident is mentioned and I have let them down very lightly compared with the real thing.' About the air cover for that same battle he wrote, with regard to orders possibly issued by the local Air Commodore, 'I don't know whether this was actually so, and I have not said so in the narrative, as I don't want to criticize even if it was so. Is the way I have put it in the narrative all right and not unfair to anyone?'

Slim's commitments were not always obligatory. He had the virtue, for a Governor-General, of inquisitiveness; 'for to behold and for to see' was his maxim. So—to take a characteristic instance—he would send for Tyrrell. 'Murray, I want to go to Cairns'—in the far northeast of Queensland—'find me a reason.' On his intelligence network Tyrrell consults an influential citizen of Cairns. 'Fine: we have a standard to present to the C.M.F.'* Tyrrell then proceeds to Cairns. Arrangements are made for special trains to bring in the men, and their families, from the country districts, and for the pubs and cinemas to be opened (illegally and without permission) on a Sunday. Slim arrives, to take a parade of 600 men which, he tells Tyrrell, is the finest of its kind he has ever seen. As he gives his address he is near to tears. He would never be forgotten in Cairns.

But his human touches were always memorable. Australians, like the veterans of 14th Army, have an endless store of personal reminiscences. The son of the man who came weekly to tend the Slims' beloved wire-haired fox terrier cherished the fact—astonishing to his father—that thereafter the family always received a Christmas card. In the Australian Club it is still remembered that when Slim finally retired one of his last acts was to pay a special visit to the barber and thank him for his attention. And when they landed after their last flight down to Melbourne Slim made a point of taking on one side his personal flight-steward, Sergeant Aveling (whose log-book recorded

---

* The Commonwealth Military Force—Australia's Territorial Army.

all those 1,100 flying hours), presenting him with a silver tray and saying: 'We've three things in common, Taffy—I shall call you Taffy for once. We're both Pommies, which we won't say too much about here. And we're both servicemen, though there's some difference in our rank. But above all, and this is something no one can take away from us, we're both 14th Army.'

Aveling, later custodian of Admiralty House, had served over Europe as an air-gunner in the RAF, and then, under Slim, as a General Transport driver at Imphal. After the war he found himself, by coincidence, again under Slim at British Railways. In 1950 he joined the Royal Australian Air Force as a steward, and in 1954 came to No. 34 Special Transport Squadron at Canberra, whose Dakotas and Convairs were the Governor-General's essential air-lift. Utterly devoted to his master, he had a unique opportunity, afforded by the intimacy of a Dakota's cabin, for observing him *en pantoufles*, observing his passion for steak and onions, in flagrant disregard of Aileen's interdiction on the grounds that they were not good for him; his curious preference (when on his own) for salmon served *in the tin*; his constant courtesy, even though the uneasy flight of a Dakota was hard on his splintered back. During those hundreds of hours in the air Aveling never received a bark or bite.

'They were model passengers,' was the verdict of Squadron-Leader Kilby, Slim's personal pilot. Before they left at last, from RAAF Fairbairn, the Governor-General's standard was lowered by a Warrant Officer, and for a short while the flag-pole remained bare until a new régime began, and Dunrossil flew in from New Zealand. One of Slim's quirks, curiously enough, was a fussy concern about the flying of his personal standard wherever he went. Just as, in 14th Army, he was tolerant about his soldiers' dress but insistent on their saluting, so in Australia he was generally easy-going, especially on tour, but sharp in requiring a proper respect for the insignia of the Queen's Representative. His Field-Marshal's baton was another symbol. Woe betide the officer who ordered a General Salute before the Governor-General had performed the correct gyrations and shifted his baton to the appropriate ceremonial position. But there is a Caribbean saying:

You shake hands, you don't shake hearts.

Slim proved the opposite, just as his effect was the opposite of Macbeth's:

> Those he commands move only in command,
> Nothing in love.

Quirks and all, he had won hearts by his hand-shakes, and love by his commands.

Had there been any doubt, the scope of the affection he had generated was warmly demonstrated during the last days of farewell, at the receptions and dinners, in the speeches and the press tributes, and above all by the cheering crowds lining the streets to wish Uncle Bill 'Godspeed!'. The universal tone was one of admiration, of attachment, of kinship. 'Good on yer, Bill.' Australia had accepted him as 'one of us'.

This sense of identity was subsequently marked by the Australian Government in an unprecedented fashion. After Slim had returned to England Menzies began to worry about the possibility that he might lack the means to live as his distinction deserved. The Prime Minister's sense of propriety had been offended by the treatment McKell experienced as a former Governor-General. 'Such a man', he felt, 'should not be reduced to attending official functions in a taxi.' He therefore initiated, and carried through his Cabinet without difficulty, a proposal that the retiring Governor-General (and his widow) should receive from Australia a generous pension. Considering that Slim was British (even though he represented the Queen-in-Australia), and considering that financial rewards of this kind might well have been held to be the responsibility of Whitehall, Menzies's innovation was an open-handed recognition of the *entente cordiale* which had developed between his country and its Governor-General. From Burma Slim bore a Samurai sword; to Britain he now brought a passport and a pension—and they were both Australian.

When John Buchan went to Canada as Governor-General in 1935 his function was already uncertain. 'Since the Statute of Westminster, many Canadians in public life had wondered if anybody could successfully carry out the office of Governor-General now that it had become so much more difficult in its new and almost indefinable stage. The job had not lost its meaning, but the meaning had now largely to be created by the individual who held it.'* For Field-Marshal Lord Alexander, when he went to Canada ten years later, the meaning was even harder to find, and the method of his success, which was undoubted, may be deduced from *The Times*'s description of his term of office as 'a triumph

---

* Janet Adam Smith, *John Buchan*, 1965.

of personality'. How much greater was the problem for Slim in the Australia of the fifties! One of his successors, Sir Paul Hasluck, has described the basic requirements for an effective modern tenant of Government House, Canberra.*

> The influence of the Governor-General in the government of Australia will vary a good deal according to the degree of respect in which a Governor-General is held. If he is thought to have some depth of experience, to have some degree of wisdom, some measure of tolerance and understanding of various points of view and to be worthy of confidence and trust and able to keep his own counsel and the counsel of others, his influence will be much greater than if he were held in a lesser degree of respect. His influence would disappear altogether if he were thought of as one who would do whatever he was told without asking the reasons why.

Slim passed all these tests. But there was something more. Just as confidence in his ability, his integrity and his humanity mysteriously filtered down to the lowliest soldier in his 14th Army, binding it together into a family, so the Queen's Representative contrived, by an even greater triumph of personality than Alexander's, to overcome the formal limitations of his role and give it a fuller meaning and relevance. To the average Australian he was a person, not a figurehead. His wisdom and guidance were respected in the councils of state, but his real achievement is still to be remembered in Australia as a man.

---

* In the William Queale Memorial Lecture delivered at Adelaide University on 24 October, 1972, and entitled 'The Office of Governor-General'.

CHAPTER EIGHTEEN
HOME AND AWAY

HEN SLIM returned to England he was nearing seventy. The big
things lay behind him—defeat and victory in war, the highest
post and rank in his profession of arms, outstanding service in a
remarkable proconsulate. In the future he could scarcely hope for
similar great offices or commands, but he faced it four-square—a little
tremulous, as ever, about his value in the civilian market, but a man
who by now had seen all his capacities, practical, emotional, intellectual,
put to the most stringent tests in which he had failed neither his
country nor himself. That thread of self-doubt which can be traced
right back to the beginning of his career was never to vanish, but as he
took up a new life in the London of 1960 its effects were transient and
superficial. His great gift was for seeing things in proportion, and
though his humility ran pure and deep his personality was essentially
stable; the challenges he had accepted and mastered as Army commander,
CIGS and Governor-General had made him master of himself. A true
standard-bearer, he kept the flag flying in war and peace while he
upheld, by thought and deed, the strictest code of personal integrity.
That microscopic scrutiny of a man's life enjoyed by a biographer who
has been able to search his papers and discuss his subject in intimate
frankness with his family and friends has revealed not a single action
on Slim's part which was the result of mean or unworthy motives. He
would be at ease with the Recording Angel.

And yet, how Slim himself would have hated a paragraph which
appears to present him as a paragon! His dignity and air of authority
were natural and instinctive—if necessary, quelling—but he had no
false pride; the anecdotes he most enjoyed were those he so frequently
told against himself. The Field-Marshal who, as a young officer on
leave from India, once invaded the stage of a music hall had grasped

the great music hall truth; he was aware, and aware with relish, that the banana-skin can bring us all down. The honesty with which he admitted his errors as a commander made him frank, open and humble about his limitations as a human being, and his sense of the ridiculous survived the years unquenched, as it had survived the monsoon and the jungle. The word 'wholesome' has been devalued from its early dictionary definition of 'sound in condition or constitution; free from disease or taint; healthy', but this is the feeling which his character most evokes. He was clean-run. To think of Slim is to recall that surprising and lyrical outburst by a Spaniard about the Englishman: 'He carries his English weather in his heart wherever he goes, and it becomes a cool spot in the desert, and a steady and sane oracle amongst all the deliriums of mankind. Never since the heroic days of Greece has the world had such a sweet, just, boyish master.'*

Out of this strong man came forth sweetness because, of all the standards he had upheld, truth-to-oneself was the dominant. He loathed sham. His range of friendship was enormous, but it had no room for the pretentious or the *faux bonhomme*, and that 'common touch' which endeared him to millions of men and women who were never close to him owed its power to an instinctive reaction—they warmed to a man who seemed straight, honest, all-of-a-piece. Once in 1952, nine days before he retired as CIGS, he gave a lecture at the University of London in which he summarized his creed: 'Some people seem to think that if they put badges in their caps they are Monty. They are not. They think that if they carry an onion in one hand and an alarm clock in the other they are Wingate. They are not. It is the essentials and not the frills that count.' And ten years later, when Bernard Fergusson's book on Wavell appeared, Slim wrote in a review words which apply to himself: 'Nowadays young people sometimes refer to their seniors, who do not altogether share their tastes, as "squares". In this they differ from the ancient Romans, who used the word "quadratus", when applied to a fellow citizen, as a compliment. The picture of Wavell that emerges, clear and true, is of a man who, standing four-square to whatever favours or buffetings fate brought him, remained true to himself, who neither strutted in success nor in misfortune blamed others.'

But though his laurels were abundant, freedom from the responsi-

---

* George Santayana, *Soliloquies in England.*

bilities of service to the state did not mean that he would rest on them. Slim's arrival in London simply marked the opening of a new campaigning season—and in territories, as it turned out, which were new and strange. There was an obvious need to earn, for though his pensions provided a cushion they were not enough to sustain his position. But far beyond that was the fact that Slim enjoyed the challenge of activity, the adventure into fresh fields. His whole life had been one of effort. It was habitual; it was his way. Judy Hutchinson had a poignant reminder. 'I went to see him a short time before he died, and as he got up and came to the door of his room to say good-bye, unable even to see clearly, a sad and rather wistful expression crossed his face. "You are lucky," he said, "you can work."'

The preliminaries to the next phase in his career had occurred while he was still Governor-General. Sir Paul Chambers describes how Imperial Chemical Industries drew him into the world of the City board room.

> My predecessor as Chairman, Lord Fleck, was greatly impressed by Lord Slim's capacity to take a broad view and to make sound judgements about important issues which had nothing to do with military matters, and following a visit to Australia in the year before he retired from the chairmanship he suggested that I should give the matter of asking Lord Slim to join the Board serious consideration. This I promised to do, and in a visit to Australia shortly before I was elected Chairman I spoke to Bill Slim about it. He explained that he would be delighted to accept such an invitation but as a matter of good form I ought not to invite him until after he had ceased to be Governor-General of Australia. My Board readily agreed and by a happy coincidence the first day that I was Chairman was the first day that it would be proper to send an invitation to Lord Slim to join us. I sent the letter that day. He accepted readily and I found that he was all that we expected.*

So did many others among the best judges in the City. Further invitations to take up directorships followed, and Slim was soon immersed. They were not sinecures. The kind of man who sought him out was looking for ability and reliable advice, not for a famous name with which to dazzle shareholders. The name was of course a convenience, but the magnates really went to Slim for sound judgement

---

* Letter to author, 25 November, 1975.

and that indefinable element of common sense, something more deeply rooted than shrewdness, which he had always possessed. He was never a sleeping partner—he would not have accepted so passive a role. His commitment to the organizations whose Boards he joined was solid, and they in turn came first to respect and then to feel a positive need for his contributions to their discussions. He made no pretence about mastering financial techniques. He never entered early into a debate, but when it had run its course, and the gist of the issue was clear to him, he would speak briefly, decisively and with an accepted authority. One Chairman noted that during Slim's directorship Board Meetings had a greater tautness and discipline than was usual, for in his formidable presence fellow directors seemed to avoid by instinct anything time-wasting or ill-considered. Unconsciously, Slim put the City on its mettle.

Few of its leaders had a more expert eye for the quality of judgement required than Harald Peake, who throughout most of Slim's last decade was Chairman of Lloyds Bank. It was he who, even before Slim arrived in Australia, had spoken about him to the Chairman of the National Bank of Australasia in Melbourne. In a natural consequence, on his return Slim was appointed to the London Board of Advice of the National Bank,* where his great practical experience of Australian affairs and personalities was of special value—as was his gift for interesting and entertaining important visitors from the Antipodes. That same year, 1960, Peake was Governor of the London Assurance, whose Court Slim also joined. In 1965 the London Assurance amalgamated with Sun Alliance (itself an earlier combination of the Alliance and Sun Life groups). This merger had a consequence which vividly illustrates how the City came to respect Slim's acumen. The triple union of the big insurance societies meant that instead of one Board functioning for the whole, a senior Board with junior off-shoots was established. As a relative newcomer to the former London Assurance Slim took his place at one of the junior tables. But Sir Roy Matthews, who had been much responsible for bringing Slim to the London, told

---

* Slim had a fine disregard for fringe benefits, expense accounts (except where the Army was concerned) and all the perquisites of the Managerial Society. Sir Harald Peake was impressed by his indifference to remuneration once he had undertaken a task. But Slim was deeply grateful to the National Bank of Australasia for this immediate appointment and for the provision of an office and secretary, which gave him a firm base to cope with the complex business of regaining his bearings in England.

the author that it was not long before the main Board felt his absence
from their councils, and in consequence he was elevated. It was an
accolade as significant, in its way, as the dubbing he had received on
the plain of Imphal. Slim had proved his worth on yet another battlefield.*

One thing led to another. He joined the Board and became Deputy
Chairman of the property company, Edger Investments, under the
aegis of Sir Edwin McAlpine. His Australian affiliations brought him
to Dalgety and New Zealand Loan, Ltd; in 1965 he was appointed
President. But it was his old ADC in the ALFSEA days, Lord
Brabourne, who persuaded him to undertake the least predictable of
his ventures. Since the war John Brabourne had established himself
firmly and with great distinction in the contentious world of film and
television productions. As the sixties advanced, the time seemed to
him ripe for pegging a claim in what looked like being the new gold-
field of 'pay television'. Determined that his organization should be
soundly based and wide in scope, he created British Home Entertainment Ltd, with an active Board including such representative figures as
Lord Olivier and Dame Margot Fonteyn. For Chairman he picked and
obtained Field-Marshal Lord Slim.

This was a subtle move. From Brabourne's point of view Slim's
chairmanship endorsed his organization in the eyes of the City—a
critical factor in the early days of fund-raising and getting-off-the-
ground. Slim provided the right image. But the benefits were mutual.
The man who, as a young subaltern in 1915, had solemnly corresponded
with his friend Philip Pratt about a film scenario, and who had always
preferred writing to war, blossomed in an atmosphere where the arts
were treated as serious business. It would be absurd to pretend that
conferences aimed at making a corner in pay television were wholly
devoted to aesthetics. Still, the company Slim now kept was largely
drawn from the world of theatre, film and television. He was dealing
with the practitioners, and it was a stimulus for one already over seventy
to hear and share the experience of younger but distinguished artists
and producers. Not surprisingly, more than one difficult personality
surfaced, and Brabourne found Slim's authority and wisdom invaluable

---

* His election as Master of the Clothworkers was another instance of the City's
respect not simply for his trappings, but for his ability. The Master of one of these
great City institutions faces not merely banquets but many tough decisions in the
conduct of financial or charitable business.

at such times. His Chairman, he observed, was a great nonsense-stopper.

Now that he was permanently settled in England Slim was able to devote himself again to the cause which, next to his family, was closest to his heart—fostering the Burma Star Association and attending, each spring, the great Burma Reunion in the Albert Hall, where thousands of his old comrades of 14th Army would converge from all over the British Isles. At each reunion he spoke to them with the voice of a leader, skilfully playing on the emotions of the moment to persuade them that the fortitude with which they had tackled the Japanese and the jungle was a capital reserve, on which they must draw to overcome their personal problems in the present and future. He would pull out every stop—humour, pathos, praise. What he was essentially trying to do was to touch a fibre in his men, to stir a memory of days when courage and self-sacrifice were normal and to suggest that what they had discovered about themselves in war they must keep alive in peace. Sometimes he spoke of the dead. In the spring of 1960, his first appearance at the Albert Hall for eight years, he began:

> Lady Louis, Lady Louis Mountbatten, is not here tonight on this platform as we have so often seen her. She has given her life, as so many of our comrades gave theirs, on active service. She died in the front line of unselfish and unsparing service to the weak, the sick, the poor and the desolate. She went to their help wherever they were; no journey was too arduous, no conditions too hard for her. Thousands all over the world, and not least the countries of South-East Asia that we knew, mourn her.
>
> But with us, who wear the Burma Star, she had a special link and our hearts kept for her a special affection. There can hardly be one of us who, when things were toughest, has not seen her vital, graceful figure in her trim St John's uniform, moving from bed to bed in a basha hospital, standing on a sunbaked airstrip to meet the wounded, lurching about the sky in an old Dakota on some errand of mercy, passing down a muddy jungle track, reaching, ahead of most of us, the ghastly prison camps. Wherever we saw her she brought us courage, hope and real practical help.
>
> The other day after her Memorial Service as I paid off my taxi, the driver asked me if I had been to the Abbey? When I told him I had, he said, 'A woman like that ought never to die!'
>
> She won't. She will live in all our memories and still, I know, inspire us with something of her own courage, vitality and unselfishness.

I would ask all of you now, in her memory and in her honour, to stand in silence for a moment.

That was from the heart. The Albert Hall must have been very quiet. But there were times when, with a quick anecdote, Slim could make it explode with laughter—as in his 1961 address:

Do you remember the Gurkha who suddenly came face to face with a Jap officer in the jungle? The Jap took a mighty swipe with his double-headed sword at the Gurkha. The Gurkha ducked under it and said, 'Ha! Ha! Missed!' Then he in turn took a lightning sweep with his kukri. 'Ha! Ha! Missed!' jeered the Jap. But the Gurkha only grinned and said, 'Try shaking your head'.

Slim's humanity, though warmed by emotion and enlivened by humour, was always strictly controlled by a compassionate realism. He knew that the rigours of the Burma campaign would have their effect on many men later in life, and that his veterans would face problems of mental and physical health as well as the economic stresses of the post-war world. For members of the Burma Star Association he therefore initiated a Relief Fund, insisting, in the spirit of 14th Army—'God helps them who help themselves'—that the monies should be raised and administered by the Association. When he sent out appeals to firms connected with Burma he gave a pledge, never broken, that every penny raised would go on welfare; unlike most charitable organizations, the Burma Star has no administrative overheads. (It was notable, incidentally, that Burmah Oil, whose wells and installations Slim and his men had destroyed, made a handsome contribution.) From the launching of the Fund until his last years at Windsor he stayed close to the scheme, ensuring that all needs were being met and following up individual cases until a satisfactory conclusion was reached. It is right that the men of 14th Army should speak, as they do, not of having served 'under Slim' but of having served 'with Slim'; the ties between them and Uncle Bill were indissoluble. In the spring of 1976 a plaque commemorating Slim's name was unveiled in St Paul's—a lasting tribute from the Burma Star Association, given by men who, more than three decades ago, were ready, under his leadership, to give their lives.

This identification with his veterans was not simply nostalgic. Their futures concerned him as much as their past. And during his remaining years it was a sense of the future that preoccupied him in his work for the Fairbridge Society, of whose Council in England he became Chairman in 1961. The imaginative, compassionate South African, Kingsley Fairbridge, first visited England in 1907 as a youth of 17. So distressed was he by the suffering of the poor and orphaned children in industrial cities that he dedicated his life to establishing schools in the Commonwealth where they might grow up and develop their potentialities in healthy, happy and beautiful surroundings. That dream is now a triumphant reality; in Canada and Australia several thousands of children whose life might otherwise have been stunted have enriched the Dominions as farmers, doctors and nurses, priests, business and professional people.

Here was a concept of special significance for Slim. His first-hand experience of poverty and deprivation in the slums of Birmingham and the Black Country left a permanent mark on his mind. In any case, as he wrote in *Defeat into Victory*, 'Children and soldiers always go well together'. His first contact with the Fairbridge scheme took place on the *Strathnaver* in 1953, as he sailed for Australia. A party of Fairbridge children, his fellow-passengers, awakened his interest and, as Governor-General, he was assiduous in visiting and staying at the Australian schools. One can see how the man who was meticulous about taking gifts to the lonely children of the outback stations never, as he later confessed, 'came away from a Farm School without great refreshment of spirit'.

So, during his Chairmanship, no less than 1,055 children were sent out to Australia. Judy Hutchinson, who had shared the Australian experience and sailed on the *Strathnaver* as Aileen's private secretary, was closely associated with the Fairbridge venture. She recalled Slim in action.*

> It was a fascinating experience to see him take a meeting. He made them such fun, with flashes of humour and human understanding, and had always done his homework down to the last detail. Even more remarkable, as one would expect, was the quality of his mind. He cut through our sometimes rather woolly ramblings like a knife through butter—though never unkindly; and he made the answer to each problem seem so simple and obvious that one could not imagine how it had ever been a problem at all. His fine brain instantly saw the essential point in any situation, whether it was human, financial, or one of

---

* Letter to author, 10 October, 1975.

policy; his sense of priorities was sure. In the Annual Report he wrote, 'The end product, what comes out of the mill in the end is what matters, and in that Fairbridge need not fear comparison with anyone.'

Even when he became ill he showed concern for other people, offering committee members lifts in his car, and sending, in his own handwriting, a cheering and of course very amusing letter to one who was in hospital after a big operation. He came up from Windsor to London for the farewell party given for Miss Dorothy Hall, the devoted assistant secretary, when she retired after 35 years' work for Fairbridge. Typically, he kissed her good-bye as he made the presentation!

In the midst of these many preoccupations with old soldiers and young people, a demanding life in the City, expanding friendships and the inevitable inroads on his energy made by functions and ceremonies, speech-making, committees and consultations, he was suddenly required to take down the trumpet in the hall and execute on behalf of the Government a military-diplomatic manoeuvre of notable delicacy. At the beginning of 1963 the Conservative administration's decision that the country's future commitments could be met by an all-regular Army of 180,000 meant that, over the next three years, the Brigade of Gurkhas would have to be reduced from 14,600 to 10,000. Trivial figures: but not so for the Kingdom of Nepal, whose economy relied directly on the earnings, pensions and training of its soldier-exports, and which was linked with Britain not only by written and un-written agreements about recruitment, but also by a unique and generations-old record of service under the British flag. Moreover, the 'lobby' of former Gurkha officers is a potent force, and proposals to reduce the Gurkha contingent have always been politically 'hot'. In this case extra warmth had been generated by certain actions on the part of the Major-General, the Brigade of Gurkhas (Sir Walter Walker), whose cavalier efforts to 'save the Gurkhas' earned him Slim's disapproval and a chilling interview with the CIGS.*

Three Field-Marshals, Slim, Harding, and Templer (Slim the former and Templer the present Colonel of the 7th Gurkhas, and Harding a former Colonel of the 6th) met with some sympathy from a hard-pressed War Office in their plea that reduction in numbers should not

---

* See Tom Pocock, *Fighting General*, Ch. 5 for an extensive account of this episode.

involve a loss of identity for the eight existing Gurkha battalions. But there was an embarrassing time factor. The Secretary of State for War, John Profumo, was due to speak in the Army Estimates debate on 13 March; the rumours of recent months had made the Gurkha affair a matter of political concern, and as yet no agreement had been reached with the King of Nepal which could be presented as a *fait accompli* to the House of Commons. Slim was therefore asked to undertake a sudden and secret mission to Nepal and obtain the King's acquiescence—a mission so secret that not even the British Military Attaché in Katmandu was to be informed of its purpose. The last-minute arrangements were such that there would only be time for Slim, as he was advised, 'to convey news of the King's attitude by telegram from Katmandu and the Secretary of State for War will have to base his statement on whatever information you can give him by that means'. On 28 February, 1963, Profumo sent him a Personal and Secret letter, attaching an Aide Memoire and ending, 'I shall keep my fingers well crossed until we have a signal from you. With warmest wishes and gratitude, for I know very well at what personal inconvenience you are going on this journey.'

Slim's cover for his mission was perhaps the most implausible disguise attempted by a famous figure since Churchill, faced with the need to change transport at Gibraltar during one of his wartime journeys, suggested to Alanbrooke that he should hide behind a grey beard. The late commander of the 14th Army flew to India as 'Mr Phipps', ostensibly on a business visit for ICI. But as Churchill himself once observed to Lord Moran about Slim, 'Oh yes, he has the hell of a face.' It was hardly likely that he would pass from India to Nepal unrecognized, and inevitably one of his pilots, who had flown under him in Burma, gave a rapturous greeting to Uncle Bill. However, though the deception plan was less subtle than that for the Meiktila victory, the result of Slim's foray was satisfactory.

On 8 March he had an interview at Katmandu with the Commander-in-Chief of the Royal Nepalese Army—the public explanation for his presence being that, as he was in India, a courtesy invitation had been extended by the King to the most distinguished Gurkha officer alive. At this meeting, and in a later audience with the King himself, Slim's tactful explanation of the British proposals was readily accepted, after a decent period for discussion and some counter-proposals over details. And so, in plenty of time before the Army Estimates debate, he was able to signal to London that the King understood the British Government's difficulties, accepted the need for reductions and was grateful for the War Office's arrangements to minimize their impact. It was certainly a convenience that the Commander-in-Chief, Chief of Staff, Quarter-master-General and Adjutant-General of the Nepalese Army had all served under Slim as young officers!

After a token visit to Calcutta, where he made the gesture of calling on various ICI factories and offices, Slim returned to London and submitted his report. Apart from filling in the detail of his negotiations, it included a useful confidential assessment of the Nepalese attitude towards India and China, and a frank picture of the feeling among his old friends in the Indian Army after their recent experiences at the hands of the Chinese. On the 15th, after the debate, Profumo sent him a Personal message in his own hand. 'Dear Field-Marshal,' it began, 'I hope perhaps this letter may arrive to greet you on your return, for I want to take the earliest chance of congratulating you on your great success with the King and the Nepalese Government. A most skilful performance, which, as I do hope you know, has made all the difference in what was a most difficult operation. . . .' The job had been done, loyally and efficiently; but Slim's private opinion was made plain in a letter he wrote to Field-Marshal Lord Harding on 1 April. 'I again told the Secretary of State for War that I thought anyone who reduced the Gurkhas in the present world situation was "crackers", and I still believe that. The amount of money we shall save out of a £1,700 million Defence Budget is not worth it. We would do better to cut one rocket!'

One more official journey overseas awaited him. In April, 1964, he flew to the United States to attend the funeral of General MacArthur as the Queen's Representative. The conqueror of Burma paid his respects to the overlord of the Pacific. But Slim was already restored to regular service under the Crown. Towards the end of 1963 he had been appointed Deputy Constable and Lieutenant-Governor of Windsor Castle.

CHAPTER NINETEEN

THE CONSTABLE

'It was like a magnificent uplifting paragraph at the end of a marvellous book'.

Slim on Churchill's funeral

THE FIRST Chief of the Imperial General Staff was appointed in 1907, the first Governor-General of Australia in 1901: but when Slim returned to service under the Crown and took up residence in the Norman Tower of Windsor Castle in 1963 he was entering into an inheritance of great antiquity. His first appointment was that of Lieutenant-Governor and Deputy Constable, a post which had existed for several centuries, but not so long as the senior post of Governor and Constable—first recorded in 1087, when it was given to Walter Fitzother. Since the mid-19th century this had become a largely titular distinction, usually bestowed on a member of the Royal Family, and last held by the Earl of Athlone, who died in 1957. In the year following Slim's arrival at Windsor the Queen did him the signal honour of conferring the senior appointment on him, so that from that date until his retirement in 1970 his formal title was that of Governor and Constable. At the same time the junior post was conferred on the Governor of the Military Knights of Windsor, Major-General Sir Edmund Hakewill Smith.

The role of a modern Governor, though less onerous and martial than that of his earlier predecessors, is nevertheless a reminder of ancient and more realistic responsibilities. He is the Monarch's liege, embodying the security of a Castle which, though now a royal home, was also once a fortress. Thus when the Queen is officially in residence with her Court it is the Governor's duty to meet her inside the Sovereign's Entrance on her arrival. On State occasions, when foreign

Royalty or Heads of State visit Windsor it is equally the Governor's
task to meet them at the entrance to the Castle. Such ritual gestures are
a symbol of days when it was possibly of vital importance for Kings
and Queens of England to be assured that their castle was a safe
stronghold. And the Governor's place in the ceremony of the Garter,
his seat in the Chapel of St George, carry into the twentieth century
powerful overtones for a man like Slim who saw the past as part of the
present. To sit beneath the banners of the Garter Knights in St George's,
with the sunlight winking along the walls from the serried plaques
commemorating the arms and styles of their predecessors, and the
magical fan-vaulting sprayed delicately overhead, was more than
conventionally emotive. Slim had always been the liegeman of his
sovereign and warmed by a sense of history. Now, at Windsor, he had
come home, and the benison of being able to spend his last years there
was indeed 'like a magnificent uplifting paragraph at the end of a
marvellous book'.

To catch the tang of the past he had no need to move from the study
in his apartments above the archway of Norman Tower. Set into one
wall was the great oaken portcullis which used to drop plumb down its
grooves, like a guillotine, to block the arch below and exclude the
unwelcome. Carved into the massive stonework of other walls, visible
and eloquent, were the names incised by Cavaliers imprisoned there
during the Civil War . . . Bowen, Stradling, Bayly, Powell, Laugharne
and Browne Bushell.* But the imagination could range much further
back. As Slim looked out of his window, over the gardens and courts
and outworks of the castle, beyond the intervening Thames to 'a distant
prospect of Eton College', he was standing in the room where, it is
said, the young James I of Scotland watched from his place of detention
the daughter of the Earl of Somerset walking below and fell in love
with what he saw, so that when he returned to his realm in 1424 Lady
Joan Beaufort was already his consort. This was the very room,
indeed, L-shaped in a corner of the Tower, where James is presumed to
have composed his remarkable poem, *The King's Quair*, over five
centuries before Slim came to Windsor.

---

* Major-General Laugharne with another Roundhead, Colonel Poyer, deserted
to the King's side. With Colonel Powell, who like them was a leader in the
Welsh Rising, they were taken from Windsor to Whitehall and condemned to
death. An act of clemency allowed them to draw lots to select one out of the trio
for execution. Poyer drew the short straw and went to the block.

Perhaps his most intense pleasure during these years came from his intimate association with the Order of the Garter. To be of the fellow-ship of 'Knights of the Blue Garter', that select company of 26 men of renown which Edward the Third instituted in commemoration of his victory at Crécy, was itself a matter of pride. Many of the contemporary Knights were his friends and fellow-commanders, retrospectively honoured with this distinction because, by service to the state, they had fulfilled the precepts laid down on the first members of the Order at their installation. 'Tie about thy leg for thy renown this noble Garter; wear it as the symbol of the most illustrious Order, never to be forgotten or laid aside, that thereby thou mayest be admonished to be courageous, and, having undertaken a just war . . . that thou mayest stand firm and valiantly and successfully conquer.'

But as Governor, and a resident at the Castle, with the Knights' private chapel of St George's but a few yards from his door and the Order's whole history and heraldry displayed before him every time he attended a service, Slim was drawn far more directly into the inner life of the Order than if he had been, as it were, a 'country member'. He loved his part in the discussions, the arrangements, the diplomacy and even the little animosities involved in the conduct of the Order's affairs. Not even Edward the founder was a more passionate champion of its rights.

Membership of the Order of the Garter was not, however, merely a matter of mediaeval ceremony. It directed Slim straight into the problems of the present and the future. He had not been at Windsor for long before practical steps were taken to establish there what is now known as St George's House. Conceived initially as a centre where meetings and discussions might improve ethical and moral standards in government and industry, and thus refine the quality of leadership throughout the country, St George's was formally launched at a full gathering of the Garter Knights. Prince Philip, Robin Woods (as Dean of Windsor and Register of the Order), and Slim as Governor of the Castle and a KG himself, became *ex officio* Trustees, while other Council members from the Order included Field-Marshal Lord Alexander and Lord Salisbury.

The project stimulated Slim's imagination. As his exchanges with Attlee had shown in 1948, and his experience with British Transport had taught him, the issue of effective management—particularly manager/worker relationships—was as central in the post-war years as it had been on the battlefield. The more general question, of moral standards, was one which perplexed and haunted him as he watched a new generation evolve or sometimes, it seemed to him, disintegrate. He put his large shoulder to the wheel. In raising the necessary £350,000 to set up St George's House within the bounds of Windsor Castle he was indefatigable. And it was typical of his down-to-earth approach that he arranged for Robin Woods to visit the Staff College so that he could study the system of instruction employed for the future leaders of the Army. He would have been gratified by the long-term results. On the one hand, St George's has matured into a true 'Staff College' for the higher ranks of the clergy, and though it is unlikely that future Deans and Bishops will append to their names, as in the Army, the meaningful symbol 'p.s.c', to have 'passed Staff College' at St George's can prove a critical preliminary to advancement within the Church of England. And in the field of management and government it is certain, though it is impossible to quantify their results, that the shrouded but regular week-end meetings at St George's of the most fertile and forward-looking brains in industry and Whitehall are beneficial in ways that Slim would have endorsed.

The 'community of Windsor' instituted by Edward III contained two main elements, which still survive—the clerics of the Chapel, and the Military Knights. With the Dean and Canons of Windsor, over whom his writ as Governor in no sense ran, Slim maintained an amiable if slightly detached relationship, warmed by the mutual affection which he came to share with Robin Woods. But then, Robin had been a chaplain with 4 Indian Division during the war and they spoke the same language from the start. If Slim detected a certain inwardness among some of the ecclesiastics, it will be recalled that his concept of religion was a practical mingling of faith *and* works. On the eve of the great Meiktila battle he had asked Donald McDonald to make his chaplains pray 'flat out' for victory as if, in the most literal way, he was ordering up extra ammunition, and it was in this realistic spirit, for example, that he responded to the pragmatism of St George's House.

He was faithful in his attendance at Chapel services, though he never took communion. Long ago, as has been seen, he had come to rest on a set of simple beliefs, child-like, perhaps, in their innocence but strong in conviction. This *anima naturaliter Christiana* still rejected dogma, ideology and complicated creeds. In his Indian summer he became, if anything, still more antipathetic towards the Catholicism of his youth, and though close observers were aware that towards the end he was troubled, from time to time, by some private turmoil, this was more the result of a *crise de conscience* over abandonment of the Catholic Church to which his mother committed him than a sense of estrangement from the Mother Church of Christianity itself. As his health began to decline, he was plagued by the thought of death not because of his own unreadiness, since death and he had long walked together, but because of Aileen. St Philip's, the school of his boyhood, was an off-shoot of the Birmingham Oratory where Cardinal Newman's spirit, tortured on the racks of Victorian controversy, had once found peace. Appropriately enough, therefore, one must turn to Newman's famous description of the character of a gentleman (in his lectures on the Idea of a University), a description true of Slim at many points, to find a sentence which perfectly catches the Constable's mood in his last years: 'He is patient, forbearing, and resigned, on philosophical principles: he submits to pain, because it is inevitable, to bereavement, because it is irreparable, and to death, because it is his destiny.'

The Military Knights were another matter. When Edward established at Windsor his college of canons, associated with St George's Chapel, he also made provision for maintenance within the Castle of a select number 'of poor Knights chosen from the humbler ranks of chivalry for their valour and need'.* These praying Knights, as they came to be called, had as a main duty punctilious attendance in Chapel at the services of the day. Though their duties diminished, and their title modulated into The Military Knights, a dozen senior officers who have deserved well of their monarch still find a place of retirement, with their own Governor, inside the walls of Windsor Castle. Not unnaturally, Slim felt a special sense of obligation, affection and concern for the soldiers of his neighbourhood; for their part, their esteem was touchingly demonstrated on the day in 1970 when their Constable at last withdrew from the Castle, and the Military Knights formed guard in his honour.

The first years at Windsor were halcyon. His seventies found Slim strong in both body and mind. Regular attendance in the City's boardrooms was diversified by endless visits from old and new friends and constant entertainment, particularly of visitors from Australia and elsewhere overseas. (By a wise provision, the Constable of Windsor has tended, latterly, to be a distinguished officer with live Commonwealth connections; like Slim, his predecessors Lord Gowrie and Lord Freyberg had close links with Australasia, and his successor, Marshal of

---

* Arthur Bryant, *The Age of Chivalry*, p. 323.

the RAF the Lord Elworthy, is intimately associated with New Zealand.) Though Norman Tower is essentially a segment of a fortress designed for medieval war, and with its 234 stairs scarcely offers a rest-home for an old campaigner, Aileen as usual created a home—though not without initial problems, which she described to Betty Foott in July, 1964:

> This has been the hardest six months of my life! I AM WORN OUT. . . . At last this house is becoming fairly normal and responding to all the efforts of many people. It had to be done from the grass roots. The Ministry of Works decided the moment had come to bring it in line with the other Castle residences and the central heat and all domestic heat and all electrical wiring etc. were dug out and re-done. With total chaos and 40 men at work for four months. Then began *our* few and quite restricted ideas. . . . Bill is to have two weeks at Osborne doing nothing.

That summer they were visited by a new acquaintance, Joel Egerer, a distinguished American professor of English Literature—who, as an ex-Captain of the US Marines in the Pacific, was disturbed to find himself being closely interrogated by a Field-Marshal on his recollections of war with the Japanese. Egerer observed that 'there was no feeling whatsoever of a family just moved into a new residence; they were completely settled and at home, the result of their having lived in the most disparate circumstances and under various conditions in a great many parts of the world'.* Aileen had not made homes out of 'mud-walled hut or Government House' for nothing.

During this and subsequent meetings Egerer was particularly impressed by Slim's perennial concern for human relationships.

> I became more and more aware of his tremendous interest in people; not only top-flight people, but all kinds of people. He had met many of the former—he was especially interesting on General Eisenhower and Mrs Lyndon Johnson both of whom attracted him tremendously —but he seemed interested, and concerned, about 'people'.
>
> He was fascinated, and horrified, at my account of the student eruptions of the late sixties of which I had had some experience in my own academic life. He asked me numerous questions about what

---

* Communication to author.

Americans thought on certain topics, especially political and socio-logical subjects. He always seemed interested in what I had to say to my students about things British. Again, he was always drawing me out on what I had said to American students about the British tempera-ment, the British approach to any number of issues from the day-to-day problems of life to the larger international aspects of what was going on in the world.

This fostering concern for youth—a concern which waxed strong when, as CIGS, the Army's National Servicemen were his responsi-bility—stemmed directly from his days as a pupil teacher in the Birmingham slums. He enjoyed nothing better, at Windsor, than wandering incognito among the tourist crowds and talking on equal terms with the younger ones—delighted, above all, when he could report that he had been asked if he was the Head Gardener and he had replied 'Yes—in a sort of way'; or when two long-haired characters, having elicited that he was in fact the Governor, announced that he presumably didn't think much of them. 'Why?' 'This hair . . . effem-inate?' Slim indicated tactfully that they were right. 'Well, we've been walking round . . . looked at a statue, Prince Rupert or someone. He'd long hair, over his shoulders—and *he* weren't a bad soldier, nor bad with the women, neither!'

Slim relished such ripostes because he believed that youth has its own point of view which should be heard, understood and respected, even if it could not be accepted. Nothing could have been more alien to his loyalties than the attitude of the anti-nuclear demonstrators, yet when one of their marches arrived at Windsor and threatened to invade the Castle it was Slim, as Governor, who refused to close the gates. Instead he went down and chatted to them, let their views have an air-ing, and defused the situation just as he had done fifty years earlier when, as a raw subaltern in the Warwicks, he scotched a mutiny by his reasonableness and fair dealing. It was the same with the Windsor Leatherjackets—those roaring boys on their screaming motor-cycles who made certain parts of the town a nightmare. Uncle Bill went down from Norman Tower and tackled them in their clubs, on their own ground.

From the Leatherjackets to the royal court was a wide span which Slim bridged effortlessly. The regard in which he was held by the Queen and her family only strengthened with the years. But the Governor is not *ex officio* part of the Royal Household, his formal duties are slight, and apart from an appropriate attendance on ceremonial occasions, on dinner-parties or some occasion of state, there was little to restrict Bill and Aileen from going their own way and living their own life.

When her Constable began to fail, however, the Queen was at pains to stroll over to Norman Tower wearing, like any neighbour, a simple head-scarf, and call on him privately and alone. For the halcyon days were inevitably darkened. In Australia there had been the very slightest intimation of a stroke. One morning when Aileen was absent from Norman Tower, attending the birth of a grand-daughter, Slim left Windsor for London. His dressing-room was found to be in a wild disarray, as though in confusion of mind he had been turning things over in a helpless search for some ordinary object—a stud, perhaps, or a tie. At Imperial Chemical House Sir Paul Chambers observed the next stage:

> He had attended a small meeting (which dealt with high level salaries) and which, as usual, was held in my room as chairman of that meeting; the meeting finished a few minutes before the full Board meeting was due to start. When a few minutes later I took my seat at the Board I looked round as usual to see whether all Directors who were expected were in their places. Only Lord Slim's seat was empty, so I waited a minute or so and in answer to a question I replied that as he had already been at a meeting which had just finished I knew that he would not be more than a minute or two. Eventually I asked somebody to go and look for him. He was found walking along a corridor only a few yards from my room. He came in at once and took his seat without a word and the meeting started without further delay.
>
> At a later stage of that meeting I specifically asked him for his opinion on a matter on which I thought his opinion would be valuable. He made no reply and I realized at once that he was 'not with us'. So without comment I turned quickly to another Director.
>
> He attended Board meetings subsequently after that but made little contribution to our discussions or decisions.

The clinical sequence at Windsor was in fact a gradual but one-way process. In July, 1965, some difficulty with his sight and balance, from which he soon recovered, was a foretaste of the definite small stroke in June, 1967, which deprived him permanently of a segment of his field of vision. An impairment of his speech became evident in August, 1968, and in the next two months there were further attacks, one severe. Then, at the beginning of 1970, his actual powers of comprehension

became slowly and intermittently weaker. By the time he left Windsor
he was, to all intents and purposes, blind.

Yet Nature, who so gently withdrew his bodily strength, was
gracious in allowing him to remain himself until the end. Nobody
reading Lord Moran's revelations about Churchill's last days can fail
to feel a certain sadness as he observes how senility can erode even the
greatest of our time. But whether in the close circle of his family, or
while receiving old friends, Slim was still what he had always been—
thoughtful, dignified, courteous, considerate. Milton's great chorus
about the blind Samson in Gaza has a special relevance:

> All is best, though we oft doubt,
> What the unsearchable dispose
> Of highest wisdom brings about,
> And ever best found in the close.
> Oft he seems to hide his face,
> But unexpectedly returns
> And to his faithful Champion hath in place
> Bore witness gloriously. . . .
> His servants he with new acquist
> Of true experience from this great event
> With peace and consolation hath dismist,
> And calm of mind all passion spent.

Of course life was sometimes irksome. It was deflating for a Field-
Marshal not to be fit enough to take his part in the Garter procession,
and to have to watch from Norman Tower the gay pageant moving by;
but as the ranks of Garter Knights drew opposite the Constable they
made a gesture which seemed to incapsulate five hundred years of
history. Before the man who embodied the first principles of the Order
and its oath, who had stood firm and valiantly and successfully conquered, they gestured and quietly called their greeting.

By now he seemed a permanent part of the Windsor community. To
all the staff, to the Castle police, to the people on the telephone exchange he was a familiar and beloved figure. Arthur Johnson, his
faithful valet of Australian days, who would come down to Norman
Tower to 'lend a hand', made him a white stick, and he would stroll
peacefully about the grounds talking, in his egalitarian way, with
anybody he happened to meet. There was nothing to prevent him from
ending his days peacefully in the Constable's Tower.

But Slim thought that this was wrong, and unfair to the Queen. He

was well abreast of reality, and he knew that in their latter stages some
of his predecessors had so declined that they were unable to fulfil the
small requirements of their office. He himself was not prepared to exist
as an incompetent pensioner. With reluctance his point was taken, and
in mid-1970 he was permitted to retire. Nor did the old soldier simply
fade away. The last Guard at the Castle before his departure was
mounted by the Field-Marshal and Constable, with his son John acting
as ADC. Slim's back was a ramrod.

Aileen took him to a flat at Eaton Mansions in Chelsea where all was
arranged for his comfort. The friends and fellow-officers of a lifetime
could conveniently call for carefully rationed talks. Then, early one
morning, there was a collapse. Arthur Johnson, who had served in
Arakan as a medical orderly, was fortunately present and able to lift
him on to his bed for the last time.

On the 14th of December, 1970, the late Commander of the 14th
Army died.

BIBLIOGRAPHY

All five volumes of the *War against Japan* series in the British Official History (Supervising Editor the late Major-General S. W. Kirby) have been frequently consulted, as well as relevant volumes in the *Grand Strategy* series, and other campaign studies with reference to Slim's operations in East Africa and in Syria—Iraq—Persia. The following books were also helpful:

Acheson, Dean, *Present at the Creation*, Hamish Hamilton, 1969
Arnold, Ralph, *A Very Quiet War*, Hart-Davis, 1962
Barker A. J., *The March on Delhi*, Faber, 1966
Bateson, Charles, *The War with Japan*, Barrie and Rockliff, 1968
Bond, Brian (Ed.) *Chief of Staff: the diaries of Lieutenant-General Sir Henry Pownall*, Vol. II 1940–44. Leo Cooper, 1974
Brett-James, Antony, *Ball of Fire: the Fifth Indian Division in the Second World War*, Gale and Polden, 1951
Bryant, Sir Arthur, *The Turn of the Tide* and *Triumph in the West*—the Alanbrooke papers. Collins, 1957 and 1959
Calvert, Brigadier Michael, *Prisoners of Hope*, Cape, 1952
—— *Fighting Mad*, Jarrolds, 1964
—— *Slim*, Pan/Ballantine, 1973
Chaplin, H. D., *The Queen's Own Royal West Kent Regiment, 1920–1950*, Michael Joseph, 1954
Chester, Sir Norman, *The Nationalization of British Industries, 1945–1951*, Her Majesty's Stationery Office, 1975
Churchill, Sir Winston, *The Second World War*, Cassell, 6 vols. *passim*
Connell, John, *Wavell: Scholar and Soldier*, Collins 1964
——*Wavell: Supreme Commander* (ed. M. R. Roberts) Collins, 1969.
Crisp, L. F., *Ben Chifley*, Longmans, 1961
Darby, Phillip, *British Defence Policy East of Suez, 1947–68*, Oxford University Press, 1973

Davis, Patrick, *A Child at Arms*, Hutchinson, 1970
Evans, Lieutenant-General Sir Geoffrey, *Slim as Military Commander*, Batsford, 1969
——, and Antony Brett-James, *Imphal*, Macmillan, 1962
Fergusson, Brigadier Bernard, *Beyond the Chindwin*, Collins, 1945
—— *The Wild Green Earth*, Collins, 1946
—— *The Trumpet in the Hall*, Collins, 1970
Gibbs, Lieutenant-Colonel H. R. K., *Historical Record of the 6th Gurkha Rifles, Vol. II*, Gale and Polden, 1955
Hart-Davis, Duff, *Peter Fleming*, Cape, 1974
Jackson, General Sir William, *Alexander of Tunis as Military Commander*, Batsford, 1971
Kennedy, Major-General Sir John, *The Business of War*, Hutchinson, 1957
Lewin, Ronald, *Churchill as War Lord*, Batsford, 1973
Liddell Hart, Sir Basil, *Memoirs*, Cassell, 1962
Lucas Phillips, Brigadier C. E., *The Raiders of Arakan*, Heinemann, 1971
Mackenzie, Compton, *Gallipoli Memories*, Cassell, 1929
Macksey, Kenneth, *Armoured Crusader: Major-General Sir Percy Hobart*, Hutchinson, 1967
Mason, Philip, *A Matter of Honour*, Cape, 1974
Masters, John, *The Road Past Mandalay*, Michael Joseph, 1961
Menzies, Sir Robert, *Afternoon Light*, Cassell, 1967
Montgomery, Field-Marshal the Viscount, *Memoirs*, Collins, 1958
Moran, Lord, *Winston Churchill: the struggle for survival 1940–1965*, Constable, 1966
Nicolson, Nigel, *Alex*, Weidenfeld and Nicolson, 1973
North, John (Ed.,) *The Alexander Memoirs 1940–1945*, Cassell, 1962.
Owen, Frank, *The Campaign in Burma*, HMSO, 1946
Pocock, Tom, *Fighting General*, Collins, 1973
Rhodes James, Robert, *Gallipoli*, Batsford, 1965
Roberts, Brigadier M. R., *Golden Arrow: the story of the 7th Indian Division in the Second World War*, Gale and Polden, 1952
Romanus C. F. and Sunderland, Riley, *Stilwell's Command Problems* (United States Army in World War Two: China-Burma-India Theater), Office of the Chief of Military History, Department of the Army, Washington D.C., 1955
Shaw, James, *The March Out*, Hart-Davis, 1953
Slim, Field-Marshal the Viscount, *Defeat into Victory*, Cassell, 1956

Slim, *Courage, and other broadcasts*, Cassell, 1957
—— *Unofficial History*, Cassell, 1959
Smith, E. D., *Britain's Brigade of Gurkhas*, Leo Cooper, 1973
Smithers, A. J., *Sir John Monash*, Leo Cooper, 1973
Stilwell, General Joseph W., *The Stilwell Papers* (ed. Theodore White), New York, Sloane, 1948
Swinson, Arthur, *Kohima*, Cassell, 1966
—— *Four Samurai*, Hutchinson, 1968
—— *Mountbatten*, Pan/Ballantine, 1971
Sykes, Christopher, *Orde Wingate*, Collins, 1959
Terraine, John, *The Life and Times of Lord Mountbatten*, Hutchinson, 1968
Thompson, Edward, *These Men Thy Friends*, Benn, 1927
Tuchmann, Barbara W., *Stilwell and the American experience in China*, Macmillan, 1971
Tulloch, Major-General Derek *Wingate in Peace and War*, Macdonald, 1972
Vincent, Air Vice-Marshal S. F., *Flying Fever*, Jarrolds, 1972
Wavell, Field-Marshal Lord, *The Viceroy's Journal* (ed. Penderel Moon) Oxford University Press, 1973
Wingate, Sir Ronald, *Lord Ismay*, Hutchinson, 1970

INDEX

Compiled by F. H. C. Tatham